A HISTORY OF
ANCIENT
BRITAIN

Neil Oliver is an archaeologist, historian, author and broadcaster. He made his television debut in 2002 with the ground-breaking *Two Men in a Trench* battlefield archaeology series for BBC2, and he has since become a familiar face as the lead presenter of the BBC's award-winning series *Coast*. He was also the presenter of the 'bold, pugnacious and authoritative' ten-hour series *A History of Scotland*, screened on BBC1 and BBC2. *A History of Ancient Britain* is a major eight-part series for BBC2.

By Neil Oliver

A History of Scotland
A History of Ancient Britain
Vikings

A HISTORY OF
ANCIENT
BRITAIN

Neil Oliver

PHOENIX

A PHOENIX PAPERBACK

First published in Great Britain in 2011
by Weidenfeld & Nicolson
This paperback edition published in 2012
by Phoenix,
an imprint of Orion Books Ltd,
Orion House, 5 Upper St Martin's Lane,
London WC2H 9EA

An Hachette UK company

5 7 9 10 8 6 4

Copyright © Neil Oliver 2012

The right of Neil Oliver to be identified as the author of
this work has been asserted by him in accordance with
the Copyright, Designs and Patents Act 1988.

All rights reserved. No part of this publication may be
reproduced, stored in a retrieval system, or transmitted,
in any form or by any means, electronic, mechanical,
photocopying, recording or otherwise, without the prior
permission of the copyright owner.

A CIP catalogue record for this book
is available from the British Library.

ISBN: 978-0-7538-2886-1

Typeset by Input Data Services Ltd,
Bridgwater, Somerset

Printed and bound in Great Britain by
CPI Group (UK) Ltd, Croydon, CRO 4YY

The Orion Publishing Group's policy is to use papers
that are natural, renewable and recyclable products and
made from wood grown in sustainable forests. The logging
and manufacturing processes are expected to conform to
the environmental regulations of the country of origin.

www.orionbooks.co.uk

To Tom Affleck,
who was there at the start

Contents

List of Illustrations

Chapter 4

Chapter 5

Chapter 6

Acknowledgements

I was soaked to the skin and shivering in what I earnestly believe to have been the outskirts of hypothermia. I was in the middle of a peat bog in the west of Ireland and the freezing rain was sweeping across the landscape in great cloaking sheets. I might as well have been under water. We had been filming for hours, one of the cameras had already given up the ghost and I was asking myself, quite seriously, what on earth I was doing standing ankle-deep in mud, with rainwater running down my skin inside my clothes. But then I looked around at the crew – director, cameraman, sound recordist, researchers – and reminded myself of something important: my discomfort in the rain and wind would one day be seen by an audience; someone, somewhere would see that it had happened. But while my misery was being recorded for posterity, everyone else's would go unnoticed. And no one was complaining. Not a single word.

As often as possible – sometimes several times a day, in fact – I remind myself how lucky I am to have this job. Bad weather might be an occasional blight, but after all it's only an occupational hazard for folk who mostly work outside. I also try and bear in mind that my job is made possible only by the unstinting efforts of others.

This is the time therefore, long overdue, when I get to thank those who also stand miserable and drenched on sodden bogs (sometimes bearing flasks of hot tea), or on wind-blasted cliff tops, or in the wheelhouses of little boats wallowing in big seas. I have not forgotten!

Just like a television documentary, a book is the product of the hard work of many different people. One with a grand title like *A History of Ancient Britain* is dependent upon the efforts of a whole range of thoughtful and painstaking professionals.

A mountainous debt is owed to Michael Dover, my editor and publisher at Weidenfeld & Nicolson. Unless and until you have listened to his always calm, constantly reassuring and encouraging voice, you cannot begin to imagine what a steadying presence he provides for anyone struggling to face down the unforgiving stare of the blank page. Thank you, Michael.

Linden Lawson's brilliance as a copy-editor and proof-reader deserves nothing less than whole pages of appreciation. I am constantly stunned by her attention to detail and by her ability to fine-tune and fettle, so that the final version is as close as humanly possible to what I actually meant to say all along.

Grateful thanks are also due to editorial assistants Nicki Crossley and Jillian Young, and picture researcher Caroline Hotblack has shown great imagination and sensitivity in sourcing all of the illustrative material that enlivens the text. My experience of Weidenfeld & Nicolson over the past few years has been a real treat and the whole team there has my admiration.

It almost goes without saying that the book would never have happened without the BBC Television series of the same name. Cameron Balbirnie was the series producer and somewhere along the way he has become a good friend as well. No mortal could have given more of himself in pursuit of the creation of a series worthy of the name of *A History of Ancient Britain*. Not content with sweating blood to create the best television possible, Cameron also found time to read through the proofs of this book to help ensure we were all singing from the same hymn sheet. Executive producer Eamon Hardy was an ever-present champion of the series and grateful thanks are owed to him as well.

Also crucial were the five producer-directors – each of whom contributed hugely to the content of the book. So to Paul King,

Arif Nurmohamed, Dick Taylor, Jeff Wilkinson and Simon Winchcombe – a huge and heartfelt thank-you.

Series researchers Sarah Ager, Ellie James, Poonam Odedraand and Mark Williams worked wonders – sourcing and checking information, finding contributors and fighting the forces of error and falsehood on a daily basis. I just hope I have the chance to work with them again.

Without the organisational genius of Dominic Bolton, Sarah Vickers, Alice Pattenden and Sue Ng, the wheels would have come off the *Ancient Britain* wagon long ago. Dominic in particular was and is a marvel to me. How he patiently stayed on top of the mountain of arrangements – and, more importantly, the *re-*arrangements he had to make day after day and week after week – is quite beyond my comprehension.

The epic look of the series was for the most part the work of the principal editor Martin Johnson. Thanks to him, the finished article had the feel, in my opinion, of a Hollywood blockbuster.

Camera operators and sound recordists are special breeds of human being. While the rest of the team struggles up mountains, through caves and tunnels and across rivers and streams, the camera and sound crew must cover the same terrain while lumbered with the heaviest and most cumbersome technical kit imaginable. Cameramen Patrick Acum, Toby Wilkinson, Neville Kidd, Ben Joiner, Justin Ingham, Michael Pitts and John McIntyre and sound men Sam Staples and Mike Williams would surely thrive in the SAS. And then, when they arrive in the desired spot, be it summit or seabed, they are required to be creative and adept, making everywhere look wonderful and me heroic! On top of all that they were possessed of senses of humour that didn't just make each hard day tolerable, but a positive pleasure. For all the laughs – almost more than anything else – a thousand thank-yous.

Sophie Laurimore, my television agent at Factual Management, and Eugenie Furniss, my literary agent at William Morris Enter-tainment, fight the good fight on my behalf every day. I honestly don't know what I would do or where I would be without them. Lots of love to both, as always.

Finally, and most importantly, I must acknowledge the biggest debt of all, to my wife, Trudi – who soaks up all the strain, takes care of the family and runs the whole show at home while I waft around the world on the magic carpet of television. How she puts up with me and all of this, I really don't know. But she does, and I don't forget that either.

Introduction

There is a sequoia tree in the Sierra Nevada of California known as the Great Bonsai. The men and women of the US Forest Service are protective of their charge – as they are with all sequoias – and prefer its precise location to remain less than well known. Sequoias grow only in the Western Sierra Nevada and are therefore something of an endangered species. There are no sequoia forests as such – they occur only in 'groves' within forests of lesser, more plentiful species, a handful of giants standing here and there like members of an exclusive clique, surrounded by hoi polloi. Their apparent disdain for the fir trees crowded around their waists is almost palpable.

A handful of celebrity sequoias like General Sherman and the Grizzly Giant are on the tourist trail and get most of the attention – which means many others are left in relative peace. That is the way the rangers like it.

Despite having reached a height of over 200 feet, the Great Bonsai is a long way from claiming the title of tallest sequoia (the loftiest of them tower well over 300 feet high), but it is unusually immense in the sheer volume of wood it contains. Many of its individual branches are themselves larger than full-grown trees of other species. In terms of the mass and reach of its canopy, the Great Bonsai is one of the largest trees on Earth.

More impressive than its size, however, is its great age. Tree scientists estimate the Great Bonsai has been occupying its perch, on a rocky summit overlooking deep valleys, for at least 2,000 years. That much would already be newsworthy: a tree as old as

Christianity itself, alive in California before the Romans conquered Britannia.

There is only one way even to try to calculate the age of such an ancient specimen and that is to cut it down and count the rings. No one is proposing to go to such lengths to total the years of a character as precious as the Great Bonsai, though; and even if they did, experience suggests they might find the inner section so rotten that ring-counting would, anyway, be impossible at worst and inconclusive at best.

Those scientists familiar with the greatest sentinels of the sequoia species will quietly confess another possibility: that the elder specimens may be much older than 2,000 years. Some will even allow that the Great Bonsai may be over 4,000 years old. There is simply no way to be certain.

But just consider the suggestion that some of those sequoias might have been living and growing for the last four millennia and more. It would mean that while people in Britain were still making and using bronze axes, and while the finishing touches were being put to monuments like Avebury and Stonehenge, the Great Bonsai was taking root in the high sierras of California.

The story of humankind – at least the comparatively recent chapters – may therefore have unfolded in the shadow of those trees. It might well be the case that 200 generations of people have come and gone while a handful of sequoias reached steadily skywards, oblivious to the rise and fall of kingdoms, empires and entire civilisations. The existence of giants like the Great Bonsai makes our species the very epitome of ephemeral. Millions of us have certainly been born, lived out our three score and ten and returned to the soil while a single tree drew water, made oxygen and starch from sunlight and carbon dioxide, and grew.

The Scottish conservationist John Muir, who emigrated to the US with his family when he was 11 years old and spent much of his life championing and defending the wild places of the world, was among the first to stand up for the sequoias. When he first encountered them, in the middle years of the nineteenth century, they were being felled for lumber – a pointless exercise as it turned out, because the timber shatters into matchwood when the trees hit the ground. He was thereafter in the vanguard of those seeking to protect the remaining giants for posterity; that any survive today is due in no small part to the efforts of one stubborn Scotsman.

For much of the twentieth century the US Forest Service battled valiantly to protect the sequoia groves from what they considered the greatest threat to the species' continuing existence: wild fire. They were very successful, and kept the flames away from the giants for many years – until someone realised the trees actually depended upon fire as a key element of their reproductive cycle. Sequoia wood is naturally saturated with a chemical the foresters call tannin – which, as well as repelling insects and other parasites, also makes it virtually fireproof. Blazes that will clear away all other species like so much tinder generally leave little more than a few patches of charring on the lower parts of the sequoias. The heat also serves to encourage the tiny sequoia seeds to pop from the otherwise tightly clenched fists of their pine cones; these then fall into freshly cleared soil that is newly bathed in life-giving sunlight and free from any competing plants. Some people call the sequoias 'fire trees'.

A person could be forgiven for thinking all the advantages are stacked in favour of that one species – a species that has evolved to thrive in conditions that destroy the competition.

One other characteristic of sequoias, however, is worth bearing in mind: despite their massive girth and great height, they have extremely shallow root systems, and the prime cause of death among them is simply falling over. Their huge bulk actually works against them whenever a high wind blows through the sierras – and when one giant falls it usually takes a neighbour or two down with it.

Within the story of the Giant Sequoias, therefore, lies a warning for humankind. For long we believed we too had grown high and mighty – that our own long, long history was proof of our invincibility. We had come through it all. Some or other ancestor of the mammals had emerged from the shadow of the dinosaurs, evolving and learning for millions of years until an ancient, distant relative straightened its spine and stood up on two legs. Thereafter a series of trials and errors laid a path leading all the way to the first people, and beyond.

It seemed to many that our seeds had been sown by the fires of creation itself and that we had grown and grown until we were head and shoulders above all others. Masters of nature, we were therefore beyond its reach, we thought – fireproof, so to speak.

But the truth is altogether different and far less reassuring. *Homo sapiens sapiens* has been alive and conscious on Earth for no more than 200,000 years. Born and bred in Africa, we found the need to leave that continent's warmth just a few tens of thousands of years ago. We spread north first, and then east into Asia. Some of those adventurous souls crafted boats and made the sea crossing from the land that would be south-eastern Asia to the continent that would be Australia, something like 50,000 years ago. While all that was happening, yet more made inroads into Europe; others continued into north-eastern Asia and from there found their way to the continent of North America. Sea levels were lower and what is now the Bering Strait was then a land bridge – indeed an entire landmass – known to geologists as Beringia. Between perhaps 40,000 and 20,000 years ago those farthest-flung of the pioneers penetrated all the way down into South America and on to Tierra del Fuego, the land of fire at the ends of the Earth.

A person might be forgiven for thinking that if we were a plant we would be some sort of smothering ivy, crawling across the face of the planet until our tendrils threatened to throttle the very life out of the place. When astronauts take pictures of the globe from space, after all, the artificial lights conjured by humankind are seen glowing from every nook and cranny.

But Earth is four and a half billion years old – and for all the miles we have travelled as a species during the last 60,000 years or so, we are effectively as new to the place as this year's swarms of mosquitos. Our spread has certainly been astonishing – in terms of its speed if nothing else. There are more than six billion of us now – more people alive at once than at any other time in history. But for all that we are more numerous than before and reaching levels of population density that may one day bring about our own extinction, in some respects we are of no more consequence than a sprinkling of dust. The truth is that every last one of us – all six billion and more – would fit, neatly stacked like lumber, into the space currently occupied by Windermere, England's largest lake.

While the sequoias – and the rest of the Redwood family to which they belong – are nowadays restricted to the Western Sierra Nevada, they are relics of another time entirely. It was during the Jurassic period, which began 200 million years ago, that the first of them put down their roots. Once upon a time they were represented on every continent on Earth and it is only in the relatively recent past that their territory has become restricted to one small part of California.

So while we human beings have been tenants of the Earth for 200 millennia, those giant trees have been here a thousand times as long. In terms of the history of the planet we squat upon, our roots are shallower by far than those of any sequoia. We need not look for a John Muir to save us either. The next big gust of wind – global warming, climate change, sea level rise or whatever – might bring about our downfall.

In *The World Without Us* American journalist Alan Weisman wrote about what would happen in a world suddenly devoid of human beings. Plants quickly sprout through roads and motorways, turning them from grey to green within years. River water flows unchecked through the tunnels beneath the cities, undermining foundations so that homes and buildings are toppled. Within decades, or a few centuries at most, towns and neighbourhoods are swallowed up by forests. Time sees to it all, until even the bundled copper wires of our telecommunications networks and the lead, steel and iron pipes that carried everything else, are crushed by geology – turned back into metallic veins running through rocks. Our radioactive waste and our plastic bags may well last longest of all – but eventually the world will quietly deal with that mess too.

Long before then the books, CDs, DVDs – as well as every last hard drive of every last computer server – will be dust in the wind. Our recorded history will not outlive us. To all intents and purposes it will be gone in the same instant the last of us closes our eyes.

And if our species falls, deep in the forest of years, not one of the other creatures that walk or crawl, swim or fly will care a jot.

We matter only to ourselves and that is no bad thing; this is why our history must be central to our understanding of the world and our time upon it. Its dependence upon our attention, and ours alone, should remind us that our past is something immediate, fragile and fleeting as a flash of inspiration – and as potent. We must pay it heed now – not because it has been long but because in the scheme of things it has been the stuff of moments. The accomplishment of many years is this way turned into an hour glass, as the Bard said. We must watch the play.

1

ICE

'Of the extreme tracts of Europe towards the west I cannot speak with any certainty.'

Herodotus

'And the Lord said unto her, two nations are in thy womb, and two manner of people ... and the one people shall be stronger than the other people; and the elder shall serve the younger ... And the first came out red, all over like an hairy garment; and they called his name Esau. And after that came his brother out, and his hand took hold on Esau's heel; and his name was Jacob ... And the boys grew: and Esau was a cunning hunter, a man of the field; and Jacob was a plain man, dwelling in tents.'

Genesis 25:23–27

'Ginger people! D'you know what they are? Our aborigines ... that's what! GINGERIGINES! Look at 'em ... they were 'ere first. All this is theirs!'

Al Murray, Pub Landlord

Until the arrival of human beings, people more or less like us, there was no meaningful time in the universe. Astronomers and physicists say different and measure the age of the cosmos by the billions of years (around 13.7 billion, in fact). But before there was intelligent life, the mindless comings and goings of galaxies, stars and planets had no witness. Nothing existed even to notice, far

less reckon the passing of all those moments. There was no awareness of the past and certainly no sense of a future – just a meaningless, disembodied *now*.

Time is beyond even the comprehension of the cosmologists
who make it their preoccupation. They have called the firing of
the universal starting pistol the Big Bang – but it seems it was
neither big, nor a bang. Time, space and everything else in the
universe were contained within a 'singularity' – something infinitesimal, immeasurably tiny – that appeared for reasons unknown
and in a place unknown.

Seemingly driven by the inevitability of physical laws, it began
spontaneously to expand, like a balloon inflating, and it continues
to do so. There is apparently no sense in asking what happened
before the singularity appeared and began to grow because until
it did, there *was . . . no . . . time*. At the very moment the singularity
began to expand, it made room inside for time along with everything else. As if all of that were not baffling enough, the universe
is not expanding into space because all the space there will ever be
is not outside the universe – somehow surrounding it – but *inside*
it.

During those first moments there was unimaginable heat –
billions of degrees centigrade of heat that cooked the available
particles into simple elements like hydrogen and helium, the two
elements that, by themselves, account for 99 per cent of all visible
matter in the universe. (The Russian cosmologist George Gamow,
towering champion of the Big Bang theory, suggested all this
happened fast – very fast – so that the first course of our universe
was served in minutes: 'in less time than it takes to cook a dish of
duck and roast potatoes'.)

It is the heat inside stars that has cooked the gold, carbon, iron,
uranium and the rest of the 118 other known elements which in
time conspired to make planets and spiders, flowers and us. Only
in their death throes do stars release the stuff of worlds and so,
depending on your point of view, we are made either of stardust
or nuclear waste. Along with everything else in the universe we

are still inside that expanding dot: a place at once incomprehensibly huge and yet – since it is expanding into and inside nothing at all – immeasurably small.

Who on earth can deliver all of this with a straight face, far less claim to understand it?

After eight billion or so uncounted, unlamented years came planet Earth and, three and a half billion more years after that, a soup of life began to simmer in her oceans. A slow procession followed: plants grew, fish swam and lizards crawled. Tectonic plates – the great rafts of rock that encrust the planet – drifted upon the currents of its molten core, the continents we know today trapped shapeless and as yet unsculpted within. The rocky components of Britain, at first scattered far and wide, were clumsily crushed together during the course of a trans-global odyssey that began several billion years ago, not far from the South Pole. They reached their present location, in roughly recognisable form, around 60 million years ago.

While Britain's component parts travelled north, dinosaurs ruled the earth, before a collision with a meteor all but wiped the planet clean of life once more. Birds and mammals emerged stunned and blinking from the chaos, not quite the creatures we know today but reasonable likenesses, and yet still none of it mattered because not one of those beasts had the wit to notice each had had a beginning and that all of them would come to an end.

Not until the advent of creatures with a sense of their own mortality, of infinity and their place within it, did the aeons weigh at all. Before the coming of human consciousness, all the years from the Big Bang passed in an instant; unmarked and forgotten as though they had never been. Like the tree that falls in an empty wood, making no noise, so the billions of years were accounted for in less than no time.

As far as we know, we human beings of planet Earth are the first and only animals to have felt the unbearable weight of infinity, the first to remember and to mourn. At the moment of our awakening as a species Earth – even the universe itself – awoke too. The clock started ticking and someone, somewhere, counted one day more . . . one day less.

Time, therefore, starts with us. It starts with us and holds us in servitude to it. This is our blessing and our curse. And so history starts with us as well. Only we have bothered to wonder what came before – and to keep a record of events as they unfold. This urge to keep track is part service to the future and part vanity. In addition to informing our descendants of the back-story that will give a context to their present, we hope to be remembered there – to have been noticed and to have mattered.

Memory . . . remembering . . . history . . . these are uniquely human. We are Earth's youngest apes – feeble, without claws or fangs, with neither speed nor strength, naked of feather or fur – and yet beneath thin caps of bone we are possessed of minds that reach backwards and forwards in time. It is a predicament. In all the universe we alone are troubled by *when*?

But in the end it is our awareness that our time is short that drives us to find out who we are and where we came from, while we have the chance. It is this pursuit of knowledge of the past, our desire for *history* to fill the void of all the time that came before that makes us human, and that will enable us to cope with whatever is coming.

Fittingly for a history of ancient Britain, it was a *Briton* – in fact a Scot – who was first to feel the weight of time, to sense just how old the planet might be. Born in Edinburgh on 3 June 1726, James Hutton eventually shone among the brightest stars of the Scottish Enlightenment. He was part of that gilded age when Scotland was Europe's philosophical and scientific leader. He walked the same streets as the economist Adam Smith, author of *The Wealth of Nations*; the same as the chemist Joseph Black and the engineer James Watt, whose combined efforts developed the universal steam engine; the same as the philosopher David Hume and the poet Robert Burns, among scores of others.

Hutton was variously a student of agriculture, chemistry, medicine, meteorology and philosophy, but it is for his contribution to the science of geology that he is best remembered. Though educated in a world still in thrall to the belief that God had created everything in six days (completing the job, according to the seventeenth-century Irish Archbishop James Ussher, on 23 October in the year 4004 BC), he was a born observer who took, as his principal teacher, the landscape around him.

It is worth noting that Hutton's hometown is shaped more than any other in Britain by its geology. Born in the shadow of Edinburgh's Salisbury Crags, he seemingly absorbed their significance into his DNA – read for the first time the truth they had been broadcasting to the world for millions of years in letters made of basalt and standing 150 feet high.

The Crags loom over the lower part of the city's Old Town like a fossilised wave, and that is what they are. Hundreds of millions of years ago molten basalt surged upwards from deep within the planet's core but failed to burst out onto the surface. Trapped underground, it cooled between two older layers of soft, sedimentary rock. Many more millions of years later an Ice Age glacier scoured the land – easily stripping away the softer rock and leaving the hard black Crags exposed to the light for the first time.

All of this is accepted truth today, but it took a son of the Scottish Enlightenment to see those towering cliffs for what they were – evidence of geological time as we understand it. As well as the landforms around his hometown, Hutton travelled throughout the rest of Scotland and into England as well, in pursuit of understanding. In 1788 he published his *Theory of the Earth* – a work that was to travel across the world with an elemental force equal to that of any glacier. A full 70 years before Charles Darwin rewrote the history of life on Earth in *The Origin of Species*, Hutton's logic bulldozed away centuries of religious dogma to reveal the natural truth of Earth's great age lying unbreakable and immovable beneath.

Rather than a creation of six divine days, when Hutton considered the making of the Earth he saw 'no vestige of a beginning and no prospect of an end'. Though he did not use the term himself, Hutton had laid the foundations for 'Uniformitarianism' – a philosophy which assumes that the natural processes shaping the world and the wider universe today are exactly the same as those that held sway in the past. Hutton's way of looking at the world in the eighteenth century is the way we see it now. He is remembered as the father of geology but he was also part of the greater revolution that first invited humankind to gaze into the bottomless abyss of 'deep time'.

For all his glacial powers of reasoning, the realisation that ice had sculpted Britain's landscape was not Hutton's. It was another Edinburgh Scot who was first to bring this next revolutionary theory into the public domain. Charles Maclaren was editor of *The Scotsman* newspaper in 1840 when he received a letter from Professor Robert Jameson, a geologist and mineralogist working at Edinburgh University. It was a young Swiss naturalist turned geologist named Louis Agassiz who had actually written the letter, in the hope that Jameson would publish it in his *Edinburgh New Philosophical Journal*, but the letter arrived just as the journal was going to press. Jameson was so impressed by its contents, however, that he immediately passed it on to Maclaren – so that it might quickly reach public attention via the city's newspaper.

The resultant scoop was nothing less than earth-shattering. Published on 7 October 1840, the letter expressed Agassiz's conviction that Scotland had, in ancient times, been completely submerged beneath an enormous glacier of ice. It was the culmination of years of observations by the scientist, of glaciated valleys in his homeland. There it was common knowledge that the existing glaciers had once extended further towards the lowlands. Though the ice was gone from the lower reaches, the evidence of its passing was plain to see in the deep gouging and polishing of the visible rock surfaces, along with great heaps and scatterings of rocks and boulders – erratics – carried and deposited far from home. When Agassiz subsequently learned about similar evidence on mountains in Scotland – where no glaciers either existed or were ever known to have existed in the past – the truth of it all was instantly obvious to him: Scotland's landscape had been sculpted by ice.

In 1840 he travelled to Scotland and there, in the company of friends, toured the Highlands to see for himself the evidence of ancient glaciation. Following the publication of his letter in *The Scotsman*, on 7 October, Agassiz travelled to Edinburgh later that month where he joined Maclaren for a tour of the geological features surrounding the city. Some impressed him more than others but when he was taken to Blackford Hill, on the southern outskirts, he immediately spotted telltale horizontal striations etched into the surface of a distinctive wall of andesite lava on the lower slopes. The wall is popular today with climbers keen to hone their skills and it is known as 'Agassiz Rock', for it was there that the Swiss geologist excitedly declared: 'That is the work of ice!'

Agassiz did not stop there either, with the suggestion of an Ice Age only in Scotland's past. Rather he saw in his mind's eye a glacier covering all of Europe, if not the rest of the planet, at some time. Today it is hard for us to appreciate how revolutionary this breakthrough was. Despite its publication in Scotland in 1840, it would be another 20 years before the wider scientific community, let alone the God-fearing public, accepted Agassiz's theory. Until then geologists, mineralogists and antiquarians alike had been trying faithfully to reconcile what they saw in the world around them with the Biblical tale of creation most of them still carried in their fearful hearts. In the middle years of the eighteenth century, scientists struggled to comprehend natural phenomena in the context of the six-day Creation and The Flood – the apocalyptic deluge with which God had punished all but Noah and his family.

It must have been a strange agony for many of those eighteenth-century thinkers – at once sensing deep time and yet hobbled by their religious faith in a near-instantaneous Creation. Surely as fascinating as the scientific discoveries sweeping Europe and the world in those enlightened decades is the fact that the natural truth had been lost in the first place? After all, at least some of the

Ice Ages were witnessed and indeed endured by modern humans. People exactly the same as us were driven from their lands as the climate deteriorated – and then generations later their descendants stepped gingerly back onto the new landscapes revealed by the glaciers' eventual retreat. At times in our past therefore we must have known all about the ice – its comings and goings – and for generations those facts must have been passed, parent to child, as part of the lore of the tribes. And then at some point, for some reason, that part of the story was left untold by some father to some son. Over time fewer and fewer children heard it until finally it was lost to the minds of men.

When and why did a story so huge cease to be worth the telling – so that the truth of it had to be relearned centuries or millennia later, discovered as though for the first time by scientists like James Hutton and Louis Agassiz? We will never know.

The same can be said for the rest of the truth of Britain's ancient history, which we still struggle to piece together today: how we came to till the land instead of hunt ... the thinking that inspired people to build great houses of timber, earth and stone for their dead ... the nature of the religion that made them raise avenues and circles of stone ... the reason why Stonehenge was built and what it was for – all of it. A day came when the need for Stonehenge finally passed. After all those centuries of meaning and understanding it was left alone. But for generations after the last ceremony, the last gathering in the shadows of those trilithons, people would still have known the story – the explanation for all that work. Why did they stop passing it on? That so much has been lost and forgotten is every bit as astonishing as the discoveries that gradually fill in the gaps.

By his insight, Hutton had exposed the reality of an ancient world – millions upon millions of years in the making – and Agassiz had found it shaped most recently not by God's wrathful flood but by pitiless ice. There were consequences from all this new understanding, a price to be paid. Since the world was so very old there was suddenly unexpected time to be filled. It was surely inconceivable that the place had been empty for all these hitherto unexpected ages. Something must have lived there all the while and as well as some*thing* perhaps the world had also been home to some*one*.

In *The Origin of Species*, published in 1859, Darwin would connect all species with the concept of common descent. In the distant past, alongside all manner of animals, there had been some ancestor, some relation of modern humankind. The implication of this suggestion – for human origins in particular – was plain to see. But in 1871 he would go further – alarmingly so, as far as more conservative minds were concerned. The conclusion to *The Descent of Man* has within it the claim that, 'man is descended from some less highly organised form', a line that allowed caricaturists and others to infer he saw man connected in relatively recent time to some or other monkey.

Even as he was putting the finishing touches to *The Origin of Species*, Darwin had felt the shadows of older, more primitive humans looming over their modern descendants. Good scientist though he was, the absence of much physical proof in the form of fossilised early human remains discouraged him from saying so in print. But even before he put pen to paper, people had been finding human remains – fragmentary, enigmatic proof of earlier, older populations. The evidence was there; what was needed was an explanation . . . a story that fitted.

Louis Agassiz had been invited to Scotland in 1840 by his colleague and friend the Reverend William Buckland, the eccentric but brilliant Reader in Geology at Oxford University. Buckland had been a man of God first and a scientist second. But he was clever enough – and open-minded enough – to make a long personal journey from belief in the literal truth of the Old Testament to an acceptance of at least some of the scientific facts revealed during his lifetime. (Buckland was as fascinating as he was fascinated. He kept a hyena for a pet – as well as other animals just as dangerous. Throughout his life he pursued an ambition to taste the meat of every creature in existence and found something to commend in most; only the bluebottle was entirely without merit apparently, and moles had little to be said in their favour either.)

While studying divinity at Oxford he had found time to attend lectures in geology and mineralogy. Fascinated by rocks and fossils since childhood though he was, his faith convinced him the findings of geology would confirm rather than undermine the Book of Genesis. During the first decades of the nineteenth century he travelled all over Britain on horseback, clad always in his academic gown, to try and prove it and in 1821 his attention was drawn to a cave discovered at Kirkdale in Yorkshire by a squad of quarrymen. Large quantities of fossilised animal bone had been found inside and when Buckland visited he was able to identify dozens of species – including tropical exotics like elephant, lion, hippopotamus and hyena.

A literally Biblical interpretation of the find would have suggested the animals were victims of The Flood, that their carcasses had been swept into the cave's recesses – all the way from the tropics where they had lived and died – as the deluge swirled across the entire surface of the globe. Buckland, however, was able to suggest an alternative explanation that sought to reconcile his scientific observations with his faith in the received word of God. Though well aware of Hutton, and the teachings of Uniformitarianism that had followed in his wake, Buckland adhered to a version of 'Catastrophism', a philosophy that explained Earth's development in terms of sudden, violent, often short-lived events of such magnitude they had literally changed the world.

Rather than imagining a single creation of the world during six 24-hour days, Buckland believed there might have been a whole series – each followed by a catastrophic extinction event that wiped the slate clean. He reasoned, logically, that he and the rest of modern humankind were simply part of the most recent, which had sprung into being after Noah's ark came to rest on Mount Ararat.

Buckland observed that the fossils in Kirkdale Cave were

sealed beneath a relatively thin layer of mud and concluded it was only this topmost deposit that had been laid down by the great deluge. He imagined an antediluvian Britain populated by all manner of creatures – and suggested the hyenas had scavenged their remains as carrion. When The Flood struck all traces of the earlier fauna – other than those protected inside the cave – had been swept away.

After the publication of his findings in 1822, Buckland was awarded the Copley Medal by the Royal Society, 'for outstanding achievements in research'. The following year saw the publication of his masterwork *Reliquiae Diluvianae, or, Observations on the Organic Remains ... Attesting the Action of an Universal Deluge* (known as *Relics of The Flood*), which as well as winning academic approval became something of a surprise bestseller with the general public.

Earlier in 1823, just prior to completing the book, Buckland heard about yet more elephant bones – discovered this time in a sea cave at Paviland, on the Gower Peninsula of south Wales – and immediately travelled there. As soon as possible after his arrival, in an area that is remote now and likely all but inaccessible then, he made his way down the side of a cliff known locally as Yellow Top (on account of the sallow lichen that ekes a living on its surface) and across to the entrance of Goat's Hole Cave.

The landscape there is stunning today and can only have been as breathtaking in the Reverend Buckland's time. The cliffs are of limestone and have been scoured and beaten by ice and elements, wave and tide, until only the bare bones of the world remain. There is no hiding the age of the world at Paviland; her face is washed clean of all makeup and the sunlight is unforgiving, revealing every wrinkle of a long life. The several caves of Yellow Top were cut by waves when the sea level was nearly 30 feet higher than today; the mouth of Goat's Hole itself is shaped like a teardrop, lying lopsided towards the right.

Everywhere on the approach the limestone is pitted and pocked, sculpted and carved into outlandish, otherworldly Henry Moore shapes. The possessive tides pull back just long enough to permit an hour's access to the base of the steep rock face that leads to the cave, so that any visit in Buckland's footsteps is either short – or made half a day long by the inundation of the lower slopes by deep and dangerous water. Inside Goat's Hole Cave the world of the Reverend Buckland is intact. Behind, back in the daylight, the waves boom just as they did for him on that January day in 1823, counting more of the seconds, more of the minutes that have passed since the place was transformed into somewhere eternally special. For students of early humankind in Europe Paviland is a place of pilgrimage, made almost sacred by what it once contained – by what was laid there by people who knew an entirely different world.

Although the atmosphere of Buckland's time survives, many of the physical details he recorded within the cave sadly do not. It is hard to imagine how much pristine archaeology remained, untouched and unnoticed, in places like Goat's Hole Cave as late as the early nineteenth century. So much of the British landscape has since been picked clean by professional archaeologists and trophy-hunters alike that it takes some imagination to picture a time when our more recent forebears seemingly paid scant attention to the evidence of ancient worlds lying all around them.

As Buckland walked towards the rear portion of the cave, beyond the reach of the worst winter storms, he noted that everywhere the floor was covered with 'a mass of diluvial loam of a reddish-yellow colour, abundantly mixed with angular fragments of limestone and broken calcareous spar, and interspersed with recent sea-shells'. So far so familiar, but also abundant in the mix were the teeth and bones of 'elephant, rhinoceros, bear, hyena, wolf, fox, horse, ox, deer of two or three species, water-rats, sheep, birds and man'.

Here then was a time capsule – where remnants of ancient pasts, times when other creatures altogether made this land their home – that had been left alone until antiquarians like William Buckland finally disturbed their peace.

Buckland knew previous visitors had recently collected quantities of supposed elephant bones and ivory, and it was close by the location of those enigmatic remains that he opened his own trench. What he found, though it evidently moved him hardly at all, would eventually change the world.

'In another part,' he wrote, 'I discovered beneath a shallow covering of six inches of earth nearly the entire left side of a human female skeleton.' He was admirably methodical as well as confident in his ability to identify all he saw. Scattered among the bones, and laid around them in the grave, he found two handfuls of periwinkle shells, each perforated with a tiny hole so they could be strung together as a necklace. There were scores of fragments of cylindrical ivory rods, whittled down from tusks and as thick as a finger. There were other items of ivory too: rings measuring a few inches across, pieces cut into 'unmeaning forms' and another the size and shape 'of a human tongue'. He found as well 'a short skewer or chopstick, and made of the metacarpal bone of a wolf'.

The rod fragments and rings, the shells and the wolf bone – all were stained a deep-red colour, as were the human bones. Buckland was instantly sure whoever had dug the grave and placed the body inside it had then liberally backfilled it with a great deal of red ochre: 'They were all of them stained superficially with a dark brick-red colour, and enveloped by a coating . . . composed of red micaceous oxyde of iron which stained the earth, and in some parts extended itself to the distance of about half an inch around the surface of the bones. The body must have been entirely surrounded or covered over at the time of its interment with this red substance.'

Likely because he associated jewellery with the female of his species, Buckland assumed he had unearthed the body of a woman. And given that he had spotted the ramparts of a Roman camp on the cliff top directly above and behind the cave's location, he quickly decided she had made a home for herself where she was in easy reach of the soldiers – a camp-follower, as it were. Perhaps the final nail in the coffin of her reputation was provided by the red ochre heaped upon her remains – a scarlet woman indeed. 'The circumstance of the remains of a British camp existing on the hill immediately above this cave, seems to throw much light on the character and date of the woman under consideration; and whatever may have been her occupation, the vicinity of the camp would afford a motive for residence, as well as a means of subsistence, in what is now so exposed and uninviting a solitude.'

The good Reverend was sure, in other words, that he had found the skeleton of a prostitute – whose immorality had condemned her to be buried far from civilised society in the very cave where she had conducted her business. From that moment, the remains from Goat's Hole Cave were labelled the 'Red Lady of Paviland'.

All of this Buckland wrote up for his forthcoming *Relics of The Flood* and, along with everything else he had seen on his travels, his Red Lady convinced him of the truth of a world shaped by catastrophes. Whatever and whoever she might once have been she was 'clearly not coeval with the antediluvian bones of the extinct species'. In other words, in his mind she belonged to a world much more recent than the pre-Flood animals whose bones littered the cave.

Denied any other means of dating his discovery, he allowed his religious convictions, coupled with his knowledge of history, to provide an explanation that made sense to him: 'that the date of these human bones is coeval with that of the military occupation of the adjacent summits, and anterior to, or coeval with the Roman invasion of this country'.

But in 1823 Buckland was wrong – in his view of the Red Lady as in so much else. Rather than a Biblical flood, the Reverend's world was under threat from the tide of scientific thought rising from, among other sources, Hutton's *Theory of the Earth*. He fought the good fight for another decade and a half until finally the weight of evidence made him change his mind. It is greatly to his credit – and ultimately evidence of his love of unbiased observation – that he finally went with the flow.

Buckland had become aware of the work of Louis Agassiz, particularly that on fossil fish, and in 1834 he invited the young Swiss scientist to come and study the British collections. Then, in 1838, he visited Switzerland and saw for himself the evidence of glaciation in the Alpine valleys. By the time he accompanied Agassiz on his momentous tour of the Scottish Highlands, Buckland was already persuaded by the idea that a hitherto unexpected Ice Age had shaped much of Britain and Europe in ancient times.

But while he accepted some alterations to his world-view, he remained committed to a divine creation of Man – and a relatively recent one at that. He was, after all, a product of his times and that he nonetheless investigated his surroundings as diligently as he did is more deserving of praise – for all that his endeavours left us – than of criticism for his failure to see the world through our eyes. Had it not been for his efforts in Goat's Hole, for example, the so-called Red Lady of Paviland and the animal remains that accompanied the burial might not have been available for study by the twenty-first-century world. For this service to science at the very least, Buckland is owed an enormous debt of gratitude.

The Red Lady is kept today as part of the collections of the Oxford University Museum of Natural History, and is now in the care of Professor Jim Kennedy. There was no skull even when Buckland was excavating the find, but enough of the skeleton has survived to enable modern scientists to go much further towards understanding that most enigmatic and significant of burials.

'Within a few decades of Buckland's death, people re-examined the skeleton,' said Professor Kennedy. 'They looked at the shape of the pelvis, the shape of the long bones – and in particular the shape of the articulation surfaces [of the joints]. And on the basis of those features, any anatomy student today would recognise this as the skeleton, not of a young woman, but of a young man.'

Not a Red Lady then but a Red Laddie, who had come to die sometime in his early twenties. Much more importantly, as it turns out, further forensic analysis has made it possible to determine just how long ago that Red Laddie breathed his last.

Like every other scientist who lived and died before 1949, Buckland had not the advantage of radiocarbon dating. Until that momentous breakthrough, archaeologists generally made assumptions about the age of excavated items – human bones and every other class of artefact – based on the context in which they were found. Items were 'older' than those unearthed above them in a trench and 'younger' than any found beneath. This is and was the principle underpinning so-called 'relative dating'.

But in 1949 the American chemist Willard F. Libby noticed something special about one of the building blocks of life on Earth. All living things here are made primarily of the element carbon. A tiny proportion is formed in the planet's upper atmosphere when cosmic rays from the sun bombard nitrogen atoms, transforming them into carbon – and not just common-or-garden variety carbon, but rather *radioactive* carbon. This magical ingredient, in the form of carbon dioxide, then dissolves in the oceans and enters the food chain via photosynthesis by plants.

Libby's genius was to notice that at the moment a living thing dies, the radioactive carbon within it (known as C14) begins to decay and break down, reverting to nitrogen once more. Crucially for archaeologists set on determining the age of objects, C14 always decays at the same rate. Exactly 5,730 years after something dies (or, more particularly in the case of an archaeological find like the Red Laddie, some*one*) only half the original amount of C14 remains within them. After a further 5,730 years there will be only half as much again – and so on, at exactly the same rate of decay until, after perhaps 60,000 years, the remaining amount of C14 is just too small to measure.

Libby realised that by counting the proportion of atoms of C14 remaining in an object made of organic material – a piece of wood, antler, skin or bone – it would be possible to determine exactly how long ago it had died.

A team of archaeologists at Oxford University, led by Dr Tom Higham, has subjected a tiny sample of bone from the Red Laddie to precisely this process. The painstakingly counted C14 atoms discovered within revealed he died a little over 33,000 years ago. He was therefore the first modern human being – someone exactly like us – who lived in the land we know as Britain.

The Red Laddie's Britain was a very different place, to say the least. Louis Agassiz rightly saw a world shaped by ice, but he never learned the whole truth of it. During the most recent 30 million or so years of our planet's history, glaciation has been at work. Even today its causes – the reasons why Earth has sometimes hurtled through the universe as a giant snowball – are not fully understood.

The seemingly random descent into an Ice Age may be partly a result of the shape of Earth's orbit around the sun. More than four billion years ago when Earth was a relative newborn, still a glowing, cherry-red ball of molten rock, something of similar size thumped into it like a giant fist. The force of the punch knocked out a mass of molten material that later solidified to form the Moon – and also jolted Earth out of kilter so that rather than sitting in an upright position as before, it reeled slightly backwards.

In spite of the blow, despite being juddered out of true by many degrees, the planet kept spinning. More importantly in terms of the conditions that enable continent-wide ice flows to form, the impact also changed Earth's orbit from a circular path into an oval form best described as an ellipse; and so during the course of our year-long waltz with a star we are sometimes close to our dance partner, sometimes further away. It seems that when other conditions on Earth conspire we are sometimes long enough out of the spotlight to let the ice take an unshakeable hold.

The northern hemisphere in particular has known the violence of the ice again and again during the last three million years – long, cold glacials interspersed with shorter, warmer interglacials.

The uncomfortable truth is that we are presently enjoying one of those summer holidays from the ice – and have been for the past 11,500 years or so. During the last 750,000 years the glacial cold spells have tended to be longer and more severe than ever before, each one lasting for an average of 100 millennia. The most recent – the one spotted by Agassiz – was at its peak just 21,000 years ago. What he identified was almost literally just the tip of the iceberg.

The Red Laddie and his fellows looked up at Yellow Top and the rest of Paviland from an utterly different world. He lived and died during a time classified by archaeologists as the Upper Palaeolithic – towards the end of the Old Stone Age – and may have shared his version of Europe with just a few tens of thousands of people. In his time, 30,000-odd years ago, it was a landmass on a downward spiral towards another Ice Age. Great sheets of ice were advancing from the north and, with so much water locked up inside them, the sea level was significantly lower than today. Although the Paviland caves are on the coast now, 33,000 years ago the sea was perhaps 70 or 80 miles further away. Paviland looked out, not over rolling waves but across a low-lying plain that stretched far off into the horizon and beyond.

The land now known as Britain was not an island then, but a peninsula of north-west Europe peopled by nomadic hunters in thrall to the animals upon which their very existence depended. The beasts moved in great migratory herds, reindeer and wild horse – and also another species, parts of which had been buried near the young man's grave in Goat's Hole Cave. For the skull, bones and ivory recorded by Buckland had come not from any tropical elephant, but from a tundra-dwelling Ice-Age mammoth.

In his report of his excavations at Paviland, in *Relics of The Flood*, Buckland included a careful plan that clearly showed the 'elephant' skull lying close by the human skeleton. But sometime not long after their discovery, the animal's remains became separated from those of the more infamous Red Laddie and for the best part of two centuries they went their separate ways. For almost all of that time the mammoth bones were presumed lost. Only when curators in a Swansea museum began going through the contents of some long-neglected boxes, in 2009, did the light of day fall upon the beast once more. Mammoth tusks and bones were found, together with around 300 other animal bones collected from Goat's Hole just before Buckland arrived – undoubtedly parts of the same skull he featured in his excavation plan – and during the filming of *A History of Ancient Britain* the young man and his mammoth were reunited for the very first time.

Now those red-hued bones and blackening ivory suggest a story more moving by far than the good Reverend's harlot. Instead they speak of tragedy and grief – and an attempt by thoughtful, imaginative people to move beyond loss. Perhaps a hunting party tracked a lone mammoth across terrain they knew well ...

They had wounded it already, many times, with stone-tipped spears. And there was dark blood in its tracks, from someplace deep. Patience was what mattered now – that and the stamina to stay close, bring it to bay and finish it. This was land their fathers and mothers had roamed before them, in endless pursuit of the herds – and its contours and landmarks, its scents and sounds were as familiar as each other's faces. It was also unforgiving. It had been cold for longer than memory and they sensed rather than saw the towering mass of the cliff face high above them, pitted with caves and all but invisible through the snow-laden wind. It was here in its familiar shadow they hoped to corner the beast once and for all. Perhaps the storm should have warned them – persuaded them to call off the hunt until the weather eased just a little. But the folk of the tribe were hungry and the kill was close – a kill that would bring warmth to all souls. Then all at once the ground shook and their would-be prey was among them, weakened and in agony but raging and deadly dangerous nonetheless. Taken by surprise, the hunters briefly scattered like snowflakes, all but one. Before they could make sense of the chaos, the favourite was felled. He was the one they loved best of all their number and now he was dead at the feet of the beast. Enraged, they surrounded the monster as it stood over their fallen son and brother, and buried their spears in its sides again and again – finally reaching vital organs and dropping it to its knees. It was over quickly then. Two deaths separated by moments, moments that made all the difference. Later, with the

*favourite cold and their anguish still warm, they climbed with his
body to the cave mouth. Others bore a separate burden and they huffed
and panted under its weight. In times past the tear-shaped cave had
sheltered them for nights and days and now it would be his sanctuary
for all eternity. Inside, away from the wind and snow, they dug his
grave. They laid him gently down and placed the head of the one that
had killed him close by. Let any who passed this way remember what
had happened – know that there was eternal rest here for the man
and the beast together. Two spirits united in a shared death. Then, on
this furthest outreach of Europe, the Red Laddie's family and companions bade him a final farewell and left him behind for ever . . .*

Fanciful? Certainly. But fantasy? Not necessarily. Three hundred centuries ago a young man was buried in a cave at Paviland
and a mammoth skull was laid nearby. Neither accident of Biblical
flood nor Romano-British morality brought those two together.
Rather, what was left behind in Goat's Hole Cave all those years
ago was some mother's son; and those that buried him there, safe
from the wind and the world, were at pains to leave him with
ivory tokens for his amusement and a mammoth skull for his
headstone. The rods may have had some practical function but
seem more likely to have been ceremonial, worn or carried by
someone special. The periwinkle necklace and other items of
jewellery look like gifts too, from people who loved him in life as
well as in death. These were modern human beings – the same as
us in every way. We are separated from them only by circumstances
and time. We do them – and ourselves – a disservice if we do not
see the Red Laddie of Paviland, his keepsakes and his mammoth
for what he is: one of us.

When Buckland unearthed his Red Lady of Paviland in 1823, it
was hardly the first discovery of one of modern humankind's
ancestors. Down through the centuries people have found, from
time to time, fragments that have come to be understood as
characters from earlier pages of the human story. In total, the
number of known fragments of our most ancient ancestors still
do not add up to much – but they have been just numerous

enough to let palaeontologists follow them all the way back to the beginning.

Humankind has always originated in Africa. It is our home. There have been several species of human over the millennia, as though Earth conducted experiments and trials to see what kind works best. As far as palaeontology can tell, the first actually to leave the warmth of the nursery and head out into the rest of the world was *Homo erectus* – upright man – who began spreading north, east and west, into Asia and Europe, just less than two million years ago. In ways not yet fully understood – and certainly lacking consensus among palaeontologists – *Homo erectus* was subsequently joined on stage by a closely related species called *Homo heidelbergensis*. Named after a jawbone found near the city of Heidelberg, in south-west Germany, in 1907, *Heidelbergensis* seems either to be descended from *Erectus* or from some earlier, more primitive species that is a common ancestor to both – perhaps *Homo habilis*, handy-man, or *Homo ergaster*, workman, both of whose faint traces are also found in Africa, Europe and Asia from time to time. The paucity of physical evidence of any of these species recovered from around the world so far means that certainty is as elusive as the people themselves.

Further complicating the picture is Neanderthal man. The first remains of this additional relative were found in the Neander Valley, near the town of Düsseldorf in western Germany, in 1856 and finally given the name *Homo neanderthalensis* in 1863. Some palaeontologists see Neanderthal characteristics on skulls and bones that are as much as 600,000 years old, but there is more general agreement that humans of this species inhabited Europe and Asia from around 350–400,000 years ago. More interesting than when they 'start', however, is when they finish.

Neanderthals were still roaming the European continent 25,000 years ago. While that species was evolving for hundreds of thousands of years in Europe and Asia, somewhere in Africa there was one last throw of the human dice. *Homo sapiens sapiens* – 'wise man', modern man – was the result, and had certainly evolved somewhere on the Dark Continent by at least around 200,000 years ago. Not until as recently as perhaps the last 100,000 years, however, did any of us leave the homeland and make our way into other parts of the world.

Modern humans are therefore the Johnny-come-latelies of the story but their arrival in Europe by around 40,000 years ago means they encountered a sitting tenant there in the form of the Neanderthals. For perhaps several millennia, until the last of the Neanderthals died out, for reasons unknown, our modern ancestors shared their world with a venerable old uncle of the human race.

From his office in the Natural History Museum in London, Professor Chris Stringer directs the Ancient Human Occupation of Britain Project. Stringer's name is inextricably linked with the now broadly accepted 'Out of Africa' theory and he understands more about the shadowy comings and goings of humans in Britain than perhaps anyone else.

If the mammoth-hunter from Paviland is the first and oldest modern man known to have lived in Britain, he was certainly not the first human. In *Homo Britannicus – The Incredible Story of Human Life in Britain* – Stringer describes the discovery of the individual who is the earliest known inhabitant.

Close to the city of Chichester, in West Sussex, is a gravel quarry called Boxgrove. Along with gravel, people regularly found distinctive flint tools called handaxes there, and it was these that first attracted archaeologists and palaeontologists to the area.

For those who study the ancient past, the 'handaxe' is a talisman, the word itself almost a shibboleth. In some form they have been part of the human toolkit from the very beginning. Handaxes developed from the crude (but effective) pebble tools used by the earliest humans for butchering meat millions of years ago on the African plains. Knock a couple of hand-sized pebbles together and soon flakes will be removed from one of them, leaving a useful sharp edge. But by at least a million years ago this primitive technique had evolved to produce the heart-stoppingly beautiful, teardrop-shaped tools that have been humankind's calling card all over the Old World. With a point at one end, a cutting edge down each of the two long sides and a heavy butt for crushing and hammering they became, according to Stringer, the Swiss Army Knives of the Palaeolithic.

Unless and until you have actually held a Palaeolithic handaxe, it is impossible to understand why they exert such power. They were made not by us, but by our distant relations, members of wholly separate species like *Homo heidelbergensis* and *Homo neanderthalensis*, yet they fit into our hands as though made with us in mind. It is a unique sensation to pick up one of those beautiful bi-faced stones with one hand and fit it into the palm of the other. Almost as a reflex the fingers fold around the butt, the fingertips coming naturally to rest on a barely discernible, yet deliberately crafted asymmetric ridge that makes the holding that little bit more comfortable.

Just as the fingers of an old man's hands at rest still curl inwards in memory of the time they spent balled into fists inside his mother's womb, so our hands receive handaxes from half a million years ago as though those tools were made to fill the space left empty by all the years.

Hold up your good hand and turn the palm towards your face. Relax your fingers, watch them curl towards your palm and see how your fingertips form a set of four steps rising upwards from little finger to index: that is how they would sit along the asymmetric ridge of a handaxe. Now turn your hand until your thumb is towards your face. Look at the empty space between your fingertips and your palm. That is the space waiting to be filled by the butt of a Palaeolithic handaxe. (People used to make things that fit.)

As well as many, many handaxes, what the scientists eventually found at Boxgrove, sealed beneath many feet of sand and fine silt, was a glimpse of a truly ancient Britain. The old land surface was so astonishingly well preserved it was possible to find the very spots where people had knelt down to make their handaxes. All the waste flakes created during the crafting of single tools, removed by expert hands during bursts of activity lasting perhaps just 10 or 20 minutes, are found lying precisely where they fell. Framed by the outline of the flint-knappers' legs and knees, they can be reassembled to reveal the shape of the original flint nodule – and when plaster is poured into the void it makes an exact replica of the handaxe that was the point of the exercise in the first place.

Also sealed beneath the silt are the remains of the animals those handaxes were made to butcher. Bones of bison, giant deer, horse, red deer and rhinoceros have all been recovered, many bearing the marks made as they were cut up; others have been gnawed by scavengers like hyena and wolf. All of this was fascinating enough but then, in 1993, a very special bone indeed was brought to light at Boxgrove. It was this that put the quarry firmly on the map of the human story. Together with fellow palaeontologist Simon Parfitt, Stringer identified it as part of a human shinbone from an ancestor belonging to the species *Homo heidelbergensis*. It is half a million years old.

Continuing excavation nearby unearthed two human teeth and now the remains are stored together in the Natural History Museum in London. Although there are limits to how much can be deduced from part of a shin and two teeth, they still reveal a remarkable amount about their owner, or indeed owners. Stringer explained that Boxgrove Man stood around five feet 11 inches tall and weighed in the region of 14 stone. It is a massively constructed bone (the scale of it led to the assumption it was part of a man's rather than a woman's leg) suggestive of someone used to a hard and physically demanding lifestyle. Examination of the teeth found the surfaces heavily scored and scratched and it is thought the marks were made by a sharp-edged flint tool used to hack away at meat held between clamped jaws.

Regardless of what the bone and the teeth reveal about Boxgrove Man's lifestyle, they are profoundly moving simply because of what and *who* they are. Given their value to science, I was not allowed to lay so much as a finger on them. The closest I got was holding one faintly shaky hand an inch or so above the bone, but that was enough. Those remains are half a million years old ... half a million years. That is the kind of timeframe I have in mind when I think about mountains forming, or great rivers cutting chasms through solid rock. And yet in the Natural History Museum I held my hand over the few remains of a man who lived 5,000 centuries ago in an unimaginably alien Britain, the same and not the same – one that was home to lions, hyenas and rhinoceroses.

Stringer's AHOB project has found stone tools of even older vintage at Pakefield in Suffolk, and at Happisburgh in Norfolk. At both sites the geological evidence, together with animal remains found in association with the tools, suggests occupation by some kind of human at least as long ago as 700,000 years. The search for the beginning of the human story in Britain keeps burrowing deeper and deeper.

Boxgrove Man lived during the period known as the Lower Palaeolithic, the earliest part of the Old Stone Age. While it might be natural to assume that, having reached the territory of Britain, humans of one kind or another stayed put here, in fact the truth is quite different – and altogether stranger. Boxgrove Britain was wiped away, like chalk dust from a blackboard, by the Ice Age known to geologists as the Anglian. For 100,000 years or more, while the glaciers ground out yet more trillions of tons of rock from the landscape, gouging valleys here, lowering mountains there, life here was utterly absent. And by the time humans returned they were not *Homo heidelbergensis* any more, as Boxgrove Man had been, but his younger relative *Homo neanderthalensis*.

Those step-brothers and -sisters of ours are perhaps the most fascinating and enigmatic of all the skeletons in modern man's closet. Despite more recent rehabilitation of their reputation, still the very word 'Neanderthal' has connotations of the brute animal, bringing to mind a hairy, knuckle-dragging, lantern-jawed cave man.

Books and television documentaries have sought to draw a different picture, of sensitive souls in tune with nature and therefore with something profound to teach us about ourselves. The discovery of nine Neanderthal skeletons in a cave called Shanidar, in the Zagros Mountains of northern Iraq, went some way towards reinvesting the species with the sensitivity and dignity their outward appearance had for so long denied them.

Excavated in the late 1950s and early 1960s, some of them appeared to have been given formal burials, even funerals, by their fellows. At least three were mature adults at the time of death – indeed one was aged perhaps 40–50 years old, making him the equivalent of an octogenarian at least, by modern standards. Nick-named 'Nandy' by the excavators, he was by any standards a poor soul. At some point in his life he had suffered a crushing blow to the left side of his head that would almost certainly have left him blind in that eye, as well as facially disfigured. His right arm was withered and wasted – the result of childhood injury, disease or birth defect – and the lower bones and hand had likely been amputated at some point many years before death. There was also a suggestion of wasting or deformity of his right leg and foot so that he would have walked with a heavy, painful limp. Despite these weaknesses, which would have made life very difficult for Nandy, he had obviously been cared for and valued by the tribe. Unable to hunt, he was nonetheless provided for – presumably because he was loved.

Another adult male buried in the cave had been placed in his grave lying in the foetal position. Analysis of the soil in the fill revealed unusually high levels of pollen of several different flowering plants. It is possible the pollen was introduced to the grave long after the burial – perhaps by burrowing animals – but the possibility has lingered that those mourning the dead man had filled his grave with flower heads and blossom, hardly the behaviour of grunting ape-men.

Despite evidence like Shanidar, first impressions last and for most people today it is hard to shake off the image of the

Quasimodo, the approximation of a man pictured by those who came face to face with that first skeleton in the Neander Valley in the middle of the nineteenth century.

Whoever – *whatever* – they were, it was Neanderthals who colonised the British peninsula of north-west Europe after the ice had retreated once more. Human remains were found in a gravel quarry at Swanscombe, in Kent, in the 1930s. Like Boxgrove, the site of Swanscombe had attracted the attention of palaeontologists because of the regular discovery among the sands and gravels there of beautifully worked flint handaxes. According to Chris Stringer, something of the order of 100,000 handaxes have been recovered from the Swanscombe area over the years – testament to generations of occupation. The human remains are those of a woman who lived and died – on low-level terrain beside the river that would in time become the Thames – around 400,000 years ago.

There is not much to see of Swanscombe Woman – just two pieces of bone that formed the back of her skull – but they are those of a Neanderthal just the same. To the rear of modern skulls there is a bump, an anchor point for the muscles of the neck. On Neanderthals the same function was performed by a shallow depression and that telltale hollow is there on the Swanscombe skull. Comparison with other skeletons from Europe enables a more complete sketch to be drawn of this very early Kentish woman.

She would have been at least as tall or taller than an average modern woman and more powerfully built. Neanderthal men and women alike were most identifiable not by their muscularity and width, but by their faces and heads. While the foreheads of modern humans rise almost straight up from the nose to create a domed expanse above the face, the Neanderthal equivalent was low and flat, sweeping almost straight back into the hairline behind massively overhanging, frowning brow ridges. Rather than the protruding chin of today, the Neanderthal's was receding and 'weak' by comparison. Like Boxgrove Man, Swanscombe Woman's teeth would likely have borne scratches resultant from holding meat and other material between clamped jaws so she could cut at it with a sharp stone tool held in one hand. For a while it was in vogue among palaeontologists to say you could give one of those fellows a shave and a suit – or indeed some make-up and a nice dress – and watch him or her pass unnoticed on a modern city street. Given the evidence, I still think he – and certainly she – would frighten the horses.

In 2007, geneticists extracted DNA from the bones of two European Neanderthals and retrieved from it parts of the gene that gives rise to ginger hair in modern humans. It is a separate and uniquely Neanderthal variant of the gene, called MC1R, but similar nonetheless. Ginger hair is part of the suite of characteristics that enables people living towards the northern portion of the planet to make more efficient use of the available sunlight for processing Vitamin D. Ginger people do better in cold climates, starved of daylight – especially in the avoidance of conditions like rickets – than do those with dark hair and skin. Much more interestingly, though, it means that as well as imagining them as robust, muscular and beetle-browed, we can also picture many of the Neanderthals as people with flaming red hair.

Swanscombe Woman shared her part of the land that would become Britain with a whole array of animal species including deer of various kinds, wild boar, bison and horse. She would also have been familiar with the sight of elephants, lions, monkeys and rhinoceroses. Her Britain was as outlandish and unfamiliar to us as her face.

The Neanderthals who buried their dead in Shanidar Cave were alive around 60,000 years ago, endless millennia after their counterparts in Kent. The Swanscombe bones are so much older they can be assigned to a time when *Homo neanderthalensis* was still evolving, still becoming the new species of human that would populate Asia and Europe for hundreds of thousands of years before the arrival of modern people. But clearly the Neanderthals became a success story in their own right. Though the popular image has them clad in ragged animal skins and scraping an existence in the shadow of creatures like woolly mammoths, in an ice- and snow-bound world, their remains have also been found in the context of much warmer climates, in Europe and in Asia. To some extent they were as adaptable as us – though perhaps not quite so good at moving between climatic and environmental extremes.

In Britain the warm interglacial known by Swanscombe Woman is referred to as the Hoxnian, after the discovery of handaxes and ancient animal bones at Hoxne, in Suffolk, in the late eighteenth century. No human remains were found but the similarity of the tools, and the bones of animals that were presumably butchered with them, makes it clear both sites were occupied by the same kind of people, living the same way. There are plenty of other sites too, from the same period around 400,000 years ago, suggesting that the British climate then, and the animals that thrived in it, provided good living for successive generations of Neanderthals. But for palaeontologists like Chris Stringer, the frustration lies in what apparently happened next.

After thousands of years of warmth, the cold returned again to the land – extreme cold. The Neanderthals, like the *Homo heidelbergensis* people of Boxgrove before them, were driven off, out of Britain. Given the severity of conditions during an Ice Age this is not in itself a surprise; the frustrating mystery is that, having been deserted at the end of the Hoxnian interglacial, Britain apparently remained devoid of human life for the next 300,000 years and more. At the very least, no physical evidence to the contrary has yet been found.

When Neanderthal remains are found again in Britain, they date from no more than 50–60,000 years ago. Often ephemeral, they testify to people living in a tougher world, a Britain cold enough to suit beasts like the woolly mammoth. Long before Paviland became a last resting place for a modern man 33,000 years ago, the cave appears to have provided shelter for Neanderthals. At some later point both species shared Europe, and presumably Britain as well.

Rather than *Homo sapiens*, the very earliest modern humans are known to archaeologists and palaeontologists as *Cro-Magnon Man*. Named after the remains of five individuals found in 1868 in a rock shelter in the French Dordogne called 'Abri de Cro-Magnon', they are like us in every way that matters – fully modern. But like the first edition of a book, or the first marque of a new model of car, there is something a little bit special and more desirable about these oldest of us. They should perhaps be considered our elders . . . and the best of us.

Cro-Magnons were a little taller than us, longer-limbed and slightly more robust – the sort of people who, were a few of them to walk into a twenty-first-century gathering, would turn every head in the room and make even the alpha-males lower their eyes in deference. It was Cro-Magnons who shared the world with Neanderthals for a time and saw the last of them die.

What they made of one another, those unlikely bedfellows, can only be guessed at. But while the Neanderthals themselves have most certainly gone, something remains that has unsettled us ever since. In his novel *Dance of the Tiger* the Finnish palaeontologist Björn Kurtén imagined Neanderthals as the inspiration for the trolls that populate Scandinavian myth and folklore: so that a people who lived in Europe for hundreds of thousands of years are relegated to the role of monsters, alive only in children's stories where they terrorise billy goats – before being bested even by them in the end.

Kurtén might be at least partly right. The Neanderthals must have been remembered by generations of Cro-Magnons, and later in the folklore of *Homo sapiens*, long after the last of them was gone. But surely they went into the lore of the tribe as something more enigmatic and meaningful than just dull-eyed oafs?

It seems to me the memory goes deeper than tales of trolls. The Old World's ultimate creation myth after all has, in some of its earliest pages, profound stories of the young dispossessing the old, stories of betrayal of rightful heirs by younger kin – stories, in effect, of one people displacing another. Something happened in the past – something that left the modern human race with a guilty conscience, troubled by an ancient wrong; and it has never been forgotten, or forgiven.

James Hutton, Louis Agassiz, William Buckland – like scores of otherwise enlightened thinkers in the eighteenth and nineteenth centuries – were weighed down by the immovable object of The Bible. Away from the rarefied atmosphere populated by radical thinkers, the vast majority of Britons (and Europeans besides) held that all a person needed to know about the world was contained within the pages of one good book.

The world knows better now of course and has replaced religious dogma with science. But it bears remembering that Bible stories are still part of what has been remembered and their contents should not be dismissed out of hand. The creation myth contained in the Book of Genesis is likely much older than the unknown hand or hands that first wrote it down. Long before the invention of writing, the story must have been passed generation to generation by word of mouth. Something of it, some fragment at least, must really have happened; some echo of real events and real people must have inspired it.

In Genesis, Chapter 25, Rebekah, the wife of Isaac, falls pregnant with twins. God tells her she has in her womb: 'two manner of people ... and the one people shall be stronger than the other people; and the elder shall serve the younger'.

The first to be born, the rightful heir, is called Esau. His body is covered with red hair and even as he is being lifted up from the bloodied sheets his younger brother's hand reaches out from within their mother to grab hold of the elder's heel. This is Jacob, hairless and grasping, and smooth in every sense of the word.

'And the first came out red, all over like an hairy garment ... '. Is this a memory of the people who came before, known to us as Neanderthals, many of whom according to the DNA evidence were red-haired? While Neanderthals, perhaps red and hairy, lived in caves like Shanidar, were there smooth-skinned Cro-Magnons living nearby in tents and similar shelters, watching the decline of their neighbours like the later acts in a long-running story, and failing to intervene?

As Esau and Jacob grow to manhood, they are clearly different. Hairless Jacob is 'a plain man, dwelling in tents', while his brother Esau is 'a cunning hunter, a man of the field'. In the end, the more sophisticated, more modern Jacob uses guile and treachery to trick his elder brother out of what is rightfully his – their father's blessing and worldly goods.

Is this simple tale, of one modern-living man dispossessing the wild hunter, a memory of ancient times when Cro-Magnons and the rest of more recent humankind displaced the older Neanderthals, robbing them of their entitlement to the world? Is the truth of it all even there in the background of daily life today, drifting ghost-like in the things we know, and think, and say . . . even laugh about: 'Ginger people! D'you know what they are?' asks Al Murray's Pub Landlord. 'Our aborigines . . . that's what! GINGERIGINES! Look at 'em . . . they were 'ere first. All this is theirs!'

Eenie, meenie, miney, mo . . . vestigial remnant of a counting system – one, two, three four – in a lost language that predates every 'British' tongue known to linguists. It survives because of memory – trapped like a bug in amber. The Pub Landlord's rant might also retain a germ of truth.

The hitherto unsuspected years, revealed by Hutton and others during the Scottish Enlightenment, are gradually being populated in Britain by examples of Earth's many and varied experiments with mankind. Some left their tools behind at Pakefield in Suffolk and at Happisburgh in Norfolk, at least 700,000 years ago. More of the same spent some of their years at Boxgrove in West Sussex 200,000 years later, and at least one of their number stayed behind for good. Neanderthals came and went and came again, subject always to the whim of the ice. Much more recently the Cro-Magnons joined them here and in the rest of Europe. It is reasonable as well to imagine the younger incomers learning much about surviving the increasingly cold environment by watching and mixing with their older relations. If that happened, then the Cro-Magnons assumed the wisdom of the Neanderthals along with everything else.

Some have speculated that there might have been inter-breeding of the two species but that has always seemed unlikely to me, given the manifest physical differences. Would the one really have found enough attractive in the other? Even if there were young born to mixed couples, it is just as likely the genetic differences between the species would have doomed those children to sterility – in the same way that mules are born the infertile offspring of mating between horses and donkeys.

If the ultimate extinction of the Neanderthals invoked guilt in the minds of the Cro-Magnons, it was wiped away at first by the coming of yet another Ice Age. This incursion into Britain by the glaciers of the Devensian – two-thirds of a mile deep at the height of it all, 20,000-odd years ago – is the event that separates us from all of that past. It was the world of the Red Laddie of Paviland that ended with its onset – a climate change so cataclysmic it makes our modern fears about the consequences of global warming seem, by comparison, like hysteria brought on by the prospect of light showers in the afternoon.

It was not just Britain that was affected of course. All across northern Europe the story was more or less the same. The whole planet was colder, in fact, but in the north the effects were particularly brutal. Hardy though those bands of nomadic hunters were – men and women like the Red Laddie and his family – the depths to which the climate plummeted were too great to be endured. Britain was nothing but a frozen wilderness crushed beneath the glaciers, and by the time the Ice Age reached its peak 21,000 years ago, humankind was effectively evicted from much of the continent. Pockets of population survived, in the south of France and Spain and perhaps further east in the area occupied today by the Mediterranean. For the most part, though, even the best-equipped creatures – like the woolly mammoth – were unable to cope and fled in the face of the ice.

For thousands of years it was the same – a winter so long it would have made the Ice Queen's hold on Narnia look like nothing more than a few bad days.

It was not until around 16,000 years ago that conditions eased a little, and Britain and the rest of northern Europe entered a period of relative respite – and in this context the word 'relative' is important. Conditions in Britain were still unspeakably cold by our standards but the ice did retreat to the extent that a few groups of hunters were able to contemplate a return to this most northerly peninsula of western Europe. Word must have reached those surviving hunting communities in their boltholes in the south and gradually, like the light of dawn creeping tentatively into the dark, humankind ventured onto our land once more.

From 14,000 or so years ago, people were living all across southern Britain – in and around caves in Cheddar Gorge in Somerset, in the Creswell Crags area near Sheffield in south Yorkshire, at Kent's Cavern in Devon as well as at just less than 30 other known locations, all of them in England. The tools and other evidence they left behind have been grouped together into the 'Creswellian Culture' and it has much in common with the lifestyle of folk of similar vintage living in southern Europe around the same time and even considerably earlier. On the other side of the English Channel similar material is described as 'Magdalenian' – after finds in La Madeleine rock-shelter in the Dordogne.

After the mighty handaxes of the Lower and Middle Palaeolithic, some of the Creswellian toolkit can appear fairly uninspiring at first glance. The modest little blades and points of flint knocked off a prepared 'core' are regarded by archaeologists, however, as a mark of sophistication, and of technological advance. While a handaxe was a single tool used for many jobs, by the Creswellian period of the Upper Palaeolithic, craftsmen were making specialised equipment for specific tasks. They were also making exquisite harpoon points from mammoth ivory and needles and awls from the bones and teeth of other animals. Marine amber from the coast of the North Sea and even further afield was also being collected, by a people used to ranging over vast territories in search of raw materials. The amber was made into beads for jewellery, things that show these people had the time and the inclination to make decorative items just for the joy of it. There are also some-times so-called 'batons' of carefully worked reindeer antler which, while they may have had some practical function, seem just as likely to have been carried purely as status symbols.

Back where they had presumably come from, in south-west France perhaps, or southern Spain, some of the people had been in the habit of expressing themselves in breathtaking art. In hundreds of caves – most famously at Lascaux in France and Altamira in Spain – artists conjured entire herds of bulls and horses; woolly mammoths and rhinos and the rest of the animals that shared their world, with palettes of colour prepared from natural pigments.

They are works so visceral, so potent they could only ever have been executed by painters who knew their subjects like they knew their mothers and brothers. It is even unlikely they saw as clear-cut a division between themselves and the great beasts as we do – rather they were depicting kindred spirits. Illuminated by flickering flames – as many must have been, since they are painted in chambers beyond the reach of natural light – the painted animals seem almost to move or at least to breathe. The illusion is heightened by the way the artists used the contours of the living rock to give their work the appearance of three dimensions.

The Upper Palaeolithic cave art of Europe was a tradition that lasted for perhaps 20,000 years, and it will always be rightly described as primitive. But it is upon those anonymous artists' shoulders – giants' shoulders – that later masters like Picasso were able to stand. The mercurial Spaniard himself declared: 'After Altamira, all is decadence.'

For the longest time it was believed, particularly by French and Spanish archaeologists and palaeontologists, that no such artistic talent had permeated as far as Britain. Surely any vagabonds who had reached so far into the frozen wilderness could only have evolved a culture so starved and so pared back to the basics of survival, it could never have supported anything as sophisticated as art? For much of the twentieth century this assumption was borne out by the absence of suitable discoveries here.

Until the twenty-first century, the only bonafide artwork known from Creswellian Britain was the etching of a horse head on a sliver of rib bone. Despite its size (just two or three inches in length), it is still a wonder to behold. A whole sequence of thoughts – the thoughts of an Ice Age artist – are there on the bone along with the horse. He or she had first to select the raw material and then, in the manner of a canvas, the surface of the bone was cleaned and polished in readiness for the making of the image itself. With just a few perfectly judged and executed lines, the likeness of a galloping horse has been made to leap into life, whole and breathing. The hairs of the mane stand erect like hackles raised in fear or excitement; the nostrils are flared as though by effort, the eyes wide and blazing. Despite the lack of space, the artist has even managed to suggest the animal's plunging forelegs.

At some point after completing it, the artist deliberately defaced the work – by scratching across it a series of lines and then snapping the bone in two. Perhaps it was dissatisfaction with the finished piece, or an attempt to influence future events. Either way, to hold that artwork is to hold some few moments, some of the thinking of a person who lived in Britain more than 13,500 years ago.

Sliver of a thing that it is, the horse head rib bone makes a person wonder what else the artist achieved. How much of his or her portfolio has been destroyed by bad luck and time? Imagine some Europe-wide catastrophe in the sixteenth century had destroyed every last work by Michelangelo, so that only a single crumpled scrap of paper survived, bearing a sketch made of a handful of lines. Imagine that was all we had of him. Then apply the same thought to whoever sketched that galloping horse while the Ice Age waxed and waned. What became of his Sistine Chapel, and his David?

That little treasure from so-called Robin Hood's Cave, within the Creswell Crags, was for long the sum total of Palaeolithic art in Britain. Then, in April 2003, archaeologists and cave art specialists Paul Bahn, Paul Pettitt and Sergio Ripoll began surveying the caves' interiors.

From outside the caves look almost too good to be true. Facing each other across the floor of a wide, limestone gorge – self-contained residences cut into both cliff faces so that each cave's inhabitants had neighbours either side and across the way as well – Creswell Crags appears for all the world like a prehistoric Coronation Street. It is easy to imagine lives lived there long ago, the smell of fires, the sounds of voices as people went about their business.

The caves were first occupied by Neanderthal people 40–50,000 years ago and then again by Cro-Magnons around the time of the end of the last Ice Age; and given that the tip of the ice sheet terminated just 30 miles north of Sheffield, these are closer to the sharp end than any other known sites of human habitation in Britain.

The caves have attracted tourists for well over a century and it was the Victorians who gave them their fanciful names: Church Hole, Mother Grundy's Parlour, Pin Hole, Robin Hood's Cave. It was inside Church Hole, an unpromising, irregularly shaped chamber, that the three archaeologists made the discoveries that secured Britain a place on the world map of Palaeolithic cave art. Using directional lighting to cast the cave walls into shadow, they first of all spotted what they assumed to be an engraving of an ibex. It was a stunning moment for the trio. Far beyond the known limits of such ancient creativity, in the literal shadow of the Devensian ice, a beautifully rendered work by a skilled artist had finally come to the attention of the modern world. Having seen one, it was suddenly much easier for Bahn and his colleagues to pick out the rest – as many as

90 individual engravings in Church Hole alone.

It bears pointing out that even when standing in front of the best of them – perhaps the awe-inspiring depiction of a bison, the head and forequarters of the beast taking advantage of a natural bulge in the rock wall to give added vitality and power to the piece – they are still hard to see. Maybe they were once more obvious, the lines deeper and casting sharper shadows, or picked out with pigments to give the colours of life. But there is no doubting their quality, or their great age. Now correctly identified as a stag, the 'ibex' was partially covered by cave flowstone (much the same material that forms stalactites and stalagmites). Some of this was removed and dated, by a technique called uranium-series, to reveal the stag was cut into the rock more than 13,000 years ago.

Church Hole Cave is a gallery of wonders. On part of the ceiling is an engraving that initially defied identification – in no small part because there was no way to tell at first how to view it, which part was the top and which the bottom. Then in a moment of clarity Bahn realised he was looking at the body, neck and long curving beak of a wading bird called an ibis. As with the bison, the artist – perhaps the same artist – had used the natural curves of the rock to suggest much of the bird's body and even the rough outline of the beak. He or she had then skilfully augmented what was already there to create the finished form. Modern sculptors talk about sensing a shape within an uncarved block and feeling the urge to free it by the act of carving. According to Bahn that sensation is as old as humanity: 'I think so,' he said. 'Because in fact one of the most characteristic features of cave art all over western Europe is constant use of natural shapes in the rock.'

As at Lascaux and Altamira, the artists at Creswell Crags were inspired to depict the animals they saw around them – that provided their food and the raw materials of daily life. There are nearly as many theories explaining the meaning of cave art as there are artworks. At the very least they reveal the timeless desire that is always within the hearts and hands of some people, to make realistic representations of the world. But at least some of it must have been inspired too by the need to try and make sense of that world and even to influence it.

At least one artwork found by Bahn and his fellows was made by an artist seeking to make contact with someone or something sensed but not seen. The engraving itself has been interpreted by Bahn as a series of long-necked birds, beaks pointed upwards. It is small, a few inches square, and as hard to see as the rest, but located in a spot where no one would ever have been able to appreciate it. Church Hole reaches deep into the limestone, narrowing all the while like a tadpole's tail. Much of the natural build-up of flowstone has been dug out to make the passage deeper and access easier, but in Palaeolithic times it would have taken great effort and intent to penetrate all the way back to the site of the engraving.

Picture a tunnel a couple of feet high, a couple of feet wide, reaching back into velvet darkness. Around 13,000 or 14,000 years ago an artist, presumably equipped with a lamp as well as a drawing tool, squeezed and wriggled as far into the crawl space as he could before cutting out his artwork. Having completed the job, and unable to turn round, he shuffled feet-first back into the light, condemning his engraving of a flock of birds to a presumed eternity out of sight. We have only speculation to explain whom it was for, why it was ever made. Bahn pointed out that there is an important percentage of cave art, all over western Europe, deliberately located in hard-to-reach spots. 'Palaeolithic people put themselves through this to leave images which are clearly not for human consumption,' he said. 'They're making them for something else, something non-human to see – maybe a god, a spirit, an ancestor ... the forces of nature.'

Whatever its deeper meaning (if indeed it ever represented any more than art for art's sake) the Creswell art was made during a relatively brief time – known to geologists as the Late Glacial Interstadial – when the ice had retreated, to some extent at least. Around the same time there were artists in Creswell

Crags, people of a similar sort were accustomed to using Gough's Cave in Somerset's famous Cheddar Gorge. They sheltered or lived in it, kept fires, made and used tools, butchered their kills. As well as the same types of artefacts, small blades and points, and amber from the North Sea, archaeologists also recovered human bones. Some of these made headlines across the land when it was realised they bore cut marks and the apparent evidence of butchering, and there has been much speculation ever since about what might have motivated people to dismember and perhaps even eat the flesh, bone marrow and brains of their fellow human beings.

Newspaper readers of the modern world live lives that are, in the main, kept antiseptically clean of death and corpses. We are generally unfamiliar with the sight and smell of dead animals, far less of dead people, and so it is hard to imagine living comfortably, side by side with death in all its forms. The thought of coming into contact with a corpse, let alone its consumption, fills most of us with fear, even revulsion – but all the evidence suggests these are modern responses.

In the still-recent past it was customary to see, even to handle the dead bodies of family members, in preparation for funerals, and in the ancient past corpses were left in the open to decay, to be picked back to clean bones by birds and scavengers before collection for burial or other storage. Our ancestors were also in the habit of revisiting their dead again and again, and the skulls and other bones of loved ones might well have been treated as affectionately as though they were still alive.

All of this has to be considered when attempting to explain precisely what happened to some human bodies in Gough's Cave 15,000 years ago. It may have been simple cannibalism – making use of human meat when no other was available. But any number of rituals and beliefs may have been at play as well. The notion of communion with a loved one, by eating of his body and drinking of his blood, may be much, much older than 2,000 years. The human remains from Gough's Cave should do nothing more than add to the fascination of trying to imagine life in the shadow of the ice.

The sins of that past, if sins they were, would shortly be washed away in any case. Life had been good for perhaps two or three thousand years, and the hunters had taken what they needed from the herds of deer, horse and wild cattle that roamed the fertile grasslands of a land abruptly freed from beneath two-thirds of a mile of ice. But it could not and did not last. Around 13,000 years ago, while the animals engraved in the walls of the Creswell Crags were still freshly cut, the climate rapidly deteriorated once more. During the course of as little as a few years the temperature plummeted and Britain was gripped by a time known as the 'Big Freeze'.

This was the so-called Younger Dryas, when the land disappeared once more beneath rapidly advancing ice sheets. Soon it was as bad again as it had ever been – and it was no localised event. Viewed from space the planet must have presented quite a spectacle, mindlessly, merrily whirling on its way around the sun and yet clad now in a steadily growing mantle of white. From both poles the sheets advanced, ice carving and grinding all the while and adding the finishing sculptural touches to the landscapes of today.

Severe for Britain it certainly was – for Scotland in particular where the glacier again achieved a depth of more than two-thirds of mile – but also brief. By 11,000 or so years ago, the worst was over, the ice was in headlong retreat leaving behind the landforms we see now.

And as the ice retreated, ushering in the geological period called the Holocene (just the latest spell of warm weather the planet has known in the midst of its incessant Ice Ages, our time), humankind advanced to fill the empty spaces. The first of them would have arrived dry-shod over a now long-vanished territory called Doggerland – presently submerged beneath the North Sea and the English Channel, but then a vast expanse of low-lying dry land. During the glacial periods so much water was locked up in the ice sheets that the sea would at times have been more than 100 yards below present levels and the outlines of the planet's continents would have been unrecognisable. For aeons, the tide was most definitely out.

At first it was a brutal, brutalised landscape of bare rock and melt water. Anyone hardy, or foolhardy, enough to travel north as far as the present-day Central Belt of Scotland 11,000 years ago would have arrived at the foot of the retreating glacier. A great thaw was under way and, trapped beneath the still-enormous weight of the ice, torrents of water were subjected to pressures so colossal they cut gorges and ravines through solid rock.

Immediately in front of the glacier's advance, massive ribs of rock had been casually heaped up, much like the ripples that form on a rug caught beneath a shoved wardrobe. Elsewhere were great mounds of material, boulders carried for miles by the advancing ice, now lying wherever they had been unceremoniously dumped – left behind like rubble in the wake of messy builders. Entire mountain ranges had been humbled, bulldozed entirely or roughly lowered and reshaped as jagged shadows of their former selves. Everywhere the rock bore fresh wounds, scars cut by the ice and the same that would be found many thousands of years later by Louis Agassiz during his Highland tour with the Reverend William Buckland. New valleys had been driven through the mountains as well, making ways through the landscape for rivers, animals and people alike. In places they were filled with water – either the returning sea or lochs and lakes of melted ice. The famously fiddly west coast of Scotland was being drawn too, in familiar form, as ice-cut troughs became deep fjords like Lochs Alsh, Broom and Fyne.

All of Britain was a work in progress as nature set about reclaiming the land. The period of hundreds of thousands of years known to archaeologists as the Palaeolithic – Lower, Middle and Upper – was over. The remote world of the mammoth-hunters of Paviland, even the lives and times of the Creswell artists and the butchers of Cheddar Gorge belonged to the past.

The ice of the Big Freeze had drawn a line that separates them from us, then from now. On our side, a new Britain was born. It had been a messy birth and the first centuries that followed were nearly as traumatic. Relieved of the weight of trillions of tons of ice – that had pushed it down into the mantle of the Earth like a heavy head pushing one end of a lilo into the swimming pool – the landmass of Britain began to rise up. Scotland and the north had borne the weight and so it was this portion that rebounded fastest. Like the other end of a seesaw, the English part tipped downwards into the rising sea.

It is still going on – Scotland still rising and England falling – and the process will continue for thousands of years to come. And while the land rocked and the sea levels rose, new life established itself on the dry land. Animals returned first, carrying seeds from elsewhere in their guts, and as nature took its course, new plants and trees began to grow in the freshly fertilised soils.

Before the Younger Dryas it had been a land of plains-loving beasts – wild horse, bison, the last of the mammoths. This Britain wore new clothes, forests of aspen, birch, later followed by elm, hazel, lime, oak and pine – the trees of the Wild Wood – and through its dappled shadows moved creatures styled for concealment. When the hunters returned, it was the red deer they sought, and wild cattle, boar and elk.

Along with the rest of their equipment – weapons for hunting, clothes of skin and fur, bags and baskets for gathering wild foods, tools for making and mending – those pioneers carried memories as well. In a time before writing they held their knowledge in their heads: not just what they had learned in their own lifetimes but also the lore passed down from their forefathers. Perhaps some of it was tales of the glacier, or the animals that had lived on open grasslands, animals seemingly gone from the world.

The first bands of hunters to arrive in Britain 11,000 years ago were at the front of a long line of people that had trailed all across Europe from east to west and from south to north during the preceding millennia. Back in the so-called Fertile Crescent of

Mesopotamia, the descendants of those relatives left behind long ago were on the cusp of farming – thinking about taming the animals and seeding the land. Such advances – great leaps towards the world we inhabit today – would take yet more millennia to follow that same line towards the west. For now the challenge facing the farthest-flung of the wanderers – those at the very end of the line and Britain's latest pioneers – was how to adapt to the new animals and new environments. Theirs was an ancient drama that had been unfolding for hundreds of thousands, if not millions of years, and Britain would be the stage for its last act.

If woolly mammoths and wild horses haunted their memories, along with the ancient knowledge of how to hunt them across open grassland, then the British forests must have been strange indeed. But in modifying their ways of doing things and getting the better of the animals hiding in the shadows of the trees, they changed themselves. The alterations are plain to see in what they left behind – tools, shelters, the remains of food and the rest – and prompted archaeologists to coin a whole new term to describe a new people. After the Old Stone Age of the Palaeolithic comes the Middle Stone Age of the Mesolithic.

This was also the period that caught my attention while I was an undergraduate at Glasgow University in the 1980s. The notion that these were the first people to set foot in the place after the ice was especially fascinating – like finding out the names of the people who lived in your house a century before your own family, or seeing the signatures on a brittle marriage certificate of long-forgotten ancestors. It was nothing less than an opportunity to start the story at the beginning.

My own first experience of digging – of excavating – was on a Mesolithic site beside a reservoir called Loch Doon, in Ayrshire, in Scotland. It was a life-changing experience, not least because of the character of the man who directed the dig – a former Spitfire pilot-turned-botanist-turned-archaeologist called Tom Affleck. Tom was a unique and special man: part Biggles, part joker and part professor, but gifted with the ability to infect everyone around him with his passion for his subject, which was Scotland during the Mesolithic.

The dig itself was a near-washout – blighted by summer rains so unremitting the water levels in the loch rose by several feet in a matter of days and flooded the trenches. But before the inundation there was enough time to find hundreds of flakes of flint and chert, left behind by people thousands of years ago as they made and sharpened some tools. Like most Mesolithic sites, the traces were ephemeral, all but erased by weather and time. (The term 'Stone Age' is a loaded one – a reflection of the fact that things made of stone last longest. All the other stuff – made of animal skin, fur, bone, gut, sinew, horn, antler, ivory and teeth, or of wood, bark and plant fibre – tends to disappear without a trace after thousands of years, so that we have imagined a Fred Flintstone past, made of stone, that is no more realistic than a cartoon.) But it seemed like a wonder there was any trace at all, evidence of a few inconsequential moments in lives lived impossibly long ago when Britain was still brand new.

Nobody studies the Mesolithic in Britain without hearing and reading about a site near Scarborough in Yorkshire called Star Carr. It was discovered in 1947, during the digging of a field drain, and excavated by Professor Grahame Clark of Cambridge University for several years in the early 1950s. It represents very early post-glacial occupation of Britain, not long after the end of the Big Freeze, and has been of such importance that archaeologists still excavate there every chance they get.

Unlike so many Mesolithic sites, much more has survived at Star Carr than a few flakes of flint. Melt water from the glacier formed lochs and lakes all across the landscape of Britain, and one such was in a roughly triangular hollow bounded by the high ground of the North York Moors, the Yorkshire Wolds and the Howardian Hills. Today it is a low-lying plain called the Vale of Pickering but 11,000 years ago the land there was submerged beneath a shallow lake bounded by reeds, filled with fish and a magnet for all manner of animals and wild fowl.

All that prey attracted hunters and for centuries during the Mesolithic people were in the habit of spending time living around its shores. It was no casual occupation either. Something like 10,500 years ago some of them were living in a permanent house there – a circular structure 11 feet across built of substantial posts with walls of animal hide and thatch. As well as a house – the oldest discovered in Britain so far – there was also a wooden platform extending 18–20 feet over the surface of the lake itself. Mesolithic carpenters – for that is what they were – used stone tools and wedges to split tree trunks into long, thin planks to create a stable, partially floating surface that consolidated part of the water's edge.

Partly because the people were living so close to the watery shore, and partly because many feet of peat built up over the site during the millennia that passed after it was abandoned, the preservation of organic material at Star Carr is astonishing. Items excavated from within the waterlogged deposits include wooden tools, beautifully worked harpoon points of antler and bone, and jewellery made from North Sea amber and animal teeth. There is also a piece from a wooden oar, meaning the people were using boats or canoes to get around too.

So much evidence of domestic life, of the everyday, makes the site a priceless treasure house for archaeologists; but it is for one other particular class of find that Star Carr is understandably famous. During the original 1950s excavations Clark and his team recovered no fewer than 21 headdresses carefully fashioned from the skulls and antlers of red deer. Each one represents a huge amount of skilled labour. Bone in general is hard enough to work with but antler, a specialised form of bone, is of a whole different order of magnitude – so incredibly tough that in a world without metal it must be charred with fire before it can be cut and shaped with stone tools.

In order to make each headdress a craftsman had first carefully to remove the top half of an adult animal's skull, with the antlers still in place. Presumably to keep the weight down for the wearer –

and also perhaps to stop the unwieldy points of the crown catching in overhead branches – he then removed all but the lower foot or so of the antler shafts. So that the piece could be worn, he finally carved two holes, side by side, in the front part of the skull to allow for some kind of cord or thong that could be tied under the chin.

Some archaeologists have suggested the headdresses might have been worn as part of a disguise, enabling hunters to stalk closer to their prey without detection. But the more you look at them, the less likely this explanation seems. Even pared down, the antlers would still have been a cumbersome handicap for anyone trying to move quietly through a wood. Altogether more believable is the belief that they were part of a ceremonial costume – worn by a shaman perhaps, or a priest. While wearing the headdress and presumably a cloak fashioned from the animal's hide, he would be neither man nor beast but something in between, a fusion of the two. (In the Staffordshire village of Abbot's Bromley the locals still perform a dance every year in which the men carry and dance with great crowns of reindeer antler. The origins of the ritual are almost certainly pre-Christian and in the past it was performed at the winter solstice as part of a ceremony to ensure fertility and new life in the year ahead.)

The headdresses found at Star Carr were all recovered from deposits laid down within the lake, having been thrown or placed into the water in ancient times. Harpoon points and other items had been surrendered to the lake as well by the Mesolithic hunters, suggesting the timber platform had been made so people could walk out over the water for the purpose of making offerings. The veneration of water – lakes, lochs, rivers, waterfalls – as special, magical places, is therefore a tradition as old as the recolonisation of the land itself after the last Ice Age.

Such a realisation – about the sophisticated, sensitive and complex ways in which those first hunters were thinking about the world – is crucially important. It has become almost a cliché to say the first pioneers passed lightly over the landscape, like ghosts, leaving few traces. But while the hunter-gatherer lifestyle may have made comparatively little physical impact on the land-scape, still their connection to their world was profound. Living within nature, as indivisible parts of it, meant the people of the Mesolithic were deeply embedded in their environment in ways it is impossible for twenty-first-century people like us to empathise with. They may not have influenced the land as we have done; instead they were influenced *by* it, so that the world was less something they lived *on*, more someone they lived *with*.

Steve Mithen, Professor of Archaeology at Reading University, is one archaeologist who has dedicated many years of his career to trying to see the world through Mesolithic eyes. Since a first visit to the Scottish Hebrides in 1985, much of his professional and personal energy has been focused on attempting to understand how the small islands off the west coast of Scotland were exploited by hunters in the millennia that followed the final retreat of the ice: 'My passion for the Hebrides arose from finding an engage-ment with nature that was lacking in my cosseted surroundings of Cambridge,' he said. 'In the Hebrides I could not only study hunter-gatherers who hunted deer, otter and seals, but also watch those same animals in the wild today; I myself could gather and eat shellfish from the shore just as they had thousands of years ago; I too would need to watch the weather for gathering storms and know about the tides. In effect, I could begin to walk, see and think like a Mesolithic hunter-gatherer myself. Or at least, there was the possibility of doing so.'

The Highlands of Scotland, together with islands off her west coast, have been good to archaeologists. Much of the soil is thin and poor today, as it has always been. Only the hardiest and most stubborn creatures – animal and human – have bothered to hold onto the land there. While the area was, even relatively recently, much more populous than today, there has never been anything like the levels of settlement known further south and in the rest of Britain. There has therefore been much less in the way of recent modern development – road-building, house-building and the like – so that more of the landscape, especially in the islands, has been spared the kind of damage that destroys delicate traces like those left behind by early prehistoric peoples. It is for this reason that so much evidence of the Mesolithic is still being unearthed there.

By coincidence, I formed a similar attachment to the same part of the world at roughly the same time as Steve Mithen. In 1986 I was a volunteer on the excavation of a Mesolithic settlement on the island of Rum, an island sitting 15 miles west of the Scottish port of Mallaig. Radiocarbon dates from some of the excavated material would subsequently reveal the island was a destination for hunters over 9,000 years ago, making it one of the earliest post-glacial settlement sites in the country.

Mesolithic hunters were attracted to Rum by the mountain that glowers over its north-west coast – Creag nan Stearnan. This is 'Bloodstone Hill' and the bloodstone that gives it its name is a chalcedonic silica that can be worked into stone tools in much the same way as flint. Mithen's work on the nearby islands of Coll, Jura, Oronsay and Colonsay is helping to explain how a resource like Bloodstone Hill fits into a bigger picture of life in the north-western seaboard of Mesolithic Britain.

Fittingly, for reasons that will shortly become apparent, the island of Coll is shaped like a fish, with its head towards the desolate peninsula of Ardnamurchan. If ever there was a place where Mithen could best hope to find his inner ancient hunter it is surely here on this sliver of land – just 13 miles by three. There are only two roads and the peace of the place is scarcely disturbed by its 200 or so permanent inhabitants; visitors come for the emptiness, the quiet and the sandy beaches.

Since 2006 Mithen and a team of volunteers have been unearthing the ephemeral traces of a Mesolithic fishing camp at Fiskary Bay, on the island's south-east side. The clue was in the name all along: *fisk* is fish in Old Norse and *Caraidh* is a Gaelic word for a wall, or weir. There is still a caraidh across the bay today – probably dating from the eighteenth or nineteenth centuries – and it still traps water at low tide. Mithen believes, though, that people were trapping fish at Fiskary Bay much longer ago.

Even without radiocarbon dates the site's Mesolithic pedigree is confirmed by finds of 'microliths' – tiny pieces of carefully worked flint that can be used as points and barbs. These are the classic Mesolithic artefact, so that a people and a way of life that lasted for thousands of years are identified by the tiniest, most insignificant-seeming finds imaginable. There are also beautiful, long, finely flaked blades of flint that would have been put to all manner of uses in hunting, the preparation of food, cleaning and shaping animal skins and making other tools. Perhaps the best artefact from Fiskary is a tiny piece of red deer antler – the tip, according to Mithen, of a fishing spear.

With infinite patience and thoroughness the team has also made a habit of sieving all the sediments excavated from the trenches, and it is this painstaking work that has enabled the recovery of hundreds of fish bones – cod, flatfish, haddock, hake, pollock, sea bass, whiting and, most numerous of all, wrasse. Mithen believes hunters were visiting the bay to trap and net fish throughout the year and thinks it perfectly plausible those first inhabitants built a caraidh of their own. (Here is the kind of impact on the landscape Mesolithic people are not supposed to make: their choice of the bay, their modification of it with a weir to trap prey, was echoed then by Nordic Vikings and by everyone else who has found their way to Fiskary Bay.)

Another specialist on the team has been analysing the contents of peat and soil samples pulled from the Coll landscape with a piece of equipment not unlike a giant apple corer. Examined under a microscope, the resultant cores yield tiny grains of pollen that show what plant life was growing at different times during the island's long history. It seems the present monotony of heather, punctuated only by bog myrtle, sedge and sphagnum moss, was known to the first hunters 10,500 years ago as well.

This, then, is the search for the Mesolithic – relying on sieves, microscopes and the sharpest eyes to find a people who seem identifiable always and only by the tiniest clues. Fortunately for everyone's sanity there are occasional glimpses of the people themselves.

In 1797 two men were digging out a rabbit burrow near Burrington Combe in Somerset's Mendip Hills when they broke through into a large cave. Laid out in rows across the floor of the chamber were perhaps as many as 100 skeletons. It was not until 1914 that a team of cavers from Bristol began anything like a modern excavation of the site – known by then as Aveline's Hole – and by then only 21 skeletons remained. One of them seemed to have been deliberately laid across a hearth and was accompanied by lumps of red ochre, animal teeth perforated for use as jewellery and some fossil ammonites. The whole assemblage from Aveline's Hole went on display in a Bristol museum until a fateful night in November 1940 when a German bombing raid wrecked the building and almost destroyed the lot, together with all the written records of the excavation.

It was not until 2003 that a team of archaeologists from Queen's University in Belfast re-examined the surviving fragments. Modern analysis of the remains revealed the people laid to rest in the cave had been of fairly slight stature – markedly smaller than today. There were also traces of diseases like osteoarthritis and marks on the teeth that showed the people had endured periods of very poor diet during their short lives. Most fascinating of all, however, were the results of radiocarbon dating. The cave had been used as a cemetery by people who lived and died around 10,400 years ago, not long after the final retreat of the ice. These were some of our first Mesolithic ancestors.

Only bomb-shattered fragments survive of the Aveline's Hole skeletons. But a find made in 1903 in Gough's Cave in nearby Cheddar Gorge, however (erstwhile home of the notorious Creswellian cannibals who inhabited the place before the Big Freeze), brings us face to face with a Mesolithic hunter. He is known as Cheddar Man and his is the earliest complete human skeleton ever found in Britain. He lived more than 9,000 years ago, meaning either he or his immediate ancestors were among the very first people to recolonise the land.

His skull is disfigured, just in the vicinity of where his right eyebrow would have been, by an ugly, ragged crater. It is the mark of bone disease and in life would have appeared as a large, weeping sore. It may have been caused by an injury or, more likely, by a disease that began in his sinuses and spread. As well as looking dreadful, it would have been debilitating, sometimes causing fever, always causing pain and discomfort. It may well have killed him in the end.

For the making of the television series *A History of Ancient Britain* we arranged to have Cheddar Man's skull displayed on top of a trolley piled with the large cardboard boxes that contain the rest of his bones. It was not as undignified as it sounds. The trolley was positioned on the wide landing of an imposing staircase rising up from the main gallery of his present-day home in London's Natural History Museum. For an hour or so, long after the place had closed for the night and the last visitor had gone, he was master of all he surveyed.

I spent a long time looking at his skull, considering the empty eye sockets, his still-shining white teeth, the awful hole in his forehead. By then I had seen the red-stained bones of the mammoth-hunter of Paviland, and the artwork of the people who lived in the caves at Creswell Crags between the Ice Ages.

Cheddar Man was different. In all the ways that matter he and I were born into the same world. When he was alive on the Earth, Britain was still a part of the European continent. He or his forefathers walked to Cheddar Gorge dry-shod all the way from France – and could have carried on walking straight to south Wales, untroubled by any water in the Bristol Channel. But all that really keeps us apart is the years. Cheddar Man did not live on icy tundra. His was a Britain cloaked in forests of alder and birch. He did not hunt the wild horse or the mammoth through the snow; rather he stalked red deer in the Wild Wood. By his time, the glaciers had done their work and the sculpting was complete. When Cheddar Man had eyes to see, they looked out at the same mountains, the same hills, the same valleys and the same islands as mine do now.

His ways were still those of the hunter but his relationship to the land was fundamentally different from that of his Upper Palaeolithic ancestors. During the Mesolithic, people were more settled within defined territories – perhaps being born, living and dying in the same area. By this Middle Stone Age we begin to see not just a lineage leading all the way out of the past to us, but also the first folk who could be rightly described as British born and bred.

It was in an effort to experience the world of Cheddar Man – Mesolithic Man – that I spent 24 hours on the small Hebridean island of Coll cut off from the twenty-first century. My guide into the past was John Lord, who has spent most of his life relearning the skills our ancestors took for granted. There is something older about Lord – and not in terms of his age. He is much more about doing things than talking; quiet, but in a way that leaves no awkward silence. His hands are not like mine, not soft from mobile phones and laptop keys, from spending most time outdoors shoved into warm pockets. His hands know how to make and hold tools; how to tie proper knots; to twist plant fibre into unbreakable string; where and how hard to strike one stone with another so that within minutes he is holding a knife indistinguishable from those you see on display in the prehistory section of the British Museum. I felt foolish and useless beside him. What have I been doing with my time?

Lord showed me how to paddle out into Fiskary Bay in a boat called a coracle, a versatile little craft he had made by stretching a cow skin over a basket-like frame of bent branches lashed together with cords made of tree bark. (It was boats like these – as well as dugout canoes – that enabled those early hunters to reach places like Coll in the first place.) A coracle needs only one paddle, which must be stirred in a leisurely figure of eight to provide propulsion and direction; but do it even slightly wrong and the thing just spins in place, like a bottle-top in a puddle. He showed me how razor-edged flakes, quickly knapped from a pebble of flint, could be used for cutting everything from animal hide to my own fingers.

As we stretched fresh deer skins, still soft and bloody from the carcasses, across a simple A-frame to make the tent in which I was to spend the night (in the far north of Scotland, in February), I got my first sense of what the Mesolithic world would have smelled like – a heavy, all-pervading animal odour that must have permeated everything from people's own skin and hair, to their clothes, to the shelters they called home. We charred red deer antler until it was brittle enough for shards to be split from the main. These Lord carved, with flint blades, to make elegant multi-barbed points that could be lashed to shafts with twine made from tendons cut from red deer carcasses, to make fishing spears.

All the time we worked our hands were slicked with a sheen of animal fat that steadily seeped into our skin so that we smelled no different from the raw materials we were using. We waded out into the bay in the forlorn hope of spearing fish, but the seals had chased them away. Still we tried – Lord telling me to keep the tip of the spear submerged. Light-waves change direction when they hit water so the shaft seems suddenly crooked. Let my eyes adjust to the new angle of the spear underwater, he said, and my chances of actually hitting something would be increased. (On my own I know nothing of value while hunters 9,000 years ago understood how to compensate for the effects of refraction!)

They hunted and trapped hare on Coll once, but those are a protected species now and so, in homage to the original quarry, Lord had me skin a rabbit. I did as I was told, pulling the hide from the carcass as easily as taking off a glove, to reveal a little shiny pink body that looked alarmingly like that of a premature baby. Best of all, we made fire by using a little bow rapidly to spin the sharpened end of a stick inside a shallow hole cut from a flat piece of hard, dry wood. After minutes of effort, a glowing ember was conjured into being at the tip. This Lord coaxed into the heart of a bundle of wood shavings before crouching down so he could breathe some air across it. There was a genie of smoke first and then, like ancient magic, a tiny serpent's tongue of flame that licked upwards through the shavings. It took hold with the softest sound, like a gasp, and we had fire. I would like to say I could repeat the feat now, but I would be lying.

That night, after everyone else had gone back to proper beds and heating, I sat as close to the flames as I could get without actually catching fire myself. It was a cloudless night, with a gibbous Moon, and in a bid to cheat the cold I drank too much rough red wine, my only concession to the present (apart from a four-season sleeping bag). I looked up at a million stars and wondered how many new pinpricks of light had reached our planet in the last 9,000 years – or was I looking at the same lights as they had, give or take a few degrees of parallax?

In the morning I was wretched – not cold, since the night inside the deer-skin shelter, cocooned in modern warmth while breathing freezing air, had been unexpectedly comfortable – but from lack of sleep. I watched the sun rise from behind a shoulder of Mull, just as those fishermen and women of Fiskary Bay must have done nine millennia ago, and thought about how far away their world was, and how close.

After my Mesolithic experience, it was a jolt to climb into a helicopter for a tour of the neighbouring islands. Steve Mithen has traipsed back and forth on foot across and around the coastlines not just of Coll but of Jura, Oronsay, Colonsay and Islay as well in search of lost hunters. It has been laborious, but also time well spent because it has enabled him to see how different islands met different needs for hunter-gatherers.

On Colonsay, a few hours' paddling from Coll, he has unearthed pits containing up to a third of a million hazelnut shells. 'What they may have been doing is gathering large quantities in the autumn and then storing them as food through the winter,' he said. 'If you roast them you can grind them down to a paste and then it becomes easy, nutritious food you can carry away and use later.'

The scale of the operation is staggering, though – as if every last hazel nut on the island had been collected in one go. 'It shows they weren't just living from day to day, scraping an existence,' Mithen added. 'It was really carefully planned activity.'

On nearby Oronsay the team has found evidence that shellfish were being collected from the shallows on the shoreline and then consumed in vast quantities. The scale is testified by enormous mounds – middens – of empty shells carefully heaped and piled in one place. People returned to exactly the same spot year after year, perhaps generation after generation, to gather and eat mussels, limpets, dog-whelks, periwinkles and the like before deliberately adding them to the midden until in time it would have been visible from the sea, a great white pile of shells. Maybe it was a territorial marker as well – a sign to tell any passing strangers that these islands were already known.

Although the tip of a fishing spear made of red deer antler was found at Fiskary Bay, there are no red deer on Coll. The species was not on the island in the Mesolithic period and has still not reached the place today. By contrast Islay, a larger island to the south, has always been a rich hunting ground for deer and would have been yet another stop on the shopping trip made by Mesolithic people as they systematically obtained all they needed from the world by using boats and canoes to link many islands together into a single territory they understood intimately.

Seeing that territory, learning how it provided for every human need like some Garden of Eden, makes it hard not to envy the lives lived in that cradle. There were undoubtedly hardships. Times when the fish did not come to Fiskary Bay, or the natural harvest of hazelnuts failed to ripen on the trees and bushes. Random fate, injury and disease too would lead to suffering like that experienced by Cheddar Man. Imagine tooth-ache in a world without dentists.

And yet for all that, something about the Mesolithic world of self-reliance sounds tempting and the call of it can be heard like a distant voice. As a species we lived as hunters for almost the sum of our existence on this planet. Only during the last 10,000 years at the very most has anyone thought about farming – and all that that way of life brings. For the preceding two or three million years we hunted, and the hunt still cries out to us.

On the mudflats of the Severn Estuary, at Goldcliff near Newport in south Wales, the hunt speaks with a human voice – many human voices dimly heard. Mesolithic people came here to this shoreline 8,000 years ago and more. Some of them collected shellfish, or checked fish traps. Children ran along by their mothers' sides, scattering flocks of seabirds into sudden uplifting flight. Elsewhere, the men of the tribe ran swift and silent in pursuit of deer and other prey sheltering in the reeds and long grass by the shore.

We know all of this – about the mothers and children, the birds and animals, the hunters – because they left behind the imprints of their feet. As people walked and ran on the soft wet silts at the water's edge, and as birds hopped and deer and other animals picked their way, telltale prints were left in their wake. At the end of some long-forgotten day, the tide rolled in and muddy waves gently filled the foot shapes with a layer of silt. By lucky chance the same process was repeated with every tide that followed until the trails left by humans, birds and animals were sealed, undamaged and perfect, beneath countless thin skins, like the build-up of a laminate.

Later still the shape of the estuary was altered by a change in the route of the River Severn, and the layers containing the footprints were suddenly left behind on dry land. Peat began to form on top of the laminated silts, protecting them even more, so that after thousands of years those prints (still no more than depressions in soft mud) were as fresh as the moment when the feet that made them were lifted clear.

In recent years the shape of the estuary has altered once more so that the tides have been able to strip away the protective peat, eventually exposing the layers containing the prints. Professor Martin Bell, an archaeologist from the University of Reading, is carefully recording the footprints as they appear for the first time in all those millennia and then disappear for ever, eroded by the waves. His team of volunteers use high-pressure water hoses to blast away the final layer of liquid mud so that the imprints are briefly clean and clear. If King Canute were reincarnated as a mild-mannered academic, he would be Martin Bell – wishing the waves would wait but accepting that the tide does what the tide does.

But in those last fleeting moments they are the most poignant sight. These are the prints of bare feet; the toes widely splayed by lifetimes spent walking unshod over all manner of surfaces. Some are close together, made by short strides and left behind by someone strolling. Sometimes the adult prints are accompanied by those of children. Other trails show the longer stride patterns of men running. Everywhere there are the three-toed, fleurs-de-lis of wading birds; occasionally there are the ladylike prints of deer. They are almost too much, the human footprints: looking at them, touching them, felt like eavesdropping, or secretly watching someone in an unguarded moment. I had to stare at them, but part of me wanted to look away, out of respect for privacy.

In 1978 the archaeologist and anthropologist Mary Leakey found footprints left by a man, woman and child preserved in volcanic ash on the Laetoli Plain of Tanzania, in southern Africa. They were made by members of an ancient species of human called *Australophithecus afarensis*, around three and a half million years ago. As well as the human trail, there were prints left by animals – even the impressions of raindrops that fell while the family walked that day. After the little family had gone, a subsequent eruption by the same volcano buried their prints with yet more ash, saving them for posterity.

The woman's tracks show that at one point she paused and then veered to one side for a few strides. Leakey imagined she had sensed some danger – perhaps a predator – and that she had felt the need to investigate. Maybe she thought briefly about suggesting a change of direction, before relaxing and rejoining her kin. 'This motion, so intensely human, transcends time,' Leakey wrote later, for an article in *National Geographic*. 'A remote ancestor just as you or I – experienced a moment of doubt.'

The Laetoli footprints have mostly been reburied, in hopes of preserving them. No such possibility exists for those much more recent footprints in south Wales. We can only appreciate them now, before they disappear for ever.

Our ancient past is powerful magic, strong drink – even a little shot of it can snatch your breath away and make you wonder if you can, any more, believe what you are seeing. You tell yourself over and over that these footprints are not fossils turned to ever-lasting stone, but marks as vulnerable as a name traced in wet sand with a stick. But it is unbelievable; they are unbelievable.

This Britain is the house I live in. For a long time its inhabitants mistook it for a new-build, thought they were the first and only owners of someplace made just for them. James Hutton of Edin-burgh, scion of the eighteenth-century Scottish Enlightenment, spotted the real depth of the foundations and realised it was a truly ancient dwelling. Then the Swiss naturalist and geologist Louis Agassiz saw it had been knocked down and rebuilt – and while he thought the builders had come only once, rather than repeatedly, he was on the right track.

In the years since then archaeologists, palaeontologists and other detectives have found the bodies buried under the floor – *Homo ergaster ... Homo habilis ... Homo erectus ... Homo heidelbergensis ... Homo neanderthalensis* – each evicted in turn, and all victims of time, the ultimate landlord. Then last of all, us, *Homo sapiens sapiens*, the present tenants. Britain has been built, demolished, rebuilt, demolished and rebuilt again and again and again. I am living now among the remodelled ruins, making the best of it.

The time of the first settlers – those that arrived in Britain after the ice – survives in the form of tools and talismans, pollen grains and fish teeth, bones of animals and humans; a horse's head etched onto a rib and a cave where ghostly shadows of stags and bison and birds stand breathless in the dark, awaiting the flickering light of torches. It was a time that lasted for thousands of years.

It also survives, most magically of all, in footprints on a beach, every trail the proof of a life. And like any trail of footprints in the mud, those lives were at the mercy of the next wave.

2

ANCESTORS

'The deluge overthrew the land ...'

From the Epic of Gilgamesh

' ... and these stones shall be for a memorial ... '

Joshua 4:7

'Abel was a keeper of sheep, but Cain was a tiller of the ground
... And it came to pass, when they were in the field, that Cain
rose up against Abel his brother, and slew him.'

Genesis 4:2,8

We are haunted by history, not just as nations, but also as a species. Long before there were nations or countries there were just people. We split into groups from the very beginning of course, as people do, based around families and tribes. But we were then and we are now all the same species – *Homo sapiens sapiens*. Caucasians, Asians, Negroes ... just as Labradors, Greyhounds and Mastiffs are all just dogs – so we are all simply folk, and mongrels at that.

Amidst all the ensuing complexity of race, society, religion and the rest, we have lost sight of how much we experienced together as one species. Most of the really big stuff – the making of the people and the land – happened long before we started drawing lines and deciding who was in and who was out.

All of this – all of us – began in equatorial Africa well over a million years ago as Africans with black skins and the full suite of associated physical features. Warm-blooded animals living in equatorial regions, those places most exposed to sunlight, have skins that secrete melanin to protect them from the most direct daily bombardment of ultra-violet radiation anywhere on the planet. But one of the most important functions of skin is the production of Vitamin D, which it achieves by positively inter-acting with that sunlight; and at the Equator the powerful melanin shield in black skin means black people need an hour or more of sunlight each day to make enough Vitamin D to avoid life-threatening conditions like rickets. (The Inuit people of the Arctic regions, while often darker than northern Europeans, obtain their Vitamin D – and Vitamin C, for that matter – from a diet rich in fish skin, seal liver, yolk from the eggs of birds and fish and the raw meat and blubber of seal, walrus and whale.)

As *Homo sapiens* migrated further and further north, into Europe and parts of Asia, the daily sunlight ration was progressively reduced. Individuals in more northerly latitudes also needed to wear clothing to keep warm – further reducing the amount of skin they exposed to the sun. Those humans with the darkest skin would have been at a disadvantage, suffering physically as a result of an inability to produce enough Vitamin D in less sunny climes. Factor in the added complication of the kind of climate associated with an Ice Age and you have a population of black-skinned humans facing certain extinction if they remain far north of the Equator – or rather, if they remain far north of the Equator without adapting as a species.

Fortunately for the human story it is in the nature of all species to produce mutations and in the case of modern Europeans it was, fundamentally, albinism – the congenital absence of melanin – that made the difference and saved the day.

In fact it does not take much DNA to make the difference between black skin and white and all the tones in between: a couple of switches, thrown one way or the other, and the job is done. Several genes affecting skin tone have been identified – some tending towards light, some dark – and the combination in any one individual, acquired by the mixing of genes inherited from their mother and father, will determine that individual's colour.

Anyone born with paler skin – initially as a result of mutation – would be better suited to a more northerly, colder, darker climate. The paler the skin, the less time that individual has to spend in sunlight to process Vitamin D. As a healthier specimen he or she should, in terms of Darwinian selection, be more successful in that environment in finding a mate. It follows that once the species 'realised' pale skin was an advantage in the gloomier north of the planet, so lighter individuals would be identified there as the more compatible partners. In this way, pale people would tend to seek each other out, so that what had been a recessive mutation in a mostly dark population could eventually become a positively dominant trait in an increasingly pale one. Males in particular would drive the trend, seeking paler and paler female partners.

Over generations of selection in favour of pale skin in colder, darker parts of the world, other characteristics would change too: resulting in the straightening of hair, thinning of lips, narrowing of noses and loss of pigmentation in hair and eyes. By this process human populations were able quite rapidly to change colour and general physical appearance, so that by 40–50,000 years ago there were pale-skinned people – Cro-Magnons – living in northern Europe and Asia. Natural selection had seen to it that they were able to make sufficient Vitamin D in their skins every day with just a few minutes' exposure to daylight, compared to the hour and more required by black people living at the Equator. Paler eyes – blue and green – were also better than brown eyes at making the best of low-light conditions.

Long before the last Ice Age, then, our species had adapted to the world's various climates and environments by evolving a range of skin colours: the complete set of peoples was abroad on the planet by at least 40,000 years ago, if not earlier. But while the consequences of those changes were profound, they were spread across so many generations and so many miles that none of us *Homo sapiens sapiens* could have noticed they were happening.

Much more recently, however, and in Britain, the people experienced an event that changed everything in mere moments and that has, perhaps, never been forgotten.

Natural disasters have been part of the human experience since the beginning. Ice Ages began quickly enough to be seen as disastrous, possibly over the course of just a few years, and have gripped the planet on countless occasions; the very ground beneath our feet has been shaken apart by earthquakes; volcanic eruptions have laid waste to all in their paths. But there is one particular natural phenomenon that seems to be so profoundly affecting that it has written itself into our consciousness as a species, and that is the deluge: The Flood.

As recently as 11 March 2011, the north-eastern part of Japan was hit by an earthquake followed by a catastrophic tsunami that killed thousands. On 26 December 2004 the so-called Boxing Day Tsunami killed an estimated 230,000 people. An undersea earthquake off the west coast of Sumatra, in Indonesia, unleashed waves up to 100 feet high that swept entire towns and villages into oblivion from the coastlines of 14 countries around the edges of the Indian Ocean.

Between 26 and 27 August 1883 a volcanic explosion that conjured similarly gigantic waves and killed at least 40,000 people blew apart the Indonesian island of Krakatoa, east of Java. Apart from anything else, it is said to have been the loudest noise in modern history, heard 3,000 miles away.

There are many causes of flood of course, many reasons why land is sometimes inundated by and submerged beneath water. But while it is not just tsunamis (tsunami is a Japanese word meaning 'harbour wave'), there is something about the sudden, towering wall of water that rears up out of the sea with little or no warning that is especially terrifying – and so instantly world-changing as to be unforgettable.

So-called 'disaster archaeologists' believe the Minoan civilisation, which dominated the Mediterranean world until three and a half thousand years ago, was stopped in its tracks by a volcanic explosion 10 times greater than that which destroyed Krakatoa. Dated to between 1480 and 1450 BC, the blast tore apart the island of Santorini, 70 miles north of Minoan Crete and its capital Knossos, before monstrous waves ripped across the Aegean like nothing less than the wrath of God.

Within a couple of generations of the coming of that deluge, the Minoans were gone from history. Here was a civilisation that had once placed the shadow of its hand across most of the eastern Mediterranean, its greatness centred on the vast and fabled palace of Knossos, with paved streets and running water; whose king of kings, Minos, would haunt the myths of ancient Greece for centuries to come in the company of the labyrinth-dwelling beast he called the minotaur ... all of it swatted away like a cloud of flies. Plato may even have woven his legend of the lost city of Atlantis around the wreck of all that Crete and Knossos had once been.

Going back further in time, there have been other floods – and some of a different sort entirely. By the end of the last Ice Age in North America 15,000 years ago, a great finger of ice blocked the Clark Fork River in Idaho and Montana, creating what was effectively an inland sea. Known to geologists as Glacial Lake Missoula, it was 200 miles wide and contained an estimated 500 cubic miles of water. From time to time – perhaps as many as 40 times between 15,000 and 13,000 years ago – the ice dam broke apart, sending all that ice and water surging towards the Pacific Ocean. Every time the torrent was set free it tore across the land below it with a force calculated as 10 times the combined flow of all the rivers in the world. Each time it happened the deluge might have been hundreds of feet deep and moving at up to 65 miles an hour, releasing all 500 cubic miles of water in as little as two catastrophic days – days that literally shook that part of the world. The devastation of those times survives today in the monumental channels and scoured landscapes of the so-called Scablands of Montana.

And all the while those events unfolded there were people on the land to witness them. How would such happenings have been remembered? For how long were the tales passed down through the generations before the truth of it all was finally lost? Was there a simmering fear in the minds of our hunting ancestors that a day might come when all the land disappeared beneath the waves, leaving no place at all for man and beasts to stand?

By around 6100 BC Britain had been inhabited by people living a Mesolithic lifestyle for thousands of years, since time out of mind. It is impossible to know or to calculate the population then but perhaps a few thousand is a reasonable estimate. During those millennia the nomadic hunters, gatherers and fishers would have roamed freely throughout the interior and all around the coastlines.

Since the beginning of the Mesolithic period, right after the end of the 'Big Freeze' of the Younger Dryas, Britain had been firmly attached to mainland Europe. The tens of thousands had penetrated the interior not of an island, but of a remote peninsula. (Ireland had become an island much earlier. There is no evidence that Palaeolithic hunters ever reached there before Mesolithic people made their own crossings in boats, around 8000 BC.)

Sea levels rose and the land, freed from the massive weight of the ice, rose too. There has been a long, slow dance ever since – sometimes the land has risen faster, sometimes the water – but as the Mesolithic period progressed the connection to Europe was steadily reduced to a narrow and marshy bridge of land. What is now the southern part of the North Sea and the English Channel had for thousands of years been a rich territory for hunters and gatherers. It had been perilously low-lying – dry land only while the sea level was as much as 120 feet lower than today and always at the mercy of a changing world. All the while the ice melted and the sea level rose it was steadily being inundated, whittled away little by little. But archaeologists believe the end came not with a whimper, but with an awful roar.

On a truly remarkable day around 6100 BC, the sun rose over the eastern seaboard of the British peninsula for the very last time.

All along the length of it, communities and families went about their normal round of daily activities. Perhaps it was a fishing season and people set and tended nets and traps in shallow bays and across rivers. Or maybe there were shellfish to be collected – mussels, periwinkles, cockles and the like. Some folk would have been out in their boats, coracles or dugout canoes making their way from point to point along a coastline made familiar by millennia. Children would have played in the shallows, as children do.

All of it was about to change for ever. Hundreds of miles beyond the horizon, around 70 miles off the coast of Norway, a shelf of seabed over 200 miles long and amounting to thousands of cubic miles of rock and sediment suddenly slipped free from its ancient mooring and shuddered deeper into the North Sea. It had been part of what modern Norwegians call the 'Storegga' – the Great Edge – and when it slid downslope underwater it left behind a massive void above. Into that sudden space sloshed an incalculable volume of seawater – a movement followed almost at once by an equal and opposite surge in every direction, towards Norway and Britain both. The North Sea was behaving much like a bath full of water disturbed by someone suddenly slipping beneath the surface. A great wave was on the move along its length.

Back across the sea, mere moments later, people down at water level on the coast of Britain would have noticed the strangest thing: the tide suddenly, and very rapidly, going out so that what had been sea was now seabed. All the time the wave approached land it had pulled water towards itself from the shallows ahead. Seabirds, fearing the worst, would have risen in alarm, screeching a warning that was too little and much too late. Maybe some of the most alert of the men, women and children would have dropped their gear then and turned towards higher ground. But for most there was likely nothing to do but stand still, aware all at once of a wind blowing in from offshore. And then there was a roaring noise as well, soft at first but building in volume and intensity.

For anyone close enough to the water to notice any of this, it was too late even before it began. Standing still and open-mouthed or running full tilt away from the roar, it would have made no difference. A 30-foot-high wall of water, hundreds of miles long, bore down upon the coastline of Britain at many tens if not hundreds of miles per hour. People and animals in its path would have been obliterated, smashed to smithereens. All that had been there before, all but the bedrock, was washed clean away. The force of the tsunami – believed to be the most powerful natural disaster to have hit that part of the world in the last 8,000 years or more – was such that ground as much as 50 miles inland was briefly, catastrophically submerged beneath many feet of water. Whale bones and sand found on the Carse of Stirling, smack in the middle of Scotland, have been attributed to the same event.

As quickly as it had appeared the wave withdrew, pulling in its wake the dead, the uprooted trees, everything it had torn away from the land. At a stroke a whole swathe of Mesolithic Britain – the people and all the evidence of their way of life – disappeared for ever.

It took a geologist studying post-glacial sea level changes in Scotland and northern Europe to bring the 8,000-year-old event back into the light. In 1988, Professor David Smith, of the University of Oxford, was studying a bank of sediments in the Montrose Basin, a tidal estuary on Scotland's north-east coast, when he spotted a thick layer of fine sand. Simply put, it should not have been there. It was of such a volume, and at such a height above sea level, that there could only be one explanation. This was material from the seabed, slapped up onto dry land by a giant wave and left behind when it withdrew. 'As it came on, it would have made a noise like an express train,' said Smith. 'There was no way anyone caught down there could possibly have survived. The speed is just so great . . . anybody standing out on the mudflats at that time would have been dismembered by the power of the wave.'

Apart from the tragedy of it all, the loss of life and homes, Britain's destiny had been shaped. The connection to Europe was severed. The last vestiges of Doggerland were lost beneath the waves, another Atlantis. (Millennia later, Dutch fishermen in their trawlers, boats they called dogges or doggers, would find the strangest, unexpected things in their nets from time to time. In among the fish and the crabs would be blackened mammoth ivory, lions' teeth, sometimes a lump of peat. Every once in a while they would find beautifully worked tools of bone and antler – evidence of man. They already knew the seabed was close to the surface there – the fishing ground was called Dogger Bank because submerged sandbanks just 30 or 40 feet beneath their hulls attracted the fish they sought. Now they realised it had once been dry land roamed by great beasts, and the people who hunted them. Later, archaeologists would imagine a vast territory they called Doggerland, stretching between southern Britain and Europe.)

But now and for ever Britain was an island. Shakespeare's 'scepter'd isle . . . This other Eden . . . This fortress build by Nature for herself . . . this little world, This precious stone set in the silver sea' was cut out from the main in one hellish moment that likely wiped out a fair percentage of the population there and all around the North Sea at that time.

For people living in Britain it was also the end of infancy, the end of their helpless forgetting. From now on they remembered things about themselves. They already knew there had been other people – like them and yet not like them, who had been on the land when their forefathers came – but they were long gone. Now they would remember how the waters had once risen up and taken away their land and their people. The Flood became a fixed point for our species. All across the Old World it is the same – it is floods that haunt the earliest folk memories and that are remembered as the cleansing cataclysms that ushered in everything that exists today. Atlantis has vanished more than once and we fear it will disappear again.

And so nothing has written itself into our psyche as indelibly as the threat of losing everything to the deluge. It is there in the early chapters of The Bible, the creation story for Christians, Jews and Muslims alike. Earlier still, it featured in the Epic of Gilgamesh, an even older collection of legends, from the lost land of Sumer in Mesopotamia. Before it was called the Epic of Gilgamesh, the poems it contains were known collectively by an older name – Sha naqba imuru – He Who Saw the Deep. Norman Maclean got it right in his novella, *A River Runs Through It*: 'The river was cut by the world's great flood and runs over rocks from the basement of time. On some of the rocks are timeless raindrops. Under the rocks are the words, and some of the words are theirs. I am haunted by waters.'

In the new island Britain – one haunted by waters – everything that happened next happened after that flood. Though they could not have realised it at the time the survivors, those left behind, were changed. They were the descendants of hunters who had walked north and west onto a promontory of land in pursuit of game. They had been what their forefathers were, pioneers of the north-west frontier of Europe. But those who watched the wave recede were islanders now. They had been made separate by that new sea; perhaps they had been made a little bit special by it as well.

The Mesolithic did not end with a tsunami 8,000 years ago. Far from it: that way of life would continue for yet more thousands of years. No doubt, even as the wave was smashing inland in the east, families were strolling by the sea at Goldcliff, in south Wales, unperturbed and unaware, leaving yet more footprints for posterity. Separated from calamity by enough distance, they would have known nothing of the event. The same would have been true for most of the population of Britain. The wave withdrew and life for those beyond its reach continued as before. Soil scientists believe that by the time of the disaster the British climate had been in slow decline for many centuries, becoming progressively wetter, so that what had been rich woodland turned into swampy marshland. This may have encouraged a move away from the interior and towards the coastlines, where the marine environment could be more successfully exploited for food – a migration that might have exposed even more of the population to the devastation of the wave. What had certainly changed, though, was Britain's place in the world. From now on anyone new, and anything new, would have to make the trip here in a boat. And that has made all the difference.

The risen waters did not destroy everything they touched either. In fact, a site being excavated by archaeologist Garry Momber has been preserved precisely because it has spent the last 8,000 years at the bottom of the Solent.

While the sea level was around 40 feet lower than today, the Isle of Wight was part of the dry land connecting Britain to France. The Solent itself would have been a valley, with a river running through it from west to east. Work by Momber and his team during the last decade or so has revealed that a technologically sophisticated Mesolithic population lived in and around that valley – and that they used the river as rather more than a source of food.

Known as Bouldnor Cliff, the site first attracted attention in the 1980s when divers identified traces, 30–40 feet down, of ancient woodland and also peat deposits. In 1998 the Hampshire and Wight Trust for Maritime Archaeology (HWTMA) began an underwater survey of the location and found, in a burrow dug out by a lobster of all things, some telltale pieces of worked flint. Their appetites whetted, the marine archaeologists redoubled their efforts and found more and more evidence of stone tool-making – but this was as nothing compared to what was to come.

They expected to see stumps of ancient timber sticking out of steep banks of sediment (it was, after all, evidence of ancient woodland that had brought them to Bouldnor Cliff in the first place); but as their eyes grew accustomed to the near-zero visibility of the Solent they began to spot signs that some of the wood had been cut, and even shaped, by stone tools. What has been discovered was therefore rather more than an ancient hunting camp. According to Momber it is nothing less than the oldest boat-building yard in the world.

I was the most novice of novice scuba divers when I joined the HWTMA team for the removal of one particularly interesting piece of timber from Bouldnor Cliff. Having qualified the week before, it was with more fear than excitement that I stepped off the back of a gently wallowing dive boat into cold, choppy water that looked more like broccoli soup than sea. As instructed by my dive-buddy Donny I swam, or rather dog-paddled, over to a nearby buoy, from which descended a fluorescent yellow line attached to a weight on the seabed 30 or 40 feet below. Rising and falling on the swell, feeling vaguely claustrophobic in a full face mask, I asked myself why on earth I was putting myself through it. The sound of my own, tight breathing was deafening.

So far so awful, but then I had to begin expressing the air from my dry suit – the air keeping me bobbing, safely, like a cork, on the surface – so that the lead weights on my webbing could do their job of taking me to the bottom, through steadily darkening, green murk. The bad visibility in that soup was disorientating to say the least. The density of sediment suspended in the water was not uniform; rather clouds of it drifted along on the current like banks of mist so that sometimes I could make out Donny's reassuring shape and sometimes he simply vanished, leaving my eyes trying to focus on nothing at all. Arrival on the seabed was another surprise. Since I could see almost nothing in any direction, including downwards, I got no warning of the bottom until my fins hit the sediment – kicking up yet more muck to cloud my vision.

But as I turned around and began to get my bearings, I heard my breathing begin to slow to a more normal pace. I had, at least, arrived. I was on the seabed, breathing normally and all at once it began to seem just about manageable. My anxiety about diving was suddenly replaced by the need to make sure the underwater cameraman would get the shots he needed in the brief time available. I convinced myself the worst was already over. Momber appeared from within the swirling clouds and gestured that we should follow him back along another yellow line leading off into nothingness. For no reason I could explain now, I felt quite calm – even energised by the currents of cold water flowing around us.

The thought occurred then that my earlier disorientation and near-panic in the blinding gloom had been appropriate. Part of me had always known the ancient past was another world – somewhere almost out of reach – but that was just a figure of speech. Now I was actually in another world, experiencing how difficult it is to make the crossing, to grope in the dark for some clue, some landmark to show the way.

We arrived at the spot where Momber had been working prior to our arrival. Just as an archaeologist would on dry land, he was using a four-inch pointing trowel, but in this instance he was peeling soft grey sediment from the sea floor. Clearly visible was a pitch-black piece of waterlogged timber. It was about the size of a man's thigh and even through the clouds of sediment the tool marks on its surface were plain to see. He freed it from the mud, loaded it into a plastic crate (of the sort bakers use to deliver loaves) then used a sac filled with compressed air from his own tanks to raise the whole lot towards the surface.

No sooner had our cargo disappeared into the murk above than Donny tapped my shoulder and signalled it was time for us to leave as well. In a reversal of the routine for descending, we pumped enough air back into our dry suits to let us make slow progress up towards the light. A full 15 feet below the surface we halted, letting our bodies get used to the change in pressure, before finally completing the trip and breaking through to the world of the present.

Back on the dive boat we examined our lump of timber, so recently returned to the air after eight millennia on the seabed. It bore obvious marks of ancient carpentry that Momber said made it likely they were parts of a log-boat. He produced other pieces, collected during previous dives, which had clearly been shaped and carved. Even to my untrained eye one of them, some eight inches long and the thickness of a woman's forearm, looked exactly like a gunwale – the top edge of the side of a rowing boat. Parallel grooves, carefully carved and running along both long sides, were obviously the work of a craftsman.

The anaerobic conditions of Bouldnor Cliff have preserved other organic material – including, incredibly, fragments of string identical to the sort John Lord had taught me to make from twisted fibres on Coll. It is one thing to find stone tools on a Mesolithic site – but to recover, as well, the items those tools were themselves used to make is nothing short of astounding. Had the site not been submerged beneath the sea – had Britain remained attached to Europe by dry land so that the present-day Isle of Wight was just part of the mainland – then all of the timber and the rest of the world's oldest boatyard would have decayed and disappeared long ago.

What Momber and his team are revealing is a glimpse of the sophistication and complexity of Mesolithic life. It should not be surprising – people had lived off the land for hundreds of thousands of years and needed more than campfires and sharp stones to exploit the full potential of their environment – but it is all too easy to forget they had learned to make life rich, comfortable and satisfying. Boats for navigating the rivers and coastlines may have been close to the least of it. We do not know what we are missing – the comforts of Mesolithic home – because we simply do not find it.

But while the millennia in Britain since the end of the Ice Age had seen the continuation of traditions and skills that would not have been unfamiliar to Neanderthals, let alone Palaeolithic Cro-Magnons, elsewhere the world had moved on. By the time bands of hunters were walking across Doggerland 10,000 and more years ago, curious to see what lay ahead of them over the horizon to the north-west, an entirely new way of living was being pioneered back in the east. In the Fertile Crescent of Mesopotamia and the Levant, in western Asia, people were by then experimenting with the idea of collecting and planting wild seeds, and of using pens and fences to limit the movement of herds of wild animals.

Thousands of years before Britain became an island, farming was enabling people to settle down and build towns and villages in the territories that would one day become the countries of Iran, Iraq, Israel, Jordan, Lebanon, Palestine, Syria and Turkey. It seems almost inconceivable, but while people in Britain and much of western Europe were still firmly in the middle of the Stone Age – hunting red deer and wild cattle, building middens of empty shells and sleeping in tents made of ripe-smelling animal hides – in a cradle of civilisation far to the east folk were moving closer to the modern world of permanent homes and settled villages, a world made possible only by the surplus food that comes from the growing of crops and the husbanding of animals.

Archaeologists have been theorising, for a century at least, about how and why farming came to replace hunting, gathering and fishing. On the face of it, farming is a life of grinding toil, a repetitive, limited diet and the ever-present threat of disease caused by constant proximity to too many unsanitary people. The tedium is enlivened only by the very real possibility of a failed harvest followed by famine and death. Compared to the life of the hunter-gatherer-fisher, cooking venison, beef and fish over roaring fires, harvesting wild foods and moving always to fresh ground and new horizons, it seems to have little to offer. And yet it became and still is the basis of the society we live in today.

The almost complete lack of British Mesolithic skeletons, coupled with the absence of much in the way of 'perfect' Neolithic skeletons, has made it hard to compare the two lifestyles in terms of their respective effects on health. But what evidence does exist suggests farmers did not live longer than their hunting pre-decessors. Hunters had access to a wide variety of game and wild food. Their highly mobile way of life, while tough on the elderly or the disabled, would have kept people lean and fit. Theirs was a low-fat diet – consisting mostly of gathered fruit and vegetables supplemented with occasional meat – and although they would have faced random seasonal shortages from time to time, the general absence of fat from their diets would have made them less likely than farmers to contract ailments like cancer of the bowel and breast, diabetes, heart disease and stroke. Always moving away from their own waste, as opposed to having it pile up around them, would also have helped keep them well.

The switch to farming has in fact been described as a step backwards for human health. As people settled in villages and as families grew larger on a diet of porridge, bread and occasional meat, sanitation – or rather the lack of it – would have been a real problem. Build-up of rubbish and waste would have attracted vermin. People would suddenly have been at greater risk from contracting diseases from one another and from their animals (tuberculosis, for example, is thought to have been non-existent in humans before they started living close to cattle). As fertile areas became crowded, some people would have been forced onto more marginal land where the risk of crop failure and therefore mal-nutrition and starvation would have increased. And while farmers would have been able to rely on plenty of cereal, at least during good times, such foods contain much less iron than meat. Com-pared to hunters, they would have been more exposed to iron deficiency and its consequences for health.

Farming was even a pain in the back teeth – quite literally. Wheat and the like were ground into flour on rough stones called querns, and the grit that would have ended up in the bread and other foods would have taken a heavy toll on farmers' dental health. It is all there in the nutshell of 'the daily grind' – the hours that had to be spent every day preparing enough food for the family, food that even wrecked their teeth. Farming sounds like a tough sell.

Many archaeologists and other scientists now believe that climate change holds the key. It is thought the end of the last Ice Age was followed, 11,000 or 12,000 years ago, by a 'climatic optimum' of good weather that encouraged the growth, in the lands of the Fertile Crescent at least, of reliable wild harvests of grasses related to wheat and barley. Lulled into a false sense of security by this time of plenty, hunters and gatherers dropped their guard and settled down a bit, believing they could rely on such natural bounty year on year. In effect the crop domesticated the farmers rather than the other way round.

Rather than moving around a wide territory as before, people began instead to live in permanent settlements. Most fateful of all, they allowed themselves the luxury of more children, bigger families. So when the Near Eastern equivalent of the Big Freeze, the Younger Dryas, took hold, from 11,000 to 9,500 years ago, there may simply have been too many people to permit a return to hunting. Hunters need far bigger territories than farmers and when the climate took a turn for the worse the large, near-sedentary populations may have been forced into taking a more proactive role in cultivating, and so domesticating, the wild crops they had come to depend on. Only then, with necessity having given birth to an innovation, did they slowly come to appreciate how farming might give them the certainty of fresh meat, milk, hide and horn, the hope of surplus grain. Done right, farming might offer the best chance of survival for the many.

In short, that last cold snap may have left out-of-practice hunters, now handicapped by too-big families, with no option but to learn how to farm for real. Erstwhile Mesolithic people had put all their eggs in one Neolithic basket. They were trapped in the future. Neolithic means 'New Stone Age' and was at heart a way of life centred on domesticated animals and plants. Like every age before it, the Neolithic is associated with a specific range of tools and equipment, made for different tasks. But more than anything else the new age, the Neolithic, was about a new state of mind.

From its seedbed in Mesopotamia (meaning 'between the rivers', namely the Tigris and the Euphrates) farming eventually spread westwards into Europe. One route followed the coast of the Mediterranean Sea while a second took a line across Greece and back up the pathway cut by the River Danube. One or both routes then carried the new technology – its secrets and its practitioners – all the way to western Europe and finally to Britain.

The preceding paragraph is a summary of what must have happened: farming started in the east and ended up in the west and all points in between, several thousand years later. The precise details, however – of the journey made by the technology of farming – are still being mapped and argued about by academics, and often bitterly. Most furiously debated in this part of the world is whether farming reached Britain as an idea or in the heads and hands of actual farmers who brought it here themselves as part of some kind of cultural invasion.

Most archaeologists are at least agreed that farming (together with the rest of the Neolithic toolkit of polished stone axes, knapped stone tools and pottery) was in parts of western Europe by around 5000 BC. And early farming spread because it had to. The first child of a farmer stands to inherit the parent's land. For second and subsequent children, however, there is often no option but to leave home in search of virgin woodland that can be tamed, cleared and cultivated. In this way farming nudged ever westward, spreading like a vine across the landmass of Europe, slowly strangling the life breath of the hunting way of life.

Writer and polymath Jared Diamond has suggested it was the very alignment of the European continent upon the globe of the Earth that made the spread possible. Consider the iPhone: hold it upright and all the images are displayed in portrait mode; turn it onto its side and the image flips over into landscape. All but one of the planet's continents, notes Diamond, are in portrait mode with their long axes running north to south (think of Africa, and North and South America). Only Europe is laid out in landscape mode – with its long axis running west to east – so that 9,000-odd miles of related habitats connect Asia to the west, and ultimately to Britain. Animals and plants adapted to a specific band of latitudes were able to move, strolling or sown, all the way across Europe from Asia – from Tehran to Toledo – without too much discomfort.

(When it came to domesticating animals it probably helped too that the countries of the Fertile Crescent were home to the ancestors of sheep. If you are contemplating the physical proximity required for animal husbandry, you might want to test the theory on something like an Iranian mouflon. No wonder British hunter-gatherers confronted, by way of a contrast, with red deer and aurochs – aggressive wild bulls standing seven feet tall at the shoulder – preferred to kill and eat the local beasts rather than try to stroke them.)

But in imagining the farmers, their seeds and livestock moving east to west, it is easy to overlook the impact the incomers must have had on the hunters whose territories were encroached upon. This is part of what fuels the furious debate about whether farming was forced onto hunters, or whether they sought it out for them-selves. In the British context that particular conundrum – whether the new way of life crossed the Channel by some sort of osmosis, or alongside hobbled cattle and bags of seed in the holds of an invasion fleet of French farmers' boats – might be unravelled by whoever understands the great stone alignments of Carnac, in Brittany in north-west France.

Like a marching army of giants turned to stone, they are arranged in neat parallel rows, some the best part of a mile long. Every one of the uncarved blocks (and there are more than 3,000 of them) weighs at least several tons, and some must be much heavier than that. Many tower above the heads of the visitors milling among them, like children around the feet of grown-ups. But it is the sheer scale of the alignments – the over-arching vision on the part of their creators – that boggles the mind. Stand in the middle of the rows and they stretch off out of sight, sometimes over the horizon. Silently and endlessly they make us ask: How? ... Who? ... When? ... Why?

There has been little proper excavation of the Carnac stones, but some of the most recent thinking suggests they were erected not by Neolithic farmers – the people normally associated with great monuments of stone – but by Mesolithic hunters. French archaeologist Serge Cassen has studied the monoliths and the associated stone tombs and menhirs for over 20 years and has come to the conclusion they mark a great crossroads in the human journey. According to him, some remarkable rock art inside the nearby passage grave of Table des Marchands, in the commune of Locmariaquer, illustrates the moment when the world of the hunters was brought face to face with the New World of the farmers.

The tomb was built by the farmers, part of the process of laying claim to the land. Cassen excavated the construction and its interior during the mid 1990s and it has subsequently been rebuilt – partly to give an impression of how it may have looked but mostly to protect the carved artworks within. The passage leads into a chamber tall enough to stand up in. Directly opposite the end of the entrance and completely dominating the interior is a single block of stone shaped like a massive, squat phallus. As if that were not arresting enough, its flat surface is decorated all over with what look at first sight like old men's walking sticks. These are in fact representations of throwing sticks – curved hunting weapons related to boomerangs, which would be thrown into rising flocks of birds in the hope of braining some of them. According to Cassen, these are symbolic of the Mesolithic hunters; and superimposed upon the phallus they make the strongest possible statement about masculinity.

More significant in terms of Cassen's theory is the decoration on another large, flat stone forming part of the chamber's ceiling. This is dominated by an image that brings the throwing stick of the hunter together with the archetypal symbol of the Neolithic farmer, the polished stone axe. Under closer inspection it is obvious this is no meeting of equals – far from it. Instead the axe is quite clearly on top of the stick, even cutting it in two – a depiction, according to Cassen, of the moment when the New World of the farmers rose to dominate, to cut down with the axe the Old World of the hunters.

The truth is that when it comes to interpretation, the Carnac stones are surrounded by something of a void. Despite their obvious magisterial presence, they are as mysterious now as in the early eighteenth century when antiquarians first turned their attention to them. Local legend tells of a Roman legion turned to stone for persecuting Christians. More recently they have been seen as markers tracking the movements of the stars. Even druids have been evoked – the lines becoming avenues for religious procession. But they do seem to demand serious thought, to challenge the onlooker for a meaning; and Cassen has been moved to oblige. For him they represent nothing less than the very years when the first of the farmers appeared on the hunters' horizon.

With this thought in mind, of a collision of worlds, the great alignments take on an air that is close to poignancy. The Mesolithic hunters of Brittany were a people with their backs to the wall, or rather to the sea. There on the western limit of mainland Europe they had nowhere to go (not that they wanted to go anywhere, this was their home and always had been). Onto and into that beleaguered world crept the incomers, at the forefront of a movement that had taken millennia to travel so far. Rather than arriving as conquerors or invaders, the first of them were pushed forward, unwillingly, by the crowd at their backs. Digging their heels in but too weak to resist, those tongue-tied ambassadors were made to do the talking on behalf of the horde.

The newcomers found themselves among people living the old way, by hunting and gathering in a rich habitat that offered up the creatures of the woods as well as all the fish in the sea. According to Cassen, the sitting tenants wanted nothing at all to do with the farmers, with their strange talk of clearing fields, planting seeds and ... waiting. But the incomers were just as unyielding. They had nowhere else to go either. Behind them was the rest of Europe, already in the long, slow process of conversion to the new technology. Sooner or later these new arrivals would have to put down roots – their own and those of their plants. It was in that atmosphere – of an unstoppable force meeting an immovable object – that first the stones and then later the tombs were erected.

Cassen has spent decades considering Carnac – and he has come to conclusions that are too much, too precise, too prescriptive and too involved for some. For him the stones are words and phrases of a story that was decades or even centuries in the telling. He believes that as the two worlds collided – that of the hunter with that of the farmer – both found the need to raise monuments of stone.

He has come to view the stone rows as something akin to lines in the sand, or at least in the grass. Modern visitors tend to see them as avenues that must be walked down. Cassen, by contrast, sees them as a barrier, a thin grey line of soldiers standing in the face of overwhelming numbers. Confronted by the inevitable, he believes, the hunters raised the stones as a statement of ownership: they both belonged to, and were part of, the land. But, just as there are gaps between the stones, so the hunters' defiance could never have worked to exclude the farmers. Welcome or not, farming seeped through any and all opposition, like water through the holes in a colander.

The farmers, for their part, raised their own memorials in the form of tombs for their dead. Cassen believes that once the new way of life was in the ascendant, its proponents sought to make their point in stone as well. Thus it became appropriate to envelop the hunters' symbols within their own – to take the old phallic stones, decorated with throwing sticks, and absorb them within the new womb-like tombs. For farmers concerned with fertility and the cycle of life, it made sense to bring male and female symbols together as one.

It is quite a leap, this theory of Cassen's. But stand with him among the stones, see them through his eyes, and there is somehow a sense to it all. He is believable – they are believable. The stone lines are so astounding, so outrageous they must surely have come from a momentous time. These are no ordinary monuments and therefore no ordinary explanation will suffice.

Cassen sees a symbolic gesture – a besieged community's need to leave a definite mark upon the surface of a world made uncertain and unpredictable. For as long as I was beside him, I felt I could see it too. The standing stones were a statement of defiance. It said the farmers could come onto the hunters' land – but only if those farmers acknowledged and respected whose land it was.

The Mesolithic way of life is always spoken of as travelling light, leaving little trace of its presence. Perhaps there in Brittany a community of hunters did indeed take a step that had been, for them, almost unthinkable. But by raising a permanent monument in stone they declared: 'We will not last. Our way of life will not last. But we must be remembered. You must remember us – not for a short time, but for ever.'

' ... and these stones shall be for a memorial ... '

And there may be one more thing to think about. Perhaps the hunters let the farmers work the land on their behalf. Maybe they saw the future and a way to benefit from it. After all, the hunter is still a potent image today, still associated in our society with wealth and prestige. Aristocratic landowners do not soil their hands with the work of farming – they have tenant farmers for that. And while the farmers grow the crops and tend the animals, those richest landowners don crimson coats and black hats and gallop across the land on horseback as ... hunters. Who really was triumphant in the end?

Brittany is also conspicuous for the sheer volume of a special class of super-monolith. The Breton word for these monsters is *menhir* – meaning long stones. The largest of them, Le Grand Menhir Brise – the Great Broken Menhir – lies in four pieces beside that reconstructed passage grave of Table des Marchands, at Locmariaquer. Together the gigantic fragments weigh 330 tons and when upright and intact the complete piece would have stood over 60 feet high.

Whatever they were for – and there is no more consensus regarding the menhirs than there is for the stone alignments – they were allowed to fall down (or were knocked down) by the farmers who built the passage graves. Time and again Cassen and other excavators in Brittany have found former standing stones and pieces of menhir reused as building material for tombs. Cassen believes this act – of neglect or destruction – was another attempt by the farmers to bury the past beneath the future. 'It is probably linked to this new process,' he said. 'To this new economy, to this full Neolithic where the life of animals and the life of plants is very important to the perception of the cycle of life itself.'

In contrast to the old, phallic, masculine portrayal of the hunters, the passage graves themselves may represent a movement towards an appreciation of a more feminine nature. As the fertility of animals and plants became central to the well-being of society, so the old phallic images were no longer enough by themselves. Now they were assimilated within – allowed to penetrate – the feminine shapes represented by passages and womb-like chambers.

The Mesolithic way of life was being consigned to the shadows cast by stones. By 5000 BC the technology of farming had trundled across Europe as irresistibly as a battalion of tanks. But on the north-west coast of the continent, that advance was halted. Just as it would defy Caesar, Napoleon and Hitler, the English Channel stopped the farmers in their tracks.

All of this is giving to the movement of farming, and its farmers, a sense of purpose, a grand vision. But there was no crusade. In the life of planet Earth, the actions of individuals – warlords, politicians, farmers and the like – are the twitches of ticks on an elephant's back. If there was any momentum it was of a kind so deep and so subtle as to be utterly imperceptible to mere humans. French historians working in the twentieth century were best at suggesting how to think about time in relation to human history. Beneath everything is inertia, the tendency for nothing to happen. Above that is a motion so slow its currents and rhythms could be sensed only by an immortal with all the time in the universe. These are the rhythms of geological time that move tectonic plates, raise mountains and transform mud into stone by the use only of pressure and time.

Fernand Braudel, leader of the Annales School after the Second World War, developed this as the concept of the *longue durée* – the long term. He imagined time like an ocean. On the surface are bubbles and flecks of foam that come and go in the blinking of an eye. These are the moments we humans can perceive, the actions of individuals and the stuff of years. The bubbles and flecks ride on waves that are like the lifespans of nations and empires, and the substance of centuries at least. Finally, down in the dark are the great, impossibly slow ripples within the deep that support, and occasionally move, everything above.

So the planet spun through space. Geological forces shaped continents, built mountains and lowered valleys. Climate dictated what thrived, and what perished and died upon the skin of the Earth. For a time after the last Ice Age – a time we still ride upon ourselves, mere flecks of foam – it was warm and wet enough in part of western Asia for a kind of grass to grow that attracted the butterfly attentions of humans living there. For as long as the grass grew, it changed the people and made them live differently. Flecks of foam, generations of farmers, came and went, helplessly unaware of the wave that carried them, far less the deep ocean of time that lay beneath. Decades, centuries and millennia passed until finally the plants were growing in northern and western Europe as well. It was a process imperceptible to the people involved but less than a blink of time in the *longue durée*. If the idea for farming arrived from anywhere, it came from the planet and the grass.

So the day dawned when people in the north and west of Europe looked out across the stretch of water separating them from land they knew to be out there beyond the mist and rain. They knew it was there because there had already been contact – and in both directions. People are curious and it is impossible to imagine a time when that curiosity was not compelling some of them – hunters in Britain and farmers in France – to set out on journeys just to see what was on the other side of the water.

It followed eventually that, with no greater hope than the possibility of clearing some more fields and grazing this year's

young, some or other farmers' sons put to sea in small boats to try
their luck on the island that would be Britain.

The south-east of England is closest to Europe and for a long
time archaeologists assumed somewhere like Kent would have seen
the first landings. This was the traditional version of events – the
one taught to generations of archaeology students for much of the
twentieth century: farming simply crossed the Dover Strait into
the south-east of Britain before spreading north and west in the
manner of determined Roman legionaries.

But there was a problem. The earliest Neolithic remains in Kent
had been dated to 4000 BC; and since farming was known to have
been established on the other side of Channel by at least 5000 BC
it begged the question why another thousand years had apparently
passed before it travelled the last 20-odd miles.

Archaeologists like Alison Sheridan, however, are convinced
farming followed several different routes at several different times.
And while the rival camp insists British hunters acquired the
knowledge of farming for themselves – perhaps during fact-finding
trips to the Continent – she is certain the skills were brought here
wholesale by European immigrants.

Sheridan envisages the first of them departing from somewhere
in north-west France and making landfall not in Britain but in
south-west Ireland. These earliest forays began, she says, around
4500 BC, but they were a 'false start' that had fizzled out by 4250
BC. A little later there were pioneers from Brittany who did better,
establishing themselves at various points in the west of Wales and
Scotland, and on the coastline of the more northerly half of the
island of Ireland. The earliest megalithic tombs – from 4200–
4000 BC – are passage tombs with closed chambers found in
Pembrokeshire. In shape and style these are similar to tombs in
Brittany – further evidence of the point of origin for this strand
of Neolithic behaviour. Only from 4000 BC onwards, says Sheridan, were colonists making use of the more familiar Channel
crossing, departing from the north-west of France around modern
Calais and heading for locations on the south coast of Britain.

And according to Sheridan and others, the farmers did not stop there. Colonists in this third wave travelled all the way up Britain's east coast, and then to parts of the west coast and around Ireland as well. Finally, in a reversal of the D-Day landings, a fourth wave of farmers from the Normandy area was loading boats and crossing to southern Britain from 4000 BC onwards. Sheridan's 'big picture' of the arrival of farming in Britain also allows for the possibility of a (relatively brief) time of overlapping lifestyles, with Mesolithic hunters and Neolithic farmers sharing the land – maybe sometimes even oblivious to one another's existence. But at a site called Ferriter's Cove in County Kerry, south-west Ireland, bones of domesticated cattle have been found among Mesolithic material.

A radiocarbon date from one of them suggested the cow had been slaughtered sometime between 4500 and 4180 BC – prompting the site's director, Professor Peter Woodman of University College Cork, to imagine a spot of poaching. By way of explaining such early evidence of a domesticated beast in Mesolithic Ireland, he suggested an opportunist hunter might have rustled a cow from his Neolithic neighbour. Sheridan cautiously accepts this as perhaps the last straw for a struggling pioneer. Finally discouraged, he packed his family and belongings aboard his little boat and headed off back to France.

Although woven around a handful of bones, Woodman's interpretation of what might have been happening at Ferriter's Cove 6,500 years ago is a welcome thread of story-telling. Apart from anything else it helps us visualise real people behaving in ways that are instantly recognisable, and believable. It also reminds us how resourceful archaeologists and other scientists have had to be in their search for clues to explain how, why – and especially when – people started farming in Britain and Ireland.

Sometime around 4,500 years ago, an owl flew down the stone-lined passageway of a chambered tomb on the tiny island of Holm of Papa Westray, in Orkney, before perching on a stone lintel. It had fed some hours before and now, in the near-total darkness of the chamber, it regurgitated from its gut a small, furry pellet – all that remained of the animal it had taken from among the long grass near the shore. Now the owl's prey, or its crumpled skeleton at least, would spend the coming millennia nestled among the human skulls and long bones already piled on the tomb's floor.

The tiny animal's remains were recovered from the tomb by archaeologists. They might easily have been overlooked among the more arresting human remains, but were caught in the fine mesh of a sieve used to check the excavated sediments for tiny clues. When analysed by animal bone specialist Keith Dobney, from Durham University, they were found to belong to the species *Microtus arvalis orcadensis*, the Orkney vole.

Now the Orkney vole is a special little creature – quite distinct from his cousin *Microtus agrestis*, the field vole, who inhabits mainland Britain. The Orkney vole's nearest relatives (genetically speaking) are those living in the Rhine Valley in Germany, and perhaps in Brittany, and studies have shown *arvalis orcandensis*'s ancestors arrived in Orkney at least 5,500 years ago. 'It's clear the voles aren't swimming from Europe to Orkney on their own,' said Dobney. 'Which means that humans are involved.' In fact it is thought the voles arrived as accidental stowaways inside sacks of grain carried to Orkney by early farmers – not from the British mainland but direct from the Continent.

European voles in Orcadian chambered tombs; domesticated cattle bones among the scraps left behind by an unscrupulous hunter, who had no respect for foreign prospectors – these are some of the tracks in the faint trail leading all the way back to the first British farmers.

The image of hunters and farmers existing side by side – whether happily or not – is a helpful one. There is some consensus among archaeologists that the lifestyle of the first farmers retained elements of the Mesolithic traditions. As well as planting crops like wheat and barley and herding some domesticated cattle, pigs and sheep, it seems completely logical they would have supplemented their diet by continuing to hunt.

Mesolithic hunters might even have begun the practice of opening up clearings in the woodland. Since grass would grow in the open spaces, deer and other prey would be attracted there and hunters could lie in wait to take advantage. So the earliest farmers may have planted their first crops in what were, to all intents and purposes, Mesolithic 'fields'.

There is little evidence of permanent settlement either, at least in the early centuries, and archaeologists have imagined the farmers being at least partly nomadic, herding their animals from one temporary camp to another. It is also thought that while they deliberately planted stands of wheat and barley, they were unlikely to have stood over them while they grew. Instead they would have concentrated on moving the animals from pasture to pasture, only returning to the crop when it was time for the harvest.

At Balbridie, in Aberdeenshire, however, archaeologists began excavating what they thought would prove to be a Dark Age great hall. They revealed a huge building all right – more than 80 feet long by over 40 feet wide and made of massive timber posts – but radiocarbon dates showed it had been built and used between 3900 and 3700 BC. It was Neolithic – and Early Neolithic at that. Grains of wheat and barley were recovered from the postholes and also in a considerable concentration at one end, suggesting the interior may have been partly used for storage. Whatever they did at Balbridie – whether it was a grain store, a meeting place, a setting for feasts or mysterious ceremonies – they did not do it for very long. It seems that within a generation or so of its construction the hall was burnt down.

The Balbridie hall appears out of its proper time – fully formed and without any intermediate stepping-stones to link it to what had gone before – and yet it is not alone. At nearby Warren Field, in Crathes near Aberdeen, another large timber building returned Early Neolithic dates. Excavated in 2005, the Warren Field hall was built sometime between 3800 and 3700 BC. Even more fascinating, archaeologists also found a line of pits running for nearly 200 feet along a nearby ridge. These were big holes, up to 10 feet across, and when the largest of them was excavated it was found to contain fragments of stone tools, including those of stone axes.

But it was the radiocarbon dates obtained from burnt wood in the pits that presented the real conundrum. Charcoal from the lowest levels was found to be around 9,500 years old, meaning they had originally been dug by Mesolithic hunters. They were probably still visible as depressions in the ground 4,000 years later when the farmers decided to reopen them. For reasons unknown, they put more burnt wood into the holes, along with fragments of their tools – a conscious and deliberate reuse of pits they must have known had originally been dug by people who had lived and died long before them. It was, at the very least, an act of remembrance.

While large timber buildings are conspicuous oddities in the Early British Neolithic, such structures are more commonplace on the Continent. For as much as a thousand years before anyone was digging the postholes for the Balbridie hall, farmers in parts of what are now Germany, Holland and Poland were building and using large timber structures. Analysis of the cereal grains in Balbridie suggested they too were of European origin; so it seems plausible that the land around Aberdeen was being farmed about 6,000 years ago by people who had brought with them a fully formed and sophisticated farming culture.

Across most of Britain the survival of Early Neolithic homes appears patchy, to put it mildly. It presents a confusing picture, with some built of stone and some of timber; some rectangular or square in shape while others are oval or circular. It may well be that many more structures have been scrubbed from the archaeological record by later land use and modern development, and it is also possible to build quite substantial structures that do not require deep postholes or other foundations likely to be spotted by archae-ologists. The evidence as it stands, however, suggests the first farmers were moving around the landscape much as the Mesolithic hunters had before them, using just temporary, even portable dwellings, travelling light.

But if their homes left little trace, those pioneers did implant a sense of permanence in the land by the building of monuments, and it is from some of these special places – special to those who created them – that we get a first glimpse of the people themselves.

Human bones and skulls were excavated from inside a stone tomb built at Coldrum, in Kent, around 4000 BC. The rich soil of Kent is still prime farming land – the Garden of England, as it is known – and Coldrum tomb is surrounded by fields today. But the farmers would have encountered the woodland of oak and birch that had shrouded the landscape for millennia. Among its dappled shadows moved red deer and elk, bears and wild pigs, and hunters. All of it was about to begin a steady, irresistible process of permanent transformation.

While the hunters had lived with the land as it was (give or take a few clearings) the farmers were technologists who carried in their heads an image of the way the land could be. They understood how to make the land work for them. Instead of fitting in alongside nature, they sought to rule over it. Coldrum tomb was the work of some of those newcomers to Britain and it appears today as a simple, roofless rectangular chamber built of huge slabs of local sarsen stone. Once it may have been within an earthen mound but it is no longer possible to know for sure. It contained the remains of around 17 people – adults, teenagers, young children and babies – possibly all belonging to the same extended family or tribe.

Holding one of those adult skulls, looking into the empty eye sockets and marvelling at the shine on the teeth, is a humbling experience. Archaeologists use expressions like 'the Neolithic Revolution' to describe the change from hunting to farming. But it is bones like those from Coldrum that remind us it was all the work of individual people, spending the few years of their lives trying to reshape the world. They were either among the very first to reach Britain, or perhaps those settlers' children or grandchildren, and they lived their lives against the odds. They brought a new idea, as fragile as a cutting, and transplanted it into soil that had never known the like. They crossed the sea and entrusted their own futures and those of their children to the knowledge in their heads and the skill of their hands. Apart from anything else, they were brave.

The building of tombs to house the bones of the dead was new behaviour, Neolithic behaviour that came to Britain with the farmers. Finds of Mesolithic remains are so rare – the skeletons from Aveline's Hole, and Cheddar Man in Somerset – as to make it impossible to know what funerary rituals were practised in the main by the hunters. There have been a handful of spectacular finds: a Mesolithic 'cemetery' was excavated at Vedbaek, in modern Denmark, in the 1980s and found to contain bodies laid in carefully cut graves. Some had their head or feet resting on antlers; in one a young woman wearing a necklace of red deer teeth had been buried with a baby laid upon a swan's wing. But such enigmatic rarities are exceptional and the Mesolithic approach to death remains almost a total mystery.

Along with their seeds and domesticated animals, the first farmers to arrive in Britain brought from Europe a whole new approach to death and the dead. The decision to store their remains in purpose-built chambers seems to indicate a new way of seeing the land. Having made the effort to open up the woodland for their animals and to plant crops, they justifiably felt an attachment to their own small patches of territory – made by their own toil – and wanted others to respect them. They had put down roots and as more time passed – as sons and daughters stayed in place to work the fields cleared by their parents, grandparents, their great-grandparents – the roots grew deep, and deeper still. It became important for the living to remember those who had gone before because the dead validated their continuing claim on the land. Their bones, the bones of the ancestors – or at least the bones of some representative few of them – became symbols of a tenure that had lasted for generations. The land gave them life year after year and they gave their lives to it in return. Eventually the same soil that had fed them would cradle their bones, so that the family's connection to the fields transcended death itse...

Evidence like the Orkney voles and the very early cow bone at Ferriter's Cove in south-west Ireland makes it clear the story of farming's arrival in Britain is more complex and subtle than we had ever imagined. Instead of one concerted push across the narrowest part of the Channel into Kent around 4000 BC, it now seems, as Sheridan and others suggest, that many different crossings were made from departure points all along the Continent's northern and western coastlines. In ones and twos, down through the centuries before 4000 BC, European farmers were testing the ground all around Britain, in search of footholds.

Ireland provides yet another twist. While archaeologists in Britain have found only the merest traces of the earliest farmers, on the northern coastline of County Mayo is a vast archaeological site that defies neat and tidy explanation. It appears to be the preserved remains of Neolithic farming on a truly massive scale.

Discovered in the 1930s by local schoolteacher Patrick Caulfield during routine cutting of peat for his fire, Achaidh Chéide – the Céide Fields – may contain the earliest Neolithic field system in the world. What Caulfield found was the top of a wall of large stones now buried beneath many feet of peat. The investigation of the mystery was taken up by his son Seamus, who was inspired to study archaeology as a result of what Caulfield Senior had begun to unearth; and Dr Caulfield has now spent 40 years of his life exploring the Céide Fields. What is indisputable is that the ambition of the wall-builders in this part of Ireland's wild west was, at some point in prehistory, truly heroic.

The principal weapon in Caulfield's armoury has been a steel rod with which he probes the peat. The formation of peat is still not fully understood but it is thought to be a build-up of vegetable matter on ground waterlogged by rain. Under certain conditions fallen leaves, dead grass and other plant material fails to decompose quickly enough. Instead of breaking down and being absorbed by the soil, it accumulates on the surface. Over hundreds or even thousands of years this accumulation can become several feet

...ing pattern of Neolithic walls, along with
...t was visible on the Céide Fields in ancient
...n today beneath a blanket of peat as much as 10

...riously working their way back and forth across the
...pe, Caulfield and his teams of volunteers have been able to
p... the pattern of the walls. The peat has the consistency of firm
butter and the probes slide through it easily. When they hit the
top of a section of wall a sound rings back from stones that have
been out of sight for millennia. 'Five and a half thousand years
ago somebody lifted a stone into place,' said Caulfield. 'And we
are now hearing it for the first time.'

A field system covering many square miles has already been
mapped. Pollen grains found within cores of peat removed from
the bog reveal the walls defined fields of grass – pasture for livestock. Caulfield believes Neolithic farmers were managing huge
herds of cattle and needed the field system to keep cows, calves
and bulls separate from one another at different times of the year.
There is also pollen from pine trees, showing what covered the
landscape before the farmers set to work with their axes; and also
rare instances of cereal crops like wheat.

It is the scale of the Céide Fields that has made some archaeologists sceptical about Caulfield's findings, or at least about the
early dates. The only comparable field systems in Britain and
Europe were laid out sometime after 2000 BC – one and a half
millennia later. Caulfield has also found evidence of permanent
houses on the Céide Fields at a time when pastoralists in Britain
were still semi-nomadic, driving their herds from fresh pasture to
fresh pasture. Then there is the mystery of where the Irish cattle
came from. In Britain there were aurochs, the wild ancestors of
domesticated cattle, but no such beasts existed in Ireland. So, apart
from anything else, the animals Caulfield supposes were grazing
in his neat fields 5,500 years ago had to have been imported.

The whole scale of what has apparently been discovered there
suggests it arrived fully formed, like the Balbridie timber hall. This

was no gradual process – indigenous people clearing the land a little at a time, keeping a few cattle and learning the necessary skills all the while. Instead Caulfield believes it was a grand plan executed by experienced dairy farmers from Europe.

The Céide Fields are, in short, controversial.

Whenever and however it arrived, farming eventually changed everything, in Britain and everywhere else. Despite the hardships, despite the cost to general health, it was demonstrably productive. Practised skilfully, it provided the kind of surplus and the kind of certainty of supply that hunters could only dream of. Hunters were always chasing their food, trusting nature to provide for them. Farmers had taken control of nature. As a survival strategy, it was irresistible.

It would change the land and it changed us as well. The transition to farming eventually committed every man, woman and child to a lifetime of work. The daily grind was once the chore of turning seed into flour, but we had unwittingly shackled ourselves to the millstones for all time. There could be no turning back. Because farming was productive, it fed more children. With more children a family could clear and work more land – and so produce more food, to feed yet more children.

The population rapidly increased to the point where farming was the only option; there were simply too many people ever to permit a return to hunting. They were enslaved by the grass; they had made of themselves beasts of burden. If they had been nomadic in the beginning – herding their animals, returning to clearings to harvest grain – that time passed. With all that fertility and productivity, all those children, the place gradually filled up. They could not drift around any more. Instead they had to stay put, make the best of it in one place for life. There was no room for hunters any more either. There had come a day when we were all, finally, farmers – whether we wanted to be or not.

During the millennia farming took to cross Europe, the very beliefs of its practitioners – their view of the world and their place in it – had also been fundamentally altered. Once the hunters had stood helpless while the deluges snatched the land away. Now the farmers were determined to hold onto it. Perhaps they felt that by tending the land, caring for it, they were securing it against loss.

By the time that family set about building their tomb at Coldrum, in Kent, 6,000 years ago, they were following an approach to death that was already well established elsewhere. All across Europe are burial mounds and chambers built by farmers to contain their dead and as time passed the practice became more and more elaborate. Within a few centuries of the building of the Coldrum barrow, farmers in Britain were investing enormous effort and imagination in an attempt to do right by the land and the dead.

West Kennet Long Barrow, in Wiltshire, is one of the most famous Early Neolithic tombs. The 'barrow' is a long mound of chalk rubble nearly 330 feet long and aligned east to west. At the wide eastern end a façade of enormous sarsen slabs – some twice the height of a man and weighing several tens of tons – symbolically 'blocks' the entrance to a long, stone-lined 'transepted' passage which gives access to five chambers – two pairs either side and one at the end. While the chambers are for crouching in, the passage is big enough to enable a man to walk upright and the whole interior, dimly illuminated by a small pane of modern toughened glass in the roof, is reminiscent of a chapel. It somehow demands, and usually receives, respectful quiet. The huge amount of labour involved in the construction – not to mention the imagination – suggests it was the work not of one family but of an entire community. More than a tomb, more than a memorial to loved ones, it is about creating another world – the community of the living imagining the community of the dead.

West Kennet is one of a class of tombs classified by archaeologists as the Cotswold-Severn group and the latest thinking suggests they were built and used over a relatively short space of time. With names like Wayland's Smithy (in Oxfordshire), Hetty Pegler's Tump and Belas Knap (both in Gloucestershire), they are found all across the Cotswolds and in parts of north Wales. They are also similar to monuments in the Loire: those French tombs may even have inspired the British examples.

The remains of just over 40 people were placed inside West Kennet itself over the course of as little as 25 years, and the different sexes and age groups were carefully split between the chambers. Old and young were separated from one another, as were men and women, suggesting Neolithic society was carefully ordered.

There is little consensus about how such tombs were used. In addition to the Cotswold-Severn group there are many other types and styles. Rather in the manner of awkward teenage boys with their music collections, archaeologists are committed to making lists, putting things in order and compiling classifications and groups. They have therefore identified numerous different sorts of tombs.

There are those where the internal structure is made of timber and those where it is stone; around the Irish Sea there are the Portal Dolmens with large chambers made of stone slabs; sometimes the mounds are round, sometimes they are trapezoidal, rectangular or square; sometimes single chambers are entered from the sides of long, thin mounds; in others there are passages leading to interconnected chambers from curving façades. In parts of Scotland there are Clyde Cairns, in parts of Ireland Court Cairns. Some of the variations occur within, as well as between regions and different parts of the country. But for all the lack of uniformity it is at least fair to say the care of bones was a serious matter.

They almost always contain just a relatively small number of dead and clearly were not intended as the final resting place for the whole community. Instead it seems burial within the tomb was deemed appropriate only for certain individuals or perhaps some sort of representative sample. When such a person died the body was laid out where animals and birds could do the work of removing the flesh and this may have been in the passage of the tomb, or perhaps on specially built 'excarnation' platforms. Once nature had taken its course, the bones were gathered up and placed in the appropriate chamber – and not always as an intact skeleton.

Sometimes the skulls and bones were moved around, separated from their owners and perhaps even removed from the tomb for a while.

Tombs like West Kennet were left open while they were in use. For the duration of the 25 years or so while the bodies and bones gradually accumulated inside, the living – or some of them at least – could enter as well. It might be more helpful to think of them as temples or churches. The dead are buried within and around Christian churches but that is only one of the functions of such a building.

While West Kennet and the rest of the Cotswold-Severn tombs seem to have been about the recent dead, of just a generation or so, gradually there was a move to amass anonymous piles of bones. A practice developed of sorting skulls, long bones, vertebrae and the rest into piles, so that the dead ceased to be individuals. Instead they became part of one collective entity, one presence – that of the ancestors.

We are left to imagine what it must have felt like inside such a tomb, for people who truly believed their loved ones and the rest of the honoured dead were somehow present there – that they were all around, watching and aware. Surely the faithful entered only with the greatest reverence, with the hairs prickling on their necks as they wondered what would happen next in that eternal gloom.

Eventually, within a generation of construction, the active life of the tomb was brought to an end. Having decided access to the ancestors was no longer appropriate (or required), the farmers dragged into place the great stones of the façade. Once these were raised upright, with Herculean effort, the community of the ancestors was off-limits to that of the living.

But, open or closed, tombs like West Kennet performed a more simple, earthly function as well. They are often found surrounded by fertile farmland and by building such obvious structures loaded with the potent presence of their ancestors, the incumbents were making a statement of ownership. Like farming, like making pots of fired clay, like polishing axes and building houses for the dead – this was new to Britain. From the time of the first farmers, a powerful notion took root and began to grow: this land is ours; it is mine.

Formal burial of individuals seems to have been highly unusual in the Neolithic. The truth is we simply do not know for certain what happened to most people when they died. If they were not among the tiny proportion destined for the tombs, where their remains would be preserved for the attention of archaeologists in the future, they may have been left in the open for the scavengers, or consigned to fast-flowing rivers. There were graves of a sort for some, usually in circumstances where the remains perhaps enhanced the sacred nature of some part of the landscape set aside as 'special'. As time passed, a few more of the farmers were granted graves of their own, and there was always the occasional rite of cremation; but the treatment of the general dead in the Neolithic remains a mystery. Human remains are often found in houses and within settlements, so it is possible people preferred to keep the bones of loved ones close by. Perhaps inclusion in the tombs was often temporary, so that loved ones were eventually recovered and taken home. (I have always felt cemeteries and graveyards to be lonely places and I suspect the custom of putting the dead away, out of sight, is a relatively recent one born mostly out of concerns about hygiene and disease. Surely the older human instinct is to keep the beloved dead, particularly children, near at hand.)

Farmers are at the centre of a cycle of life and death. Seeds are planted, crops grow and before they die they produce more seeds. Female animals give birth to young that in turn grow to maturity – and before they die they make new life for the future. So it was for the people themselves. Generations came and lived and passed life and land onwards into the future, to their children and grandchildren. The cycles a tribe could prove, the deeper its roots and the stronger its claim on the territory where it had all happened.

With the planting of those roots, constructing tombs and owning land came the need to ask, for the first time, 'Where are you from?' And from now on there was an answer to be given. And with the building of tombs filled with ancestors it made sense to ask the question, 'Who are you from?' as well.

The anonymous collections of bones in some tombs may have been an attempt to show how long the tribe had been there, how ancient was their connection to the land. Perhaps the best claim, therefore, was one based on a lineage – real or imagined – reaching all the way back to the hunters who had been there in the first place. Descent from ancient hunting stock may have represented the strongest claim of all, so someone known (or at least believed) to have been the direct descendant of the last of the hunters may well have been one of those considered worthy of a place within the community of the dead.

Part of all this is memory as well; there is an urge within *Homo sapiens sapiens* to remember and to recall. All of us reach a point in our lives when we feel more of our time is behind us than in front. As we get older, the remaining days and months and years seem to pass faster and faster so that they run through our fingers as uncontrollably as sand. To make matters worse, we appear to have no control over what we actually do remember. Rather than obeying our commands to retain chosen events and people for ever, memory makes its own decisions on our behalf. Memory has been described as like a dog that lies down where it pleases and, as the French philosopher Henri Bergson has said, 'It is the function of the brain to enable us not to remember but to forget.'

As a species we are therefore fighting forgetfulness all the time and so we have to prioritise and make decisions about just what – and who – needs to be remembered; we then have to find some external place where all this important stuff can be stored. Eventually it became possible to write things down, first on stone and then on paper. Now we have computer servers capable of hosting vast amounts of data. But even so, we still have to make decisions about what to keep and what to lose.

This is editing and it seems it is nearly as old as the hills. It seems to me that, as well as building communities for the ancestors

and highly visible statements of ownership, the architects of the
tombs were also creating houses of memory. Our Neolithic
ancestors realised they had no way to keep track of it all. There
was no possibility either of remembering everyone, or even storing
all of their bones. Instead decisions were made about who was to
be kept, and what each individual would represent in death. This
was part of the lore of the tribe. A tomb became a reservoir of
important things – the things that seemed to matter.

But while the need to remember is part of being human it was
the concept of ownership that had the more immediate consequences. Crickley Hill in Gloucestershire is primarily famous as
the site of an Iron Age hill fort. But people placed an importance on
high ground long before the advent of metal tools; and Neolithic
farmers armed with axes of polished stone found reasons to settle
on the hilltop as well. The view is almost a justification in itself –
out over what feels like the whole of the Severn Valley with the
Malvern Hills, the Forest of Dean and the Black Mountains all
there to be sensed out on the horizon and beyond.

Today the view is dominated by the modern city of Gloucester
itself, surrounded by satellite towns and villages dotted through a
familiar checkerboard pattern of fields. But 5,500 years ago when
Neolithic farmers looked out from their lofty summit they would
have seen a landscape comprised mostly of woodland and broken
only by the occasional farming homestead and associated cleared
fields – all the more reason to value the high ground that provided
a sense of overlordship and control. Anyone wanting to lay claim
to all of that valuable, fertile land would do well to have a presence
up on the hill overlooking it all in every direction.

By the middle of the fourth millennium BC, farmers had
enclosed a large part of the flat land on the summit by digging a
vaguely circular ditch. They left at least two gaps – causeways to
let people and animals in and out – and at some point they felt
the need to strengthen the defences by building a timber palisade
with gated entrances at the causeways, on the inner side of the
ditch. As it turned out, they were right to be worried about

security. Sometime around 3550 BC, a body of armed intruders attacked the settlement with lethal force. Archaeologists have recovered more than 400 flint arrowheads from Crickley Hill – almost all of them pointed towards the settlement and clustered around the two entrances.

The arrowheads are undeniably beautiful – flaked into exquisite teardrop shapes so perfect they briefly distract from their lethal purpose. But these weapons – together with evidence of burning of the gates, the palisade and homes inside the enclosure – are testament to a watershed in our history: the arrival of armed conflict.

Five and a half thousand years ago, the longbow was the height of fashion among discerning hunters – and warriors. The ancestor of the weapon that would reach legendary status on the battlefields of Agincourt and Crécy, it was just as effective in the hands of Neolithic farmers with a taste for conquest.

To see for myself how powerful a longbow can be – even in untrained hands – I arranged to visit the scene of the crime with an expert in ancient weapons. Will Lord is the son of John Lord, the man who had earlier coaxed me through my Mesolithic day and night on the island of Coll. Will is evidently cut from the same bolt as his father. He arrived with a longbow he had made himself just weeks before from a single piece of seasoned ash. It was a thing of beauty, but one crafted for the arms and shoulders of a man much stronger than I; it felt as though someone had put a bowstring on a telegraph pole.

Undeterred, Lord Junior showed me the arrows we would be shooting (never firing – firing is only for weapons like rifles and pistols that use gunpowder and so emit a flash of 'fire'). Like the bow, they were his own work – the shafts, the perfectly knapped points fixed in place with pine resin, the crow's feather flights, all of it. (I handle things like those – made by people who have taken the time to acquire the skills that were a matter of life and death for our species for hundreds of thousands of years – and I ask myself, seriously, 'What use am I?')

Despite my lack of strength or experience with such a weapon, I was soon stunned to discover how effective Lord's handiwork proved to be. Having hung a fresh side of pork from a tall frame of timber poles, he invited me to have a go from a distance of about 30 yards. There, on the site of a 5,500-year-old battle fought with longbows of exactly the same design, I took aim at the lifeless flesh and bone and loosed my first arrow – and watched as the arrowhead and then half the shaft passed through the meat as if it were newspaper.

Whether it had been judgement or dumb luck that guided my hand, it was a breathtaking moment. I had had the strength only to draw the bow about halfway – it was as unyielding as a doorframe – and was struck first and foremost by how slow the arrow seemed in flight. Lord said it was always the case – arrows were visible in flight and in battle their intended targets would sometimes have seen them coming.

The apparent lack of speed is mostly an optical illusion and in any case the damage is done not by the arrowhead but by the power of the bowstring, stored and carried in the arrow shaft. The point penetrates the target but the energy of the bow – over 200 pounds of it in the case of ours if it had been drawn to its limit – piles in behind the point and forces it through the target like a hammer drill.

All the archaeological evidence from Crickley Hill suggests longbows were decisive on the day of the battle. Though there is no physical evidence of actual harm done to the defenders of that particular enclosure in the form of human remains, there seems little doubt the place was the scene of vicious fighting. There is also no shortage of proof elsewhere that our ancient forebears knew all about inflicting, and suffering the effects of, extreme violence.

In the cupboards and drawers of the store rooms of the Natural History Museum in London there are numerous examples of damage caused to Neolithic men and women by grievous bodily harm: skulls caved in by hammer blows, fracture lines running from ear to ear; dimpled depressions on skulls – evidence of blows that healed. It bears remembering too that only certain kinds of traumatic injury leave evidence on skulls or bones. A severed femoral or carotid artery, damage inflicted by a flint knife, would be just as lethal but would leave an unmarked skeleton.

Archaeologists took some time to come round to the idea of ancient conflict – often preferring to imagine that our forebears inhabited a more peaceful world than our own. With this mindset, finds of arrowheads and other artefacts nestled within the bones of skeletons were routinely interpreted as grave goods, objects lovingly gifted to the dead in the hope they might prove useful in the afterlife. No doubt this was often the case but sometimes such finds, in such contexts, have to be seen as the cause of death itself.

An adult male found buried beneath a collapsed section of the rampart of the Neolithic causewayed enclosure at Hambledon Hill in Dorset had an arrow in his ribcage. This might once have been interpreted as having a ritual overtone but nowadays it is seen as proof of a violent end, possibly during a battle like the one at Crickley Hill. Similarly an arrowhead recovered from the neck bones of a male skeleton found inside West Kennet Long Barrow was no gift from a grieving relative but more than likely his ticket to a place in hallowed ground – a fallen hero, killed defending hearth and home. These are by no means isolated cases. Studies of human remains from the early centuries of the Neolithic suggest that as many as one in every 15 people had suffered a traumatic head injury. In other words, people living in the first centuries after 4000 BC would have known about, witnessed and likely suffered some sort of physical violence.

Violence is as old as humanity. For early populations, as for us, jealousy, anger, hurt and the like would regularly have exploded into fights between individuals, sometimes with deadly consequences. Isolated incidents of violence among groups are to be expected and are also manageable. Members of groups understand that frictions and passions will often end up with people getting hurt, and occasionally killed. Such violence is unplanned and

spontaneous, an instant reaction to a perceived wrong. It is sometimes even forgivable.

But the real problems for society start when violence is planned
and carried out in cold blood. Premeditated attacks by one group
upon another, with a specific objective in mind, are the basis of
war. They have something we do not ... they have more young
women than us ... they have bigger stores of food ... they are
different from us – all of these and more will motivate some people
to kill, with a view to redressing the balance. The battle of Crickley
Hill, 5,500 years ago, would have been deeply upsetting for all
those who experienced and witnessed it – not just its bloodied
victims. Violence and the threat of violence undermine everything
worthwhile.

And so for the greater good of the many – inspired by the desire
to live lives free from fear – those farmers had to set about creating
nothing less than society itself. It had been better for the hunters,
so few and far between, the different groups seldom if ever meeting
one another. Once farming led to population increase, however,
the empty space dwindled. Bigger tribes needed to expand their
territories. Contact between groups was happening more and more
until the wiser, cooler heads among them understood that they
needed to find ways for people to get along with the minimum of
skull-splitting.

This, then, was in large part the inspiration for the creation of
monuments on a grand scale. By coming together in the hundreds,
perhaps even the thousands to co-operate in great works, Neolithic
society would literally have bound itself together. Some of the
results of those efforts were so vast they remain fixed in our
landscape to this day, despite the ravages of millennia of ploughs,
wind and rain.

The Stonehenge Cursus in Wiltshire – sometimes called the
Greater Cursus – is so big it can barely even be perceived up close.
As you walk towards it, it seems like the product of natural rather
than human forces. On the ground there is little to see of the thing
at any one time except a wide, shallow ditch. It stretches towards

the horizon in both directions and anyone coming across it on a walk would be more likely to think it a feature eroded by water or just a natural ripple in the grass.

It is only from the air that the form of the cursus reveals itself. It consists in fact of two ditches running parallel about 450 to 500 feet apart and stretching for well over two miles. The ditches, which may have had banks along their inside edges, therefore enclose a long, narrow lozenge shape and when freshly cut through to the chalk – bright white lines against the green of the grass – must have been visible for miles.

Their function and meaning remain unclear. They were given their name by the eighteenth-century English antiquarian William Stukeley, who imagined they might have been race courses (*cursus* is Latin for course), and the largest of them, the Dorset Cursus on Cranborne Chase, is well over six miles long. Sometimes they incorporate other, earlier monuments like long barrows within their great lengths, but they are essentially vast, empty shapes, best seen by a god. They may have been boundary markers, places to contain some of the dead, processional ways – or all of those and more besides. Perhaps the act of making them mattered as much or even more than using them.

There is something about the apparent emptiness of the cursus monuments that makes them strangely lifeless. Perhaps it is hard to picture people in them because they were always spaces set aside, from which life itself was excluded. For that reason they seem to have less to say and are somehow forbidding, certainly less than welcoming.

A quite different experience is to be had, however, in one of the many so-called causewayed enclosures scattered across southern Britain. They are found in river valleys as well as on hilltops and other high ground. Incomplete, roughly circular ditches enclose spaces that are sometimes huge. At Windmill Hill in Wiltshire the outermost of three concentric ditches, draped casually around the summit like necklaces, is well over a thousand feet across. In some the enclosure is formed by a single circle, in others by as many as four; but always the ditches are interrupted by causeways, bridges to let people and animals come and go. The causeways are effectively the point of the exercise: the ditches may define special areas, but there are ways in and ways out. As with the lines of stones at Carnac, the barrier is permeable and only symbolic.

Today there is seldom anything to see at any of them other than the shallow traces of the ditches, but excavation has shown there were sometimes banks or even timber palisades as well. Crickley Hill had, by the time of the Neolithic battle, evolved into a settlement with permanent buildings inside; but in their original form they were never places in which people lived year-round. Nonetheless, from time to time all of the causewayed enclosures were scenes of intense and deeply meaningful activity.

Professor Alasdair Whittle of Cardiff University excavated Windmill Hill in the late 1980s and found that, while many of the Neolithic features had been reduced to shadows by centuries of ploughing – not to mention decades of excavation by earlier archaeologists – more than enough survived to reveal ancient minds at work, struggling to make sense of their world.

Between 1925 and 1929, Alexander Keiller spent five summers excavating there, systematically digging sections through the ditches to reveal how they had originally been cut and what, if anything, had gone into them as they gradually silted up. In fact the site was stuffed full of archaeological riches, including huge quantities of Neolithic pottery and flint tools. There were also large quantities of animal bone – sometimes whole skeletons – as well as small amounts belonging to humans. In all, Keiller's excavations recovered sherds from over 1,300 separate pottery vessels and the best part of 100,000 pieces of worked flint.

By any standards it was a vast and complicated assemblage and should have enabled him to put together a comprehensive report on the site. But Keiller was an heir to the vast fortune amassed by his family in the Dundee marmalade business that still bears their name (he had actually bought Windmill Hill in its entirety before starting to dig holes in it) and had a taste for women and fast cars, preferably taken together. On the last day of the 1929 season of excavation, 9 July, he was driving his secretary, a Miss Duncan, in his Targa Florio Bugatti racing car along a stretch of the A4, the main Bath road towards Savernake near Marlborough, when he smashed the thing into the side of a railway bridge.

He wrote afterwards: 'We were climbing this hill at a reasonable speed, but not by any manner of means, I consider, an excessive one, viz. some 84 miles an hour, when my back axle broke and, the car turning round rising into the air, we hurtled ourselves onto the angular portion of the bridge. It is fortunate that we hit the angle, since otherwise, considering the speed at which we were travelling, we must have burst through the brickwork and fallen another 40 feet onto the railway line below. It is of course miraculous that either of us lived through the experience.'

As a result of the crash – proof if proof were needed that archaeologists are not all dusty academics – Keiller published little of his findings. The job of writing it all up, making sense of the huge assemblage of artefacts, was taken up in part by another legendary figure in twentieth-century archaeology, Professor Stuart Piggott, who concluded that the enclosure had been operated primarily as a cattle market. He imagined animals from the wider area being herded across the causeways into Windmill Hill by farmers keen to buy and sell.

Subsequent radiocarbon dating of some of Keiller's finds placed most of them between 3600 and 3300 BC. While some of the pottery had likely been made on Windmill Hill itself, much of it had come from elsewhere – often from considerable distances. Some of the pots had been made from clay sourced on the Lizard in Cornwall, more than 100 miles away. There were also stone axes from Cornwall and even from quarry sites as far away as north Wales and the Lake District.

Such was the allure of Windmill Hill that it drew yet more archaeologists. And so when Whittle arrived in 1988 it was at the end of quite a line of investigators. Armed as he was with new techniques and new thinking, his analysis has allowed the site to shed a whole new light on the Neolithic in Britain.

For all the talk of a 'Neolithic Revolution', its agitators are strangely absent from the scene, if truth be told. Farmers came and changed the world, shaped it in their own image, and then mostly disappeared like mist in the sunshine. We find relatively few of their homes, or even of their bones. Given that their efforts laid the foundations of the world in which we live today, they have remained elusive to the end.

Despite Piggott's assessment of Windmill Hill as a corral, Whittle and others have arrived at a much less prosaic interpretation of all that pottery and bone. First of all, Whittle points out, there is the sheer physical effort of the construction of a causewayed enclosure like Windmill Hill. A large number of people had to agree to gather there at the same time, to begin the job of digging those huge ditches that loop around the summit. They had to agree the design – and what it represented – and then, working with tools of stone, antler and bone, they had to excavate countless thousands of tons of material. Just that coming-together to complete the task is significant. It speaks of co-ordination and co-operation – people spread over a wide area communicating with each other and agreeing to a plan and a schedule. The practice of building such monuments began around 3700 BC and the impact of their sudden appearance across the landscape must have been profound. Where before there had been bare hilltops, now the green of the grass was etched with great circles of shimmering white chalk, visible for miles around.

The circle is the shape that has mattered to people for the longest time. The Moon is round, as is the sun. The more observant might have noticed that the crescent forms of the Moon's phases are made by the shadow of our planet – and that our world must therefore be round as well. There was the passage of the Moon and other bodies across the night sky – regular and predictable, cyclical. For farmers, people concerned with the coming and going of seasons, the year itself would eventually have suggested a circular shape. Life itself is the ultimate circle, from birth to death and back again, endlessly repeating. So the significance of the circle would have registered early on, inspiring people to see in its symmetrical completeness the continuity that kept everything going. Life was a circle and the circle was life. 'Round like a circle in a spiral like a wheel within a wheel/Never ending or beginning on an ever-spinning reel.'

Having created their ditches, the builders of the Windmill Hill causewayed enclosure made a point of gathering at the site on a regular basis. They slaughtered animals and feasted on the meat and while the fires burnt and the carcasses roasted there was time for talk. Marriage partners could be sought, luxury items like stone axes could be admired, shown off, exchanged or traded.

After the feasting was over, some of the animal bones were placed into or even buried within the ditches, along with pottery from the eating and drinking vessels. From time to time human remains were interred there, giving even more significance to the place. Perhaps people, especially children and babies who had died during the year, were carefully stored until it was time for the gathering on the hill. Rather than being left behind, they were taken to the enclosure and made a permanent part of it. Now, whenever the family was inside the circle, its living members were reunited with the one lost.

'Such deposits seem to celebrate various dimensions of the social world: subsistence, eating, sharing and gift-giving, relations with neighbours and others, and dealings with the dead,' said Whittle. Excavations at Windmill Hill, Whittle's own and others besides, have accumulated a huge resource of this material. Compared to the paucity of finds at settlement sites, the picture painted is one rich in meaning and imagination. What archaeologists do not find of the Neolithic elsewhere, they find in the causewayed enclosures.

By gathering every year – year after year – scattered populations were able to remind themselves they were not alone. There was a unifying identity to be had from minding what was done inside those circles. People could keep track of what the majority deemed it right to do, to eat and to make. In this way was a society formed and by the repeated visits to the communal sites it could also be maintained. 'Causewayed enclosures, like barrows, may have evoked the past,' said Whittle. 'But above all they brought people together in their construction, enhanced attachment to place and seem to have celebrated relations among the living, near and far.'

Five and half thousand years ago, people living scattered through the Wild Wood in their clearings, settlements and home-steads realised it was not enough. More than just for living, life was about other people. They needed to find ways and places to meet those others, those they knew to be out there but whom they could not see.

At Windmill Hill and other similar places they were making sense of a journey their species had begun as hunters but which they were now continuing as farmers. They had travelled a great distance, in terms of both geography and time. By choosing a site on high ground, with dominion over the land below, they were making a statement about their position in the world. By digging ditches, gathering inside circles for feasting and ceremony, they were reminding themselves about who they were and what they had become. And also what they had ceased to be.

Windmill Hill comprises three ditches, one inside the other. Within the inner circle, on the summit of the flat-topped hill, was found pottery and the bones of domesticated animals like cows and bulls. There in miniature was the world the farmers were trying to create – the safe, tame, ordered world in which plants and animals did what they were told and everything was in its place. Outside the circles and far away, at the bottom of the hill in fact, they buried the bones of a wild auroch, a beast twice the size of anything the farmers dared to tend. Here was the Wild Wood – the untamed, dangerous, unpredictable world they had left behind. It was the world of the hunter and the past.

There may even be a note of resignation in it all and a touch of sadness. There was an awareness and an acceptance that they could not go back now, even if they wanted to. They had come too far. The world of the hunter was the world they had all come from but they had cut it adrift, left it outside the circle. They understood what they had done and what it meant. The men and women who designed, built and used the causewayed enclosure on top of Windmill Hill knew they had made their bed – and that from now on they would have to lie in it.

3

COSMOLOGY

'If I had to say which was telling the truth about society, a speech by a Minister of Housing or the actual buildings put up in his time, I should believe the buildings.'

Kenneth Clark, *Civilisation*

'By heavens man, we are turned round and round in this world, like yonder windlass, and fate is the handspike.'

Captain Ahab, in *Moby Dick*

We take buildings for granted. We live most of our lives indoors, inside houses, schools, office blocks, factories, shops, cinemas, pubs, clubs and all the rest. We walk down city streets lined with gigantic structures of stone, steel and glass that seem as permanent as mountains; cathedrals dedicated occasionally to God but mostly to the making and moving of money. When we look up, we see ceilings instead of sky. This is to us reality and normality.

But for the majority of our time here on Earth our species built nothing much but flimsy shelters against the worst of the cold and the wet. The decision – the need – to start designing and building permanent structures was therefore a radical one. The first of them must have appeared upon the land as suddenly and as unexpectedly as a field of mushrooms after rain. Where did it come from, this idea it was necessary to build, to have an inside as well as an outside? And once we started building things why did we start raising them higher and higher into the sky?

To begin to answer these questions we have to look back 6,000 years and more into British prehistory and to try and imagine what it was like to live during the time archaeologists call the 'Neolithic Revolution'. The human species had embarked upon the most profoundly influential ambitious social experiment there has ever been. By planting seeds instead of gathering wild harvests and by keeping animals in pens instead of hunting them in the woods, we changed everything, and every one of us as well. Instead of helplessly trusting nature – hoping the fish would come, that the fruit would ripen on the trees and bushes – we took steps to bring the world to heel.

Chemical analysis of human remains reveals that the effect on our diet was profound. After thousands of years of eating wild foods, hunted and gathered, quite suddenly we relied instead upon domesticated cereals. Depending on your point of view, we either invested in the future or made an enemy of it.

By 6,000 years ago farmers were changing the land of Britain for the very first time: clearing away the Wild Wood and replacing it with ordered fields. They were possessed of profound thoughts about their relationship with the very ground beneath their feet. Did they belong to it like the hunters had, or did it now belong to them? They were preoccupied, too, with what it meant to be alive and what it meant to be dead. They were also newly concerned about what was to be done with the dead. Since they depended upon the germination of seeds and the birth of animals from their herds, their lives were partly dominated by thoughts of fertility – how much could be taken from the soil and how much had to be given back.

It is strange to think the first people to spend time inside permanent buildings in Britain were the dead. The first 'houses' put up by Neolithic farmers were storage chambers for bones. While the living continued to move around the landscape, chivvying their herds of cattle and sheep from one patch of pasture to another and carrying their shelters with them, at least a few of the dead were tucked up inside well-appointed houses built of timber or stone, overlooking stands of wheat and barley.

So rather than places in which to live, the first houses were places in which to be dead. A handful of the living might spend some little time inside them now and again while interring a new permanent resident, or perhaps seeking wisdom from the collected ancestors, but mostly those first buildings were meant to be seen and appreciated from the outside. They were territorial markers and the claims they staked were made legitimate not by the words and actions of the quick but by the unquestioning silence of mouldering bones.

It seems likely that before there were tombs (or causewayed enclosures either, for that matter) there were simply special places. They might have been hilltops, high ground overlooking fertile land; clearings left behind by wild fires and full of flowers; stands of trees silhouetted against the sky. Such locations, pleasing to the eye and restful to the soul, may have been places of pilgrimage – where groups gathered for all sorts of reasons at particular times of year, where they brought the remains of their dead – long before anyone thought to dig an encircling ditch or to raise an upright timber, or a mound of earth, or a stone. (Maybe a tribe made a point of gathering in a natural clearing in the forest, surrounded and bounded by trees. Once they had cut down all the trees and the special clearing was no more, it may have made sense to them to recreate the feeling of the remembered place by raising a circle of great timbers or stones.)

When the farmers arrived, they brought ideas that had germinated and flowered during the millennia it had taken the new technology to cross the continent of Europe. They looked at the landscape and saw how it might be changed, moulded to suit a complicated and evolving vision of what it all meant. Long before the farmers came, hunters would have watched the movement of the sun, the Moon and the rest of the lights in the sky, noting patterns that repeated again and again. That much is human nature. But farmers are more closely tied than hunters to circles and cycles. Farmers await the coming and going of seasons with a particular, dependent urgency and if the passage of that time was marked by so many risings and settings of the sun and the Moon then it would have mattered to keep track and to count, to look back as well as forward – to remember and to predict. As they waited for the Moon to return to the sky, they might have imagined its journey and thought about how time was unwinding and unspooling all the while.

Six thousand years ago there were two worlds on the Earth, one wild and one tamed, and they were separated, one from another, by boundaries. The Wild Wood bordered and defined their fields and there were other, symbolic lines that could be drawn with ditches and lines of posts and stones. But there were also lines drawn between worlds, boundaries the farmers could not control – between life and death, land and water, earth and sky.

There are landscapes in Britain that still have the power to inspire, and to remind even the most modern of us that the world is sometimes a place of wonder. The Lake District in Cumbria, in England's north-west, has apparently been attracting people – and filling them with wonder – since the very beginning. It is a place made mostly of water and stone. Even the hunters may have understood that the stone must have been there first, so the lakes and tarns could collect in its valleys and hollows. Maybe there was still then a memory, or a remembrance, of the Ice Age – knowledge that the mountains themselves had been carved, ground, hammered and polished into shape by glaciers long ago.

For people without metal, still dependent upon stone for their sharpest, hardest edges, a place so obviously made of stone might have commanded a respect bordering on reverence. It is certainly clear that much significance was placed upon axes made of a volcanic rock called tuff, or greenstone, that occurs in Great Langdale, a U-shaped valley two miles from the village of Ambleside. Such axes have been found all across Britain and Ireland, suggesting their value was rooted in something other than their suitability for cutting wood.

Since forest clearance was integral to the spread of farming, the axe was the vital tool. It was, after all, a representation of a polished stone axe cutting a Mesolithic throwing stick in two that was carved into the ceiling of the Locmariaquer passage grave in Brittany, by a farmer, to symbolise new ways triumphing over old. Every farmer would therefore have set great store by such tools. But there are many sources of stone suitable for making perfectly good axes scattered all over Britain, without the need to secure raw material from somewhere as hard to get at as the high slopes and summits of Great Langdale.

Flint makes excellent axes and is found in countless locations. It has the added benefit of providing sharp off-cuts which can be used for other tools besides the axes themselves. Unlike flint, which often occurs at or near sea level, much of the Cumbrian greenstone is to be found towards the barren rocky summits of two peaks, Harrison Stickle and Pike O' Stickle, 2,000 feet and more above the floor of Great Langdale. The axes it produces, particularly those that have been ground and polished to give a characteristic cool, glassy smoothness, are certainly lovely. Held in the hands they have a pleasing heft and would be just as desirable as ornaments. But they are no better for cutting down trees and shaping wood than any other kind of stone axe. So why clamber for exhausting hours into the mist-shrouded mountains of the Lake District in search of a material that, on the face of it, makes the life of a farmer no easier? And why did farmers in every corner of Britain covet axes knapped and ground from that particular stone?

Archaeologist and writer Mark Edmonds has spent three decades studying and wondering about the motivations of the people who climbed among some of the Lake District's highest peaks thousands of years ago in search of the greenstone. During the course of an exhausting day we spent together, scrambling up towards those 5,500-year-old axe factories, he explained how so much more was being sought than a sharp edge.

While we were still much closer to sea level, Edmonds took me to see some recently discovered rock art that is another clue to understanding the significance of the uplands, the high ground, to ancient peoples. Just west of the village of Chapel Stile, at Copt

Howe, a pair of giant boulders nestles incongruously in a field, like pebbles dropped onto the grassy slope by a passing giant. Before archaeologists paid them any attention, they were familiar mostly to rock climbers, who call them 'the Langdale Boulders' and still find toe-holds among their fissures.

The larger of the two, formed of volcanic andesitic tuff stone, has around a dozen barely discernible carvings etched into one of its vertical faces. If Edmonds had not been there to point them out, I would have walked right past them unaware.

With the light from the right direction, casting as much shadow across the shallow grooves and peck-marks as possible, the best of them appear as multiple concentric rings or spirals. There are also faint straight lines, rough rectangles and chevrons as well as a triangle with a carefully pecked surface, giving it the appearance of long-healed acne. The most prominent marks are a number of cup-shaped depressions, but at least some of these may be the result of natural weathering.

The meaning of the carvings is anyone's guess. Concentric circles and spirals are recurring features of prehistoric art – most commonly in the Boyne Valley in Ireland but also on Anglesey and as far afield as Orkney. It has even been suggested the circular forms represent tunnels to other worlds, or other states of consciousness. People under the influence of hallucinogenic drugs often experience the same sensation – of travelling through spinning circles of light – and this has encouraged some modern theorists, or the fringe element among them at least, to imagine shamans having similar experiences in the ancient past and documenting them in stone.

Given their location – on such a visible and memorable landmark along the side of a valley leading to Langdale, and the climb up into the sky towards the greenstone – it is tempting to see the boulders as touchstones, or stepping-stones marking the way. Not quite a map but something to give direction just the same.

Cup- and ring-marked stones are a class of monument, or perhaps artwork, found scattered across parts of England, Scotland

and Ireland. They are notoriously difficult to date, but some of them at least are thought to have been made as early as the Neolithic period. Almost always on horizontal, rather than vertical, outcrops of bedrock, they are often in clusters close to other monuments like burial mounds and stone circles. The rings are sometimes pecked around the cup-shaped hollows, sometimes on their own; and, given that they were cut without stone tools, all of them represent an enormous amount of time and patience. They are often numerous, so that one plane of rock after another in the same location is found to be covered in a veritable rash of pockmarks and whorls.

If dating them is problematic, then interpreting the meaning of the things is harder still. My own favourite of the many choices on offer is to see them as marks left behind as proof of passage. For people making an important journey – maybe a once-in-a-lifetime pilgrimage or a rite performed at a certain age – there may have been a desire to leave something permanent behind, just to show you really had passed that way. And so the spirals and other shapes at Copt Howe may be something similar – perhaps started by one traveller and then continued and added to by many more pilgrims over the years.

Long before the artworks were added the boulders – distinctive and memorable – may have been counted special anyway by the Mesolithic hunters. From the perspective of our world of buildings – with clear distinctions between natural and man-made, inside and outside – it is well nigh impossible to get back inside ancient minds. In their world, short on scientific explanation but rich in memory and story, there may even have been a sense in which the natural world appeared to have been 'built' by powers unseen. Even today it is impossible to look at the tors of Dartmoor without noticing how they resemble the ruins of massive fortresses. Natural features and landmarks, like strangely enigmatic boulders that seemed placed by a giant hand, may have provided inspiration for the location and even the building materials of the first man-made additions to the landscape.

Edmonds pointed out how, from a position directly in front of the most heavily decorated face of the larger boulder, the unmistakable outline of some of the Langdale Pikes themselves – Harrison Stickle included – appear neatly framed against the sky. Did the Langdale Boulders mark a significant point on the journey of the axe-makers travelling to and from the source of the stone? 'Five or six thousand years ago, the chances are no one was living up here full time,' said Edmonds. 'They would come here because the high ground would give them good grazing. But what drew them up here was not the chance of living here full time – that would happen later. It was the stone that brought them up – it was the stone that they came for.' (Ever since the Copt Howe carvings came to light there has been disagreement about their age. Some locals even suggest they were carved as recently as 70 or 80 years ago by someone half-remembered, who camped nearby for a time. But whenever they were carved, the fact remains the boulders and their place in the world inspired someone to carry out the work. Whether decades or millennia old, they mattered to someone who cared about what and where they were.)

As we made our way higher into the hills, eventually onto the quarry sites themselves, Edmonds pointed out that there was no practical need to climb so high. On Pike O' Stickle the axe-makers concentrated their extraction on and around a narrow, precipitous ledge that is nothing less than a dangerous place to be, then as now. According to Edmonds there are exposed outcrops of greenstone much lower down, some of even higher quality, geologically speaking, than that found in the most remote quarries; and yet it was the harder-to-reach stuff that was most attractive to the Neolithic craftsmen. 'It wasn't just the stone itself,' he said. 'At least part of what mattered was precisely where it had come from – from hard-to-reach, challenging places, up high, as near to the sky as possible.'

Edmonds has spent a lot of time in those mountains, pondering as usefully as working. I first met him more than 20 years ago when I worked as one of his volunteers excavating another axe factory – that one high up on slopes above Loch Tay in Scotland, close by the village of Killin and the mountain of Ben Lawers. He was thoughtful about what it all meant then and he is even more wrapped and folded into the high ground now.

He writes about the motivations of the axe men at least as well as he talks: 'What mattered were the distance and the climb to places only seen on the horizon when the trail brought them into view,' he wrote in *The Langdales: Landscape and Prehistory in a Lakeland Valley*. 'To crags that were dangerous and sometimes unstable, that could vanish in the cloud and lead you on false trails in harsh conditions. A place of fractured stone where a wrong step could be your last, where only the swifts move in and out with ease.'

Edmonds describes the quest for stone as one that fitted within the season when grazing herds were moved up onto the remote pastures, when a few of the folk left hearth and home behind and began journeys into the high country. As well as minding the beasts they took the opportunity to climb yet higher, to where the stone was most removed from daily life, and therefore better: 'Where the goal of working was to make tools which said something about you, the journey, and a measure of separation conferred a special quality to both the act and the artefact.'

For Neolithic farmers increasingly bound to the earth – by their crops but also by their ancestors planted in the same soil – the deepest roots of all would have been those of the mountains. Thrust up into the sky, with mist and cloud for cloaks, they were surely home to more than birds. Won from the highest and most threatening of the peaks, the grey-green stone might as well have come from another world, one populated by spirits and gods. Though the axe men could not have known it, the material they sought and worked was the ash from ancient volcanoes compacted and transformed by the hammer blows of deep time.

In order better to understand the effort involved, Edmonds has also learned how to make polished greenstone axes for himself.

The job of making a 'rough-out', knocking flake after flake from a block to produce the basic shape, takes him around 45 minutes now: no time at all. But while the roughing-out was completed in the quarries (literally millions of still-sharp flakes form man-made scree slopes all over the Pikes' uppermost slopes, testament to countless generations of return to those places) the finishing of the pieces was done far away.

Back in the lowlands, back in the everyday world, hundreds of hours were required for the job of polishing the surface of the axe, grinding it first against coarse material and then with progressively finer abrasives until finally a glass-like smoothness was achieved. (Polished and also therefore 'polite' are words that originate in the jewellery trade. They apply to the work of cutting gem stones and convey the sense of something being refined and finished by laborious, patient labour, of things being made the best they can possibly be.)

But while polishing makes for a more beautiful object it does not make a sharper or better axe. Often finished polished stone axes show lines and blotches of different colour – veins running through the pieces like lettering through seaside rock, adding to their allure. Those features would have been visible in the uncut block and in the rough-out and seem always to have inspired the completion of the finished axe that contains them. And yet such veins are faults in the stone and therefore points of weakness. By rights the maker of an axe intended for chopping down trees ought to have discarded such a stone at the very beginning. The first blow against something hard would likely shatter such an axe along the fault line so that hundreds of hours of work (not to mention a life-threatening climb up a mountain) would be wasted at a stroke.

Such items, then, were never intended to be used for work. Instead they were symbols, precious objects kept and admired, given names and attributed with power; passed from hand to hand, from parent to child and from clan to clan.

Up on those lonely perches, surrounded by the evidence of

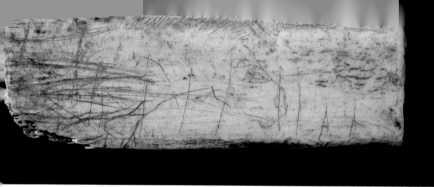

A horse head etched into the surface of a rib bone recovered from Robin Hood's Cave, at Creswell Crags, near Sheffield. The exquisitely beautiful work of a Palaeolithic artist who lived in Britain around 13,500 years ago.

The oldest complete human skeleton found in Britain. Cheddar Man, recovered from Gough's Cave in Cheddar Gorge in 1903, lived and died more than 9,000 years ago and may have been among the first hunters to recolonise these islands after the Big Freeze.

Evidence of some of our earliest ancestors – a flint handaxe from Hoxne, in Suffolk. Whoever made and used this tool lived in Britain perhaps 400,000 years ago.

Goat's Hole Cave at Paviland, in south Wales, last resting place of the so-called Red Lady – a Palaeolithic hunter interred 33,000 years ago alongside the bones of a mammoth.

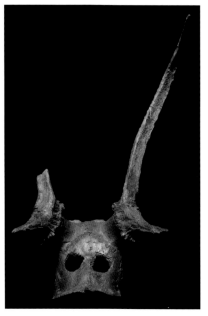

A haunting glimpse into the minds of the hunters who stalked their prey around the shores of a shallow lake at Star Carr in Yorkshire around 10,500 years ago. Ritual headdresses made from the skulls and antlers of red deer were recovered from the waterlogged deposits.

Some of more than 3,000 stones erected at Carnac in Brittany during the period when Mesolithic hunters and Neolithic farmers vied with one another for control of the land.

Inside the chamber of the Table des Marchands burial mound at Carnac, the focal point is a massive upright stone shaped like a phallus and decorated all over with representations of throwing sticks – weapons for hunting birds.

West Kennet long barrow in Wiltshire. The remains of around 40 individuals were placed in the chambers inside before the entrance was ritually 'blocked' by the erection of massive stones across the façade.

Inside the chamber of Maes Howe, on Orkney – an architectural masterpiece and a true wonder of the ancient world. The entrance passage is 23 feet long and is formed, for the most part, by two giant monoliths laid on their sides.

A talisman of the Neolithic period – a polished stone axe, representing hundreds if not thousands of hours of skilled and painstaking work on the part of its maker.

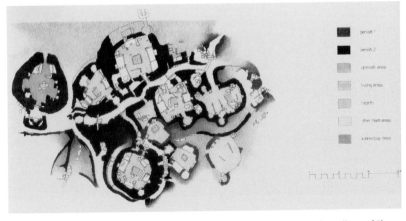

period 1
period 2
grassed areas
living areas
hearth
other hard areas
workshop areas

Like a film set for a remake of *The Flintstones*, the 5,000-year-old Neolithic village of Skara Brae was home to Neolithic farmers before the pyramids were built in Egypt.

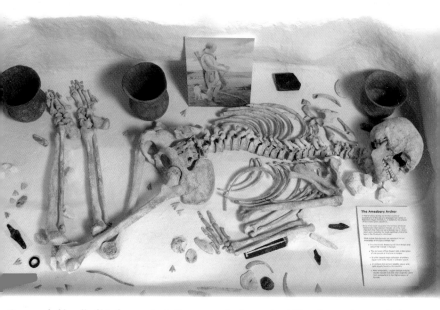

Surrounded by all of his finery – including copper knives and gold jewellery – the so-called Amesbury Archer lived and died while the finishing touches were being put to Stonehenge.

Three and a half thousand years ago, the Dover Boat – made by 'sewing' planks of oak together with twisted slivers of yew – was in use ferrying passengers and cargo back and forth between Britain and the Continent.

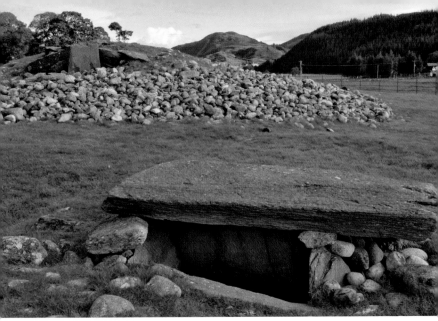

Nether Largie South Cairn, in Kilmartin Glen, Argyll. No fewer than 350 historic sites are clustered within a six-mile radius of the village of Kilmartin – indicating how much the valley has mattered to countless generations.

A rock-cut footprint near the summit of Dunadd, in Argyll. Tradition has it that by placing one naked foot into the hollow during their coronations, kings were symbolically wedded to the land they sought to rule.

Testament to the skill of an Early Bronze Age jeweller, a necklace made of Whitby Jet found in a woman's grave at Poltalloch, near Lochgilphead, in 1928.

ancient labour, the notion that people came just for stone to make tools does seem patently absurd – as though devout Catholics would travel to Lourdes to buy a pint of milk. 'What we're dealing with here is a monument,' said Edmonds. 'A place that draws people up, draws people together to make objects that say something about who they are.'

The axe factories of Great Langdale are part of a belief system centred on the relationship between people and the world, and also the nature of stone itself. But it was a belief system that continued to evolve, changing over time into something different and arguably more complex. Once you know the story of Great Langdale – better yet when you visit the place and hear it from someone like Mark Edmonds – then the scree slopes of sharp flakes suddenly matter and make sense. But they are less than prepossessing at first sight – far less impressive than the views they command. It was surely the place itself that mattered, high in the sky, as much as the work done there.

It was the farmers who first felt moved to build in Britain around 4000 BC. First came places for the dead made sometimes of stone and sometimes of timber, often enveloped within mounds of earth or rubble. Then a little later they made enclosures where they could gather to feast and to reflect, and also cursus monuments that established and maintained boundaries between wild and tame, inside and outside and between life and death.

But if the first of the buildings were about the ancestors and the dead, then as the fourth millennium BC gave way to the third a fundamentally different set of ideas began to be expressed. Rather than obsessing just about the continued role of the dead in the daily life of the tribe, some people in Britain began thinking about the living and how they fitted into society as individuals. Much more significant – and more enigmatic in terms of the monuments the new thinking inspired and shaped – they began thinking about the universe, about time and about how they were connected, as individuals, to the cosmos.

Circles mattered to the artists who decorated the boulders at

Copt Howe. They mattered to the builders of the causewayed enclosures like Windmill Hill and they mattered as well to the designers of new monuments that began to appear across Britain from around 3000 BC onwards. In the uplands, in open spaces under the giant sky they built circles of stones. These also tend to be located in those parts of the country – Cumbria and the south-west of England, Wales and the west of Scotland – where mountains pierce the sky and where bedrock is exposed and in plentiful supply. In the lowlands – of southern and eastern Scotland and eastern England, where building stone is harder to come by – monuments called henges were more commonplace.

Henges began to be built around the same time as the stone circles. At first glance, and to the uninitiated, they are similar to causewayed enclosures. But there are crucial differences between the two. For one thing henges are more straightforwardly circular in shape and are marked out by only a single, unbroken ditch. For another, the material dug out is heaped up into a bank around the outside edge – in contrast to causewayed enclosures, which sometimes have banks on the inner rim. While a bank on the inside of a ditch could have a defensive function, one on the outside – affording attackers the benefit of the high ground overlooking the interior – is useless.

Even the word henge is unhelpful, derived as it is from Stonehenge, which is a unique and special site. In Old English 'henge' means hanging or supported and refers specifically to the sarsen lintels that could be said to 'hang from' or be 'supported by' their uprights.

True henges are circles entirely without stones, and while circles of stone are generally located on high ground where they can be seen from miles around, henges are on low ground and valley floors. People approaching stone circles have a view towards the centre of the monument that is only partly obscured, even perhaps framed, by the stones themselves – and people inside can see out. The encircling bank of a henge, on the other hand, conceals people within a private and enclosed space cut off from the world. In short, stone circles show off what goes on inside, while henges hide it.

Also in Cumbria and therefore within easy reach of the green-stone are some stone circles that archaeologists regard as among the very earliest in England, dating to around 3000 BC or even a little earlier. Names like Castlerigg and Long Meg and her Daughters add to the atmosphere of the sites – and show how long people have wondered about them and their origins. Sunkenkirk is another, where local legend says folk were laying foundations for a church (or kirk) when the Devil intervened and stopped the job by making the stones sink into the earth. The circle itself is an oddity in that so many stones are involved (perhaps as many as 60 originally) they may once have formed a complete barrier. There is also a clearly marked entrance at Sunkenkirk, like a porch formed of rough stone pillars and approximately aligned with sunrise at mid-winter.

Archaeologists are usually scientists and therefore uncom-fortable talking or writing about how places make them feel. But there is no denying stone circles have an atmosphere all their own. Perhaps we bring that feeling ourselves, in the expectation that such sites must once have mattered, and had power; but it is surely impossible to walk around those, touching stones set in place 5,000 years ago, without sensing something strange?

It was partly a childhood fascination with places like Sunkenkirk that attracted me to archaeology in the first place. Growing up in the town of Dumfries, in Scotland's south-west, I made several visits as a schoolboy to the Twelve Apostles stone circle close to the nearby village of Newbridge. There the mystery lies in the fact that, despite the name, there are only 11 stones. The circle is large by any standards – over 250 feet across – and the stones that form it squat in a sloping field bounded on all sides by modern roads that add to their strangeness. Early on I learned that circles of stone – like henges – are almost unknown outside Britain. And yet well over a thousand of them survive here – not counting the unknown number that must have been destroyed or lost before

such places were deemed worthy of preservation – part of a tradition that endured well over a thousand years.

The stones of Sunkenkirk, like the stones of every other stone
circle, beg some obvious questions from even the most casual
observer. For a start they make a person wonder at the sheer
physical effort involved in finding 60 boulders, each weighing
tons, and manhandling them into position on high ground so that
they overlook hundreds of square miles of territory. Presumably
these were busy farmers with plenty of practical demands on their
time and yet they found the need to co-ordinate their manpower
and resources for the construction of a large and complicated
monument with an astronomical alignment.

Sunkenkirk also seems similar in many ways to other monuments far away. The porch entrance, for example, is found rep-
licated at the stone circle of Ballynoe on the north-east coast of
Ireland. Other similarities – including the likelihood of some kind
of levelling of the sites having taken place before the stones were
put up – hint at links to other circles, further south in the region
of the Wicklow Mountains. It is important from the outset to
appreciate how the designers and builders of such monuments
were not working in isolation. Instead they knew what was happening elsewhere and were plugged into a network that meant
they were connected to people thinking the same way, in other
places.

A glance at a map reveals that only 80 or so miles separate
Sunkenkirk from Ballynoe in County Down. The Isle of Man
appears as a handy stepping-stone between the two locations; and
something like a third of all the polished stone axes found on that
island are from the Langdale Pikes. Rather than being divided by
the Irish Sea, the communities of Cumbria and Ireland were more
than likely united by it – by links established in the Mesolithic,
long before the arrival of the farmers and their monuments.

Whatever the reasons, from around 5,000 years ago people –
living in Cumbria in the shadow of magical mountains, and
all over Britain and Ireland besides – began making spiritual

connections that had never been made before. If the commitment to the dead remained, with its associated attachment to the land, then it was joined during the Neolithic by a new connection, between the living, the dead and the sky. It may even be regarded as the very idea of Heaven itself.

To understand all this it is vital to bear in mind, at all times, the connections between people living all across Britain and Ireland. Representatives were travelling between communities, from north to south and from east to west, and ideas were being disseminated, shared and expanded.

Floating like green rafts moored in open sea almost 10 miles north of Caithness, Orkney feels remote now. For many people, even some Scots, the islands seem far enough away to be classed as another country altogether. Since the archipelago appears in its own little box on the television weather map, even pointing out Orkney's exact location, relative to Britain, is a stretch for most. For the 19,000 or so folk who live on the 20 inhabited Orkney islands (out of a total of more than 40 and a whole host of what can only be described as large rocks standing proud of the sea), the most annoying mistake made by outsiders is calling the place 'the Orkneys' – as though anyone would ever talk about the New Zealands.

But if Orkney seems remote in the twenty-first century, it is largely an optical illusion, and a modern one at that. Take a map that shows Britain in the context of northern Europe and Scandinavia and turn it upside down. Viewed from that unfamiliar and disorienting perspective, Orkney becomes once more the hub it likely was for much of its history. For people travelling around the North Sea – especially those heading south towards the long island of Britain itself and north towards Scandinavia and northern Europe – Orkney is not at the edge of things but at their centre.

Before the Romans arrived in Scotland in the first century AD and began writing things down in Latin, the people there spoke a language similar to Welsh, or Scots Gaelic. This was likely the language of the Picts – the people encountered in north Britain by the Romans – and the northern islands were the territory of a Pictish tribe that seemingly had the wild boar for their totem. We know this because Irish historians later wrote about Inis Orc – the Islands of the Orcs – and in so doing fossilised the word *orc*, Pictish for wild boar. Later still the Vikings colonised the islands and misheard their name as Orkneyjar, a Norse word meaning 'Seal Islands'. To say the least, it has been a convoluted tale.

So Orkney has mattered since the beginning and has known human habitation since at least the Mesolithic period. Until around 15,000 years ago, the islands were physically connected to Scotland by a low-lying valley that was later submerged beneath rising sea levels at the end of the last Ice Age. The history of the place is as deep and rich as any. An unnamed 'King of Orkney' was among 11 monarchs who bent the knee to Tiberius Claudius Caesar Augustus Germanicus, Emperor of Rome and Conqueror of Britannia, in Colchester in AD 43 – an event commemorated on a fragment of triumphal arch in the city of Rome itself. Until the latter quarter of the fifteenth century, Orkney was part of the Danish kingdom. But in July 1469 King James III of Scotland married Princess Margrethe of Denmark and in lieu of a dowry her father, King Kristian, mortgaged Orkney and Shetland to the Scottish Crown. In 1472 Kristian defaulted on his repayments, James promptly took possession and the islands have been part of Scotland ever since.

Orkney may not be as distant as some think, then, but it is and always was a wild place. First-time visitors are generally struck at once by the absence of trees. There is also a near-incessant wind blowing across it and it is tempting to think the trees have been swept away along with everything else that is not tied down. But more than the wind is responsible, and in fact the deforestation of Orkney began during the Neolithic period. As they did everywhere else, the farmers began cutting down the trees to make room for fields and farmsteads. Since Orkney is not a big place – just over 200 square miles of habitable land – it probably did not take long to fell every last one.

Fortunately for those determined to live there, Orkney is rich in another kind of building material altogether: stone. Strip away the grass and topsoil practically anywhere on Mainland Orkney and you reveal a brittle carapace of horizontally bedded and fractured sandstone that splits easily and naturally into slabs and sheets. From around 3300 BC Orcadians – for that is what the inhabitants are called – began employing their limitless building material in the construction of some of the most enduring and enigmatic structures in the whole of the ancient world.

Some places on Earth are mostly about the present, while others seem to belong more completely to the past. Nations and empires have their moment too; some high point that, once reached, can neither be sustained nor ever reached again once it has passed. They say time marches on, as though there were an even rhythm and an equal weight to each footfall of its passing. But in truth only a few moments weigh heavy enough to make deep prints, while most skip by leaving barely a trace.

The countryside of Flanders – those parts of Belgium and northern France devastated by the Great War of 1914–18 – is a landscape trapped by a time. All the most memorable places there are dedicated to death and remembrance. The modern world is woven throughout but seems as ephemeral as strands of a spider's web strung between the branches of a tree. The power of the past – of memories of the First World War – to overwhelm the present is undiminished by the intervening years, partly because great care has been taken to preserve the cemeteries and other memorials and special places as sacred, and therefore inviolable. More than that, though, there are the experiences and behaviour of people living in Flanders now. The events of four years of fighting long ago hang in the air around them like the aftermath of the tolling of a bell; the sound has stopped but something of it still resonates. Nothing as important, it seems, has happened in all the days since.

Something similar has happened to Orkney – but there it is about much deeper time. Whatever passions gripped the place 5,000 years ago are long cooled; no tears are shed now beside the empty tombs and no hearts beat fast in the shadows of tall stones so earnestly raised. But something lingers just the same, the memory of a memory. While Flanders has been fixed for ever in the Edwardian world that was its greatest influence, so the deepest marks cut into Orkney are those left by its most ardent trustees – Neolithic farmers asking the sky above why they were alive at all ... and what would come after.

Orkney is therefore a strange and unusual part of Britain. The volume of Neolithic sites and monuments there is exceptional by any standards, and when compared to what has been identified so far in the rest of the country it can seem as though the inhabitants of that northern archipelago were overcome, 5,000 years ago, by a mania for marking special places.

Those islands have certainly been subjected to less in the way of modern development, the arable fields to much less pressure than their mainland British equivalents, so that more sites may have survived in Orkney than in other areas. It is also worth bearing in mind that Neolithic architects elsewhere may have had freer access to timber and other organic materials for building houses of the living and of the dead, and for ceremonial circles – and that such constructions would have had a relatively short shelf life. This is in stark contrast to Orkney, where the early deforestation would have forced builders to work almost exclusively in stone, a material that is uniquely durable and much more likely to survive the millennia.

But, even taking all that into account, it remains important to allow that something especially intense happened on Orkney during the first centuries of farming. Perhaps behaviours were magnified there for some reason – made somehow louder and more vivid, so that we are able to hear and see the Neolithic on those islands long after its traces and echoes elsewhere have been dimmed and dulled, made undetectable by the passing of too much time.

One of many unique aspects of the Orcadian Neolithic is the presence of domestic houses – even whole villages. While such places are frustratingly absent from much of Britain, on Orkney they appear almost larger than life. Skara Brae is surely one of the most famous villages in the world, and deservedly so.

After spending the best part of 5,000 years buried beneath the sand dunes that had enveloped them, the houses were returned to the light by a great storm in 1850. The waves crashed higher that year than ever before and washed away a great swathe of sand and grass, exposing the dry stone walls of ancient houses. Subsequent excavation, as well as further storms, eventually revealed the marvel that has ever since drawn people to the southern shore of the Bay o'Skaill, in the western Mainland parish of Sandwick, in their thousands.

The stretch of dunes that had entombed the village had long been called Skerrabra in the local dialect, and so the site has come to be known by the slightly corrupted Skara Brae. Visitors approach it along a path that winds its way past little signs reminding them the houses they are about to see are as old or older than, among other things, the pyramids of Egypt. The route then leads them towards a grassy mound – and it is this that contains the houses.

By around 3100 BC a great midden of earth, sand and domestic rubbish had accumulated on the site. Into this cosy but undoubtedly smelly womb of insulation the builders dug their semi-subterranean homes. There are eight cellular houses today, all connected by a stone-lined passageway. The whole place is an attempt to get out of the wind and rain; and even after 5,000 years the best-preserved of the homes look like the perfect response to the Orcadian climate. There may originally have been more buildings – perhaps revealed and destroyed by other storms long ago – but what does survive is more than enough to conjure up a clear picture of the lives lived by those industrious farmers.

The individual entrances into the houses, from the passageway, are all crawl spaces, no more than three or four feet high, but the interiors beyond are surprisingly roomy. What strikes the visitor most vividly is the similarity to the cartoon homes of Bedrock, inhabited by Fred and Wilma Flintstone. The reliance on stone for everything, from beds to shelves to storage containers, is almost comical and lends the whole place a vaguely unreal feel, like a film set. But this is no land of make believe – these are Neolithic homes.

Directly opposite the entrance of every house, and therefore the first thing to be seen on entering, is a 'dresser' – like a Welsh dresser but made entirely of slabs of the familiar Orkney flagstone. Their prominent, dominant position in every home suggests these would have displayed precious possessions – the Neolithic equivalents of the best china and the family silver. In the centre of each floor is a square hearth for a fire, and since the houses are windowless the interiors would have been lit only by those fires and by lamps burning oil from fish and whales. The interiors are roughly square, with rounded corners, and against the walls are stone settings for beds. There are storage spaces built into the walls and other recesses too, with drains running behind the walls that may have been used as indoor toilets, 'flushed' with water.

But along with the dressers it is the beds that speak most loudly of Fred and Wilma and it is important, in the mind's eye, to add the soft furnishings that are absent. The homes of Skara Brae were likely warm and comfortable, with floorings of rushes and straw, bedding of animal skins and fur, roaring fires and soft lamplight. Insulated against even the worst of winter storms – and in the Neolithic the sea was several miles distant, not lapping at the walls as it does today – the farmers on the Bay o'Skaill had made a good life for themselves.

Skara Brae as it is presented today is, of necessity to ensure its continued preservation, a tidy and immaculately manicured place. Missing, though, are the sights, sounds and smells of everyday life. The place was inhabited for a long time and a bustling atmosphere would have prevailed as people went about the business of preparing and cooking food, making and mending tools, equipment and clothes, discussing plans for the harvest and other tasks, caring for children, playing, chatting and squabbling. Because of the darkness of the interiors, much of the work would have gone on outdoors, in the daylight, and it is the atmosphere of activity that has to be imagined if the place is to be seen as more than just a sterile cluster of stone cells.

Neolithic specialist Alison Sheridan had special permission to allow me into a house so pristine and so perfectly preserved (and known as 'number seven') that visitors are normally banned from its interior. Thanks to the addition of a modern roof, the inside is gloomy – completing the illusion of stepping back in time 5,000 years. The furniture is identical to that in the other houses but, safe from the wind and rain, it seems only recently abandoned, its owners momentarily distracted. I had stepped into a Neolithic house (a home that was in many ways beguilingly familiar) but any notion that it was as simple to step into a Neolithic mind was swiftly swept away by what Sheridan had to say about at least one custom of the previous owners. She explained how archaeologists excavating the interior had uncovered the skeletons of two women, side by side, buried in the floor beneath one of the bed settings – the ultimate sitting tenants. 'It's as if during the lifetime of the house they lived here, they died here and they were buried here, Granny under the bed – so that it was a house for the living but also a house for the dead,' she said.

How are we twenty-first-century people – revolted by and afraid of corpses and with our need for an antiseptic separation between the living and the dead – to reconcile ourselves to the thought of sleeping above the decaying remains of our own loved ones? It is beyond us to remember when love was so straightforward and uncompromised. Apart from anything else we must not dare to judge them. At the very least their attachment to kith and kin enabled them to look through death. For me that acceptance of the dead and therefore of death itself is part of a maturity and an anchorage in reality that we have utterly lost – to our detriment.

Around 8,000 beads were recovered from the interior of that one house, number seven, and Sheridan had brought along examples – together with an array of the kind of enigmatic jewellery and other artefacts that have been recovered from throughout the village.

Many carved stone objects, like elaborate hammers or mace-heads, have also been found. Their function is unknown but each of them represents at least hundreds of hours of skilled craftsmanship, and it is this investment of time that would have underwritten their significance in a world without metal or precious stones.

But, remarkable though it is, Skara Brae is not the only Neolithic settlement on Orkney. Dating from around 3700 BC and therefore markedly earlier is the so-called 'farmstead' of Knap of Howar, on the island of Papa Westray. There, two massively built stone houses – constructed, like those of Skara Brae, from slabs and blocks of Orkney flagstone – sit side by side. Each has an entrance through a short passageway in its southern-facing wall and the two houses are joined as one by interconnecting side doors. Unlike the homes on the Bay o' Skaill, the interiors at Knap of Howar were divided into separate rooms, or spaces, by vertical slabs of flagstone.

A more recent discovery of Neolithic home life has been made at a site called Barnhouse, back on Mainland Orkney. Only the foundation levels survive but a dozen separate houses have been unearthed. All but one are broadly similar to those at Skara Brae, with roughly square interiors, stone beds against the walls, central hearths and each dominated by a stone dresser on the back wall. One house at Barnhouse, however, is different. Generally larger and more impressive than all the others, its double cruciform interior incorporates two separate rooms, each with deep recesses in its walls.

But, for all the richness of the domestic remains, it is not for preservation of the everyday that Orkney is rightly famed. The architecture and layout of the houses is, rather, a key that can be used to unlock the door into another world – that of Neolithic religion – and the first clue, as it turns out, was back in house number seven at Skara Brae, with the bodies under the bed.

Houses for the dead, rather than for the living, were always the first buildings erected by the farmers. It was symptomatic of the way in which death and the dead were understood, how they were

to be treated. Seemingly central to the philosophy was an idea of continuity – so that death was not the end of someone, rather just a change in their circumstances. A house that had been – and perhaps continued to be – a home for the living at Skara Brae could also be a home for the dead.

Quite close to the village is a passage grave built on a truly grand scale. It is Maes Howe, huddled beneath its great grassy mound, and it is justly famous as a wonder of the ancient world. Any who would enter must first fold themselves over, like a half-shut knife, before shuffling awkwardly along a 23-foot-long passage. Most of each side of that passage is formed of a single giant monolith laid on its side – just a foretaste of the vaulting ambition of the tomb's architects. Having bowed the head and progressed in suitably respectful fashion, the visitor emerges into a chamber that is over 12 feet in height, achieved by corbelling. Each successive course of dry stone masonry overhangs the one below, until the internal space is roofed by a simple dome – in much the same way as you would imagine building an igloo with blocks of ice. It is a simple-sounding technique, but at Maes Howe it has been executed with great skill and finesse to create an elegant, almost symmetrical interior. In each of the four corners stands an upright monolith. They appear structural at first glance, like pillars, but closer inspection reveals they support nothing at all.

Almost at once you get a nagging sense you are being reminded of something else, someplace else: there is the roughly square interior but with the corners projecting inwards so that the floor plan has more the look of a stumpy cross; there are the recesses set into the walls as though for sleep (except anyone laid down in here was destined for a deep sleep indeed). Excavation revealed that the site was occupied by a house long before the monument was built and traces of a hearth were found beneath the floor of the chamber. Then realisation strikes ... you are standing inside a more grand, more stylised version of one of the Skara Brae houses (perhaps even number seven with the skeletons under the bed).

At Maes Howe it seems there was a slow, considered evolution from domestic to spiritual, from everyday to otherworldly.

And there is still more strangeness about Maes Howe. Unlike any other chambered tomb on Orkney, the mound there is surrounded by a circular rock-cut ditch and bank. Recent excavation behind the mound has found the socket of a now absent standing stone.

Two toppled monoliths forming the passage ... four uprights, one in each of the corners of the chamber ... an empty socket for another ... did Maes Howe begin life as a circle of standing stones surrounded by a bank and ditch before someone saw fit to make of it a house of the dead? It seems almost certain.

Then there is that house at Barnhouse – the one that is twice the size and at least twice as complicated as any of the others there. Its intricate, double-cruciform floor plan is also reminiscent of the stumpy cross-shape of the interior of Maes Howe – so that distinctions between tombs and houses on Orkney seem to blur, homes for the living blending into homes for the dead.

Maes Howe's builders were also astronomers. For a few days each mid-winter the setting sun seems to drop between two hills on the neighbouring island of Hoy. Before it disappears into the invisible on the solstice, the sun's rays shine directly into the passage, illuminating the interior of the chamber. Those ancient architects had therefore sited the tomb in direct alignment with a single sunset, and furthermore had taken care to ensure the occupants of the chamber received the last rays of the dying sun before it was reborn at the start of a new year.

Here were people precisely attuned to earth and sky, cosmologists sharply aware of where and when the heavens touched the land. Single monuments like Maes Howe are so entrancing they make it hard to see the bigger picture of which they are part. But take the time to look around the landscape of Mainland Orkney and you realise the ancient sites were not operating individually, but in concert with one another.

Maes Howe sits within a giant natural amphitheatre, a shallow

bowl lying low in the land and surrounded on all sides by mountains. The centre of the bowl is filled with water – Lochs Harray
and Stenness – and that gleaming mirror is straddled and bisected
by a narrow finger of land, the promontory of the Brodgar peninsula running directly through the middle of it all. It is by any
measure a stage styled for drama and the man-made sets are placed
carefully all around. Walk towards the promontory from Maes
Howe and you pass the settlement of Barnhouse and, close by, the
Stones of Stenness, thought to have been raised around 3100 BC.
A nineteenth-century farmer went to some lengths to erase the
site but stopped short of finishing the job, and while just four
upright stones survive, there are stumps and sockets for at least six
more.

What is left behind is still striking, the remaining sentinels
appearing defiant and more like an art installation than an archaeological site. A small pair of stones neatly and deliberately frames
the mound of Maes Howe, less than a mile away to the east, but
the connection between the sites runs deeper still. The stones
themselves were brought from different quarries, and some archaeologists now believe they were sourced and gathered together over
a long period of time. Like Maes Howe, the Stones of Stenness
are surrounded by a ditch, hammered and smashed through the
fractured bedrock. Archaeologists believe both were intended to
hold water, like moats. It seems possible the designers of Stenness
and Maes Howe endeavoured to create islands within islands –
miniatures of the larger world they were attempting to reshape
and influence. Finally, at the centre of the circle, are the remains
of a square, stone-lined hearth that may even predate everything
else on the site. Stenness seems to tell yet another long story,
reaching all the way from the fires of home to the infinite sky.

Before you step out onto the promontory itself, to cross the
mirror of water, you pass another stone sentinel – the so-called
'Watch Stone', 20 feet high and like the gnomon of a huge sundial.
Beyond the reach of its longest shadow, a mile or so to the north-
west of Stenness, is yet another stone circle.

The Ring of Brodgar is a true giant in the world of Neolithic monuments; in the whole of Britain only Avebury and Stanton Drew are larger. Today it comprises 22 stones – tall shards of the now familiar Orkney flagstone raised on a gentle, heather-covered slope overlooking Loch Harray. When its builders designed it they had more stones in mind. There are a dozen stumps and several others that have simply toppled (one was shattered by lightning 20-odd years ago, hinting at what may have happened to some of the others).

At least as impressive as the circle of stones is the ditch that encircles them. Just as with Maes Howe and Stenness, at Brodgar the architects felt the need to draw a line separating inside from outside. Here, though, it is on a mind-boggling scale – 30 feet wide, the best part of 350 feet in diameter and cut to a depth of 10 feet through the bedrock. Best guesses suggest the ditch alone would have required something like 100,000 man-hours to complete.

In fact the finished ditch is incomplete, bridged by two narrow causeways. If Brodgar were a clock face they would be at 3 and 9, suggesting a way in and a way out – a route straight through the circle and roughly aligned with the promontory itself. Suddenly the Ring of Brodgar seems less a destination than a portal, an elaborately designed transit station on a long walk from somewhere to elsewhere. Only in the last few years have archaeologists begun to realise quite where the path might terminate. It had long been realised that Maes Howe, the Stones of Stenness, Barnhouse, the Watch Stone, the promontory and the Ring of Brodgar seemed linked like beads on a chain. What has taken everyone by surprise, however, is the possibility that the real jewel in the necklace – the centrepiece – had been entirely overlooked.

A whale-back ridge dominates the middle of the Brodgar peninsula, roughly halfway between the Ring of Brodgar of the Stones of Stenness, and it had always been taken for a natural feature. The fact that it lies right at the centre of this great natural amphitheatre, containing all of Orkney's most famous ritual monuments, seemed purely a coincidence of geology. Then in 2002 the loftily titled Heart of Neolithic Orkney World Heritage Site Geophysics Programme turned its attention to the area, about the size of five football pitches, and began what was supposed to be a routine survey. Instead the readouts from the geophysics machines revealed countless anomalies – buried walls and other structures – across the entire area.

Archaeologist Nick Card, originally from Glasgow but for many years a resident of Orkney, is overseeing efforts to try and make sense of it all. He realised early on that, rather than being a natural feature, the whale-back ridge of Ness of Brodgar was entirely man-made – the build-up of decades or even centuries of construction and demolition. In the Middle East they call such accumulations tells – artificial mounds created as successive occupants of the same site keep building on top of the remains of earlier settlements.

Card reckons he would need more than one lifetime fully to investigate the site, but has already seen enough to persuade him the Ness of Brodgar will prove to be Neolithic Orkney's most precious gemstone. At least 10 buildings have been identified so far, some with similarities to houses like those at Skara Brae and all constructed with consummate skill by people well schooled in getting the best out of Orkney flagstone. One of them, however (prosaically labelled 'Structure 10' in the matter-of-fact language of on-site data recording), is already going by the nickname of 'the Temple of Orkney'.

First spotted in 2008, it is unlike anything seen before in Orkney, or anywhere else in Britain for that matter. Measuring 80-odd feet long by 60-odd feet wide and with walls 15 feet thick, it is a massive building even by modern standards. Card believes a pitched roof of slabs of Orkney flagstone would have extended out over the walls to create a covered walkway or quadrangle around the outside of the building – an idea supported by the discovery of a beautifully paved surface around at least three of the four sides.

While the craftsmanship of the outer walls is exquisite, Card describes the interior as 'scrappy' by comparison – so that the main impact was to be had from outside. Only a privileged few would have stepped inside to a gloomy, cruciform interior, reminiscent of the chamber of Maes Howe, where they would have encountered a stone dresser and, perhaps, painted walls. Neolithic paintwork is unknown in Britain and if Card is right, and the few smears of pigment identified so far do indeed prove to be iron ore imported from Hoy and processed into paint, then the unique nature of the 'Temple' will be enhanced even more.

All of the buildings around Structure 10 are impressive, made second-rate only by its exceptional grandeur. Their interiors have already yielded a veritable treasure store of Late Neolithic finery: beautifully decorated 'Grooved-Ware' pottery, carved and polished axes and mace-heads, flint tools. It is as though everything an archaeologist could dream of finding has been deliberately piled within the enigmatic structures.

To make matters even more fascinating, the most recent seasons of excavation have begun to persuade the archaeologists that all the secondary buildings had been put beyond use and even demolished before Structure 10 was erected. It is as though the last incumbents of the site decided to wipe the place clean in preparation for a final architectural flourish – a last hurrah. Once built, on the apex of the ridge and with nothing else around it, the Temple of Orkney would have been visible for miles around. And, best of all, even the most scientifically minded of the archaeologists on site are beginning to talk not just of a temple but of a 'temple complex'.

Excavation of geophysical anomalies north and south of Structure 10 has revealed the remains of two huge walls that once cut across the full width of the promontory, separating the buildings from the outer world either side. The larger of them, 'the Great Wall of Brodgar', was 12 feet wide in its first phase – wider than anything ever built in Britain by Hadrian – before being widened to nearly 20 feet and having a parallel ditch cut alongside. The second boundary, 'the Lesser Wall of Brodgar', was over six feet thick and both are likely to have been too tall for a man to see over.

It is already becoming hard to avoid the conclusion that all the monument-building on Mainland Orkney 5,000 years ago – the passage grave of Maes Howe, the circles of standing stones, the lone monoliths dotted through the landscape – was an overture leading to a final crescendo. 'The size, symmetry and grandeur of the buildings already uncovered, coupled with their dominant location on a raised, centrally located mound, imply a site of extraordinary importance in Neolithic Orkney,' said Card. 'When all the evidence is pieced together ... the complexity of the architecture, the monumental enclosure wall and the artefact assemblage – the term "ritual" or "temple" seems inescapable. ... We may be on the brink of a radical rethink of prehistoric religion in Orkney in the third millennium BC.'

The Grooved-Ware pottery recovered from the Ness of Brodgar is part of the key to understanding the spread of Neolithic religion and belief systems. It is found on Neolithic sites the length and breadth of Britain – but the earliest of all of it was made on Orkney. Grooved-Ware – with its intricate patterns of lines etched into the wet clay before firing – is the first domestic pottery in Britain made with a flat rather than a rounded base. Apart from anything else it was designed for display – probably on the shelves of those ubiquitous stone dressers – and whatever inspired its production and use, it all started on Orkney. Anyone studying the Neolithic of Britain is reminded at all times that the inhabitants of the northern archipelago were at the centre of something rather than on its fringe.

Having reached Britain, the farmers found themselves at the end of the line. Short of crossing the Atlantic Ocean, there was nowhere left to go. Long before Julius Caesar crossed the Rubicon, those pioneers who made it over the sea to Britain with their seeds and animals took a similarly fateful step, one that would change everything – including themselves in the end. Until their arrival in Britain the farmers always had options, the freedom to keep chasing the horizon towards pastures new, but no more. These islands were different – Ultima Thule, the ends of the Earth – and they fundamentally altered all that touched them. Whatever came to Britain was eventually changed by it so that the Neolithic here became like no other.

Perhaps it was an effect of arriving at the last and final destination. When the Roman writer and historian Tacitus put words into the mouth of Calgacus, the first named Scot, on the eve of the climactic battle with the Caledonians at Mons Graupius in the autumn of AD 84, he had him refer to that very thing: 'We the last men on earth, the last of the free, have been shielded before today by the very remoteness and seclusion for which we are famed ... there are no tribes beyond us, nothing indeed but waves and rocks'.

The remoteness for which Britons are famed ... and after 1,000 and more years in Britain, trapped against the waves and rocks, the farmers learned a new way of understanding the world and their own place in it. For generation after generation they had built great earthen enclosures, vast cursus monuments and tombs of timber and stone, claims upon the land. But by 3000 BC, a profound change had taken place. From now on there were connections between Earth and sky as well – and that was new. It was not that the land stopped being as important as it always had been; rather it was a realisation that the Earth itself was connected to something much, much bigger ... an infinity roamed by the sun, Moon and stars ... the heavens.

This need to understand and make sense of their function and purpose within the cosmos is uniquely human and it still moves and motivates people today. Proof of this, if proof were needed, is to be had by joining the multitude that gathers every mid-summer, just before dawn, in the shadow of the most famous Stone Age monument of them all.

Stonehenge on Salisbury Plain has been attracting people for millennia. I was there on 21 June 2010, dazed by the effect of getting up at 2.30 in the morning, and the whole experience that followed was vaguely surreal. Thousands of people walked towards the stones through the darkness before dawn, all seemingly as chilled and befuddled as me. Thousands more were already there, having spent the night near the stones, and the assembled throng seemed to include people from every country on Earth. Many danced (together or alone), juggled flaming torches, beat drums, or chanted, or filmed themselves and others with mobile phones.

All the usual suspects were there too: the obligatory satsuma-orange Hari Krishna devotees; the druids in their elaborate robes and headgear, easily mistaken for extras from a pantomime, Widow Twankies every one; dreadlocked hippies, waifs and strays and all the rest were represented among hordes of ordinary people who just looked as if they had got on the wrong bus that morning. Most simply stood around, seemingly unsure of what to do, or lay huddled inside sleeping bags waiting for light and warmth from above.

More than anything else I was appalled by the mess they had made of the place. It was as though half a dozen bin-lorries had backed up to Stonehenge from all points on the compass and tipped their loads into the waiting breeze. There was rubbish everywhere – papers, bottles, fast food packaging, throwaway barbecues – all being trampled underfoot. For people on a sup-posed pilgrimage to a sacred site in search of understanding, it seemed many of them found even the proper disposal of refuse too challenging a concept. There was an edge to the whole thing as well – characters roaming through the crowd apparently more in hope of trouble than enlightenment, disappointed by the almost negligible police presence. (Go to Stonehenge, it is a wonderful place; but if you take my advice you will give it a body swerve at the summer solstice.)

But there we were – human detritus of every possible sort – a river eddying around the foot of rocks set in place by farmers the best part of 5,000 years ago. The sky on the horizon turned from black to blue and finally to pink. What had been an unfocused hubbub of chatter and laughter changed steadily into something more defined and orchestrated. A broken whooping cheer began in fragments scattered through the crowd and then coalesced into a single roar of welcome for the main event. Ironically enough it was hard to see the sunrise because there were too many people and big stones in the way, but all at once she made her entrance – appearing like a diamond in the grass. Presumably the dawn of a new day meant something different to every human being on the plain, and judging by the expressions on their faces most seemed sure it had been worth the trip and the wait.

The whole overpowering spectacle was enough to make a person wonder what form gatherings at Stonehenge had taken when the stones were younger than today. Did they come in their thousands then? Did they await the dawn with fear, elation, relief or grim resignation? And when it was all over did they clear up afterwards or leave the mess to the stewards to take care of?

Some of the answers are to be found by considering a few of the stones themselves. Everyone today recognises the horseshoe of giant trilithons – the 'hanging' stones that give the place its name. But those are comparatively recent arrivals in the story of Stonehenge and anyone in search of the original look and feel of the monument must consider the much smaller, uncarved blocks of stone that mingle discreetly in the shadow of the showstoppers. While the trilithons and the rest of the largest uprights are of local sarsen stone collected from the Marlborough Downs, less than 20 miles up the road, the most unassuming elements of the whole – veritable bit-part players – are from many, many miles away to the north-west.

High in the Preseli Hills of south-west Wales the dramatically rolling landscape is broken here and there by just a few huge outcrops of very distinctive stone. It is a rock known to geologists as a particular type of spotted dolerite, and in the whole of Britain it occurs only in the Preseli Hills. Close inspection of a few fragments reveals it to be quite special stuff. When freshly broken – and wet – the surface has a distinctly blue-green colour and it is peppered throughout with glistening silvery white flecks of feldspar. Rather than spotted dolerite this particular Welsh variant is more commonly referred to as 'bluestone' and it seems its qualities persuaded at least some monument-builders that it was a must-have material.

Among the many mysteries surrounding the most famous Stone Age monument in Britain, we at least know for certain that the first stone circle at Stonehenge was built of Preseli bluestones – more than 200 tons of the stuff hacked out of the Welsh hills and transported 150 miles. But the story of Stonehenge is a complex one. People today ask, 'What does it mean?' – and the beginning of any truthful answer to that question must allow for many different meanings; must allow for a special place that changed and evolved during hundreds of years of use.

Five thousand years ago the Stonehenge we see today simply did not exist. The first human addition to the place was a circular ditch, with a bank heaped up around the outside edge, enclosing an internal space about 360 feet across. There were at least two entrance gaps – certainly one to the north-east and one to the south – and around the inner edge of the ditch was erected a circle of 56 large timber posts. So for the first years of its existence – its marking out as somewhere special – Stonehenge was an earthen enclosure, and then a wooden circle. After a while, more circles of timber posts were placed in settings towards the centre and archaeologists think it likely these would have been topped with lintels. This must not be seen as a conscious evolution by gen-erations of designers working towards a preconceived conclusion. Instead, different users of the place had their own, distinct ideas about what should be built there. Stonehenge has meant many different things to many different people.

Later still, some guardians of the site felt the need to replace timber with stone. It was then, sometime around 3000 BC, that the Herculean effort was made to bring in the bluestones – each around six feet in length and weighing a ton and a half – from Preseli. These newcomers were erected in a double circle towards the centre of the enclosure and stood in place for an unknown length of time, until yet another community decided on something even bigger.

The bluestones were eventually moved to make way for the circle of huge sarsen uprights – weighing as much as 40 ton apiece – topped with lintels. Inside that circle a horseshoe of yet bigger sarsen trilithons, like great stone doorframes, was erected as a final flourish. Fascinatingly, the builders used mortice and tenon joints – a self-conscious and deliberate rendering in stone of techniques best suited to wood. Was there a memory or knowledge of the timber uprights and lintels that had featured in that earlier monument centuries ago? And did it matter for some reason to echo the past in the later constructions on the site? Some archaeologists are even persuaded that the surfaces of at least a few of the upright sarsens were worked and carved to give facets that suggest the bark of trees – suggesting a desire to combine the appearance of a wooded clearing, a natural circle of trees, with the permanence of stone.

Having moved the bluestones out of the way to give space for the sarsen structures, the builders of the final phase of Stonehenge then brought them back in and erected them as a circle and an oval within the new larger settings. All of it represents colossal effort and commitment, but archaeologists are increasingly of the view that the sarsen-building phase may have been compressed into just a few years of fairly frantic activity. An avenue was built as well – two parallel earthen banks leading all the way from the stones to the River Avon a mile and a half away.

The intervening years have seen many of the stones toppled into the grass, so the place has a ruined look. But the likelihood is that Stonehenge was never finished. Different generations imposed their own visions on the site, but even at the end it was what it had really always been: a work in progress.

By the middle of the third millennium BC, an entrance to the circle was aligned with the solstices of mid-winter and mid-summer. But it was in the monument's final phase, towards 2000 BC, that the rising and setting of the sun was most famously – and most permanently – marked in stone at Stonehenge. The largest of the trilithons, the final stones of the avenue and an upright monolith outside the circle, known as the Heel Stone, are all in a line that forms what is effectively the axis of the monument. At mid-summer the rising sun follows a path directly along this line, indicating beyond any doubt that the architects of that final phase had been very precise in their layout of the stones and other features. Neolithic thinking – Neolithic religion – changed during its first millennia in Britain. The final form of Stonehenge paid heed not just to what was happening on Earth, but also to cyclical and predictable events.

But while revellers gather at Stonehenge to watch that mid-summer sunrise, they are overlooking something crucial import-ance. That same alignment, of trilithon, avenue and Heel Stone, also points in quite the opposite direction at the other end of the year, to sunset at mid-winter. This simple fact may make all the difference. To understand why archaeologists are increasingly sure the popular view of the place may be back to front, it is necessary to consider what was happening at another important Neolithic site nearby.

As is the case on Orkney, no single monument on Salisbury Plain or anywhere else can be understood when examined in isolation. Stonehenge was part of an entire landscape that had been sculpted and moulded, by people, into a backdrop for ritual and belief. On their own the hanging stones set within their circular bank and ditch count for just a few phrases from a long story. All around are the rest of the words, in the form of other henges, tombs, cursuses and yet more stone circles, and only when all of it is considered together do the sentences construe and finally begin to make sense.

Archaeologists excavating the interior of the great earthen henge of Durrington Walls, two miles north-east of Stonehenge, found huge quantities of animal bones, primarily belonging to pigs. Examination of the animals' teeth revealed them to be generally rotten – evidence that the beasts had been deliberately fattened up prior to slaughter. Piglets are usually born in the spring and since the vast majority of the bones found at Durrington Walls were of animals that had been killed at around the age of nine months, all the evidence there points to feasting on a vast scale . . . in the depths of mid-winter.

Farmers from hundreds of miles around were seemingly in the habit of gathering at Durrington Walls for the mother of all hog roasts. It was at that time of year when the days are short and cold, when the sun stays low in the sky, distant and aloof. Thoughts might turn dark, like the sky, and so people made a point of gathering together at the lowest ebb – on the day when the sun's visit was briefest and most desultory – to seek reassurance and solace from one another's company instead. If ever there was a time for great fires, and great feasting by the light of towering flames, it was when the heavens had only cold comfort to offer. And as the old year died – as the old sun rose and set for the last time before being renewed – thoughts might have lingered too upon the whereabouts of souls departed during the months since the last mid-winter, of those most recently dead.

It is thought now that the earthen bank and ditch of Durrington Walls enclosed a little world of the living. People gathered there to share a grand celebratory meal together before accompanying the souls of their loved ones towards the world of the dead. Archaeologists have only recently discovered a 100-foot-wide avenue leading from the settlement of Durrington Walls right down to the banks of the River Avon. It is believed the cremated remains of the dead were transported downriver on boats, a gently meandering journey along the purifying waters, leading from one world to another. The route then returned to dry land once more for a final procession along another avenue: the one leading into Stonehenge from the north-east.

In stark contrast to what happens at the site every 21 June, Neolithic pilgrims faced the setting sun of mid-winter as they approached the stones, as they walked hand-in-hand with the memories of those they had lost. As well as raising circles of timber and stone at Stonehenge, it turns out the farmers were in the habit of burying the cremated bones of their loved ones there too. The remains of hundreds of individuals have been found buried throughout the interior, and the assumption is that death and the dead were part of the place from the very beginning.

The most recent work on Stonehenge and its surroundings has been carried out by the wide-ranging Stonehenge Riverside Project and Josh Pollard, one of its directors, took me on a guided tour to help me see the site from a chilly new perspective. 'One thing we've realised from recent work is that Stonehenge has a very close relationship with rituals to do with the human dead,' he said. 'We know, from very early excavations, that there are at least 300 cremation burials within the area of the bank and ditch. We also know of many other unburnt human bones that were placed within the monument. So effectively the site was being used as a gigantic cemetery.'

'What you've got to realise is that we're looking at communities who probably didn't conceive of life as coming to an end at the point where they died,' he said. 'But that basically this was a transition into another state of being, into a state of ancestorhood – so we think that, from that perspective, the mid-winter solstice was probably very important because this of course marks the point where you have the death of one year and the regeneration of another.'

Pollard said that the modern preoccupation with mid-summer at Stonehenge, with life at its zenith, was in all likelihood misguided. 'I think celebrating life, celebrating the seasons is fine,' he said. 'But in a way what they should be doing [at Stonehenge] is celebrating the dead, the ancestral dead, and they should be doing that at mid-winter.'

The farmers who created Stonehenge lived and died by the seasons. The extremes of mid-summer and mid-winter must therefore have been powerful reminders of time passing, from one year to the next and from generation to generation. Everyone has an image of Stonehenge in their mind's eye. It is one of the fixed points that holds the landscape of Britain in place, like a drawing pin in a map. Like the *Mona Lisa* or the Great Pyramid of Egypt, our image of Stonehenge is so familiar it has become hard to see it through fresh eyes. But that is precisely what we must do now if we are to regard the stones and the earthen circle they sit inside as Neolithic farmers once did.

Go there in the winter time if you can, in deep mid-winter if possible, when the golden warmth of a summer's day is as distant as a rumour, impossible to believe. There is still a charge in the air around those stones, like the ozone-rich tang that tingles on the tongue after lightning. You can feel it, taste it. And if you walk near them on mid-winter's day itself, you can feel it just a little bit more. Stone is cold in the dark, a product of the same qualities that make it last for ever. The monoliths of Stonehenge reach up from the grass like a skeletal hand from a grave and that open, treeless landscape makes them all the more stark, unforgiving and unyielding. Stand then in their shadow, while there is snow on the ground and as the sun sets at the end of another year. Feel the warmth of life drain through the soles of your boots and down into the ground and all at once you realise the stones belong not to the living but to the never-ending days of being dead.

It was also while looking at Stonehenge that I thought again about Serge Cassen and those megaliths of his at Carnac. Cassen has said he believes hunters raised the lines of megaliths in the face of the farmers' advance. He regards the seemingly endless rows as a last defiant cry rendered into stone by people who had seen the future and realised it did not include them. But thinking about the centuries swallowed up by the different moods and meanings of Stonehenge brought me to a simple realisation: that stones are raised not by losers but by victors.

Memorials in stone are pushed up towards the sky by unreasonable men – those who have seen a world that does not suit them and who have decided to alter it again and again until it finally fits. Perhaps the hunters were triumphant in Brittany, at least for a while. Far from surrendering their hold on the land, they tightened it, weighed it down with the heaviest stones they could find. Maybe they had their first generation of tenant farmers do the job for them.

In *The Ascent of Man* Jacob Bronowski held that farmers were always prey, at least at first, to bands of marauding nomads. War was the nomads' business, he said, and they waged it with men and women trapped upon the land, those unable and unwilling to flee because of their servitude to their crops. But Bronowski also argued that if war has one weakness it is that it can only ever be a temporary condition. Regardless of the wishes even of its keenest practitioners, it cannot be sustained indefinitely.

Accept for a moment that the hunters waged an early and shapeless sort of war in Brittany, clumsily but forcibly relieving the farmers of their surplus and making them do their bidding. But as Bronowski said, they could neither maintain their nomadic ways of life nor their antipathy to those who had settled among them. One day the hunters awoke to find the farmers all around. Finally there was nowhere left to roam. And so at last those unreasonable men and women resorted to the only course open to them – to allow themselves to be seduced by ways they had once despised. By then, though, it suited them. They had grown tired of resisting and wanted peace for its own sake. While moss grew upon the rows, they accepted their role as masters and landlords in a world inherited by the meek. Then and only then did the stones that had marked their victory become their memorial.

Today we are used to being surrounded by man-made things that dwarf us. But in our modern world they are seldom dedicated to spiritual matters, and more often to money, power and earthly prestige. The motivation of the people who built the first great Stone Age monuments 5,000 years ago was more or less the same. The new age – an age of astronomy and concern with the goings-on in the heavens above – was about more than a spiritual awakening. It was also about a new society, one in which we start to see social hierarchy for the very first time. The builders of those first monuments were every bit as competitive with each other as the architects of modern skyscrapers, and they wanted to show off.

Grooved-Ware pottery – of the sort found on Orkney – has also been recovered from Stonehenge, which means there must have been a connection between the sites. The chamber of Maes Howe is briefly illuminated by the setting sun of mid-winter, another world of the dead aligned with the dying of the light. Experts therefore believe people must have travelled between the great sacred places of Britain, and that this would hardly have been the experience of the average Stone Age farmer, but the privilege of a new elite, people at the top of society who would have voyaged the length and breadth of the country on a kind of Neolithic Grand Tour.

When that King of Orkney travelled to Colchester in AD 43 to see with his own eyes the face of the Emperor of Rome, the near-certainty is that he made the journey by boat. It is entirely believable as well that the craft that carried him all that way down the coast of the long island of Britain was a relatively simple one. On the Hebridean island of Coll I spent some precarious time in a little coracle, a boat made by stretching an animal skin across a basket-frame of bent saplings. These were certainly among the vessels of the hunters of the Mesolithic, as much as 10,000 years ago, and there is no reason to believe the technology would have evolved much over the ensuing millennia: if it ain't broke, don't fix it, as the saying goes. So prehistoric hunters, pioneering farmers, first-century kings and everyone else in between would have relied upon sea-going vessels made from plentiful everyday materials.

In County Meath in the east of Ireland, a woodcarver and dreamer by the name of Clive O'Gibney has set himself the task of proving that sea travel in the Neolithic was rather more sophisticated than has been previously thought. In the yard of his workshop beside the River Boyne, within site of the world-famous tourist attraction that is the passage grave of Newgrange, O'Gibney has completed a mammoth task: the building of a large sea-going vessel, longer than a Transit van and about as heavy, using only materials and techniques known to have been available in the ancient past.

What English speakers call coracles, the Irish call curraghs. The two craft are essentially one and the same, in that both comprise animal skins stretched over frames formed of slender saplings; but the Irish version is often larger and more reassuringly boat-shaped. Sea-going curraghs, powered by oars, have been used in Ireland for longer than anyone cares to remember. Legend has held that one St Brendan made it all the way across the Atlantic Ocean to Newfoundland in one in the late sixth century AD. (The English adventurer Tim Severin recreated St Brendan's voyage in 1978, successfully completing the crossing accompanied by four like-minded friends.) But until O'Gibney entered the fray no one had tried to imagine how sailors contemplated journeys of perhaps several hundred miles 5,000 years and more ago. Most intriguingly of all, the Irishman is convinced the longer voyages – and certainly those linking Ireland to Britain – would have been undertaken in curraghs powered by sails.

In the Neolithic period, however, there was no cloth; and so O'Gibney's greatest challenge was to think himself back into the mind of a long-distance mariner of the ancient past, and then set about tackling the problem of how to make what is essentially a large sheet. His solution was a logical one: employ precisely the same materials that were available for the hull of the curragh. Using hazel rods and strips of cowhide he managed to fashion a 'sail' he was convinced was large enough to power his super-curragh.

I was with him aboard the vessel (thankfully accompanied by a crew of expert curragh-men – O'Gibney was the first to admit that, while he had worked out how to build a curragh, he had not the first clue about what to do with one in the water) when we put his Heath Robinson means of propulsion through its paces for the very first time. To begin with we simply rowed the vessel in the time-honoured manner and even the purists among the curragh-men were soon loudly agreeing that O'Gibney had built a fine boat. Curraghs have no keel – no single timber running the length of the bottom of the craft – and so tend to sit very high in the water. Even laden with men and a heavy rolled-up sail made of hazel and leather, we rode the soft swell as naturally as a seabird.

Fortunately for all concerned it was a perfect sailing day, for soon the moment came when we had to work out how to raise our Neolithic sail into position. It had been lying along the bottom of the curragh all the while – as heavy as a man and half again as long – but O'Gibney is a fellow with the energy and enthusiasm of half a dozen and he was quickly to the fore with a plan.

'This'll be a bit of fun lads,' he said, a master of understatement. 'So we'll all just have to stay calm.' He had worked out a tripod arrangement in lieu of a single mast. Once we had manhandled the thing into an upright position – a feat involving much anxious stumbling and grabbing at ropes as seven men and seven oars jockeyed for position aboard a wallowing craft without a deck – we lashed a leg of the tripod into place either side of the craft and placed the third into a specially prepared leather socket at the stern. Using all of his considerable strength, O'Gibney then hauled on a rope arrangement that slowly raised the woven sail towards the top of the tripod. Satisfied it was high enough, he secured the ropes and carefully encouraged the stiff cowhide to stretch fully down and so catch the best of the wind.

I cannot recall seeing a happier face than that of Clive O'Gibney as the vessel gently, but perceptibly, began to pick up speed through the waves. 'I'm thrilled, delighted,' he said. 'All the hard work that everyone put in, everyone coming from every part of Ireland because they'd heard this fella was trying to make a sail out of wicker.' The skipper, comfortably ensconced in the stern, man-oeuvred the steering oar with a practised hand and set us fairly skipping away from shore. 'But it's one thing imagining it – it's another to see it working,' added O'Gibney. 'I wanted to hear it, feel it – and that's what we're getting now. It's one of the best experiences!'

Sat there among the crew it was suddenly easy to imagine boats just like O'Gibney's, powered either by oars or makeshift sails, carrying people between the great megalithic sites of Neolithic Britain – along with ideas, beliefs and, sometimes no doubt, precious artefacts.

On display in the Museum of Dublin is one of the most breathtaking Neolithic objects ever found in Britain or Ireland. It is a 5,000-year-old ceremonial mace-head made with astonishing skill and imagination. The raw material was quite obviously part of the inspiration for the finished piece – a fist-sized lump of creamy white flint with veins and blotches of a reddish toffee colour seemingly stirred through it, so that it has the appearance of a giant boiled sweet. Apart from anything else it looks good enough to eat.

But the natural beauty of the stone is at least matched by the artistic genius of whoever undertook the hundreds, perhaps thousands of hours required to make something so perfect. Using only tools of stone, wood and antler, the artist had first to shape the nodule into the symmetrical proportions of the basic mace-head. The mace's two supposed 'striking' surfaces were worked anew to create scores of diamond-shaped facets that catch and reflect the light so that they seem to shimmer. Countless hours and days were then spent drilling the perfectly smooth hole to take a wooden shaft. For a craftsman without metal this would have entailed endlessly patient effort with a wooden bow-drill, the spinning of the bit made more abrasive and effective by the use of sand or ground quartz.

As well as technical expertise, the artist has also demonstrated a level of imagination that even manages to hint at a sense of humour. In addition to the hole for the shaft he, or she, has added two intricately worked, interconnecting whorls – so that together the three clearly suggest two wide eyes and a gaping, astonished mouth. The effect is enhanced even further by the way the artist has exploited the location of two splotches of ginger-red veining, to make it look as if the head has wild ginger hair and a ginger goatee beard. By any standard, in any era, it is a pocket-sized masterpiece and reveals a level of sophistication and refinement that is not seen on any other artefact of the period.

The making of such a mace-head 5,000 years ago hints at nothing less than the existence of a privileged elite able to commission and own such objects. It speaks, in fact, of the emergence of an upper class – of chieftains or even priests, who carried symbols of power that advertised their prestige.

The mace-head was found buried at the heart of yet another ritual landscape. The Brú na Bóinne – the Palace of the Boyne – is the collective name for the complex of tombs, standing stones, stone circles and henges scattered across County Meath. Together they add up to one of the most important ancient megalithic landscapes in the whole of Europe, a palace indeed. The megalith-builders were at work in the Brú na Bóinne, however, as early as 3200 BC – before the bluestones were imported to Stonehenge, before the circles were raised on Orkney – and some archaeologists believe this part of Ireland may be where that special brand of Neolithic religion actually began.

Easily the most famous site is the giant passage grave of Newgrange, just the other side of the Boyne from Clive O'Gibney and his curragh-sailing dreams. Full-scale excavations were conducted there by the archaeologist Michael J. O'Kelly from the early 1960s until the mid 1970s, after which he had the mound and its 'façade' reconstructed in exuberant style. A larger quantity of quartz and granite pebbles had been recovered in front of the entrance, leading O'Kelly to believe they had once formed a shining white wall extending either side of the opening to the passage itself. With this vision in mind, conservators set to work with a will – but found it was only possible to realise O'Kelly's interpretation by reinforcing the interior of the mound with concrete.

The site as it appears today is certainly striking – and popular with tourists – but has been described as looking like the prototype for a new style of hat to be worn by stewardesses on some Irish airline. More recent analysis of the original excavation results has prompted the suggestion that the quartz and granite pebbles may simply have formed a bright pavement in front of the mound. Around the outside of the mound are about 100 large boulders described as kerbstones. Almost a third of these are decorated with the spirals, circles, chevrons and zig-zag lines that characterise the megalithic art of western Europe.

Controversial though the reconstruction undoubtedly is, it should not detract from the wonder of the interior of the tomb. The long, low passage is instantly reminiscent of that at Maes Howe – which it predates by perhaps hundreds of years. It opens into a cruciform, corbel-vaulted chamber 20 feet high with three recesses that once contained the remains of the dead. This too recalls the Orcadian tomb, but Newgrange is more primitive, more rough-hewn – somehow more 'Stone Age'. It feels like a very early realisation of a dream or a vision – one that would be refined over time and in other places.

Best of all at Newgrange, there is clear evidence of ancient commitment to venerating the voyage of the sun. Long before the excavations of the 1960s and 1970s it was known locally that a decorated lintel stone was to be found in a position above and behind the entrance. Careful work by O'Kelly and his team revealed the stone was, however, part of what they subsequently called a 'roof-box', a window to let light into the passageway. The architects of Newgrange had possessed such skill and accuracy they had been able to align the passageway with the mid-winter sunrise – a feat in itself but complicated here by the fact that the chamber floor is six feet higher than the ground level at the entrance. By carefully aligning the angle of the roof-box to compensate for the gentle slope of the passage, they could coax the rays of the last sun of the year all the way to the back wall of the chamber.

Even on a crystal clear 21 December – and those are few in County Meath – the effect lasts only 17 minutes or so before the chamber is plunged once more into darkness. But on those occasions when it works, the rays penetrate far enough to illuminate a very special carving, pecked out on the wall of one of the recesses. It is the earliest known example of something called a triple spiral – one continuous line, winding and unwinding with no beginning and no end. Interpretations of its meaning are too numerous to list but there is surely a link between the form at Newgrange and the coils and whorls at Copt Howe in Great Langdale and every other Neolithic circle and spiral worked into rocks and mountains all across the land.

So the spiral is about time, and the lives it governs. Individual lives begin and end but life flows through us, from one to another down the generations so that together we are something more, something infinite. Sun and Moon rise and set in an endless cycle of light and dark, life and death. As well as containing the remains of the dead, places like Newgrange, Maes Howe and Stonehenge also held the promise of rebirth. If the old sun was dying then the new sun, with its promise of spring and summer to follow, could not be far behind.

Archaeologists are increasingly of the opinion that the great circles of Brodgar and Stonehenge, and the passage graves of Newgrange and Maes Howe, are all memorable phrases within one splendid conversation between the people, the stone, the land and the sky. From the Orkney Islands of Scotland, to the Preseli Mountains in south Wales, to Stonehenge in the south of England and to Brú na Bóinne in the east of Ireland – it is all connected.

The exquisite mace-head staring wide-eyed and open-mouthed from within its case in the Museum of Dublin insists, by its very existence, upon a powerful person to bear it. And that object too is evidence of connections; because although it was found at Brú na Bóinne the flint from which it was made likely came from Britain, even perhaps as far away as Orkney. Whether it was exported in finished or unfinished form can never be known but there is enough evidence to suggest that the great sites of Britain and Ireland inspired successive generations; and as the Neolithic elite moved between Orkney and Wiltshire and the east of Ireland and elsewhere, so ideas spread.

Within sight of Newgrange lies another passage grave – Knowth, surrounded by 17 smaller chambered tombs like chicks around a mother hen. Stunning though Newgrange undoubtedly is, it is knocked into second place by its near neighbour. A total of around 400 decorated stones adorn Knowth, some as a kerb of boulders around the outside of the mound, and many more incorporated into the internal structures. It is believed to comprise, amazingly within this one location, around half the megalithic art in all of western Europe.

Knowth contains not one but two passage graves, non-identical twins lying back to back within the same womb. The western tomb is the lesser of the pair, with a chamber that is simply wider and taller than the passage leading to it. That on the eastern side, however, is a marvel of Neolithic engineering and it is there that the mace-head was found, together with a decorated pin of bone or antler.

The task of excavating Knowth has effectively been the life's work of Irish archaeologist George Eogan, who has studied the site for over 50 years. The passages and chambers are not normally open to the public, but Eogan granted me privileged access. Now a man of advanced years, he was nonetheless fearless in leading me into the partially collapsed eastern passage – all 140-odd feet of it – the far end of which can only be negotiated using techniques normally required by pot-holers. The reward for all the effort in those last several claustrophobic feet of the passage is the corbelled chamber beyond – a space in which only a relative handful of people have stood in the last 5,000 years.

Eogan first breathed the air inside that hallowed vault nearly 50 years ago, and has described the experience of reaching the end of the passage that day with all the excitement and anticipation of a latter-day Howard Carter. 'It suddenly came to an abrupt halt, and I felt as if I were suspended in mid-air,' he said. 'But, still not suspecting what might exist before me, I flashed my lamp around. And there was an astonishing sight: a great space with corbelled sides narrowed beehive fashion to a single closing slab at the top.

That was only part of the structure. When I flashed the light downward, what I saw was even more remarkable: a great chamber with a rounded ground plan. I descended into the chamber, how I did so I cannot think, but I must have jumped two metres or more from the top of the orthostats.'

Like that at Newgrange, the chamber Eogan landed in during the summer of 1968 is cruciform in shape. (He had actually made his final approach through a void leading up and over the lower course of upright stones forming the walls of the interior – a product of the partial collapse that makes the approach so uncomfortable today.) But once he had regained his bearings he found something particularly special – a basin more than three feet across, carved from a single block of stone and elaborately decorated, with deeply incised lines around the outside and on the inside with arcs and rays, as though representing the risen sun. Lying in the basin and scattered around it were cremated human remains.

Stonehenge was eventually a cemetery for burnt bone; but at the time when Knowth and Newgrange (and the neighbouring passage grave of Dowth) were being built, such a rite was highly unusual. This was an innovation of Neolithic society and the remains found at Knowth are some of the earliest evidence of ritual burning ever found.

Forensic examination revealed that the remains of perhaps 121 people were placed inside Knowth during the course of a period as long as three centuries. With just one cremation every two to three years, it was clearly an unusual event, one presumably reserved only for people regarded as special. The likelihood that the rite was restricted to the few – together with the discovery of that prestigious mace-head – strongly suggests it was an honour bestowed upon those who in life had occupied the very highest stratum of Neolithic society.

Put simply, if you were important then your mortal remains were consigned to the flames of a great pyre. Presumably it also meant that those practising the cremation believed the spirit, the soul of someone whose body was treated in that way, was being sent somewhere different as well. Lesser members of society were left behind on Earth to be buried, or just picked over by the crows.

With the help of two Dublin firemen – professionals more comfortable extinguishing blazes than deliberately starting them – I conducted my own experiments in the art of cremation in the very shadow of Knowth. The destruction of a human body by means of fire is no easy task and a temperature of around 1,700 degrees centigrade must be maintained for several hours to get the job done. With that effect in mind we carefully built a square tower of timber, layer upon layer of branches criss-crossing one another, until we had a fairly solid pyre. For good measure we had incorporated some straw bales at the centre and these we doused with petrol.

For want of any human volunteers, I visited a local butcher and acquired the carcass of an adult pig weighing around 11 stones. (About a third of that was fat and Donal, one of the firemen, explained this was key: although the wood, straw and petrol would get things going, the main fuel for a cremation is provided by the body itself.) After much struggling, during which I came fully to appreciate the meaning of the term 'dead weight', we managed to position the victim on top of the pyre. Given the lingering smell of petrol fumes it was with some trepidation that I at last stepped forward, armed with a lit blowtorch, to ignite the whole. There was a satisfying 'whump' of combustion and then slowly, reluctantly the flames took hold.

As it turned out, the burning took many hours and as the sun set behind the great mound of Knowth there was nothing but time – time to reflect on what such a ritual must have meant to farming communities 5,000 years ago. Our modern sensitivities are such that we have ordained that our cremations must happen out of sight. It is a quite different experience, therefore, to watch what actually happens. As night came on, the glow from the pyre became hard to look at. The heat was intense and overwhelming, almost frightening to see on such a scale, and quite soon the body of the pig became less distinct, less identifiable as that of an animal.

Within an hour it was easy to imagine a human body was being consumed, turned into smoke. The smell of roasting flesh was pervasive too, strangely sweet, but in spite of it I found the process oddly comforting. There was something clean about it all as well, as the flames got about their work and a grey column rose high into the dark.

Ultimately I was left to wonder what impact all of this would have had on people reflecting upon the life of a great leader, or a priest, as something ethereal parted from the body and flew away. Next morning there would be nothing left and the sun would rise into a day and a world from which the priest was utterly absent, the body consumed and reduced by around 12 hours of burning to only a cupful of brittle fragments.

During the later part of the Neolithic a new society was emerging in Britain and Ireland. It dictated what objects a person might possess in life and also how the body would be treated in death. Assumptions were being made and if there ever had been a time when people were truly equal, then that time had passed. Some of those people, the most valued and therefore the most powerful, were now in the habit of making journeys far from home. Along with precious objects that might be exchanged or left behind in the special places, they also carried ideas that were to take root like the seeds of a new species of plant. Enough was preserved – the monuments themselves and the things interred within – to enable us to glimpse the birth of a whole new concept of existence.

The world had changed. Once there were only earthly concerns. First the hunters stalked their prey. The first farmers came next and tilled the fields or lay dead upon them in houses made of stone. All eyes were focused on the ground, all minds preoccupied with what it might give, what it might take. Then those simple truths were left behind, or at least set aside by generations newly transfixed by the sky, who believed their fates were written by the sun, Moon and stars.

From now on what mattered was forever out of reach. The best that could be done was to get up high, stand on tiptoes and stretch out a hand. Between 3000 and 2500 BC, people were making it plain, in the form of the monuments they built, that they had become aware of their place, not just on Earth but within the cosmos.

The tombs, the circles, the swirls cut painstakingly into the bedrock with tools of bone and stone ... all these were about trying to make sense of the movement of the lights in the sky, of the universe that shapes and governs our lives and our time on Earth. Those forces went way beyond the reach of the ancestors – so much so that from now on, when some people died, they were sent to a new place, a different place.

High among the Langdale Pikes, where people once climbed in search of magical greenstone, the land had seemed far away, while the sky was almost close enough to touch. It seems that during the later Neolithic people first conceived of an idea that changed everything and endures to this day, that somewhere beyond the mountains, beyond the clouds – way out where the sun and Moon lived their lives and made their endless journeys – was Heaven.

BRONZE

'He for one had never been given a toy as a child but made his own toys, as everyone did then, out of blocks of wood and string and whatnot, and was content with them, so the thought that a boy needed a large tin garage with gas pumps out front and a crank-operated elevator to take the cars up to the parking deck was ridiculous to him and showed lack of imagination.'

Garrison Keillor, *Lake Wobegon Days*

'They that go down to the sea in ships, that do business in great waters; these see the works of the Lord, and his wonders in the deep.'

Psalm 107: 23–24

Once upon a time there was more than enough for everyone – in Britain certainly, and in the rest of the world besides. It is hard to know precisely how many people there were, however. Estimating, far less accurately calculating, the population of Britain or anywhere else at any given moment in prehistory is so devoid of certainty as to be little more than a game. For one thing no one was counting yet and for another there was no way to note down any totals until as recently as five or six thousand years ago when people in parts of Asia began recording words and numbers on tablets of wet clay, the birth of writing. In short, for almost all our time our species lived in ignorance of how very few we actually were, and therefore how fortunate.

Not any more. Now the consequences of our own fecundity, our ingenuity and productivity are impossible to ignore. The evidence is all around and pressing in from every side more irresistibly and threateningly than any Ice Age glacier. There are six billion of us *Homo sapiens sapiens* alive today – far more people living and breathing at the same moment than the world has ever known before.

The most credible estimates suggest as many as 100 billion people have already lived and died, so that the six billion of us living on the planet now are actually less than seven per cent of humanity's total. None of us has ever really left the place either. All the atoms that were once assembled into those billions of individuals are still here – part of the living, or peppering the ground beneath our feet, or floating in the air ready to become part of something new. At times it feels as though the world must be growing fatter with it all, layer by layer, like an onion. Grass, trees and plants grow from the soil, then die and in time become more soil – good for the burying and hiding of more of the dead.

Old buildings, towns and cities are bulldozed so the rubble can become foundations for the new. Everything is buried in the end and those of us alive today are dancing on the ruins and bones of everything and everyone that went before. We live on top of one gigantic rubbish tip, the detritus of all that has lived and died and been turned to mulch. But all of it has been here all along, in one form or another. What happens is constant shuffling and reshuffling of the same deck of cards. Planet Earth is one giant reprocessing plant and we, and all the rest, are just temporary manifestations of the stuff of which it is made. And so it goes on and somehow the planet has coped, neatly disposing of the dead while providing the living with everything we have ever needed.

In planetary terms it has taken no time at all for us to crowd this particular dance hall with a mass of heaving, sweating humanity. If we allow for four or five generations per century then we are, at most, only the 500th generation to have walked the Earth since people first recolonised northern Europe after the melting of the ice 10,000 years ago. The same basis of calculation means there have been no more than 150,000 generations since the very first hominid stood upright three million years ago. For the majority of that time, despite the fertility of all those generations, we were few and very far between across the country, let alone the planet.

But for all that, we are now finally and undeniably too many. The day will surely come, and soon, when the latest empty mouths and naked backs demand food and clothes from the world – and the world will have nothing more to give.

For all the time we hunted and gathered, the world was a bountiful place. The herds and shoals were as numerous as grass and the fruit bowed all the branches. Eventually those first farmers of 10,000 years ago taught the trick to all the rest and from that moment we were doomed. One hundred and fifty thousand generations have passed since then and yet it has taken only the last few to ruin it all.

The population of Britain is just 60 million – a mere one per cent or so of the world – and for now, some of them at least are blessed with space in which to live and breathe. But 60 million is still a huge figure – by far and away the greatest density of humanity ever known in the archipelago.

The archaeologist who directed my first dig, in Ayrshire in the west of Scotland in 1985, was only half-joking when he suggested the Mesolithic population of Scotland might have fitted, at times, inside one double-decker bus. Even the most generous estimates of the hunter-gatherer population of Britain in the centuries after the final retreat of the ice run to no more than the many hundreds, or at most a few thousand souls.

By any measure it was an almost empty land and the natural resources must have seemed limitless – wild animals for meat; hides, feathers, furs and sinews for clothing and shelter; bones, antlers and horns for tools; wild foods of every kind; trees for timber and bark; plant fibre for strings and ropes; flint, chert and pitchstone for axes and blades of all kinds, other stones for hammering, crushing, grinding; amber and jet for jewellery.

But sometime towards the end of the Neolithic someone some-where made a momentous discovery – in its way more momentous even than the discovery of farming. Where before we had made do with what the physical universe had given us, now we were about to alter its forms. We had already tamed the animals and the plants and now we would warp and bend the elements as well. Call him or her a genius, or a visionary, scientist, magician or meddler, but the result was the foundation of the world we live in today. It was the discovery of metal – and that metal-making was regarded as having the stuff of dangerous magic about it is clear from all the associated legends and stories.

Wayland's Smithy is the name given to a transepted passage grave of the Cotswold Severn type just over a mile from the famous Uffington White Horse, in Oxfordshire. Wayland is an English corruption of Wolund, the name of the semi-divine blacksmith of the gods, but the Germanic legend likely came to Britain with the Anglo-Saxons, several thousand years after the tomb was actually built by Neolithic farmers. At Wayland's Smithy the local story goes that any rider whose horse throws a shoe must bring the animal and tether it to the capstone. Provided he or she leaves a silver coin for Wayland's trouble, they will return next day to find the horse reshod and the money gone.

According to the larger legend, Wolund's skills with metal were coveted by King Nidud of Sweden, who sent a troop of horsemen to capture him. Having brought him to his castle, Nidud first had Wayland hamstrung so he could never leave his forge, never stop making tools and weapons; and the notion of the lame smith is one that occurs again and again. In Greek tradition there is Hephaestus, god of the blacksmith's fire and worshipped by crafts-men of all sorts. Alone of all the pantheon, Hephaestus was imperfect – ugly and lame. The son of Hera, Queen of the gods, he had made the mistake of intervening in a quarrel between his mother and her husband Zeus. Zeus was enraged and threw Hephaestus from the top of Mount Olympus. His fall from grace lasted for a whole day until he landed on the island of Lemnos where, forever broken, he built his forge inside the fires of a volcano and set to work.

It seems that from the very beginning metal was seen as something that came at a price.

The Britain in which metal first arrived was still at the height of the Stone Age. By around 2500 BC farming had been established for centuries and people were living lives that were still, at least in part, nomadic. Fixed settlements and villages were in the main the stuff of the future and for now it was about moving, season by season, in search of new grazing and fresh soil. Everything a family needed and possessed – food, shelter, clothing, tools and the rest – was obtained directly from the natural world.

Still central to everything was flint – the same that had been sourced and worked for uncounted thousands, even millions of years, and by the Late Neolithic period it was needed in vast quantities. Farming had enabled the population to grow into the tens if not hundreds of thousands and with more and more people came the need for more and more cleared and prepared fields. By the middle of the third millennium BC, the demand for tools to get all that work done was approaching a point where only industrial levels of tool production could sustain the pace.

A real sense of that Neolithic demand is to be had from a visit to the flint mines known as Grime's Graves, near Brandon on the Norfolk-Suffolk border. Now in the care of English Heritage, the site encompasses almost 100 acres and the whole place is protected as a Scheduled Ancient Monument. No wonder. From around 3000 BC and for more than a thousand years thereafter miners dug at least 433 separate vertical shafts – some as much as 40 feet deep and 30 feet in diameter – to reach thick seams of flint. (Flint is a mysterious material in its own right, chiefly found as nodules or larger masses within sedimentary rocks like chalk and limestone. Even now geologists are unclear about precisely how it forms but it seems likely that at some point, millions of years ago, a thick, gloopy material trickled inside gaps and cavities bored into harder

sediment by sea creatures like molluscs. Chalk itself is the accumulation of the skeletons of trillions upon trillions of tiny sea
creatures that lived short lives in warm tropical oceans before
dying and sinking to the seabed. Their skeletons were made of
calcium and over time built into thick layers that were eventually
compressed to form chalk. During subsequent millennia, pressure
and time conspired to change the consistencies of that layer-cake
of sediments – and in the case of whatever thick mineral soup
leaked into those cavities in the chalk, the end product was the
glassy, brittle material called flint.)

At Grime's Graves (an Anglo-Saxon name meaning 'the quarries
dug by the masked man') the miners knew precisely the kind of
flint they wanted – because in places they dug straight through
shallower seams of lower-quality material in search of what lay
many feet beneath.

The sheer physical effort involved in the excavation of the
mines almost beggars belief. Working primarily with picks made
from red deer antlers, Neolithic miners removed thousands of
tons of chalk from every shaft. Archaeologists have worked out
it was likely that no more than perhaps a couple were open and
in use at any one time – so that the resource was carefully and
methodically exploited. As they dug deeper, the miners must
have built wooden platforms connected by ladders and then, on
reaching the flint, began working horizontally to create rabbit
warrens of galleries and tunnels. They would have encountered
the flint as whole thick floors of material, like solidified spills
of toffee and treacle, and this they would have smashed into
pieces, with stone hammers, ready for removal to the surface.
Back in the daylight other specialists worked the raw flint into
blanks for axes that were then distributed far and wide throughout the country for finishing and eventual use. For a world of
farmers, the endless work of cutting down trees, building shelters
and tools and all the rest of the daily grind of toiling over crops
and animals, axes were the essential item. It has been estimated
that thousands of tons of axes were mined from Grime's Graves

during the millennia when the area was actively exploited.

Now several of the shafts have been reopened so that it is possible to climb down into the ancient dark. And what you find there is more than just a mine – it is a glimpse of a surviving part of the Neolithic world. Some of the tunnels are so tiny and confined they could only ever have been worked by children. Here and there archaeologists have found hearths, human remains and what have even been interpreted as shrines. Bones and skulls and also personal items including finished axes and other tools and belongings were intentionally left behind from time to time, before the shafts were finally backfilled.

As well as stabilising the landscape above, the act of backfilling may have mattered on a more spiritual level. It seems possible the miners understood they were taking something from deep inside the living body of Mother Earth – and that they were concerned to make amends, to pay for the harvest. They may also have been at pains to try and ensure there would always be more flint to mine. Perhaps they believed the flint was something else that 'grew' from the Earth, no different in many ways to an edible root or tuber. For farmers used to reseeding the ground with some portion of the latest crop to ensure next year's harvest, it may well have seemed logical, vital even, to put back the odd axe in the hope of 'growing' more.

All of it smacks of a highly ordered and organised activity. The season's work at the mine would have required the marshalling, in one place and at one time, of a large group of like-minded people. Having set aside the tasks more directly related to farming, they had to gather for weeks at a place like Grime's Grave and set about tool preparation on a near-industrial scale. Rather than relying on hunting for the supply of antlers for picks they may have corralled a herd of red deer somewhere close by so that the material could be guaranteed. As well as the miners there would have been a whole community working on the surface – preparing the clothes, food, shelter and tools required by the men toiling below ground. It seems, too, there was a holy man or woman – someone whose preoccupation was the well-being of the mine and its contents.

So, long before there was metal, when it came to obtaining the essential material of flint, the Stone Age farmers had already developed sophisticated approaches to meeting their own needs, and those of the planet. It was into such a world that there came, around 2500 BC, a technology that would blow even those sensitive, inquiring minds. Metal arrived with such momentum it would eventually catapult Britain right out of the Stone Age, where it had languished, in truth, since human time began. When 'British' society landed again after that explosive impact, it was well on the way towards the world of today.

It seems the earliest landfall by the metal-makers – those who carried in their heads and hands the wondrous knowledge of how to take special rock and transform it into something utterly new – was not in Britain but in south-west Ireland. At Ross Island, surrounded by the Killarney Lakes of County Kerry, archaeologists have identified the source of the metal used to make the very first metal tools found anywhere in Britain.

Irish archaeologist Billy O'Brien has spent decades learning about the lives and times of people who gathered there as early as 2,500 years ago to exploit rich seams of copper. O'Brien explained that the first copper mines were dug in the Balkans, as much as 6,000 years ago. By 3000 BC pockets of copper technology were appearing further west, in northern Italy and elsewhere along the Mediterranean coast. It took another five centuries for knowledge and understanding of the potential of copper deposits to reach north-west Europe and when it did so, it arrived fully formed in the heads and hands of experts. 'Copper metallurgy first appeared in Ireland at a relatively advanced level, probably through contacts with metal-using groups on the Continent,' he said.

People equipped with lifetimes of metal-working experience were therefore prospecting in south-west Ireland when they spotted what they were looking for in rock formations at Ross Island. Copper ore is relatively unremarkable and the sight of it would only mean anything to someone who had had it pointed out to them before. Having located the naturally occurring seams, the foreigners set to work with a will, likely aided and abetted by the locals. Seams were exploited by lighting fires against rock faces to make them brittle enough to shatter with stone hammers. In this way gaping quarries were created as miners smashed their way into the seams. Anyone visiting the location today would take the deep gashes and fissures as natural features – but they are the work of the earliest copper miners in either Britain or Ireland.

As well as the extraction sites, O'Brien has also identified and excavated various processing areas, where stone hammers and anvils were used for pounding the large lumps of ore into coarse powder ready for transformation into the metal itself. It bears mentioning that apart from a single droplet of smelted copper, not one metal item has been recovered from Ross Island. Instead the processed ore was taken or sent elsewhere, to be made into axe-heads and other tools.

Wherever it was taking place, that processing – smelting being the correct term – would have been a magical wonder for people watching it for the first time. I grew up in a world from which men flew to the Moon and back. Like everyone else alive in the developed world of today I take for granted wonders like mobile phones, computers, the Internet, wi-fi, Skype, the Large Hadron Collider and talk of quarks and String Theory – but with my hand on my heart I will swear I have never witnessed anything more viscerally amazing than the transformation of powdered rock into molten metal. No matter how carefully the science of it all is explained, I defy anyone to watch the process without a lump forming in the throat. It is magical enough to make a man cry.

The secret lies in heat – the kind of extreme heat that can be coaxed from a fire only by using bellows. Just a pair of leather bags suffices and, provided they are pumped rhythmically for long enough and their manufactured breaths funnelled into the flames by a tube of fired clay, then the temperature can be pushed high enough to make the magic happen.

Copper ore is called malachite and appears as a faintly greenish

rock, sometimes shot through with black bands (the Romans'
principal source of the stuff was Cyprus and it is from cyprium,
or *cuprum*, 'the metal of Cyprus', that we get our version of its
name). As well as copper, the ore contains atoms of both oxygen
and carbon that must be removed to leave pure copper behind.
The powdered ore is first 'roasted' in a fire, a process that drives
off any carbon dioxide, leaving just copper oxide – which is a
chemical combination of copper and oxygen. The copper oxide is
then heated a second time – to nearly 1,100 degrees centigrade,
using the bellows – in a fire composed primarily of charcoal.
Charcoal is rich in carbon and as it burns it creates an atmosphere
around the ore that is low in oxygen, so that the oxygen within
the ore is drawn out and consumed by the oxygen-starved flames.
With the oxygen gone, only copper then remains.

If this is complicated to explain and to understand, then imagine
how much trial and error must have been employed by the very
first people to attempt the miracle in the first place. Who even
thinks up such a possibility – that of changing the very chemistry
of stone so that it becomes another material entirely – far less finds
a way to make it real? It must surely have taken hundreds, if not
thousands of years of experiment by people before the process was
finally nailed down; and it was the possession of such knowledge,
so hard won, that set the metal-makers apart from other men and
women.

On a number of occasions now I have had the privilege of
standing beside some of those who have learned to replicate the
techniques of ancient copper smelting – and every time the miracle
has taken me by surprise. When the temperature is just right, for
just long enough, what had simply been dry powder heaped
into a crucible of fired clay turns spontaneously into liquid. It is
impossible to describe the colour or the consistency of that liquid.
Suffice to say that when the crucible is fished out of the glowing
embers using a pair of tongs, and tipped up to let the copper pour
out, it seems to be filled with something alive.

If molten copper is like anything, then it is a little like

blood – but rosy-orange blood, viscous and with a perfect sheen on its surface, reflective like a mirror, or a living eye. No matter how delicately that crucible is tipped, the liquid seems suddenly to leap up and out of it, lightning fast and darting like a lizard. Its life, if life it is, is less than brief however, just a few moments between crucible and mould before it seems to die before your very eyes – so that what had been quick and nimble like a flash of inspiration is suddenly still again, for ever. The sheen that had been on its surface dies too, leaving behind a steadily dulling patina that becomes first pink, with a hint of green, before passing through many shades of red. It is elemental stuff – like a glimpse of what must happen inside the heart of a star – and for want of anything else to burn while you watch, the living metal draws your breath towards it and consumes that as well, so that you gasp.

This first stage of the arrival in Britain of metal-working technology is known by archaeologists as the Copper Age – or the Chalcolithic, from *khalkos*, the Greek word for copper. As well as their understanding of how metal was to be made, the incomers seem to have brought with them an entire culture – one represented by a set of objects they were in the habit of burying alongside their dead. Typically there are distinctive drinking vessels called Beakers, copper knives, arrowheads, wristguards to protect an archer's forearm, boars' tusks, stone tools and special 'cushion' stones for putting the finishing touches to metal items. Sometimes there are even pieces of gold jewellery.

As well as equipping their loved ones with specific grave goods, the practitioners of the new technology liked to place them in their graves lying on their left sides and slightly curled up, as though sleeping, their faces towards the north. The graves containing people positioned that way and accompanied by some or all of those bits and pieces are therefore like a trail of footprints archaeologists can follow all across central, western and Mediterranean Europe. (I said 'culture' in the preceding paragraph and from time to time it has been fashionable to use that word to imply a unified people, all thinking and acting the same way. When I was a student we were taught about the 'Beaker People' and it was tempting to see them almost as missionaries, travelling throughout the Continent spreading the word and enlightening Stone Age farmers with the message of metal.)

The Beakers are shaped rather like upturned bells (so that they are often referred to in the archaeological literature as 'Bell Beakers') and have been interpreted as part of male-dominated drinking rituals. Viewed from that perspective much of the rest of the kit – the arrows, wristguards and knives – seem similarly masculine, related to hunting. Perhaps even after millennia of farming, real manhood continued to be associated with the ways of the hunter, so that men felt the need to incorporate at least a ritualised form of hunting into their lives. If they had to be farmers in life, perhaps in death their souls were freed to return to the trail, bow and arrows in hand.

In all likelihood, however, there was probably no single 'people' and no single explanation for the inclusion of Beakers and the rest in graves scattered all across Europe. Instead there were probably many explanations, as different peoples acquired the new science and adapted it to suit their lives and circumstances. By the time metal-working reached Britain, it had travelled for thousands of years and over thousands of miles, a technology that was flexible and malleable and ready to take on whatever shape and use was required of it.

Sometime between 2500 and 2300 BC, a boy grew to manhood in the Alpine region of Europe, among people who had made and worked metal for centuries at least. He had the skill himself and even among his own people it made him worthy of note, since it was known only to that caste of specialists who kept the secrets to themselves. It is impossible to know if he was actually born there in that swathe of territory incorporating modern Austria, France, Germany, Italy, Slovenia and Switzerland – but he spent enough of his childhood and early adulthood in the vicinity to ensure that, as his teeth developed in his jaws, they incorporated the very atoms contained in the earth and water of the place. The Alpine region was therefore quite literally in his bones. As an adult he stood around five feet eight inches tall and, completely unbeknown to him, he had a highly unusual and benign malformation of some of the bones in his feet.

It was as a fully grown man that he left that part of Europe and headed north-west, either walking on his peculiar feet or riding a domesticated horse. It is possible he travelled alone, but more likely he was part of a group that had found reasons to leave the place they knew best and set out towards new horizons. There is only so far a person, or indeed a group of people, can travel in a day and the journey from its beginning to its end would ultimately have taken many months, if not years. We will never know if he or they had a final destination in mind and they may have spent unknown days, months or even years in any number of places along the way. Finally, though, their route reached the Channel and a boat was begged, borrowed, made or stolen in order to make the crossing.

By the time of that life, and that journey, there was a place towards the extreme north-west of Europe – on an island across the sea – that was already special and famous. It may even have been the inspiration for the journey in the first place. We cannot know what it was called then – even whether it had one name or many – but it was a special location where circles of timber had become circles of stone and those circles were themselves set inside a bigger circle dug out of the ground, the fill heaped into a rounded bank that underlined the separateness, the apartness of the space within. Some people said it was a world of the dead and that even the sun was born and died there every year.

A long time before the man died, on one side of the Channel or the other, he suffered a terrible injury to his left knee. It was crippling and meant that for at least part of his life he was partially disabled and would have walked with a halting limp. If it happened in the Alpine region where he grew up, then the journey or journeys he made in adulthood seem even more remarkable. If it happened in England, it may explain why he died there rather than back home.

How long he spent living close by the place known to us as Stonehenge is anyone's guess. Also unknowable is whether, having arrived, he spent the rest of his life there or if he made many trips, sometimes returning home to the Alps or journeying elsewhere in between. (Given the nature of his knee injury, it seems unlikely he would have enjoyed covering long distances, but you never know.) Maybe he believed the stones in their circle had healing properties and visited them from his home over and over, like a modern-day pilgrim to Lourdes, before eventually dying in their shadow, aged no more than 45 and still unhealed, still uncured.

He was buried in the manner of his people, a few miles to the south-east of the great monument. First they dug him a grave and lined it with timber. They laid him inside it on his left side, the side of his withered leg, and took care to curl him neatly into a foetal position so he seemed less lost to them, more likely to return. His face was turned towards the north, as was their custom. But if that much of the burial tradition was familiar – common to countless graves of his kind, their kind, all across Continental Europe – then the wealth they heaped upon and around his body was nothing less than startling. Into the grave went a whole quiver of arrows, 15 of them, tipped with beautifully worked, barbed and tanged heads of flint, all of which appear to have been made by the same craftsman. On one of his forearms was a wristguard of grey-black sandstone – a practical item to protect an archer from the painful recoil of the bowstring but also a mark of status – and on his chest a precious copper knife. By the wristguard, or bracer, was a bone pin, the fastening for a cloak. At his back the mourners placed a Bell Beaker that, before firing, had been decorated with lines scratched into the wet clay with a comb. Beside it they set a handful of flint tools, some used and broken, a so-called 'cushion stone' for finishing metal and a pair of boars' tusks. Close to his face they put two more decorated Bell Beakers, more flint and flint tools, another pair of boars' tusks, some red deer bones and pieces of antler and a second copper knife. A fourth Beaker was placed in the crook of his bent knees, a fifth at his feet, together with yet another copper knife. The belt around his waist was strung through a ring carved from shale. Also near his feet was a second wristguard, this one of red sandstone. Most wondrous of all – at least to our eyes – the burial party laid at the man's feet two tiny pieces of fine, beautifully worked gold jewellery. At first sight they look like little basket-shaped earrings but are more likely to have been decorations designed to be worn in long hair. Content they had done right by him, they backfilled the grave and topped it with a low mound, so they would always know where their metal-worker lay.

For thousands of years he lay at peace – thousands of years during which his world disappeared and was replaced, again and again, by others. Long ago the mound marking his grave was eroded away by years and neglect so that for the longest time no one even knew he was there. Other peoples settled the land, including Romans in the centuries following their invasion of Britain, and they buried their own dead in a careful cemetery close to the long-forgotten metal-worker. Perhaps the mound was still visible then – and drew them to the place – perhaps it was only coincidence. During the time of the Anglo-Saxons a village was established there, called Amesbury, a possession of the kings. Most recently it has been a simple market town, but popular enough to create demand for new houses and a new primary school. And so it was that in the spring of 2002 archaeologists, mindful of the Romano-British presence in the area, conducted a programme of excavations in advance of the construction work.

To begin with they found what they had been expecting – evidence of burials related to the time of the Roman Empire; but as spring gave way to summer they turned their attention to some depressions they thought might be no more than cavities left by the root bowls of trees fallen long ago. Instead, from within one of them, they unearthed the metal-worker in all his Early Bronze Age glory.

Given the arrowheads and wristguards it was not long before he was being referred to, at least by the writers of newspaper headlines, as the 'Amesbury Archer'. It was soon clear to the archaeologists that they had found the richest burial of the period in the whole of Britain, indeed one of the richest in Europe. By then the tabloids were speculating about the 'King of Stonehenge'. One of his teeth was removed and taken for isotope analysis – a process that finds elements like strontium and oxygen in tooth enamel and allows scientists to pinpoint where a person lived his or her early years. The rock of a place becomes the soil of a place; rivers and streams run over the rock, acquiring the elements too. Plants absorb them; the animals that eat them and drink the water do the same, so that a child makes himself from the very stuff of the land on which he grows. That the Amesbury Archer was found to be no local but a man who had reached maturity south of the Alps confounded all expectations.

And there was a further twist. Excavation of a second depression just 15 feet or so away from the first revealed a second burial, this time of a man aged between 20 and 25. There was nothing on the scale of the wealth that had accompanied the older man, but in addition to some flint tools and a single boar's tusk, a second pair of golden hair tresses was found stuck to the jawbone of the skull. At first it seemed they might have been placed inside the young man's mouth during his burial, as some kind of ritual act, but it has subsequently been thought more likely they were simply placed on a cord around his neck. Nothing more than time and decay of the body had seen to it that the precious items found their way to a position between his jaws. It was examination of the skeleton itself, however, that delivered the real surprise: the younger man had the same, extremely unusual deformity of the bones of his feet. This was no coincidence – the pair had to be related by blood.

Radiocarbon dates are always tricky to interpret, but those recovered from both skeletons are compellingly similar, and suggest in fact the younger man lived and died just a little later than his older relative. He has gone into the literature as the

Amesbury Archer's 'companion', but he must be family – a close relative, maybe even the older man's son.

The same isotope analysis that revealed a central European childhood for the Archer showed his companion, or son, probably grew up in southern England – maybe close to Amesbury and Stonehenge and the rest of the great Stone Age monuments. Taken collectively, the evidence is fascinating: it suggests the older man, with his debilitating knee injury, not only reached Stonehenge but rose to prominence within the society he found in its shadow. Perhaps he brought his wife and other followers with him, and after settling in the vicinity of modern-day Amesbury she bore him a son. Whatever the relationship between the men, both of them were valued, in life as in death, by the people they lived among. Both were accorded the kind of burials reserved only for men of real status.

There is as well the story to be told by the Archer's grave goods. The copper from which his three knives were made came originally from Europe, possibly Spain, and the gold for his hair tresses (in fact the earliest gold jewellery found in Britain so far) is also from a Continental source – all suggestive of a life and a man connected to other metal-making communities far from where he and his belongings ended up. The people who buried him took care to ensure he had that cushion stone with him too. It was smoothed and burnished by much use and may have belonged to the Archer in life, proof he was a man accustomed to making and shaping metal. If he was not a metal-worker himself, then the inclusion of such an item may indicate he was a man who had the power to control access to the magical material.

The radiocarbon dates obtained from his skeleton and that of his companion mean they may even have been living and breathing in Amesbury while Stonehenge was a scene of frantic activity – during the few years it took to source the giant sarsen stones and to raise them into position at the centre of the circle. They certainly lived while all the great monuments of the area were in use – Durrington Walls, Woodhenge and the rest – so suddenly that newspaper headline about the King of Stonehenge seems less fanciful. Was he indeed part of a kind of Early Bronze Age royalty – one of an elite that travelled throughout Europe, visiting all the great religious and spiritual centres of the age, Stonehenge being perhaps the greatest of them and the place where he decided to pass not just the last years of his life, but also eternity?

Most fascinating of all is the possibility he had a hand in that final building phase. Maybe he was drawn to the already famous, sacred location, a place of pilgrimage – only to find himself involved in the design and completion of its most famous form. Perhaps rather than the King of Stonehenge, he was one of its architects.

Or did his journey to Stonehenge culminate in a wedding? It has been suggested by some archaeologists that so-called Beaker Culture spread by means of marriage alliances – husbands and brides being exchanged between communities, even over great distances, along with the knowledge of how to make metal. Maybe the Archer travelled from central Europe to Britain as a husband-to-be, promised to the daughter of a powerful man living close to this magnificent stone monument.

I even wonder about that wounded, wasted leg of his. How strange and how appropriate that one of the first men to arrive in Britain with the ability to source and perhaps also to work metal – a true pioneer in every sense of the word – should have been disabled like the smiths of later legends. Like Wayland, overseer of the tomb that bears his name, and Hephaestus of Greek myth, the Amesbury Archer was lame. Like the fictional characters that would follow him – the creations of imaginations yet to be born – our metal-worker may have ended up unable to stray far from his forge.

The French anthropologist Claude Lévi-Strauss went so far as to say all creatures born of Earth understand that they are lame by nature – that they know the Earth does not easily give up those things taken from her. Just as the flint miners of Grime's Graves left offerings to pay for what they had taken, so perhaps the metal-makers understood there was a debt. It seems people in the Late Neolithic and Early Bronze Age were among the first to sense that their very existence in the world had consequences and that their actions were capable of changing things for ever.

Wrapped up in it somewhere, it seems to me, is something that smells like guilt. If there ever had been a time when *Homo sapiens sapiens* lived as guiltless as a child, then it was over by the Early Bronze Age. As a species we were growing more mature. We had become aware in a way we had not been before. As well as learning to worry about the welfare of ancestors, and paying attention to the cycles of the sun and the Moon, we began to see ourselves as active rather than passive participants in it all. We could change the world – and so, maybe, we should. In times to come the metal-workers – the world's first scientists and alchemists – would be portrayed as lame, perhaps symbolic of how they were weighed down, tied more tightly to the Earth than other men, by what they owed her.

All in all the Amesbury Archer offers many questions and few definite answers. His skeleton, surrounded by all his finery, is on permanent display in the Salisbury and South Wiltshire Museum, in Salisbury. The display of human remains is a controversial subject now. There are many who find it distasteful, for all sorts of reasons, to have the dead on show inside glass cases. They argue there is no justification for such a morbid practice, irrespective of whether the body has been dead for hours or for thousands of years. As an archaeologist I find nothing morally wrong with such exhibits; in fact I will confess a fascination for looking at the remains of our ancestors. But there is nonetheless a strange feeling to be had from coming close to the dead, however ancient – a feeling you have crossed a line. Seeing those Mesolithic footprints in the mud of Goldcliff, in south Wales, made me feel I was prying, viewing private moments I was never meant to see. There is undeniably something similar to be experienced while looking at, or handling, the bones of people who had every reason to expect they would spend eternity unmolested by other mortals.

The Amesbury Archer lies in a low case that contains a reconstruction, as far as possible, of the condition and position in which he was found. Curled on his side he seems more human, somehow, than if he was on his back. It is such a familiar position, that of sleep, that even a curled-up skeleton seems strangely less dead. And then of course there are his grave goods, those things the people he left behind felt he should have with him on his final journey. I was even allowed to handle them – always a nerve-wracking experience – and the first thing that struck me about the copper knives was how small they were. At just a few inches in length, they are the size of penknife blades and yet, while the Amesbury Archer had them, they would have been of incalculable value.

Think of the store we set by new gadgets today – the latest mobile phone or whatever – and then consider the impact of owning something made of an utterly new material, something never seen before by the people you show it to. Most breathtaking of all his belongings are the golden hair tresses. Until you see them for real you cannot fully appreciate how tiny they are, and how fragile; when you hold one in your hand it weighs almost nothing at all. Aware at all times of their value, how irreplaceable they are, I felt my hands jangling with nerves. After just a few moments I had to put the things back down in their case, for fear an involuntary twitch of thumb and forefinger might crush them flat.

But there he lies: a man who, 4,500 years ago, was accustomed to international travel. When he came to die he was over a thousand miles from the land in which he had grown to manhood, a stranger in a strange land. He was among the very first to show metal to the people of Britain, a man who, more importantly, knew how the precious material could be obtained. He had ridden the wave that brought the future, even the modern world, to these shores. Despite a terrible injury to his leg, a wound that lamed him for life, he had risen to prominence among his peers and when he died they saw to it he had the richest funeral imaginable. In life and in death he was nothing less than extraordinary and even now his bones, in a glass box, surrounded by a few scraps, have the power to enthrall and to make some of us long for a world in which a little copper knife was more magical than any Excalibur drawn from a stone.

Whatever the truth of the Amesbury Archer, he was certainly part of that movement of people and ideas known sometimes as the Beaker Culture. Its arrival – their arrival – in Britain was a landmark moment in the history of the islands. Before the Beaker People all of the materials of day-to-day life were simply gathered from the natural world. Stone, bone, shell, wood, antler, animal sinew – all these and more besides were used in countless ingenious ways. By the time of the Early Bronze Age, people in Britain had also been familiar, for a thousand years and more, with the idea of using fire to harden clay. But along with their metal, the Beaker People brought new ways of thinking about themselves and their fellow human beings.

Due in no small part to the birth – or at least the coming of age – of the science of archaeology in the 1960s, the subject has always been coloured by some of the politics of that time. For those who had grown up in the aftermath of the Second World War and who were living through televised conflicts like Vietnam, there was a comfort to be had in looking into the distant past and imagining people had lived differently there. Not for the hunter-gathers the horrors of war, or the oppression of the weak by the strong. Instead it was popular among 1960s archaeologists to imagine our ancestors in the Stone Ages enjoying vaguely egalitarian existences, sharing the stuff of the natural world and happily co-operating with one another. If they had been savages, at least they were noble savages – and with left-wing sensibilities to boot.

Caved-in skulls became, for a time, mere aberrations – either exceptions to the rule or evidence of some or other ritual practice. Arrowheads within ribcages were not proof of cause of death, but rather grave goods, symbols lovingly placed on top of the dead bodies to identify them as hunters, archers.

But even the most ardent, 'right-on' archaeologists had to admit something changed in the ancient world under the influence of metal. For one thing there was the conspicuous evidence of altered burial practices. By the Early Bronze Age, the communal tombs of the Early Neolithic were ancient history, sealed and long forgotten. Gradually it was to become more about single burials, of a few individuals being treated to an elaborate send-off while the rest were left out for the birds and foxes. The tendency towards singling out special people for special treatment – like the occasional cremations associated with tombs such as Knowth and Newgrange, or at Stonehenge – had begun in the Neolithic. But the undeniable existence of social hierarchies became more blatant still once there was metal to play with. From then on the centralising of personal wealth in the hands of the few – together with the status wealth confers – was unmistakable. They had not only enjoyed it in life, but also had the clout to ensure they took it with them into death.

Metal-workers like the Amesbury Archer were apparently able to transform more than just ore from the ground. They changed the nature and shape of society itself, from one in which all men had been more or less equal into another, in which wealth and power created them ... and therefore us.

Stone Age Britain had reached a peak of sorts with the creation of those massive, cosmically aligned monuments. There was still then some relic of a belief in the collective entity that was the ancestors. But the incomers, with their Beakers and other oddities, brought a sense of self, a sense of individuality. The Amesbury Archer was buried on his own, and with valuable possessions that told eternity who he had been, what he had done in life. His funeral and afterlife were a statement about his status. For the Beaker People all of those things mattered – but for the British people they first encountered, it was radical thinking.

Communal burial in stone tombs was soon passé, to be replaced in the Bronze Age with a near-obsession with barrows – round mounds centred on individual burials. A handful of other souls might be incorporated within the same mound later on, like satellites held in place by the gravity of a planet; but it was the planet that mattered.

But for all their impact – the arrival from far-off lands of foreigners capable of making stone into metal, who carried themselves with the haughty demeanour of those who think themselves a cut above – the earliest Beaker People were peddling a substandard product. The smelting of copper is certainly magical, a showstopper by any standards, but copper's effectiveness as a material for making tools is distinctly limited. It looks wonderful but try cutting down a tree with an axe made of the stuff and see how far you get. It is simply too soft. It blunts easily and is also tricky to cast. From a purely practical perspective, flint is superior to copper in almost every way; and if copper had been all the incomers had up their sleeves they would never have lasted.

Copper, therefore, was only the appetiser. Some of the Beaker People knew how to make an even more extraordinary substance, another metal – one that took and held a sharp edge, that poured easily into moulds, that could be used to make bigger, longer, better things. That metal was bronze and it would transport Britain from the shadows and anonymity of the Stone Age into the technological forefront of Europe.

Bronze is an alloy – a mixture of around 90 per cent copper and 10 per cent tin – and tin is hard to come by. Because it mixes so readily with others, metallurgists describe tin as a 'sociable' metal. The problem is its scarcity, occurring as it does in just a few places on the planet. In prehistoric Europe it was to be found only in the area between modern Germany and the Czech Republic, in Spain and in Brittany. A particularly rich new source however was Cornwall and Devon in the south-west of England, and the discovery there of such a valuable resource meant ancient Britain was all at once transformed into a focus of international attention.

Unlike copper, pure tin does not occur naturally anywhere on Earth. Instead it is always within a compound of other materials. In prehistoric times it was obtained exclusively from the ore cassiterite. (Indeed, when the Greek historian Herodotus was writing in the fifth century BC he referred to a group of islands lying in the sea to the north-west of Europe, certainly Britain, as the Cassiterides, the 'Tin Islands': 'from which we are said to have our tin'.)

When cassiterite does occur, it is often in association with igneous rocks like granite; and it is likely that ancient metal prospectors, sailing alongside the south-west coast of Britain, spotted black ribbons of the stuff running down through the Cornish cliffs. That discovery was to make all the difference – a stroke of geological luck. Some part of the process of the making of the British Isles, millions and billions of years in the planet's past, had seen to it there was tin within the rock of their south-west tip. These islands had been latecomers to the Copper Age, but the discovery of cassiterite, so much more rare and therefore so much more valuable, would propel them to Europe's technological forefront.

A lump of cassiterite is strangely heavy, almost more like metal than rock, and the tin it contains, once extracted, is quite beautiful. An ingot of tin is as bright as silver but much, much softer – so that it can be bent in the hands. If you hold it up to your ears, as you do so you can hear tiny sounds, crackles from within – the so-called 'cry of the tin' – and in fact you can persuade yourself the sound is like someone far away shouting the very word, 'tin!' in a high-pitched voice.

Rather than just looking at Bronze Age artefacts in a museum, I had the privilege of spending time with Neil Burridge, who specialises in reproducing such objects himself, using traditional and ancient materials and methods. While I worked the bellows, keeping a steady flow of air passing through the flames of his workshop fire, Burridge described the superiority of bronze over copper. 'Copper is no match for bronze,' he said. 'An impact that would crumple a copper point will have no effect whatsoever on one made of bronze. It was simply the hardest metal of the ancient world.'

I had met up with Burridge in the hope of watching him cast a bronze sword – and found I was to be a much more active participant than I had initially imagined. He had pre-prepared a two-part sword mould of fired clay and this he heated in a gas furnace to ensure it would not shatter on contact with the molten metal. Once he was content that all the temperatures were correct – a moment reached only after several hours of careful fire-tending – he stood the glowing mould upright in a cylinder packed with sand, ready for the all-important pour. Liquid bronze is every bit as mesmerising as copper: again there was the illusion that something alive jumped from the crucible and down into the mould. There is a hot smell too, wholesome and somehow reminiscent of baking. After just a few seconds we were able to sink the mould into a cauldron of cold water, to cool it. I was afraid it would explode, that the change in temperature would be too abrupt, but it just hissed and sizzled like noise from chipped potatoes lowered into boiling fat, and released a coiling wreath of steam. Once it was cool enough, Burridge let me use a chisel to knock the fired clay away in chunks to reveal the sword.

Again the mystery was all around, the disbelief that accompanies anything that confounds mind and eye, or at least asks for more than a scientific explanation. How can it be? What had been a glowing orange liquid, moments before, radiating heat like the sun, was now an elegant green sword, shaped like a long, thin tongue and already hard enough to chop wood with. How could that be possible?

No wonder we have ended up with legends like the sword in the stone – a mighty weapon created by magic and drawn from the rock only by the once and future king. Without the benefit of schoolboy science, no witness to the creation of a sword from a pile of dust balanced within a fire could ever hope to understand what has just happened. Even Burridge, as modest and unassuming an expert as you will ever meet, was happy to admit he was nervous every single time – even after making hundreds of swords. The possibility that the process will fail, for some reason, is ever present and the emergence of an intact, perfect sword is always greeted with relief. It was, and still is, about some volatile, mysterious magic.

Unlike copper, bronze was for much more than just show. It could be made into all manner of very useful, very effective items – knives, axe-heads, tools of all descriptions, swords. In the hands of master bronze-workers Britain would be led into a whole new age.

The spread of metal had all sorts of consequences for every level of society. For one thing, the time was now past when everyone had to spend every waking hour working in the fields to grow enough food. For a few individuals, those with an entrepreneurial bent, say, or the brute power and determination to get their own way, metal opened up new worlds of opportunities. Sources of copper and tin were limited, and scattered far and wide across Britain, Ireland and the rest of Europe. Inhabitants of previously overlooked places, who had once been on the periphery, were thrust suddenly centre-stage, purely because of the nature of the rocks beneath their feet. People wanting bronze had to gain access to copper and tin as well – had to find ways to move those raw materials around, bring them together – often across considerable distances. For the first time society was vulnerable to modern-sounding concepts and preoccupations like 'supply and demand'.

Specialist metal-workers, metal traders and, most importantly of all, those who could control the new trade routes, would create positions of power for themselves; and where there was power there was the potential to obtain personal wealth. For that new, self-made elite of the Early Bronze Age the Stone Age must have seemed a quaint and distant memory.

In this New World it was no longer just the ancient, sacred landscapes of monuments and tombs that mattered either. Now there was an importance and a value placed upon practical, natural features like harbours, river routes and valleys. First the causewayed enclosures and then later the great stone circles and monuments of the Late Neolithic had given scattered communities reasons to meet up – and the places at which to do so. There had been husbands and wives to find, binding ties to establish and maintain for the good of body and soul. With the advent of metal the need for ties became practical and lucrative as well. Beautiful, desirable polished axes of rare and special stone had been exchanged over great distances, given names and treasured, passed within and between clans as powerful heirlooms. Now there were other things to covet – metal objects – and the making and obtaining of those new objects of desire demanded even stronger links between disparate locations and more clearly defined and ordered ways of moving between them.

Some of the earliest bronze items in Britain have been recovered from sites in the north-east of Scotland – axes created from a union of Irish copper and Cornish tin. They were cast around 2200 BC, very early in the story of British bronze, and whoever it was that had the authority to co-ordinate such an operation at that time, to obtain and move the necessary ores around the country, was elevated into a position of power; and that power was rooted in the control of one particularly well-defined natural feature of the landscape.

The Great Glen slashes diagonally across Scotland, from south-west to north-east, like the scar left by a Jacobite's broadsword. It separates the Highlands from the Lowlands and has, from the very beginning, shaped the destinies of those people born either side of it. In fact it is nothing more or less than a geological fault line. The landmass of Scotland – like that of the rest of Britain and Ireland – has been bundled together from assorted bits and pieces during billions of years. Other continents came and went, formed and disintegrated as the tectonic plates making up Earth's surface floated aimlessly across the planet's molten core from south to north and east to west. Occasionally they knocked lumps from one another in the course of that endless bump and grind and eventually a handful of those fragments came together, like pastry scraps crumpled into one lump, to form the dry land we know today as Britain. Scotland's Great Glen is the most obvious physical evidence of it all and that sword wound is where two of the plates come together. The fracture was later exploited by an Ice Age glacier that ground its way along the fault line from north-east to south-west, and all of that upheaval has resulted in one huge valley – a convenient, low-lying straight line that cuts across the country more directly than any motorway ever could.

The south-western entrance to the Great Glen (the slip road onto that motorway, as it were) is called Kilmartin Glen and runs through Argyll between the town of Oban and the village of Lochgilphead. The landscape is of such breathtaking beauty it is easy to see why people were drawn there from the earliest times, and in fact the hunter-gatherers of the Mesolithic were regular visitors as soon as the ice sheets withdrew 10,000 years ago. Some places are just good for the soul.

Something like 350 monuments are clustered within a six-mile radius of the modern-day village of Kilmartin – everything from tombs to standing stones and from cup and ring marks to medieval castles, proof of how much the place has always mattered, to countless generations.

It was during the Neolithic and Bronze Ages, however, that people began really to go to town, developing what can only be described as an entire ritual landscape in which individual monuments are best seen as parts of one elaborate scheme. It is even thought onlookers might once have gathered on the natural terraces on the valley sides to watch ceremonies and processions performed among the henges, stone circles and burial cairns on the valley floor below. Needless to say, Kilmartin Glen has been a destination for generations of archaeology students, and I was lucky enough to have archaeologist Alison Sheridan as my guide. I first worked for Sheridan – who showed me around those Neo-lithic houses of Orkney's Skara Brae – when she codirected the Kilmartin axe factory dig with Mark Edmonds, the Langdale axe-man, in the early 1990s. She is one of those academics who wear their knowledge lightly.

She explained how Kilmartin Glen was like a roundabout, a hub where copper from southern Ireland and tin from Cornwall were brought together for onward passage to bronze consumers living in Scotland's north-east. For those tribes whose territory Kilmartin Glen was – those whose ancestors had long ago settled the area simply to exploit its fertile soils – the fledgling fashion for the new metal provided a new and wholly unexpected source of wealth. Picture a kind of prehistoric customs post, where people wishing to pass through the portal in either direction had to declare whatever goods they were carrying and pay the necessary duty. Simple geography had dictated that the people controlling Kilmartin Glen were in a position to demand a share of the constant flow of metal items

It almost goes without saying that those metal traders likely resented the demands of the inhabitants of Kilmartin – and would surely have preferred to pass through without parting with so much as a crumb of their valuable wares. In other words, it would have been beholden upon the locals to demonstrate the ability to back up their demands with the threat of force – leading inevitably to the rise of those with the confidence to throw their weight around.

The most visible, and arguably the most famous, prehistoric feature of Kilmartin Glen is the so-called 'linear cemetery' – a sequence of tombs strung out for more than three miles along a line running south by south-west from Kilmartin village; it is uncertain precisely how many there were in ancient times. Ploughing and field clearance during the intervening millennia may have destroyed much of what was created in the Bronze Age, but five tombs are still visible today and their scale indicates that those interred within were folk of substance.

Unlike the communal tombs of the Neolithic, those of Kilmartin's linear cemetery were built to contain just one or two individuals, each within a stone-lined cist or grave buried beneath a vast cairn of boulders. One of them, called Nether Largie North Cairn (10 feet at its highest point and about 70 feet across), was reconstructed following its excavation. Inside is a single grave cut into the floor. Propped up alongside, leaning against the wall of the modern-built chamber, is the massive capstone that once sealed the grave, and it is another marvel. Carved and pecked into the surface that was once the underside – the one the departed loved one was meant to spend eternity looking up at – are at least 10 axe-heads, as well as dozens of cup marks.

Here then was a man or woman of great importance – one at the very top of the society that had grown rich from controlling the passage of metal through its territory. The last axes he or she would look upon were plainly for his or her eyes only, an eternal reminder of the object the new wealth was built upon: the bronze axe.

Excavation of a stone cist inside a burial mound at Poltalloch, near Lochgilphead, in 1928, unearthed over 100 individually carved and drilled beads and trapezoidal plates of Whitby Jet lying among fragments of cremated human bone and lumps of charcoal and ochre. This was the grave of someone special, someone worthy of honour in life and death. Once the beads and plates had formed an elaborate necklace, in fact a masterpiece of the jeweller's art. Strung on multiple cords, each shorter than the last so that the whole formed a near-complete breastplate of black, it would have been as captivating as a quadrant of the night sky. It is now on display in the National Museum of Scotland, in Edinburgh, and makes a person wonder just who would have owned such a treasure 4,150 years ago. (When Queen Victoria, mourning the death of her husband Prince Albert, commissioned black mourning jewellery made of Whitby Jet she was just the latest, in an extremely long line of wealthy women, to covet a particularly unusual and special material. The fossilised wood of Monkey Puzzle trees, Whitby Jet has been prized for thousands of years on account not just of its shiny appearance but also because it feels quite unlike anything else. Rather than being cold to the touch like stone, jet feels almost warm, like varnished wood. It also has electrostatic qualities, so that when rubbed against the skin it will attract small particles of dust and chaff – surely a magical property for people living in a pre-scientific world.)

She – and such delicate finery was surely intended for a woman rather than a man – had had time during her few decades of life to develop refined, even exotic tastes. She also had the wealth to indulge them. Whitby, on the Yorkshire coast, is over 300 miles from Kilmartin and yet she was able to order up a bespoke item of jewellery from a specialist craftsman there, as remote, in modern British terms, as one living somewhere in the Far East. Did she commission it herself so she could power-dress to impress? Was she then a woman of substance in her own right, a female head of a dominant clan? Or was it a gift from a loving husband, father or mother who wanted to show how much the woman mattered to him or her by adorning her with jewellery made of stone as black as night and imbued with magical powers? And when she died what more fitting item could she wear on her last journey into that dark than a necklace made of a blackness that attracted motes of dust like eternity pulls the sun, Moon and stars?

Kilmartin Glen, at the start of the second millennium BC, may be a snapshot of a moment in time – when Britain found within herself the wherewithal to produce the kinds of raw materials and finished products that had currency in the wider world. Sheridan goes further – arguing that by around 2100 BC the communities of Kilmartin would have attracted international attention for their metalwork and for prestige items like the jet necklace. She happily describes that part of Scotland, at that time, as 'the epicentre of cool', as though communities thousands of miles away to the south and east – back in the lands of the Mediterranean and the rest of Europe – would have suddenly become aware that smiths and craftsmen working in the British archipelago were producing items of the highest quality.

Looming over the southern end of the Glen is the rocky outcrop of Dunadd – 'the Fort of the River Add'. Nearly 180 feet high at its summit, its natural terraces are wrapped and wreathed with the remains of ancient walls as much as 30 feet thick. Its brooding presence is exaggerated out of all proportion to its true size by the flatness of the valley floor from which it rises, so that it sits proud like an upturned cup on a saucer. The fields around are often waterlogged, but their lyrical-sounding Gaelic name, Moine Mhor – pronounced Moin-yah Vawr and meaning 'the Great Moss' – adds a romantic burnish to what is little more than a weeping, heather-covered bog.

Fortification of the rock began in the last few centuries before the birth of Jesus Christ, but sometime around AD 500 the place was made the capital of the emergent Gaelic kingdom of Dal Riata. Legend has it that a great chieftain called Fergus Mór mac Eirc – Big Fergus, son of Eirc – crossed the water from his Irish home in search of new lands to dominate. In his day the sea level was higher than now and the rock of Dunadd more an island than a hill. From its summit he and his tribe could look out upon the waterway that was their connection to their homeland, and oversee the comings and goings of their ships.

At the start of the sixth century AD, the Gaels of Dál Riata were just one of the peoples occupying lands in the northern third of Britain. If the legend has a basis in truth, and the Gaels did indeed arrive from Ireland, then it may explain why they have gone down in history with a name that translates as something like 'pirates' or 'seaborne raiders'. In any event, it seems likely they did not call themselves 'Gaels' but had the name foisted upon them instead. Latin scholars referred to the Gaels as *Scoti* – the root of Scot and therefore of Scotland itself.

Excavations at Dunadd have found that the people centred there were skilled goldsmiths – for delicate moulds have been recovered. The find of a single piece of Mediterranean orpiment – a yellow ink – suggests they may have been in the habit of making illuminated manuscripts as well.

By the time there were Gaels at Dunadd, there were Picts in the east and north and Britons in the south. The Picts were the descendants of those native tribes that had refused to co-operate with the Romans, preferring to fight and make mischief for the invaders instead. They occupied much of the best farming land in the territory that would one day be called Scotland and the most powerful of their leaders styled themselves as kings. The Picts had contacts far and wide and traded natural resources as well as ideas about art and religious beliefs.

To the south were the Britons, sons and daughters of those tribes that had chosen to accept Roman rule. Their territory was spread between fortresses like Din Eidyn – Edinburgh – in the east and Alt Clut, mighty Dumbarton Rock, in the west.

Relations between the three were complicated. There were marriage ties to bind them and blood feuds to put them at each other's throats – all the threads so twisted and interwoven that the tapestry was likely as confusing to the peoples themselves as it is to historians and archaeologists today.

Like the leaders of the Picts, the foremost of the Gaels had aspirations to kingship. On a terrace below the summit of Dunadd they carved a footprint into the living rock ... an anvil upon which to forge their kings. Each heir apparent would be crowned with one naked foot placed within the print so that he was literally joined, wedded to the land he sought to rule.

For the next few centuries there was war and peace and war again between Gaels and Picts – until at last, around AD 900, the two became one by means still not fully understood. In time, though, the sons and daughters of the new union adapted the old nickname for one of them to form a new identity for all: from now on they were the Scots.

Orkney was once a central point around which much else revolved. Time moved on, however, leaving the place high and dry, like a rock pool. Rather than the centre, that little archipelago north of Scotland now feels like somewhere remote and on the very edge of nowhere. The same is true of Kilmartin Glen. Drive into that valley today and the overriding feeling is of travelling far off the beaten track. But that is an impression to be had only from our time in the world. Kilmartin was once nothing less than a true capital – somewhere that mattered as much or more, in its own time, as any London or Paris. Perhaps the most helpful view of the glen is the one from high above. Sitting as it does on the neck of the Mull of Kintyre, Kilmartin is suddenly, obviously, in control of the great strip of dry land between the Irish Sea and the inland lochs of western Scotland, a dry-shod shortcut for people heading north-east and south-west. (In his most important work, *Vita Columbae* – the Life of Columba – the seventh-century hagiographer and abbot of Iona, Saint Adoman, wrote about his more famous predecessor. In it he mentioned travelling to 'the head of the region' – likely Dunadd – and there meeting with traders from Gaul – France – so Kilmartin Glen was an important destination then for sailors from as far away as France, and even Spain.)

Kilmartin Glen is therefore a little wonder of the Scottish world, a reminder of heydays long past. That it once absorbed an Irish tribe and cradled them in its rocky fastnesses – making them, in the end, into the first Scots – underlines how the east of Ireland and the west of Scotland have always been closely tied, almost one country at times. For peoples more accustomed to travelling by boat than overland, a waterway like the Irish Sea was always going to be a shortcut between sister islands rather than any kind of barrier.

The story of Dunadd and Dal Riata is therefore another chapter in the long chronicle of connections between the islands of Ireland and Britain – and the rest of Europe besides. That the very name 'Scot' is rooted in vagabond sea travel serves as a memory of how the water has always mattered to the people at least as much as the land it surrounds.

Of course that sea has been guilty of treachery – stealing away the land by stealth as well as by ram-raiding tsunamis, and forever conjuring up storms to swamp and sweep away curraghs and coracles. Just a handful of miles west of Kilmartin and Dunadd, in the narrow strait between the islands of Jura and Scarba, lies the monstrous whirlpool of Corryvreckan. One of the largest such maelstroms in the world, its name surges through Scottish legend. The Gaelic name is Coire Bhreacain – meaning 'the cauldron of the plaid' – and the folk tale has it that the Hag of Winter, called Cailleach, used it to wash her tartan shawl. Dangerous all year round, the vortex is the result of Atlantic tides forced through the narrow channel and swirling around the peak of an undersea spike of rock they call An Cailleach. When conditions are worst, during the winter months, the swell is often huge and unforgiving and the roar of it all can be heard miles away – perhaps as far as the summit of Dunadd itself.

Despite the risks, boatmen and sailors had been braving the waters around Britain since at least the Neolithic; and by the Bronze Age, trade with folk on the European mainland demanded regular crossings of the Channel at least, as well as the wider North Sea.

Such journeys are commonplace to us. The volume and regularity of ferries and other vessels plying back and forth between Britain and the Continent have rendered such journeys about as meaningful as jumping on and off a bus. So it is important to try to imagine how perilous an undertaking such a crossing must have been in the Neolithic and Early Bronze Age – and therefore how laden with significance and meaning. Britain and Ireland are set apart by the sea and the millennia of separation have made the people and the society utterly different from those found on the Continent. It is just 20-odd miles from Dover to Calais, and yet the differences between south-east England and north-west France are profound and instantly apparent. As is often said, the British and the Irish are island races and islanders are a breed apart.

If those differences, those made and maintained by the water, are still so discernible today, how great must they have been when the separation was much, much more significant as well? Peoples in the past may have been accustomed to making crossings; but such journeys may have been imbued with meaning and significance that far exceeded the purely physical. Island races are made special and separate not by the land but by the sea; and we have to attempt to imagine how that water was perceived in ancient times, and what it meant.

As early as the Mesolithic period it seems people viewed the coast and the sea as a boundary between worlds. Archaeologists and anthropologists use the word 'liminal' (from the Latin *limen*, meaning threshold) to describe a place set apart, or situated between two other places. People on rites of passage must cross over liminal zones as they pass from one state of existence to another – from childhood to adulthood; from single to married; from impure to clean; from life to death, and so on.

With archaeologist Steve Mithen I visited giant mounds – middens – of shells left behind on the shorelines of islands off Scotland's western coastline. As well as the accumulated rubbish created by years of harvesting and eating shellfish, the middens were also markers – possibly territorial markers – deliberately located on the shining white boundary between land and sea. Elsewhere in Scotland such middens were occasionally used by Mesolithic people as places in which to bury a few of their own dead. Food, life, death, land and sea were all mingling in that special zone where states of being were blurred. If the land represented life, then the sea was something or someplace of the dead, or the ancestors, and the coastal strip between the two was the porous boundary keeping them apart, the threshold.

For ancient peoples, therefore, islanders especially, the sea was more than just a body of water, and voyages undertaken across it may have mattered in ways we can only guess at.

'They that go down to the sea in ships, that do business in great waters; these see the works of the Lord, and his wonders in the deep.'

The earliest boats known to archaeologists are the so-called 'log-boats' – dugout canoes made by hollowing out large tree trunks, Robinson Crusoe-style. Gary Momber and his team are excavating what they believe to be the oldest boat-building yard in the world, under 30 feet of water in the Solent, and it was log-boats that were apparently being built there. But at the time when Momber's Mesolithic craftsmen were living and working, there was no south coast, no England, no Isle of Wight and no France. Rather they occupied a river valley in the body of land that then joined Britain to the Continent. The remains of log-boats are always found in rivers and lakes, suggesting they were used for getting around within the interior of territories and seldom if ever on the open sea. Such vessels, made and used by hunter-gatherers, are found all over the world. But in Britain, during the Bronze Age, a unique class of sea-going boats came into play. These are the 'sewn-plank' boats, built of carefully shaped oak planks (and they are always made of oak) literally sewn together with 'withies' of twisted yew saplings. As far as we know, sewn-plank boats were made and used in Britain and nowhere else in the world.

This is appropriate for an island race, after all. As islanders off the north-west coast of Europe, the proto-British and Irish were subject to a unique set of circumstances. They were well aware of and heavily influenced by fashions and cultures on the Continent – from farming to changing tastes in pottery and fine jewellery – and if they wanted to be active participants in it all, then they had to evolve sophisticated approaches to crossing the sea that would otherwise have isolated them. So the land that would in due course witness an armada humbled, before eventually producing the greatest navy the world had seen, discovered early on that serious thought had to be applied to the business of matters maritime.

Between 1937 and 1963 a total of three sewn-plank boats were discovered on the banks of the River Humber in the East Riding of Yorkshire. Local man Dr Ted Wright found two of them, in 1937 and 1940, and they are impressive vessels even by modern standards. Measuring over 40 feet long by five and a half feet wide and made of oak planks three to four inches thick, the first one Wright unearthed, known as Ferriby 1 or F1, is big enough to carry as many as 20 people. The individual planks had first to be split from the tree trunk before the long edges were shaped and bevelled for a neater fit. Holes bored at intervals along the length of the planks enabled the yew withies to lash them tightly together into one composite hull. The lateral joints between the planks had been caulked with moss to help keep the water out and then topped with neatly fitting, slender laths of oak. Ferriby 2, or F2, was found by Wright in 1940 just tens of yards from the first, and was almost identical in terms of its construction. The last of them, F3, was discovered close by F1 and has yielded a radiocarbon date of 2030 BC, making it the earliest boat of its kind in Europe.

When Danish Vikings found their way to that part of the East Riding around the start of the ninth century AD, they called the place 'Ferja Bi' – meaning a 'place beside a ferry'. Given the prehistoric boats, the tradition of navigating the Humber was already ancient by then. Communities on either side of the estuary – in Yorkshire in the north and in the Lincolnshire Wolds in the south – clearly found it easiest to stay connected, one to another, by using the water rather than the land.

Another sewn-plank boat was found at nearby Kilnsea in 1996, two or three miles from the neck of Spurn Point, the appendix of sand that dangles into the North Sea and forms the northern bank of the mouth of the Humber Estuary. The remains of the Kilnsea boat were less to look at, essentially just a single, long oaken plank; but the evidence of integral cleats and other woodworking features meant it was clearly part of the tradition that had produced Ferriby 1. Of greater interest to archaeologists than the remains themselves, however, was their location. The Kilnsea boat had finished its last journey at what is a perfect point of departure to – or arrival from – destinations on the other side of the North Sea. Its resting place was a tantalising position at the beginning and end of sea-going voyages, within a landscape rich in the remains of prehistoric human habitation.

Nearly 6,000 years ago Neolithic farmers were at large in the area. Archaeologists have found at least one house as well as hearths that are suggestive of several more. Later the farmers built a circular monument, possibly a henge, and, later still, during the Bronze Age, a handful of burial cairns – one over the ruins of the house and another over one of the hearths. There is no obvious reason for the Neolithic and later occupation of the area subsequently used by the boat-builders. What has been found so far simply indicates the early farmers and their successors were colonising, exploiting and trying to make sense of their place in the area for hundreds if not thousands of years.

The practice of some kinds of ritual behaviour there, in that part of the Holderness region – monument-building, the burial of the dead alongside possible Bell Beakers and other grave goods – is made even more intriguing by the general absence of such activity in the rest of that part of Yorkshire.

Archaeologist Robert Van de Noort has suggested it was the building of boats and their use for voyages back and forth across the hostile North Sea that inspired the Bronze Age residents of Ferriby to bury their dead and think about the ancestors there. In a paper published in 2003 he wrote: 'Seafaring was imbued with "special meaning", and as an activity stood clearly outside the rhythm of daily life.' (Robert Louis Stevenson wrote, in *Virginibus Puerisque*, in 1881: 'Little do ye know your own blessedness; for to travel hopefully is a better thing than to arrive, and the true success is to labour.' The part of that thought, about travelling hopefully, has become a virtual cliché. But if Van de Noort and other like-minded archaeologists are right, then notions about the import-ance of the journey itself began in some people's minds as early as the beginning of the Bronze Age.)

He goes on to suggest that an elite group at the top of Bronze Age society may have sought further to underline their legitimacy by undertaking perilous journeys across the sea. It was not enough for such people simply to command and be in receipt of prestigious items from Continental Europe, like bronze axes and swords, and jewellery of gold. Some immeasurable part of the value was drawn from the hopeful journey itself, the journey to meet the makers and personally collect the items they had made, to benefit from the well of knowledge and experience from which such objects had sprung.

'If my suggestions are correct,' wrote Van de Noort, 'then the sea was perceived principally as a boundary. This was not a physical boundary, as the sewn-plank boats were able to navigate successfully across the sea in favourable conditions, but a liminal boundary. Without such a boundary function, the religious, social and political value of goods exchanged over long distances would have been severely lessened ... Crossing the boundary may have formed part of a rite of passage essential for young members of elite groups in Britain whose eligibility to rule and lead could be measured by the time spent away from home and the distance travelled.'

By far and away the most impressive of the sewn-plank boats found to date, however – and the single most moving and impressive archaeological artefact I have ever seen – is the so-called 'Dover Boat'. Given the significance of Dover today as a point of departure, and arrival, for millions of travellers, it is entirely appropriate that it was there, in the shadow of the White Cliffs, that archaeologists discovered such startling evidence of the sophistication of Bronze Age seamanship.

Dover has controlled the English Channel for longer than history records. It was once known as the 'Lock and Key of England' and has been an object of desire for many a would-be invader – from Julius Caesar to William the Conqueror and from Napoleon Bonaparte to Adolf Hitler. But today, with threats of foreign invasion long past, it is the safe harbour of Dover that still matters. As well as being a major port for every kind of trade good imaginable, Dover is the busiest passenger-ferry terminal in the world.

It was work to build a new section of road between Dover and the nearby town of Folkestone, in the autumn of 1992, that exposed the Dover Boat to the light of day after 3,500 years. Part of the job required the construction of a pedestrian underpass and so it was that archaeologists from Canterbury Archaeological Trust (CAT) found themselves slopping around in the cloying, clayey mud at the bottom of a 20-foot-deep waterlogged hole in search of any exposed evidence of the town's long history. Steel piles and concrete would shortly occupy the void and the team had just days to find and record any archaeology before it was obliterated for all time.

They had already carefully revealed, cleaned, photographed and drawn parts of Dover's medieval wall, then traces of a Roman-built harbour wall, when archaeologist Keith Parfitt began paying close attention to a piece of wood protruding from one side of the hole. Much to the inconvenience of the road-builders, the timber was quickly identified as part of the hull of a boat and construction work was initially called off for the day to let the essential work of excavation and recovery get properly under way.

Within hours the CAT team had established they were dealing with another sewn-plank boat, identical in many ways to Ferriby 1 and astonishingly well preserved. After eight frantically busy days – during which the road company had to absorb an expensive delay and allow for the construction of two coffer-dams to permit the removal of as much of the boat as possible – the team had done all they could. By 19 October the archaeologists had carefully lifted out between half and two-thirds of the whole vessel – around 30 feet of it. Dr Wright, discoverer of the Ferriby boats, had been consulted and had recommended the surviving timbers be cut into sections for easier removal from their tomb, and so in the end it was an enormous 10-piece jigsaw that had to be reassembled back in the lab.

The first priority was conservation. Three and a half millennia sealed deep underground within mud and clay had protected the timbers from almost all ravages of decay, but as soon as they returned to the light, the clock began ticking. When the Ferriby boats were discovered in the 1930s and 1940s, conservation was in its infancy – with the result that relatively little has been saved for posterity. But thanks to more modern expertise, the Dover Boat is now a jaw-dropping wonder of the archaeological world. The timbers were first soaked in liquid wax, which permeated the wood and so consolidated it and protected it from decomposition. The pieces were then quickly freeze-dried – a process that meant the boat could safely become a permanent exhibit in Dover Museum, within a huge, purpose-built, air-conditioned and temperature-controlled display case.

You have to go and see it – it is as simple as that. Any attempt at describing the feeling of standing beside those glossy timbers, blackened by their millennia underground, must fall short of the actual experience. I had known the Dover Boat existed and had seen both photographs and televised coverage of the discovery, but none of that prepared me for the impact of the artefact itself. While visitors are restricted to walking around the outside of the display case, I was allowed inside. Perhaps it was something to do with stepping from the museum gallery into the rarefied atmosphere that protects the wood and withies, but as I crossed the threshold and closed the door carefully behind me, I got the unmistakable feeling I was suddenly in the presence not of something, but of someone. I am an archaeologist, by nature drawn to old objects and likely to be impressed by them. But I can only say that the Dover Boat is different. You would not have to believe in ghosts to get the sense the thing is somehow haunted – if not by the people who designed, built and used it, then by their intentions. Something tangible of another age, like the atmosphere within the tunnels and galleries of the Neolithic flint mines at Grime's Graves, hangs in the air.

And again, as at Goldcliff beside the Mesolithic footprints, and in the company of the bones of the Amesbury Archer, there was that sense of intruding, of seeing something that had been put away out of sight, entitled to remain there. Like Goldilocks we enter the homes of others and pick over private things, casting aside those that do not please us in search of what is just right.

It is believed that when complete the Dover Boat would have been as much as 60 feet long, and part of its power to enthrall is in its sheer size. With around 30 intact feet on display it has an overpowering presence. Things made and crafted by mankind are utterly unlike treasures and glories of the natural world. To place your hand on a surface worked by another person, the same and not the same, and thousands of years ago, should be and is deeply moving. Above all, when you look at something as sophisticated and complex as the Dover Boat, you are gifted a glimpse of how people thought, how they identified challenges and set out to meet them.

The vessel is comprised essentially of four long oak planks, each carefully worked with axes and tools of stone and, of course, bronze. It is thought people who had been part of a tradition of making curraghs and coracles – by stitching animal hides together with sinew around a wicker frame – simply adapted the same technique so they could stitch wooden planks together with twisted saplings. In the case of the Dover Boat, those withies survive in the same condition in which their Bronze Age users last saw them. They are humbling – the knots fixing them in place tied 3,500 years ago by hands the same as ours.

Unlike Clive O'Gibney's ocean-going curragh, it seems there was no sail in the sewn-plank boats. Instead they were powered by oars or paddles – perhaps as many as nine or ten pairs. The interior is big enough to permit a fairly large cargo: some passengers as well as a considerable volume of goods like textiles, or metal tools and weapons. It would have needed skilled handling even in inland waters, and the prospect of taking such a vessel across the North Sea hardly bears thinking about. For one thing, no amount of moss caulking could have kept such a construction truly watertight. So for the duration of any voyage, some of the passengers and crew would have been required to help in the constant, anxious job of bailing.

The excavators of the Ferriby and Kilnsea boats were generally of the opinion they had been hauled ashore and left on dry land – perhaps with a view to carrying out repairs, or just to wait for further journeys that were never made. The near-perfect preservation of the Dover Boat, however, enabled archaeologists to imagine an altogether more thought-provoking final chapter for their own find. A closer examination of the yew withies – the 'threads' holding the planks together – showed that some of them had been deliberately sliced through. The bow end of the boat revealed a missing section as well – as though some large, perhaps carved and decorated figurehead had been removed too, maybe to be used again.

In short it seemed the Dover Boat had been scuttled. The archaeologists had noticed during the excavation that the vessel's final resting place had been in the shallows of a stream, one long vanished and buried beneath many feet of sediments that had built up on top during the intervening millennia (it was that same build-up, in fact, that had so safely sealed and protected the timbers).

At some point while the boat was still perfectly serviceable someone – presumably the kind of high-status individual who could commission and command such an impressive craft – had decided the day had come to repay a debt. The same belief that had convinced Neolithic flint miners to return some of their axes to the Earth, from which they came, moved a Bronze Age boat owner to give back his prize.

People in the ancient past seem to have accepted they were in a constantly evolving relationship, one that tied together their belongings, the landscape in which they lived and also something unseen. They understood too that that relationship carried an obligation. Death followed life and debts had to be repaid – so that a treasured and priceless bronze axe had, at some point, to be buried in the ground or thrown into a river; a polished flint mace-head, symbolic of incomprehensible power, had finally to go into a tomb alongside the ancestors; and a perfectly good boat, crucial for connections to people far away, must one day be put beyond the use of man.

It is hard to understand. Early bronze swords – rapiers really, a foot or so long and tapered to use a minimum of the precious metal – must have been as valuable and as cherished as a gold pocket watch handed from a father to a son. And yet we find them again and again, deliberately snapped and thrown away, usually into rivers or lakes. Picture the scene, as some warrior or chieftain led a procession down to a riverside. There on the bank he took his sword from its sheath and, after facing the crowd and holding it above his head, he suddenly turned his back on them. All at once he crouched, fiercely bent the blade across one knee, repeatedly, until the thing snapped in two. These pieces he then cast into the waters, never to be seen or touched again by man or woman. This is a glimpse of Bronze Age religion. We know about it only because of the things recovered, but water was certainly central to it. In England it seems that rivers flowing into the east were deemed particularly special, perhaps because they headed back towards some ancient homeland of the ancestors. It is from such waters that offerings and gifts are recovered – swords and cooking pots of metal that, although still prized, had been given back to the world.

By around 1500 BC, something like a thousand years had passed since the arrival of the Beaker People, with their metal magic. During those centuries Britain had become home to a wealthy, internationally connected elite. All of the available evidence suggests the rich were few in number and while they sat at the top of society, the practicalities of life had changed hardly a jot for the vast majority of the population of perhaps half a million people.

A sense of something spiritual was all around for sure, and had been since time immemorial. There were ancestors to consider, heaven also. By the middle of the second millennium BC there were earth- and water-bound gods to take into account too – those that had to be appeased and appealed to by the giving of gifts.

Great trees that had been on the land as long as the reach of tribal memory, rocky outcrops, boulders, mountains – any and all and more besides may have seemed special and likely to be home to deities worthy of worship. Water and watery places appear to have been held in even greater reverence, perhaps suggesting portals between worlds, and in one form or another command some vestige of respect even today. Natural springs that were once home to this or that god are still revered in locations the length and breadth of the country. Islands and islets were chosen as retreats for hermits and other holy men and women right up into the modern era. Wells and fountains are still offered coins in return for good fortune and even bends and meanders of rivers became home to great abbeys and churches.

But almost all of the people were still farmers, and despite the technological advances they were seemingly still fairly mobile, moving within the landscape as the seasons dictated. Apart from a few exceptions there is scant evidence of permanent homes or settlements. During the centuries following 1500 BC, however, all of that began to change.

Archaeologist Francis Pryor began excavating the site of Flag Fen, near Peterborough in Cambridgeshire, in 1982. A writer too, Pryor is first and foremost a working farmer who grew up within a large, rural family living among the chalk hills and fields of Cambridgeshire and Hertfordshire. Like the Bronze Age and later peoples he has made his archaeological speciality, he has the land in his bones.

There is really no other site in Britain quite like Flag Fen. Sometime around 1300 BC there was a man-made timber causeway running for about two-thirds of a mile across what was then an increasingly waterlogged landscape. The climate at the time was becoming wetter and wetter and farming peoples had to build such walkways as means of getting between the steadily shrinking areas of land dry enough to support crops and animals. Ironically it is modern drainage, to reclaim the land for farming, that has dried out the landscape of which Flag Fen is a part – and which is threatening the survival of timber and other organic material that had been preserved for thousands of years precisely because it was under water.

Pryor and his team have found many examples of personal items cast or carefully placed into the water either side of the walkway, and one theory has it that Bronze Age peoples were asking their gods to stop the rain, stop taking away the land. In addition to metal items there are animal bones and also many white beach pebbles – suggesting people were coming to Flag Fen from far away in order to make their votive offerings.

As well as evidence of ritual and religion, Pryor's work has also found plentiful traces of the day-to-day. A section of the timber walkway has been preserved in-situ, covered by part of a purpose-built visitor centre and protected from drying out by a steady, comforting spray of mist that keeps it waterlogged.

But in many ways the most instructive part of the visitor experience at Flag Fen are the reconstructed Bronze Age houses. Archaeologists find traces of foundations of such structures, but the only way to get even a hint of what life within must have been like for the occupants is to use the available evidence – and best guesses – to rebuild a few.

Those at Flag Fen are a collection of roundhouses, with walls of timber posts and wattle, daubed with dry clay-mud. Families or extended families of perhaps a dozen people shared the large circular room, with its central hearth. The interior might have been partly subdivided, perhaps around the perimeter, but it was undoubtedly a more communal way of living than anything we are used to, with much less importance granted to personal space or privacy. The roundhouses are roofed with turf and thatch and in the gloom of the windowless interiors it is just possible to catch a glimpse of at least the setting for Bronze Age family life. 'People were very relaxed, they knew their place in society, they ate well,' said Pryor. 'The archaeological evidence doesn't suggest that there was, let's say, an underclass – a lower class that wasn't properly nourished. I mean, whenever you dig up a Bronze Age burial, nine times out of ten or ninety times out of a hundred, the body is well nourished, the bones are well formed, so they had plenty of calcium and they ate a decent diet. One of the things that there isn't much evidence for in the Bronze Age is actual strife. The population hadn't got so big that people were at each other's throats. You know, everyone knew what land they owned ... people lived in families ... your week was organised. Life, I think, in the Bronze Age would have been pretty good.'

The idea of living in families within permanent homes – houses that are built to last a lifetime and that are themselves part of permanent settlements – sounds utterly unremarkable in our modern world. But it was all a construct, a concept that was invented in the Bronze Age and matured and became ever more complicated from that time on. Whether we choose to live in a village, a town or a city, our circumstances are altered only by scale. Unless you live in some remote location, out of sight of other houses or the roads that connect them, then you are living in a way that was unknown in Britain until around 1,500 years ago. The decision to stay in one house for years, perhaps a lifetime, is entirely at odds with the approach to existence practised by our kind for almost all of human history.

Now we settle for the same views, through the same windows, day after day and month after month. We tolerate neighbours on the other side of the wall, or separated from us only by a few feet of garden and a fence. We see the same faces, the same people walking the same streets. This is, to us, normality; but until 3,500 years ago at the very most, it was shockingly new.

The best-preserved evidence in the whole of Europe of the advent of this radical new way of living is on the windswept moors of Dartmoor. Covering over 360 square miles of the county of Devon, Dartmoor today is a wild and intimidating landscape. No doubt the trees began falling to Neolithic stone axes, but during some later period of improved climate a steadily expanding population started spreading into upland zones like Dartmoor, a place that might once have been on the periphery. The most visible features now are the tors, the exposed granite summits of the hills. They are other-worldly, strangely angular and even up close have something of the look of ancient masonry. Natural cracks and fissures in the rocks seem too straight and ordered and often the effect is of looking at the massive foundations of giants' castles, rather than anything natural.

Threaded between the tors, though, and running for miles in faint criss-crossing straight lines that turn whole areas into enormous patchworks, are walls built by Bronze Age farmers. These are the Dartmoor reaves – boundaries of earth and stone that enclose the land into regular squares and rectangles. More than anything else, it is the scale of the endeavour that boggles the mind. This is a field system that covers tens of thousands of acres and, even more astonishingly, it does not appear to have grown piecemeal. Instead the whole is so ordered it was most likely a grand scheme laid out in advance, and then set in place all in one go by a highly organised society.

Some of the reaves are aligned on older structures, such as Late Neolithic or Early Bronze Age burial mounds, but in the main they pay little heed to the natural topography. It is as though the plan was drawn up by someone, or some group, who had not even seen all of the land their scheme would cover – so that the reaves crossed rivers and leapt off cliffs.

Archaeologist Richard Bradley is one of many who have studied the field systems and noticed how some of the major lines seem to have been orientated on the winter and summer solstices. Where visible, this alignment has been followed even when it has meant some of the resultant fields are cast into shadow by the natural topography.

Partly because field walls are so utilitarian, so simply functional, and partly because the passage of time has diminished much of the scheme to the point where it can only be properly appreciated from the air, the Dartmoor reaves were for long overlooked as evidence of great endeavour or effort. For a long time too they were thought by many archaeologists to have been the work of later societies – at least those of the Iron Age. But more recently both their early date and the colossal achievement they represent have begun to be fully realised.

In *The Prehistory of Britain and Ireland*, Bradley wrote about how generations of archaeologists were lulled into underestimating what they were looking at on Dartmoor because burial mounds – the monuments more traditionally used as markers for the ambitions of ancient society – became less impressive during the Bronze Age: 'It is easy to be misled by the evidence of burial mounds which became much smaller during this phase, for the amount of labour invested in the subdivision of the land was probably equivalent to that devoted to monument-building in earlier periods,' he wrote. 'It would be quite wrong to suppose that workforces could no longer be mobilised for large-scale projects – it is the nature of those tasks that had changed.'

I visited the Dartmoor reaves with another Bronze Age specialist, archaeologist Niall Sharples, who carefully explained how much the evidence of the reaves – and more particularly the houses clustered within them – has to say about the social revolution that was taking place while they were being planned and built.

In contrast to the timber, wattle and daub houses reconstructed by Francis Pryor and his team at Flag Fen, those on Dartmoor were built, at least in part, of the naturally occurring granite. No doubt this was for straightforward reasons – a general absence of trees but plentiful boulders – but the circular floor plans defined by walls of huge stones only add to the air of permanence, the intention to stay put for a lifetime.

Sharples explained how the interior would have been lived in as a communal space, but one lightly subdivided into areas of different activity – sleeping, weaving, tool-making, cooking. The point though was that a man and his new wife would have moved into such a house and then spent their adult lives there. Gone were the days of moving through the landscape from pasture to pasture, opening up new fields on virgin soil. Settlements were not entirely unknown before 1500 BC, but from that time on they became increasingly commonplace, spreading onto every part of the available arable land as the population steadily expanded.

There was something else new as well. For the first time there was a seeming determination to impose a man-made design onto the natural world. The Bronze Age communities that divided and subdivided Dartmoor were fundamentally different, in terms of their thinking about the world, from all those that had gone before them. It appears that less importance was being placed on the great monuments that had overshadowed people's lives for thousands of years. Rather than congregating within a circle of standing stones to listen to a priest interpret the cosmos for them, now people were making their homes and fields the centre of their existence.

If there was praying to be done – favours asked of the gods or precious things surrendered – then that kind of thing could go on now within the home. It is almost as though, as the Bronze Age wore on, 'English' men (and presumably 'Scots', 'Welsh' and 'Irish' men as well) began to see their homes as their castles. Ties to the land that were once tribal and ancestral had become personal and practical. Domestic life was at the heart of everything those people thought and believed and did. Britain had come a long way since 2500 BC and the arrival of the first metal-workers. During the course of 10 centuries or so people had begun to settle down and to build the kind of lives more familiar to us today.

Archaeologists like Sharples believe there could have been something of a sexual revolution as well. Now that there were fixed settlements, people became familiar not just with those living right next door but also with the inhabitants of farmsteads and hamlets over the hill, in the next valley, or even further afield. If you sent a daughter or a son to be wed to the son or daughter of a neighbouring family, then you would have an ally. Over generations your family, your clan, might build whole networks of alliances – friends who could be called upon for help when times were bad: Bronze Age insurance policies.

Those early settlements on Dartmoor did not last, however. During the next few centuries – and probably as a result of a deteriorating climate combined with over-farming of the land – the upland moors and other peripheral areas were rendered infertile. Permanent though they had seemed, built of stone and imbued with lifetimes of meaning and significance, they were nonetheless abandoned, and for ever. The field systems, laid out with such optimism and so much vision, were left to be submerged beneath the tireless, ever-advancing peat.

Through thousands of years of prehistory the building blocks of the world we know today had all been invented and set in place: society and class; religion and trade. Between 1500 and 1000 BC – the later Bronze Age – the seeds of the first permanent villages were sown. In time, cities would grow too. From the strange, distant, almost unknowable days of the first hunters, a Britain recognisable to us had begun to emerge.

The ice retreated for the last time around 10,000 years ago. Shifts and innovations in technology and in belief had laid the foundations of modern Britain. In so many ways it was as though we had reached a kind of young adulthood. We had the keys to our own front doors. The world beyond was there to be shaped in our own image, by us as individuals, looking after our own families. But with that realisation around 3,000 years or so ago – that we really could impose our own vision of the world onto the Britain we had claimed – came a suitably grown-up responsibility: What kind of world did we want to shape? What kind of Britain did we want to build?

Today we live with the consequences of the answers our ancestors found to those questions – because in the great scheme of time we are still busy trying to find ways to relate to one another. And their responsibility has been handed down to us as well, like an old oak clock that has counted the passing of all the years from then to now and that keeps on ticking.

During the later years of the time we have called the Bronze Age we came into our inheritance. Once upon a time there was more than enough for everyone. As the Stone Age ended, giving way to worlds of metal, some few of us realised there were consequences, accounts to be reckoned and prices to be paid. Despite their caution and their thrift, too many of us began to squander what we had been given. Whether the debt is too great now ever to be settled in our favour, only time will tell. Soon we will pass the inheritance on again – or at least what remains of it – to our own descendants. What will they think? How will they remember us?

5

IRON

'No man is an Iland, intire of itselfe; every man is a peece of the Continent, a part of the maine; if a Clod bee washed away by the Sea, Europe is the lesse, as well as if a Promontorie were, as well as if a Manor of thy friends or of thine owne were; any mans death diminishes me, because I am involved in Mankinde; And therefore never send to know for whom the bell tolls; It tolls for thee.'

John Donne, Meditation XVII,
Devotions upon Emergent Occasions

Our ancient past is to me a *Mary Celeste*: so much of the stuff of those long-ago lives has been left behind, sound and usable – often, it seems, by owners who had every intention of returning to pick up again where they had left off.

Before she became a byword for mystery, the *Mary Celeste* was a US brigantine merchant ship bound for the Straits of Gibraltar in November 1872. She was found perfectly intact but abandoned in the mid-Atlantic on 4 December of that year. She had been at sea for a month and still had six weeks' worth of food and water on board. Her cargo was untouched, along with all the personal possessions and valuables belonging to her passengers and experienced crew – none of whom were ever seen or heard from again.

As in the case of that infamous ship, the places and possessions of our ancestors sometimes appear to await the return of folk who have only this moment walked away, briefly distracted. The stones, bones, vessels and the rest of their detritus make us ask: 'Where did the people go ... when, and why?'

It is archaeologists who seek to board the silent past, in the manner of a salvage team, in hope of discovering what happened there. Often they find the places still set upon the table, the food half-eaten on the plates. All seems well and only the people are missing. The absence of the inhabitants of those moments and millennia that went before is sometimes made all the more poignant by the seeming richness of the cultures and societies left behind. Often it is whole villages, like Orkney's Skara Brae, where unanswered questions pace the flagstones like ghosts. Anyone walking around that place today must surely wonder why such a perfect home, filled with precious belongings, was cut adrift.

By the Bronze Age, in Britain, our ancestors had created an obviously complete and complex world. Not just technologically advanced – with all the practical necessities of farming life – but socially and psychologically sophisticated as well. By at least the Late Bronze Age, from around the start of the first millennium BC onwards, the peoples of Britain were deeply embedded within home-grown societies, many of which were intricately connected to Continental Europe and perhaps the wider world beyond.

Some of the people had found satisfactory (to them at least) answers to many of the eternal questions thrown up by life and the universe. All in all it was a world that was beginning to suggest some of the forms and structures of our own. People had grown used to living in permanent settlements – in hamlets, homesteads and even villages – surrounded by neighbours whose faces were almost as familiar to them, on a day-to-day basis, as those of their own families. They had accepted the need for daily, weekly, monthly rounds of chores – accepted too that they were dependent upon their land and therefore bound to it. For a species that had spent the vast majority of its time living the nomadic life of the hunter and the gatherer, just these steps alone had made for a profound and deeply transforming social revolution.

Archaeologists have also established that much of the Bronze

Age in Britain unfolded during a climatic golden time, so that lives then were cradled in a reassuringly warm and settled world that was kind to crops, livestock and humankind alike. It was a climate that helped generate and sustain a sense of permanence, a feeling that this was the way things had always been and also the way they would remain.

That time of plenty had led to steady population growth and with more people came both the opportunity and the wherewithal to clear yet more land and grow yet more crops. Settled civilisation seemed irresistibly on the rise and a safe, domesticated world was spreading across the land – even into upland and other zones that had previously been unproductive, if not sterile.

It would be wrong to imagine the living was easy, by our standards at the very least; but for a people coming of age and into their own it was a time of relative calm and security after thousands upon thousands of years of dramatic struggles for survival and of often turbulent upheavals in society. You might justifiably say the people living in Britain in the centuries either side of 1000 BC had never had it so good. The crops were in the fields, the animals too; bronze finery spoke of friendships and ties that spread out over the land like spiders' webs; sun, Moon and stars moved above, counting the passing years as reliably, as comfortably, as the heart-beats of an old grandfather clock. Perhaps our Bronze Age relatives felt they were masters of the universe itself.

But all those advances towards a world we would recognise as somehow modern were the product of more than just the passing of time. It had not been enough for the species simply to survive all those uncounted hundreds of thousands of years; technological and social advance are not the rewards for just beating the odds and staying alive. Ever since I was a teenage student of archaeology I have been troubled by one nagging question above every other: how come we advanced at all? That I have been born into a world of space travel, modern medicine, particle physics, smart phones, budget international airlines, the Internet and all the rest of it, is a constant wonder to me, and a mystery. How – and more importantly why – have some of us come so far?

Of course, the advances are not uniform. The world of man-made wonders that we inhabit is not evenly spread across the face of this Earth. All around, in parts of Africa, India, Asia, Australasia and even the northernmost parts of North America, are peoples still living lives that would, in large part at least, be recognisable not just to our Bronze Age ancestors but even to our most distant hunting and gathering relations as well. The world of our ancient past is therefore not nearly as far off as we sometimes allow ourselves to believe. We have been primitives before and maybe we will be cast down there again in the future, by hubris if nothing else.

Ferdinand Magellan was the commander of the first fleet of European ships to encounter the land and inhabitants of the most southerly extremes of the continent of South America. Portuguese by birth, he had nonetheless thrown in his lot with King Charles I of Spain in order to secure the backing for an expensive voyage in search of a westward route to the so-called 'Spice Islands' of Indonesia.

Having departed the city of Seville in August 1519, Magellan and his men finally succeeded in finding a way through the southern tip of South America, from the Atlantic Ocean and into the Pacific, by the end of the November of the following year. Having passed All Saints' Day (1 November) en route, Magellan named the 370-odd-mile passage from east to west 'Estrecho de Todos los Santos' – All Saints' Channel. The way is known nowadays, however, as the Magellan Strait.

It was therefore from the bridge of his flagship, *Trinidad*, that Magellan became the first European to lay eyes on those lands just east of the Pacific side of the strait. Because the new ocean he encountered there seemed so calm he called it 'Mar Pacifico', but he was at least as curious about the myriad fires he saw dotted all along the forbidding coastline of the archipelago making up the continent's southernmost tip, off the *Trinidad*'s port side. So numerous were the bonfires and campfires, so much a part of the landscape did they seem, he named the place 'Tierra del Fuego' – the Land of Fire.

Magellan correctly assumed they were lit by native peoples living in those lands; and in fact he feared the locals had gathered to prepare an ambush for any landing parties. It was therefore Europeans on subsequent voyages through the Magellan Strait who first spent time among the tribes that had passed the millennia since the Old World's Ice Age facing the challenges of 'the uttermost part of the Earth'.

They are mostly gone now, those original inhabitants of the Land of Fire – dispersed like the smoke from their ancient hearths. They are remembered collectively by history as the Fuegians, but once upon a time they had names of their own, like the Yaghan and the Haush, the Alcaluf and the Ona. All of the tribes on those islands were nomadic, living by hunting and gathering, but there were considerable differences between their individual cultures, languages, lifestyles and temperaments.

No lesser an observer than Charles Darwin spent time, during the voyage of the *Beagle* (1831–6), documenting the ways of the peoples he found clinging to life in that unforgiving and often inhospitable environment. He found the Ona, who lived inland, to be physically larger than their neighbours and to be given to warlike and terrifying behaviour, so he named them 'the wretched lords of this wretched land'. The Ona at least wore clothes of animal fur and shoes of skin or leather, and adorned themselves both with jewellery made from the bones and tendons of the animals they hunted and also with body paint. Fighting was their principal distraction, however, and they spent as much time as possible making life miserable for their more peaceable neighbours, like the Yaghan, who greatly feared them.

The Yaghan spent as much time in their canoes, exploiting the marine resources, as they did on land (maybe in no small part to steer clear of the Ona). With harpoons they hunted sea mammals and fish, as well as collecting shellfish from the shallows. Unlike the bellicose Ona, however, the Yaghan wore almost no clothing. Despite the hardships of biting winds, and of ice and snow encrusting the landscape for much of the year, they made do by smearing their bodies with oil from fish and other prey. The fires that had been spotted from offshore by Magellan were absolutely central to the lives of Yaghan and Ona alike – the Yaghan even going so far as to keep fires burning within their wood and bark canoes while they braved the coldest sea crossings.

Darwin himself wondered at the hardy nature of people he watched moving about nearly naked and barefoot in an often frozen land; and it is important to remember that the members of these tribes continued to live that way right up into the nineteenth and even the twentieth centuries.

The discovery of gold, and then oil, would eventually bring an intolerable flood of Europeans, as well as Chileans and Argentinians from further north, into the undisturbed fastnesses of the tribes. What hitherto unknown Old World diseases like smallpox and measles could not accomplish by themselves, the genocidal practices of land- and mineral-hungry incomers completed. After more than ten thousand years on the archipelago the native peoples – the peaceful Yaghan and the warlike Ona alike – were wiped out in a few decades, so that today not even their languages survive.

But it is not the end of those tribes, who lived out of sight and out of mind of our complicated modern world for so long, that should fascinate us most of all. Rather we should be preoccupied by any people, like the Yaghan, who survived as long as they did in such a physically demanding, even cruel environment without ever finding either the need or the wherewithal to make clothes to proof themselves against the always enervating cold? Some anthropologists have supposed life was so hard there on that southernmost tip of South America that material culture was reduced to an absolute minimum. The constant demands of hunting and gathering food, and tending the fires around which they erected their flimsy shelters, apparently left no time for anything but the barest accomplishments.

For all the absence of personal belongings, of things, the cultures of the Fuegians had allowed for complex mythologies and attempts at understanding the world around them. The stories they told each other as they huddled by their fires were populated by fantastic heroes who had carved the islands, and the waterways that separated them, and by sacred hummingbirds and sea lions, albatrosses and foxes.

Yaghan and Ona alike had shamans in their midst – priest-like figures gifted with special powers such as healing and foresight. But for all their thinking and dreaming, understanding and questioning, not one shivering Yaghan ever bothered to make him- or herself a blanket, or to take up an animal skin for a cloak.

The Fuegians' realm remained trapped in a Stone Age while the Old World of Europe was convulsed, down through the millennia, by one technological or philosophical upheaval after another. Magellan's sailing ships arrived on their horizon like craft from a distant planet. And so perhaps the Fuegians' lack of technological invention in the face of what most of us would consider necessity is better explained by their remoteness from all others.

However their earliest ancestors reached the end of the Earth (explanations for their presence in the archipelago include everything from descent from far-travelled Australian Aborigines to long-forgotten connections to native American populations further north), they established themselves upon a group of islands that are remote even from much of South America itself. While they managed to survive and to perpetuate themselves among the windswept, icy plains and waterways, they were and remained forever cut off from other humankind. Denied the throughput of the new ideas that comes from contact with incomers, their material culture remained basic and primitive. Not for the Yaghan or the Ona the arrival of immigrant farmers, itinerant metal-workers or evangelists of new religions. The possibility of food surplus and craft specialisation never came and in their absence there was no time for social sophistication.

We in the north and west of Europe have benefited, for

millennia, from the constant arrival of the new. At the end of the last Ice Age our hunting ancestors penetrated the land that would become Britain. They were alone there for a long time but were eventually joined by those who could teach them the skills of agriculture and stock-rearing. Later came the magicians who could source and conjure metal, and after them a steady flow of incomers, bringing more and more of the modern world. Ideas of all kinds blew in like seeds, and kept on coming. No doubt revelatory ideas occurred to individuals among the Yaghan from time to time as well; but for want of enough like-minded fellows to help and to encourage the thoughts, the seeds fell on stony ground and failed to germinate.

By luck the people of Britain are descended from populations that learned ways to grow so numerous there was both the time and the opportunity for ideas and technologies to take root and flourish. Furthermore they found themselves, by a fluke of geography, at the end of a long road – one marched over again and again by travellers moving from east to west, technological evangelists carrying the future in their wake. While the natives of Tierra del Fuego had lived – and then died out – in stultifying isolation in a cul-de-sac, the inhabitants of Britain prospered at one end of the busiest cultural motorway the world has yet seen. Then as now it was connections, or the lack of them, that made the difference.

It has been estimated that Late Bronze Age Britain, from around 1000 BC onwards, was home to about half a million souls. Since at least the onset of the Neolithic, perhaps 4000 years BC, people there had been finding ways to make and maintain connections between one another – with neighbours close at hand, populations on the mainland of Europe hundreds or even thousands of miles away, and many others in between.

It had started out with the designation of special meeting places in the landscape – huge enclosures where scattered families and tribes could come together at certain times of the year to share food and ideas, find marriage partners, settle territorial disputes and generally catch up with one another's lives and times. Gradually the ways in which people sought to maintain those connections became more and more sophisticated. Eventually many of them found it most effective to demonstrate and reinforce their ties by giving and receiving gifts. At first it was objects of stone – axes in particular, and preferably made from rock obtained from distant mountaintops – that were passed between groups. But archaeologists have long accepted that the advent of metal technology served to intensify the obsession with the exchange of special possessions. Eventually it was items fashioned from bronze that became crucial to society – the metal acting as a kind of glue that held the whole intricate system together.

And along the way towards the establishment of that Bronze Age status quo, there had been a subtle realisation for at least some of the people: it was not just the metal objects that were portable and transferable. So too were the power and prestige that special things represented. Once it had been a priestly class that emerged as society's elite – those whose understanding of the movements of the heavens, and apparent sensitivity to the moods of the ancestors, set them apart from others. By the later stages of the Bronze Age, however, it was the control and movement of metal that separated the haves from the have-nots.

Some of the grassy slopes at Deckler's Cliff, in the East Portlemouth area of Devon overlooking Seacombe Sand, are marked by a patchwork of fields. The boundaries that define them are best viewed from a distance. On closer inspection it turns out the straight, dark lines, so obvious from a mile away, are swathes of bracken growing downslope from long, low banks of heaped earth and stone. It is the banks that are the true boundaries but those have been so eroded and reduced by the passage of time, smothered by encroaching pasture, as to be difficult to appreciate up close. They are in fact the remains of field systems laid out by farmers during the Bronze Age, and would once have been used for growing oats and rye, or managing sheep and cattle. The portion that survives (largely because it is on land too steep to have been of interest since) may be as little as one sixteenth of the original system. Only the Dartmoor reaves were more ambitious. These are yet more survivals of ancient everyday life – the lifestyle of the mass of the population, and one that changed hardly at all for thousands of years.

Evidence of part of what was new and different about the later Bronze Age is, however, to be found not on land but beneath the sea, further along the Devon coast. The South West Maritime Archaeological Group began diving the clear, shallow waters off the coast at Salcombe some 15 years ago and were accustomed to finding metal items and other artefacts dating from various historical periods. In 2009, armed with their specialised underwater metal detectors, they began recovering small lumps of copper scattered near the base of a rocky reef. Soon the number of finds had increased to the point where it became apparent they had to be part of the cargo of a sunken vessel.

Shipwrecks are hardly unusual off the Devon coast (or indeed any other part of the coastline of these British and Irish isles) and the SWMAG divers are familiar with many. This one was different, however. During the past couple of years the volunteers have recovered over 300 ingots of copper and tin, bronze knives, fragments of gold jewellery and an almost perfectly preserved bronze sword blade. Analysis of the finds has established that the cargo they have been recovering belonged to a vessel that foundered a few hundred yards offshore from Salcombe no less than 3,000 years ago.

Having made my first real dive on Garry Momber's Mesolithic boatyard, in the notoriously soupy conditions of the Solent, Salcombe Bay sounded positively Caribbean by comparison. There was talk of white sand and no less than 10 metres of visibility on good days and I was persuaded to double my tally of open-water dives by going in search of a Bronze Age shipwreck.

Dave Parham, a marine archaeologist from Bournemouth University, was my guide for the day – and the man tasked with persuading me it was perfectly reasonable to go into the sea with a battery-powered metal detector. No matter what they tell you, there is undoubtedly something surreal about donning head-phones 30 feet underwater and listening for telltale electronic bleeps and squawks – evidence of lost metal – in precisely the same way any metal detectorist would do in a farmer's field. Strange or not, the simple fact that three millennia had long since done for the vessel itself meant it was only by finding more of its cargo of metal that we could hope to pinpoint the location of the wreck.

The water was every bit as clear as I had been promised (and also mercifully free of the powerful tidal pull that had added to my overall anxiety when I had floundered around, half-blind, in the sediments on the seabed off the coast of the Isle of Wight), so that I was even able to relax and pay attention to the sub-sea terrain. Clearly visible, rising up from the white shell-sand of the seabed were vertical cliffs of rock – presumably some of the same that had contributed to the demise of that Bronze Age ship. No doubt bad weather had been the primary cause of the disaster that had befallen vessel and crew, with waves agitated by reefs of rock conspiring to overwhelm them and send men and metal alike straight to the bottom.

My own attempts at submarine metal detecting proved fruitless: neither bleep nor squawk was to be heard and I even began to wonder if the whole exercise was an elaborate practical joke at my expense. But after just a few minutes one of Dave's diving col-leagues approached and signalled we should follow him. He led us along the face of a reef and made straight for a large boulder on the seabed. Underneath it he had planted his most recent finds, made just moments before. Into my Neoprene-gloved hand he dropped what looked at first glance like a couple of sea-worn pebbles, except their weight was out of proportion to their size – they were strangely heavy. They were in fact lumps of copper about the size of gaming chips. Three millennia spent rolling around among the sands and rocks of the seabed had given them knobbly, irregular shapes – like candle wax that had melted and then hardened once more. But they were, unmistakably, pieces of metal.

Through the earpiece in my diver's mask I heard Dave explaining they were fragments of a large copper ingot – part of the stock in trade of men who made their living transporting the raw materials of bronze around Britain and Europe 3,000 years ago and more. Though their vessel had long since broken up, I imagined them aboard something like the Dover Boat.

Back on the dive boat we returned our finds to the air for the first time since the tragedy that had consigned them to the deep so very long ago. In the summer sunlight they had that familiar warm, rosy glow that makes copper instantly recognisable. Dave said the total weight of copper and tin recovered by the team already amounted to something like 13 stones – a huge amount to have survived so long on the seabed – and that they had found much more than just ingot fragments.

Next he revealed the beautiful bronze sword blade, elegantly shaped like a lizard's tongue – the same that had done so much to prove the age of the cargo. If the ingots were strangely impersonal, like any scrap metal, the sword spoke of an owner, and of a life lost at sea. Dave suggested the crewmen aboard the vessel would have been well aware of the colossal value of the material they were transporting, and would have armed themselves so they could fight off any would-be pirates bent on helping themselves to the loot. No Bronze Age man would willingly have been parted from such a blade.

It turns out the ingots tell their own story – one almost as engaging as thoughts of ancient mariners and their forgotten fates. Analysis of the copper and tin recovered from the Salcombe wreck reveals they were not mined from the south-west of England – nor, in fact, from anywhere in Britain. Copper is not all the same and varies in composition from place to place. Science can therefore reveal the place of origin for any given sample. The atomic signature of the Salcombe finds suggests the majority of the metal had come originally from locations scattered across the European mainland.

By the time of the Salcombe wreck, trade and exchange of bronze had created an intricate network of connections reaching throughout Britain and Continental Europe. While it is possible the men lost off the Devon coast had been moving their cargo around Britain as part of a domestic supply chain, it is just as likely they were part of a long line of international trade. The Salcombe wreck is therefore a snapshot of metal trade in action. Scattered on the seabed off that part of the Devon coast is a cargo actually en route – heading either to or from Britain. Given the volume of metal on board it is reasonable to think of the Salcombe craft as a sort of bulk carrier. That the metal is a collection of material from many countries is as clear a demonstration as we could wish for of just how interconnected the disparate populations of Late Bronze Age Europe actually were.

Trade is a concept easily understood in our own modern world – but generally only on our own modern, consumerist terms. Commodities that are either necessities of life – like fuel, food, clothing and means of shelter – or innumerable luxuries – like white goods, electronic gadgets, jewellery and toys – are sourced at their point of production and transported into the hands of those able and willing to pay for them. At the moment money changes hands the commodity – be it a bag of coal, a barrel of oil, a mobile phone or a cuddly toy – is seen to belong to the buyer. He or she has established ownership of it. It is all quite cold-blooded, straightforward and devoid of any deeper meaning.

But in order to begin to understand what started to happen during the period of time archaeologists have called the Late Bronze Age, it is vital to allow that, for perhaps thousands of years, people in the past may have interpreted the comings and goings of things in a profoundly different way from us – and that ownership often had nothing whatever to do with it.

Many archaeologists are increasingly open to the possibility that individuals in the ancient past might not have seen themselves as owning much of anything. The land they lived on and from which they produced their food, the food itself, the stone and timber from which they built their homes, the fuels they collected to provide warmth and light – none of it belonged to any given individual in quite the way we understand. Land and resources were held in common by the whole group.

This much is straightforward enough, but the concept becomes more challenging when extended to objects. If we follow the theory to its logical conclusion, then the items so treasured by archaeologists and museum curators and which are used to categorise whole ages of our history – polished stone axes; carved flint mace-heads; bronze axes, knives, cooking pots and swords – can only be fully understood if seen through ancient eyes. More and more archaeologists are of the opinion that many, or even most, of those objects were moving between groups, often over great distances, not as commodities but as symbols of relationships, dependencies, obligations and friendships. From this perspective it is therefore all but meaningless to look at a bronze axe and see it just as a mere personal possession, or something for working wood – likewise a sword, a brooch, a cauldron or indeed perhaps any other portable object.

It seems that when two groups sought to establish a relationship between one another, they would mark the connection by exchanging valuables. The items themselves were almost meaningless without the relationship – so that a bronze axe might be better viewed as a signature on a contract: without the agreement it confirms it matters hardly at all.

The groups may have exchanged people at the same time – perhaps the one providing a wife for a son of the other. Items offered then would have had some vague similarity to wedding gifts. (Were archaeologists in a thousand years to unearth a twenty-first-century canteen of cutlery it would be a shame if they only marvelled at the workmanship of the knives and forks and overlooked the fact that it marked the beginning of a lifelong union between two families.) It follows as well that, once established, the relationship between the groups would be ongoing; the return of the canteen of cutlery would hardly be sufficient to annul the marriage. For the duration of the relationship established by the first giving and receiving of gifts there would likely be further gift-giving, so that a whole chain of obligations and debts would develop, binding groups and their descendants inextricably.

In the final paragraphs of his novel *Metroland*, Julian Barnes wrote that 'Objects contain absent people'. And there is the point: if we are to have any hope of understanding the world of the Bronze Age, sometimes we have to see beyond the objects to the people who both made them and invested them with meaning.

I will happily admit I have struggled with all of this – what often seem like fanciful concepts – for years. To me an axe is mostly just an axe and surely the primary reason for having one is to make it easier to cut down trees? But that is the thinking of someone born in Britain in the last third of the twentieth century. How can I avoid seeing objects as just useful or desirable possessions, when that is what my world has taught me?

And it is of course important and sensible not to let the trees completely blind us to the existence of the wood. Hard though it might be to grasp, an appreciation of the ancient grammar of gift exchange is vital to any attempt at understanding the Bronze Age. But tools and weapons would clearly also have been desired and acquired for their obvious uses. The evidence from the Salcombe wreck paints a clear picture of metal-traders engaged in the movement of the raw materials of bronze; and surely at least some of the products of that trade would have ended up in general use in the hands of craftsmen, warriors and housewives.

What must not be overlooked, however, is the certainty that many objects in the archaeological record were invested with meaning and significance that far exceeded their value as metal tools. I think about my own consumerist point of view – how things are mostly just things to me – and then I remember losing my wedding ring just three months after we were married. To this day I do not know exactly what happened to it. I had been out

shovelling snow and ice off our front path, taking my gloves on
and off as I did so, and it seems likely the ring slipped from my
cold finger at some point when my hands were bare. But it was
only when I was back in the house hours later, looking at my
hands as I typed something on my laptop, that I suddenly spotted
the absence. We made a claim on our insurance and within a few
weeks I was able to replace the original with one exactly the same.
But of course it is not the same. The ring I lost was the one my
wife put on my finger, along with a promise. The identical plat-
inum band I wear now is just a ring.

We should also try to look beyond the so-called 'Three-Age
System' of classifying the past, pioneered by the Danish antiquarian Christian Jürgensen Thomsen (1788–1865). Surely everyone has heard about the Stone, Bronze and Iron Ages – and how
archaeologists once sought to rank ancient civilisations in terms
of their tool-making technologies? The assumption underlying all
of it was that humankind was on a steady path leading towards
ever-greater sophistication, so that people living in the Stone Age
might be said to look up to people in the Bronze Age – but not as
much as they looked up to those in the Iron Age.

Bronze may have made for more refined objects than stone, but
that was not the only reason people opted for the one over the
other. Having access to bronze – particularly for the majority of
people, living in areas where neither copper nor tin occurred
naturally – implied precious connections to people far away.
Bronze was the visible proof that they were rich and powerful; but
their wealth and power were really based not on what they knew,
but whom.

During the Bronze Age it became highly valuable to know
people living in two particular parts of Britain. The south-west
tip of England was hugely important to the whole of the Old
World as one of the very few European sources of tin. Not for
nothing would the ancient Greeks learn to refer to our archipelago
as the 'Tin Islands'. But another, smaller finger of land pointing
out to sea further north – beside the modern-day Welsh town of

Llandudno – was enormously rich in the other half of the bronze equation.

The Vikings called it the Great Orme – meaning great worm, or more likely great serpent. Viewed from the deck of a boat approaching Llandudno from the sea, the limestone headland, pointing north-west into the Irish Sea, does indeed suggest the shape of some giant sea monster slithering offshore. The place is rightly popular with tourists who come to take in the views, and perhaps glimpse some of the herd of feral Kashmir goats acquired from Queen Victoria; but the Great Orme has mattered to humankind in another way for more than four millennia. It was likely the largest copper mine in the whole of the Old World.

Copper was first collected there as surface deposits around 4,000 years ago – an entire millennium before the time of the Salcombe wreck – but once the naturally exposed material had been exhausted, some brave and resourceful souls began to follow it underground. Using only tools of stone and bone, the pioneering miners somehow found the strength and the will to burrow more than 60 feet below the surface through solid limestone, in pursuit of the magical green rock. What they left behind is truly a wonder to behold – a wonder of the ancient or even of the modern world.

Many of the shafts and tunnels are big enough for adults to walk through while fully upright; but beyond the section of the mine that is open to tourists there exists a honeycombed warren of serpentine passages so tight they must surely inspire nightmares in all but the most self-possessed and cold-blooded of explorers. I was granted privileged (if that is really the best word to describe access to a place of mental and physical anguish) to just a sample of the five and half miles of tunnels excavated by archaeologists and mining engineers during the past 20-odd years. More than half of the network still remains to be exposed and investigated, but it has already been possible to estimate that enough copper ore was mined from the Great Orme to produce around 2,000 tons of bronze. No other prehistoric copper mine yet discovered anywhere in the world is on anything like the same scale.

As I put on my regulation navy-blue boiler suit and bright yellow hard hat, complete with head torch, a guide in the visitor centre offered the following advice: 'This may sound blindingly obvious, but do try and bear it in mind when you get into some of the tight bits,' she said, while I struggled to adjust my chinstrap. 'If you feel you're getting stuck, you really have to try and not panic.' I felt my stomach shrivelling, and all the while she kept talking. I knew she was only trying to help but I really wanted her to stop. 'If you get stuck, and you allow yourself to panic [that's actually the word she used – allow] the first thing your brain will do is signal to your body to take a deep breath. It's part of the flight reflex but it's the worst thing you can do in a tight spot – because it will just make your body bigger. And if you really are stuck before you breathe in, imagine how stuck you'll be after!'

I nodded sagely. Part of me knew what she was saying made perfect sense, but I am still not sure it was what I most wanted to hear during what I felt might yet prove to be the last moments of my life spent in daylight. The sections of the mine open to the public – those tunnels around five or six feet in diameter – were absolutely fine. Strung with lightbulbs as they were, it was possible to persuade yourself you were walking through part of a theme park experience. Beyond the ropes, though – beyond the signs reading 'No Public Access' and well past the reach of mains electricity – the ceilings quickly lowered to the point where it was only possible to proceed on hands and knees, and then flat on the stomach.

Throughout the mine there are hammer stones and picks of bone, lying precisely where they were dropped thousands of years ago. It beggars belief that 10 or more miles of tunnel were excavated through solid limestone using just human muscle, large pebbles and the rib bones of cattle, but those are the facts. The hammer stones fit naturally into the hand and the ends are chipped and crushed by hours, days and weeks of use.

The miners followed the veins of copper ore as they twisted and wound through the limestone – so that the tunnels left behind are often crazily corkscrewed. Every ounce of ore and every lump of unwanted limestone had to be kicked and shoved back down the tunnel, in the miner's own wake as it were, as he or she inched steadily, wearily onwards. The mind-numbing, bone-crushing labour of it all is almost as staggering as the knowledge this was how so many generations spent their waking lives.

In the worst stretches I had to wriggle desperately onto my back, or onto one side and then the other as dictated by the helter-skelter contortions of the tunnel walls. For some reason I can still vividly recall the rough and strangely amplified sound of my cotton boiler suit scraping inch-by-inch past the limestone, and the slightly more distant accompaniment provided by the desperate flailing of my steel toe-capped boots. If barely contained panic has a sound, then that is it.

All the while I struggled, puffed and moaned, I had to battle to stop my mind confronting me with the reality of my situation: that I was deep underground in a tunnel fractionally wider than my shoulders; that the only way to go was forwards – perhaps 30 feet towards the next space wide enough to turn round in; that if I was to get stuck there would be nothing to do but wait, trapped like a rat in a trap and deafened by the sound of my own pained breathing, while someone wriggled towards me, taking up even more space, blocking out more of the light and breathing more of the air; that even when they reached me there would be precious little difference they could make; that it would still boil down to my finding a way to free myself and carry on. As I say – I did my utmost not to let those thoughts crystallise in my head. On the plus side, the guide had informed me, was the privilege of knowing that since the Bronze Age no more than a handful of souls had ventured through the tunnel I was in now. I was joining an elite club. I could easily understand why. All in all, it was hellish.

Some of the tunnels are so narrow and so deep underground that modern mining engineers have wondered just how much breathable air would have been available to prehistoric miners working in them. Their only means of providing themselves with light would have involved fires or oil-burning lamps and it has been suggested such luxuries would have consumed too much of the oxygen the miners themselves depended upon. In short, the Bronze Age men, women and, presumably, children who spent their days in the Great Orme mine may well have passed much of their time head first at the end of the tiny tunnels no wider than their bodies, scraping and chipping away at the rock in total, smothering darkness.

The centrepiece of the visitor experience in the Great Orme copper mine is an enormous, rock-cut chamber. It is right in the heart of the mine and marks the point where many of the copper veins once converged in a giant Gordian Knot of geology. As a by-product of removing the rock and the ore, those ancient burrowers inadvertently created a subterranean space as large as a modern theatre auditorium. It is a vast, towering, echoing cavity and yet every cubic foot of it was excavated by humans working with rocks and bones. It is thought to be the largest man-made chamber anywhere in the world and it is nothing less than humbling. Spend some time considering the inch-by-inch effort involved down there and you will never again be quite as impressed by the machine-cut Channel Tunnel, or the London Underground.

Back on the surface – back in blessed daylight – the over-whelming impact of the Great Orme mine is the industrial nature and scale of it all. That so much copper was sweated and toiled for in just one location is a measure of the Old World's appetite for bronze in the millennia between 4000 and 1000 BC. The amount of raw material available as the Bronze Age progressed makes a person wonder what use it could all have been put to. There are, after all, only so many bronze axes a community can absorb, so many brooches its women can wear, so many swords and shields its men can wield.

It was the sheer quantity of the metal in circulation as the Bronze Age approached its climax that prompted archaeologists to question whether it could all have been for practical purposes. Here, then, was the inspiration for the application of gift-exchange theory – the realisation that somewhere along the line the wealth associated with the control and possession of bronze had become divorced from its utility as a metal. Once objects of bronze were being treated as a kind of proto-currency, those individuals with the power to obtain them simply wanted more and more. As so often happens where human nature is involved, enough was never enough.

The Neolithic, the New Stone Age, had been about much more than just objects and structures made of stone. The people living through it were hardly to be defined by a raw material alone. Rather the Neolithic encapsulated the revolutionary technology of farming as well as whole new systems of belief and entirely new ways of looking at the world and the cosmos. Far from simply being obsessed with a technology, a population of busy farmers struggled to come to terms with what it meant to be alive in a mysterious universe. Likewise the period of time archaeologists have labelled the Bronze Age was about much more than a pre-occupation with a golden-coloured metal. In fact that metal was only a symptom of humankind's overall condition during those particular centuries of our ancient history.

Part of the story of the Late Bronze Age seems to be steady change – a deterioration, in fact – in the climate of Britain and perhaps other parts of northern and western Europe as well. While there had been a 'golden age' – of weather as well as social relations – lasting for hundreds of years, it seems that after perhaps 800 BC or so things began to take a rapid turn for the worse. In the latter years of the Bronze Age there was more rain, winters were longer and colder and the summers shorter and cooler.

Whole swathes of farmland in upland zones and throughout northern Britain – particularly in Scotland – became less and less fertile, less and less productive. For a population that had expanded during the good times, this steady reduction in the amount of available farmland posed some obvious problems. As time went on, the still-productive lowlands, as well as lands further south, came under increasing pressure from dispossessed communities that had found their own territories no longer capable of supporting them.

During the Bronze Age there had been a trend towards laying out large-scale field systems, like those that still survive at Deckler's Cliff, at East Portlemouth in Devon. This had certainly been the practice in upland areas like Dartmoor. But in the Late Bronze Age and Early Iron Age these fields were steadily abandoned.

The way in which people lived on the land began to change as well – possibly as a direct result of the changes in the climate and soil fertility. While it was not universal across the whole of the landmass of Britain and Ireland, settlements in many areas became more substantial. During the Late Bronze Age, more and more people seem to have felt the need to build with massive timbers or stones. As the buildings became heavier, with a greater presence in the landscape, so too the homesteads and villages were often surrounded by ditches, banks and palisades. Communities seem to have been drawing in upon themselves, staking more visible claims on what territory they believed was theirs. Farmland was also more and more defined by boundaries. Where before there had been chaotic scatterings of fields, increasingly the landscape of the Late Bronze Age featured pre-planned layouts that were the product of co-ordinated efforts to formalise claims on the available land.

Approaches to death underwent changes as well in the Late Bronze Age, particularly in southern Britain. Just as in every other age, the majority of the dead were likely disposed of by leaving their corpses exposed in the open, possibly in special places, where nature could take its course. But from at least the Neolithic period, some people's remains were selected for careful treatment. During much of the Bronze Age the predominant fashion, when it came to those special individuals, had been for burial in and around round barrows that acted as focal points in the landscape. But as the centuries wore on it seemingly became more common for those ritually significant bodies to be cremated, and the fragments buried inside pottery urns. Whole cemeteries grew up, known to archaeologists as 'urn fields', and their apparently egalitarian nature – with all of those special dead treated the same way – suggests yet another change within society. Where rich burials, filled with weapons and jewellery, declared the status of the dead person loud and clear, the spread of urn fields might mean the power of a hitherto wealthy elite was on the wane.

All across the board it seems people living through the later years of the Bronze Age were facing altered circumstances – perhaps even some kind of burgeoning crisis. While there was still plenty of bronze in circulation, it came from different sources than before. The cargo of the Salcombe wreck contained metal that had its origins not in Britain but on the Continent. From 1000 BC this seems increasingly to have been the case. The Great Orme was still a busy source of copper in 1500 BC – and for several centuries to come – but more and more of the metal changing hands in Britain was imported rather than native.

In fact, by the end of the period the production of items fashioned from home-grown material had apparently ground to a halt – replaced by metal originating from all over western Europe. There is something oddly familiar about this Late Bronze Age dependency on imports. Today Britain frets about the kind of nation she has become – one that makes next to nothing and depends on imports from abroad. It seems that 3,000 years ago it became a land that looked abroad for its metalwork, the substance upon which so much was based. Despite the presence of tin in Cornwall and resources of copper in northern Wales and elsewhere, by 1000 BC many people preferred to acquire their bronze from European sources. It is yet another demonstration of how complex their relationship to the metal had become. What mattered most was not that the object was made of bronze. Much of the real cachet lay in its source, where and from whom it had been obtained. There is something almost deliberately awkward or contrary about what was going on. Often it is in those areas furthest from any natural sources of copper and tin – south-eastern England, for example – that the largest volumes of hoarded bronze are found. People in Ireland, Scotland and Wales, on the other hand – parts of the country where bronze could easily have been made locally – preferred to import the stuff from abroad.

It was not just the source of the bronze that changed, either. The things people were doing with their belongings changed too. Where before they had accompanied the dead in their graves, in the later centuries of the Bronze Age objects made of the precious metal were increasingly deposited in special locations in the landscape, and never reclaimed. For reasons not fully understood, individuals or communities began burying valuable metal objects in holes in the ground, or throwing them into bogs, streams, rivers, lochs and lakes. Deposits of valuables had been made in the preceding centuries as well; but as the Bronze Age approached its climax, the practice intensified to the point where it almost smacks of collective madness.

It is hard to come up with hard and fast rules for what people thought they were doing by discarding precious things, but in general terms metal tools were buried on dry land, jewellery and other personal effects went into bogs and weapons were cast into rivers. And they were not being discarded individually either: whole collections of items that must have represented huge material wealth to their erstwhile guardians or owners were being put out of reach of man.

For long it was suggested that hoards on dry land represented efforts to lay aside stores of valuables – savings that could be dug up and used at a later date. Archaeologists imagined they were finding those deposits that had remained in the ground only because bad luck had prevented their rightful owners returning to collect them. Understanding what was going on is not made any easier, either, by the use of the word 'hoard', with all its connotations of a store set aside as security against a future need. In many, if not most, instances the objects were being put away for ever, never to be reclaimed.

More recently it has been accepted that the story must often be more complicated than 'hoarding' in the manner of squirrels laying down winter supplies of nuts. Given that so much material was being consigned to fast-flowing rivers or to the deep sediments of bogs and marshes, surely it was never the intention to see such items again. Rather than being set aside for a rainy day, they must have been intended for the gods alone.

Much of what was going on in the Late Bronze Age of Britain has been interpreted as human responses to a time of crisis. Set against a backdrop of worsening climate and reduction of fertile land, the changes to settlement patterns and burial practices – and the new sources of and final destinations for the bronze itself – begin to suggest societies fighting to find new identities to replace old, as well as new ways to live with themselves and with one another.

Cast into eternity within one hoard are two objects that reveal another factor that came into play during the first millennium BC. In 1913, during the construction of a reservoir at Llyn Fawr, in the Cynon Valley in south Wales, workmen began finding scores of bronze objects in the waterlogged peat. In the end they recovered more than 60 artefacts, including a large cauldron, a spearhead, many socketed axes, chisels, sickles, horse harness equipment and razors.

Long before the decision to make it into a reservoir, Llyn Fawr was a small, naturally formed lake. Looming over the water on one side, and giving the place a palpably gloomy air, is a steep, heather-covered slope. All in all the lake has the appearance of a watery stage in front of a dark purple backdrop. It seems that, well over two and a half millennia ago, a Bronze Age community had chosen the overshadowed depths of Llyn Fawr as the final resting place for a collection of their most valuable possessions.

The items within many hoards are deliberately broken – as though to underline the fact they are no longer the property of any living community. Those found at Llyn Fawr, however, were deposited in generally good condition. Furthermore many of the pieces are of the highest quality and may have come originally from several locations across Britain and Continental Europe. The cauldron is particularly fine, formed of four beaten plates of bronze joined together by scores of rivets. Those encircling plates are in turn secured to a circular base and the whole is fitted with a pair of individually cast circular bronze handles from which the cauldron would have been suspended.

Cauldrons are loaded with meaning and significance that goes way beyond their function as cooking vessels. Such objects have traditionally been seen as powerful symbols of fertility and of regeneration, so that to partake of food prepared in such a vessel was to be counted into a ceremony that celebrated the giving and the taking of life itself. That such an item – and such a beautifully made and clearly valuable example – was chosen to be thrown for ever into the dark waters of a lake is an indication of powerful magic and belief at work.

Throughout much of Britain's ancient history, water was seen as special, magical in its own right. The smooth surface of a lake like Llyn Fawr, darkly transparent yet simultaneously reflecting land and sky, may once have seemed like a portal between worlds – one belonging to the living and the other to the dead, the immortal and the gods.

The Llyn Fawr hoard is on display in the National Museum of Wales in Cardiff, and it is breathtaking. The cauldron is instantly captivating – for its sheer scale alone, too big to be encircled by a man's arms – as are the axe heads of various sizes and weights, edges worn and chipped by much use. But it is some of the smaller pieces that seem to have more to say. The bronze razors are especially moving, given that they imply the life of someone interested in the finer points of personal grooming, the need to appear in a particular way in order to fit in.

But while the vast majority of the items are of bronze, archae-ologists have placed the Llyn Fawr hoard at the beginning of another age entirely. There among all the familiar golden-hued finery are two very special items – a socketed sickle and a sword – made not of bronze but of iron, some of the earliest iron objects found so far in the whole of Britain. The Llyn Fawr hoard is therefore especially precious to archaeologists since it seems to straddle the two technologies.

The little iron sickle is particularly revealing because its creator quite obviously sought to make it appear as though it were made of bronze. For one thing he bothered to form a raised central ridge or spine running down the centre of the curved blade. Such a feature would have been necessary to strengthen a cast bronze sickle but was completely redundant on one of hammered iron. For another he fashioned a socket, to receive the end of a wooden handle, by painstakingly hammering and shaping part of the iron into a hollow tube. Although the socket gives the finished article much of the appearance of one cast in bronze, it would have been infinitely easier – not to mention more practical – to have beaten out a simple tang that could have been slotted into a notch cut in a wooden shaft. It is altogether fascinating. Either the ironsmith was keen to make his sickle appeal to a customer familiar with the shapes and forms of bronze tools, or he was a bronzesmith determined to make the new material mimic the finished products he was used to casting in the old familiar metal.

Some archaeologists have consigned the Llyn Fawr hoard to a period they call the Earliest Iron Age. While the earliest iron objects in Europe were actually being made in the eastern Mediterranean, around modern-day Turkey, from approximately 1200 BC, their spread into northern Europe and Britain took several centuries.

The working of iron – from naturally occurring ore to finished object – is a challenging prospect even for people used to casting bronze. For one thing, iron has a much higher melting point than copper or tin (around 1,500 degrees centigrade, compared to 1,100 for bronze) and so could not be poured and cast like bronze until the advent of blast furnaces that were well beyond the technological reach of the first smiths.

Instead the early iron-workers found they could use charcoal to achieve temperatures inside their simple clay furnaces that were sufficient to coax powdered iron ore into a lump of metallic iron.

While never quite becoming liquid, the ore could nonetheless be persuaded to form a solid clump of material. This lump, called a bloom and looking like a cross between a misshapen loaf of black bread and a sponge, was a mixture of iron and various impurities known collectively as slag. The bloom was then reheated in a fire – one agitated by bellows to achieve the highest possible temperatures – and hammered and hammered upon an anvil until as much as possible of the slag became molten again, so that it could be separated from the iron. The continual working and reworking of the bloom in this way, driving out more and more of the impurities, produces a reasonably pure metal that is properly described as wrought iron. It is this that can be reheated until white-hot and then beaten and shaped by a blacksmith into just about any weapon or tool imaginable.

I had the great good fortune to spend a day with a man called Hector Cole, a blacksmith and an expert in the production of ancient iron tools and weaponry. I defy anyone to stand in front of the gaping maw of a blacksmith's forge (hearing it breathe, like Darth Vader, the air from its bellows, watching the flames pulse from red to orange to dazzling white and back again, as though driven by a beating heart) and not believe there is more going on in there than simple physics.

Iron-working happens in a half-dark world of giant shadows and dancing sparks and always to the accompaniment of the bell-like ringing of hammer on anvil. There is magic there too, but of a different sort than that which attends the casting of bronze. The alloy of copper and tin completes its metamorphosis – from liquid into ringing blade – in seconds. The transformation of shapeless bloom into regular, even bar and then to finished object, however, is the work of muscle and sweat – part coaxing and part bullying – and all of it a race against time. The metal is malleable only while close to white-hot and as its lustre fades, to orange and then ever darker red, so it becomes less and less amenable to change.

Watching Hector cajole and persuade the raw material, stooped over his anvil with hammer and tongs, was hypnotic. Having begun his apprenticeship as a child (legend has it he made his first iron piece aged four and a half!), he has partly forged himself. He makes iron, and iron has made him. His hands are not like mine – nor like those of anyone else who has spent a cosseted life shuffling paper around a succession of desks. His look like men's hands used to, fingers and joints enlarged and toughened by proper work. They also look clever somehow – capable and sure.

Hector's working day is all about rhythm and perseverance, nudging the reluctant iron bar ever closer to the desired shape. He has also to mind his fire all the while, managing it and tending it. Without the right kind of fire there can be no ironwork and he always has at least half an eye on the mood of the flames. I was there with a second hammer, ineptly handled, while Hector made a sickle for me. It was in the moments after the final hammer stroke, while the newly finished article glowed cherry-red and perfect, that it appeared best of all – not just a tool for harvesting a crop but a testament to the dogged, restless inventiveness of man.

For all its challenges and difficulties, the practical beauty of iron is that hematite, or iron ore, is infinitely more plentiful than copper or tin, the constituents of bronze. Instead of depending on complex exchange networks – bringing together rarities like copper and tin – usable iron ore could be collected from the surface of just about every other ploughed field. While the scarcity of its ingredients had made bronze a material controlled by an elite, iron had the potential to become the metal of the common people.

Hector explained how the blacksmith would have been much more use to his neighbours than a man skilled only in the casting of bronze. 'They would get far more out of an ironsmith,' he said. 'For those sorts of tools they needed every day – sickles and so on – iron is much better than bronze. It's that little bit more elastic, so it's not going to break if you hit it against something hard. If gets bent you can straighten it, if it breaks you can weld the two pieces back together. If an edge gets blunt you can sharpen it – it's much more versatile.'

The Bronze Age had lasted for more than a thousand years. More than just a metal for making tools and weapons, bronze had become the foundation of society itself. Relationships between individuals, between families, between tribes and clans and between peoples scattered all across Britain and Europe rode upon, and were therefore dependent upon, a ceaselessly flowing river of bronze. Long before the advent of money, it was bronze that made the world go round.

Iron, however, was utterly different. It could be used to make the same objects as bronze, but it would never have the same cachet. After all, anyone could get their hands on iron. It was commonplace and cheap and could never appeal to any self-regarding elite for whom exclusivity was everything. And if it was bronze that made the world go round, it empowered that elite and forced people willingly or unwillingly into contact with one another over great distances; if it was bronze that oiled the cogs and wheels of human interaction, what would happen now there was a rival material?

The answer to that question takes us on a journey into one of the most mysterious periods of our ancient history. Just as the first people to board the abandoned *Mary Celeste*, adrift in the mid-Atlantic, struggled to make sense of all they beheld, so the Late Bronze Age and Earliest Iron Age of Britain seems to defy all attempts at rational explanation.

For over a thousand years it had been bronze that had made sense of society. But over a relatively short space of time, after about 800 BC, the magic apparently stopped working. At first there was still plenty of the metal around, of course; the Great Orme and every other copper mine in Europe had been working solidly for countless generations, churning out thousands upon thousands of tons of copper. In Cornwall, Brittany and Iberia the other part of the equation – tin – had been exploited just as enthusiastically. Whatever else was going on, there could have been no shortage of the stuff itself.

In Britain, from around 1000 BC onwards, bronze was

increasingly being recycled – melted down and recast over and over again, and it was increasingly of European origin. But it was to hand and it was plentiful. Progressively, however, the once unassailable bronze was being dumped, quite literally thrown away – and in vast quantities. While the deposition of collections like the Llyn Fawr hoard could be said to have a certain logic to them – earnest attempts to win favour with the gods or the ancestors, or both, by offering up valuable gifts – more and more bronze objects were ending up in holes in the ground, around the same time, in circumstances that are only bizarre.

Around 600 BC or so, a smith or a team of smiths in Dorset sweated and toiled to produce more than 300 socketed bronze axes. It must have taken considerable effort and guile just to get enough of the raw material in the same place at the same time even to embark on the job. Then there was the skill and time required to produce the items in such numbers. Analysis by bronze specialists indicates the axes were not mass-produced – from moulds capable of making several items at a time – but cast one by one in a process just about as time-consuming as it sounds. This is the Langton Matravers hoard, found by a metal detectorist in the Purbeck region of Dorset in 2007. We can only imagine the expression on his face as he turned them up. A signal that returns just one bronze axe would be cause for celebration – but 303!

Most of the sockets are still plugged with clay – a result of the casting process – and that they were left in that unfinished condition makes it clear they were never used, or even intended for use. The ancient patina still visible on their surface suggests they may have been polished to look their best, but the very high tin content would have made them brittle and next to useless as tools. Not to put too fine a point on it, everything about them is odd. Oddest of all, however, is that as soon as they had been shined up they were carted into a field and buried in four large pits.

So far so strange, but in fact the Langton Matravers hoard is far from unique; it is not even unusual. All over Britain and northern and western Europe it was the same. Vast quantities of just about the most sought-after material in the world at the time was being thrown away. In parts of France archaeologists have found literally tens of thousands of bronze axes in massive pits – all of them seemingly put into the ground as soon as they were cool enough to handle after their casting. Usually, in these finds, the copper alloy is so corrupted with excessive amounts of lead or tin as to make the axes formed of it every bit as useless as those in the Langton Matravers hoard. (It has been suggested that the hoards are simply collections of axes rejected as sub-standard. But it would have made more sense simply to melt them down and start again.)

Archaeologists have been trying for decades to come up with sensible explanations for all of this. More than 30 years ago the Bronze Age specialist Colin Burgess suggested the ubiquity of the metal had driven down its 'value'. If its power was based on exclusivity, then in a world increasingly awash with the stuff it may have become a challenge to keep people hungry for it. Keen to push the price back up again, he said, the bronze elite extracted as much bronze from the marketplace as possible. The hoards were therefore a consequence of Machiavellian manoeuvrings on the part of the ancestors of unscrupulous modern-day commodity traders. Burgess's explanation has been heavily criticised, however, on the grounds that it implies a level of international co-ordination and co-operation that was unknown – and impossible – until the modern era.

The sudden wholesale dumping of an erstwhile valuable material has been dubbed the 'Bronze Crisis' – as though confidence in the importance of the metal was somehow undermined. Like Burgess's suggestion of manipulation of the market, this too sounds altogether modern. For it to make sense we would have to accept that confidence was as important to the functioning of the Bronze Age economy as it is to our own. We must therefore imagine the power of bronze being undermined in a manner not unlike the fate that befell the emperor in his new clothes. After more than a millennium in which the exchange of bronze objects had made everyone happy, one small voice is supposed to have piped up with the opinion that they were all the victims of a grand hoax – that bronze was nothing special after all – and so Bronze Age society began to collapse like a house of cards.

Neither of those two explanations seems satisfactory. For one thing, the only tangible evidence of a 'crisis' is the existence of the hoards themselves – a circular argument if ever there was one.

Perhaps a different point of view is required, one that looks beyond the metal and takes into consideration what else was going on in Britain and the wider world during the first centuries of the first millennium BC.

For one thing, thousands of years of relationship-building with populations scattered across Europe meant the inhabitants of Britain and Ireland had made themselves vulnerable to changes hundreds of miles away. From around 800 BC, there began to emerge in the Mediterranean a trio of civilisations that would shortly, and inevitably, change the world – for ever.

Of the three emerging polities it was the Phoenicians who originated from the furthest east, in the territory occupied today by Lebanon and Syria; the Greeks were centred on lands surrounding the Aegean Sea and the Etruscans lived in what is now northern Italy (in time they would be first mimicked, and finally overwhelmed, by the people of nearby Rome).

All three began vying for control of the seaways – around the Mediterranean at first but eventually into the Black Sea and the Atlantic Ocean as well. What was happening in Mediterranean Europe from 800 BC was nothing less than the formation of states, organised groups of peoples with distinct identities and, more importantly, with international agendas focused on gaining and maintaining control of commodities ranging from metals to textiles, from ivory to wine, from cattle and sheep to wheat and corn; and from olive oil to slaves.

From 800 BC, those emergent states began to generate the equivalent of a gravitational pull that attracted precious metals like bronze (as well as anything and everything else of value) away from the periphery and towards the centre. A sudden and worsening shortage of bronze would have been felt first and keenest in northern France, and on islands like Britain and Ireland. For a while the shortfall in the north and west was taken up by bronze supplies emanating from the Atlantic coast, but of course it was not the metal that was the point of the whole exercise – it was the contacts and relationships the metal conferred.

And so perhaps, at least in part, the shock felt on the northern side of the English Channel in the years after 800 BC was akin to the disorientation that has to be endured following the break-up of any relationship. And if not a break-up then at least a reassessment of existing ties. Continental Europe was transfixed by what – or rather who – was happening in the Mediterranean. There was a new flame, capturing hearts and consuming all the oxygen in the room. Attention began to focus on the emergence of what would become the empires and nations of the Classical world and, unaware, Britain and the rest of the populations on the northern and western peripheries found themselves out in the cold.

Because the people of Britain could no longer lay their hands on the right sort of bronze, from the right sort of people, more and more of them seemingly decided to try to get along without it altogether. Society still mattered and people still mattered – it was as important as ever to have contacts and allies as insulation against the chill of an often hostile world. The challenge in the Earliest Iron Age was to make new friends, in new ways.

For a start, it would seem reasonable to imagine that if the shine had, quite literally, gone off bronze – if it was no longer desirable and therefore no longer being exchanged – iron would swiftly have taken its place. But here is where the story grows curiouser and curiouser – because the main thing to notice about the first two or three centuries of the Iron Age in Britain is the almost complete absence of anything made of iron. With the notable exception of a handful of rarities like the Llyn Fawr sickle and sword, there is simply no trace of the new metal or the new technology in Britain or Ireland between around 750 BC and 550 BC.

How often do we allow for the possibility that lives in the ancient past were every bit as riven with stress as our own? It appears that in Britain 2,700 years or so ago people were struggling to cope with unexpected changes. After a so-called 'Golden Age', climate change was making the country colder and wetter. What had been fertile land in the time of parents and grandparents was now sterile. Hundreds, even thousands of people were on the move – forced to abandon upland farms and trying to eke a living elsewhere, on land already occupied. To cap it all the very fabric of society itself was unravelling. Bonds between families, tribes – bonds made of bronze – were suddenly brittle and unreliable. Even the great and the good were at a loss as to how to explain the root causes of the malaise, far less to find a remedy. Late Bronze Age Britain was a world in flux, in which the old order was undermined and the old certainties were gone. What was to be done?

Archaeologist Niall Sharples has been pondering the so-called Bronze Crisis for many years, and says that to understand what was going on we need to see past the metal. 'When the bronze goes, for whatever reason, you have to find something else with which to structure society,' he said. In Sharples's opinion the 'something else' in question was food. While people during the earlier centuries of the Bronze Age had measured wealth in terms of the control and display of bronze objects, the end of the period saw a new preoccupation with livestock and grain stores.

Giving bronze to the gods had been one way of using the metal to demonstrate power and wealth. What better way to show off to the neighbours than by snapping some swords in two and throwing them into a lake along with half a dozen knives and the same again in axe-heads?

But once bronze lost its cachet, might not the same shock and awe be generated by the throwing of decadent feasts instead? Sharples has been excavating a site at East Chisenbury, in Wiltshire, that seems to make his point for him. There is almost nothing to see at first. Because the site is located within a vast Ministry of

Defence firing range, the territory of Challenger tanks and heavy artillery pieces, the experience of arriving at the location is already strange. But at first glance the archaeology seems as well concealed as any camouflaged gun emplacement. It is hard to see, however, because it is spread over a huge area.

East Chisenbury is described as a midden – a dump of rubbish – but it is on a scale that almost beggars belief. So much material was allowed to accumulate during just a few years of the Earliest Iron Age that the midden is many feet thick and spread over whole acres of what might otherwise be farmland. 'Under our feet are thousands upon thousands of fragments of pottery, broken-up pieces of bone, carbonised plant remains – all the tools, implements and debris of life,' said Sharples as he led me on a meandering walk across the site.

He would stoop down every once in a while, seemingly at random, and straighten up holding a sheep's jawbone, or a shard of pottery, or a cow's rib. The stuff is everywhere, all of it mixed within a matrix formed in the main of uncountable tons of animal dung. People were clearly gathering at East Chisenbury in great numbers, accompanied by huge herds of animals, primarily sheep, and it would appear that only the people went home again. Everything else was either consumed or thrown onto the ever-growing rubbish heap – even the pots and eating utensils. 'What I think we're seeing is an attempt to create relationships between people scattered over a very large region, based upon feasting,' said Sharples.

In addition to the persuasive archaeological evidence at East Chisenbury – and at similar sites including one at Runnymede Bridge near Windsor, and two more at Potterne and All Cannings Cross, in Wiltshire – there are compelling parallels to be found in the modern world as well.

Among the peoples of the Pacific North-west – tribes like the Haida, the Kwakiutl and the Tlingit – the word 'potlatch' is used to describe grand ceremonies that are all about giving away or destroying huge quantities of items including blankets and foodstuffs, in front of as many guests as possible. Among some tribes in Papua New Guinea there are similar events, at which a 'big man' seeks to underline his status by collecting as many pigs and other valuables as he can before giving them all away, as 'mocha', to the members of a neighbouring tribe.

Anthropologists have coined the term 'conspicuous consumption' to describe the behaviour, but in all instances the principles remain the same. Status and prestige are there for the taking by those in a society with the clout to lay hands on huge amounts of valuable food and belongings and then give it all away. By their apparent disdain for the trappings of wealth, they parlay mere blankets and pigs into something deeper and more lasting. The food is consumed in a matter of hours, but the memory of such largesse might last a lifetime.

Although the potlatch was once commonplace, the practice is now largely abandoned, even outlawed. In days past, the ceremony was essential when two high-ranking individuals were vying for the position of top dog – and it might take weeks or months to acquire. Relationships would be exploited, favours called in and debts settled, in order to ensure the rival would have neither the time nor the opportunity to collect as much – or more – 'ammunition' at the same time. If one claimant to the throne timed his potlatch just right, his rival would be powerless to respond in kind. Such acts were therefore acutely competitive – about losing and saving face – but in the end they boiled down to the bare-faced destruction of wealth, rather than its hoarding.

Sharples has argued that people in the past sought to achieve precisely the same effect at places like East Chisenbury. The importance of a person was being measured in terms of access to surplus crops, access to the finest livestock, the best pottery. He also believes it is possible to see evidence of fine pottery taking the place of bronze as a commodity suitable for exchange. The best wares seem to have been moving between communities – although relatively locally, rather than over often great distances as before. He has suggested it may have been the case that, as well as forming and defining relationships with their neighbours by inviting them to feasts, hosts might have expected their guests to bring food along, contained in their best ceramics. While the food was eaten, the bowls were left behind with the hosts.

Sharples is even open to the possibility that the conspicuous consumption tactic might have arisen even before bronze went into decline as a basis of order and power. He has suggested there might have been an attempt to subvert or to overthrow the bronze elite by finding a new way to show off. Scattered populations still needed connections; but instead of forging them with distant groups by means of exchanging bronze axes and swords, in the Early Iron Age there was a premium placed upon relationships closer to home.

It is not hard to imagine, either: for years there must have been have-nots condemned to obscurity and powerlessness by their inability to access the bronze networks. Now there was the prospect of a revolution – or at least a concerted attempt by some in society to turn their backs on the old ways and find their own path through life.

There are even the mortal remains of some of the festival-goers themselves. On land belonging to Suddern Farm, at Over Wallop in Hampshire, archaeologists have excavated what was effectively an Early Iron Age cemetery. Unlike the urn fields of the Late Bronze Age, here people were interred intact. One of the bodies – that of a man – has been dated to around 600 BC. If he was a farmer, as seems likely, then he was probably dealing with a tougher climate than any experienced by his forefathers. To try and cope with the colder, wetter conditions, he may have experimented with new crops. Perhaps he kept more animals than before, using meat to compensate for the comparative shortage of grain. If he was primarily a livestock farmer then it is highly likely he would have been in the habit of attending ceremonial feasts, at which some of his own animals would have been slaughtered and consumed.

More interesting than those suppositions about his life, however, are the facts of his funeral. Like all the others in the cemetery, he was buried in a pit. But if that sounds casual, as though he had been almost thrown away, then it is important to note there was a degree of thoughtful ritual at play as well. He was buried in the foetal position with his knees drawn tightly towards his chin, suggesting he went into his grave bound in some sort of shroud. For a long time the tradition had been for cremations. The switch to inhumation is therefore noteworthy – because a change in the way people were being treated in death usually implies a difference in their way of life as well. By 600 BC, in southern Britain at least, death, and so life, had changed.

Some of the giant midden sites also contain evidence that things were being made there as well as consumed. Traces of metal-working, textile-making, pottery-firing – all these and more besides have been found mixed in with the rest of the rubbish. This was new behaviour. During most of the Bronze Age, production of valuable items, pieces suitable for exchange, seems to have been restricted, controlled within specialised settlement sites. If pots, metal, textiles and the like were now being made out in the open, among huge gatherings of the general population, then this might be yet more evidence of the weakening of a previously all-powerful, controlling elite.

All these ideas are fascinating to me, suggestive as they are of thoughtful and sophisticated approaches to the business of getting along with the neighbours. We can only ever hope to know the half of it, but we can imagine a whole etiquette, so that in the Early Iron Age human relationships were conducted with the precision and attention to detail required by the most complicated dance steps. There might have been all manner of nuances – together with endless possibilities for faux pas and unintended slights.

But if all of these eccentricities sound as though they might chime happily enough with twenty-first-century morals and sens-ibilities, at least one aspect of Iron Age behaviour requires a stronger stomach entirely.

At some point around 450 BC, people living at Fiskerton in Lincolnshire found the need to build a long wooden causeway over ground that was either waterlogged or completely flooded. It was maintained for generations to come and from time to time people using the thing were in the habit of making offerings of precious items by dropping them over the side and into the water. When archaeologists excavated the site in the early 1980s they found hundreds of artefacts, including spears and swords as well as tools for working wood and metal.

Also dropped in among the weapons and the rest, however, was the rear portion of a man's skull. Other than a couple of other small bones, nothing else of his body was recovered so it is not possible to say exactly how he came to die. At some point someone had hit him on the back of the head with a sword – hard enough to remove a section of bone – but a forensic expert decided the blow would not have been enough to kill him.

Since part of his head had ended up in the same place as other votive offerings – precious objects surrendered to the gods – the archaeologists on site allowed themselves to imagine 'Fissured Fred' (those dealing with human remains have a tendency towards dark humour) was a human sacrifice. If that really was the case, if those were the remains of a victim of a deliberate, ritualised and stylised killing, then Fissured Fred was not alone. There have been numerous finds – some in Britain but most in other parts of northern Europe including Ireland, Denmark, Germany and Holland – of Iron Age people deliberately killed, their bodies consigned to watery graves.

It is the very fact they were placed in watery contexts that has led to their preservation. What were once marshes or lakes have subsequently turned to peat; and within the peat their remains are sometimes so perfectly intact it is often possible to tell exactly how they died. Hanging and strangulation were apparently popular means of disposing of such people (often the noose or garrotte is still there around the neck); but plenty of others were simply hit over the head with blunt objects or had their jugular veins laid open with sharp knives so they bled out.

Always those dead are in special places – watery places of the sort that mattered to our ancestors for millennia. As well as bodies, such locations usually offer up swords and axe-heads and the rest of the items apparently deemed acceptable to the gods. And since people were placed there too – immediately after being killed – it seems likely they were sacrificed for the greater good as well.

The most famous British example was found in Lindow Moss, in Cheshire, in 1984. Peat-cutters spotted the remains and specialists from the British Museum were called in to complete the man's return to the daylight after thousands of years. The acidic, oxygen-free conditions within the peat had conspired to stop most of the forces of decomposition in their tracks. He had been squashed by the weight of material that had formed above him, but in many ways he was perfect, with skin, hair and even some internal organs intact.

When he died, sometime in the second century BC, he was at least 25 years old and, but for the presence of some parasitic worms in his gut, in generally good health. His beard and moustache had been carefully trimmed and his fingernails manicured – suggesting that for at least the last few months or years of his life he had been a stranger to hard work.

So well preserved was Lindow Man, as he came to be known, that even the contents of his last meal were intact inside his stomach. In the hours before he was dispatched he had eaten unleavened bread. Something else he had consumed contained the pollen of the mistletoe plant, which was sacred to Iron Age peoples in Britain and elsewhere in Europe.

He had been hit twice on the top of his head with something heavy and sharp, maybe an axe. The position of the wounds suggested he might have been on his knees when they were delivered and they were forceful enough to drive fragments of bone into his brain and to crack one of his back teeth. Someone also hit him hard enough in the back, perhaps with a knee or a well-placed foot, to break one of his ribs. A thin cord had been used to throttle him, snapping his neck in the process. It is not hard to imagine the rib breaking as someone used knee or foot to gain enough leverage for the strangulation. The cord, a thin piece of leather, was left in place, the slip-knot still pulled tight against the skin of Lindow Man's neck. He was already dead when his throat was cut with a sharp blade; his body was then placed face-down into a bog, naked but for a fox fur cuff around the top of one arm.

It was the almost elaborate sequence of events – the level of violence inflicted and the nature of his final resting place – that prompted archaeologists to see him as a sacrifice rather than a murder victim. Their case is made stronger still by the fact that Lindow Man was not the only soul to end up in that particular patch of bog: partial remains of two more men have also been recovered from the Lindow Moss. One of those had six fingers on one hand and since other so-called 'bog bodies' from elsewhere in Europe have been found with physical abnormalities – oddly shaped spines, short arms or legs – it is thought their physical appearance in life may have singled them out for ritual killing.

Two bog bodies found in Ireland in 2003 provide yet more evidence of massive violence, as though the desire was to kill each victim more than once – to inflict what has been called a 'multiple death'. It was peat-cutting that brought Clonycavan Man back into the fresh air – although the machinery had taken his legs and hands before he was spotted. It is thought he was between 25 and 40 when he was put to death, sometime between 400 and 200 BC. In life he wore a moustache and a goatee beard, but it was his elaborate hairstyle that captured most attention – an upswept quiff of long hair held in place with a gel of pine resin and vegetable oil.

Calculations based on his surviving body parts suggested he stood around five feet five inches tall, and so maybe he styled his hair to give himself a little extra height. It turned out the pine resin in his hair had come either from south-west France or northern Spain – so he had access to what could only be described as a luxury commodity. He had been struck repeatedly on the head and chest with a heavy-bladed axe, many more times than were necessary to kill him. Soon after death a gaping wound, more than a foot long, was opened across his stomach, as though to disembowel him.

Clonycavan Man was found in February 2003. Less than three months later and only 25 miles away, peat-cutters found Old-croghan Man – also dispatched with excessive force. He too had been a mature adult, between 25 and 40 years old at the time of death, and had also been done away with during the middle centuries of the Iron Age, between 360 and 175 BC. Oldcroghan Man, however, was a comparative giant – fractionally less than six feet tall and with a powerful, muscular build to boot.

Only his torso and upper arms were recovered, but in his case it was deemed likely his killers had cut him into pieces before depositing just part of him into the bog. Since his head was missing, it was impossible to say how many injuries he might have received in total, but a knife wound visible in his chest would have been enough to kill him. The pathologist was able to say the assailant delivered the blow while standing right in front of his victim, no doubt while looking him in the eye. His arms had been pierced from front to back so that twisted hazel withies could be passed through – likely so they could be used to pin his body into position in the bog. Like Lindow Man he was naked but for an armband. Again like Lindow Man his manicured fingernails suggested he had been from a stratum of society unaccustomed to manual labour.

Stabbed through the heart, decapitated, dismembered, pinned underwater into the mud of a bog – whoever Oldcroghan Man was, someone made sure he wasn't coming back.

We cannot know what was motivating the killers. Perhaps it was felt the gods had grown bored with gifts of metal. Maybe life itself had to be offered up – not just the lives of animals but those of people too. The Iron Age eventually became a time of plenty – surplus food, surplus livestock – and a rapidly growing human population meant there were plenty of surplus people as well.

The changes to society that had begun in the Late Bronze Age continued apace in the first centuries of the Iron Age. From around

800 BC, the climate was in a downward spiral for at least two centuries and people sought new ways to understand themselves and the altered world around them. The new circumstances – not least the economic collapse prompted by the devaluation of bronze – were felt by everyone. People responded in different ways in different parts of the country but were seemingly united in a determination to find alternative techniques for creating and maintaining the ties binding them to their neighbours.

The effects of climate change were not uniform – nor was the erosion of bronze as society's firm foundation. Southern Britain had always been closer to the Continental supplies of the special metal and so the impact of its demise was felt more keenly there. Likewise, climate change had different effects in the east of the country than it had in the west and the responses it prompted from farmers in the uplands were different to those in the lowlands.

What shines through all of it is something we can still recognise in the Britain of today – and that is the growth of distinct regional identities. Whatever else was happening, life became more locally focused. The solutions people found were local ones – local to them, wherever they happened to be.

From around 600 BC the climate began to improve, and in the warmth of longer summers the differences between the regions grew yet more pronounced. People living in the north and east of Scotland felt the need to build massive, hollow-walled circular towers of stone, called brochs. The inspiration for their construction eludes archaeologists still. Often they are on the coast, prompting some to suggest they might have been a response to a perceived threat of invasion from the sea. Others believe they were symbols of power, ordained and commissioned by chiefs or petty kings as highly visible demonstrations of their might. It has also been said they might have been places of refuge for communities that spent most of their time in lesser dwellings nearby. In times of need – when under attack from stock-rustling neighbours perhaps – they could shelter with their beasts inside the local broch and wait for the trouble to pass by.

Whatever their function, they remind me always of cooling towers – broad bases, a narrowing at the waists – except the architects of the brochs achieved that elegant shape with dry stone rather than poured cement. From time to time modern architects and builders have sought to construct their own, but their best efforts collapse in no time. The expertise required to build so high and so massively without mortar is beyond us now.

As often as not, the surviving examples stand alone in the landscape, like the statue of Ozymandias. At Gurness on Orkney, however, there is a famous broch at the heart of something more complicated and involved. There a bank and ditch surrounds an entire stone-built settlement – the massive broch acting as a hub for the lesser buildings radiating away from it, as though on the spokes of the wheel. The tower stands nearly 12 feet tall today, but would once have been nearly three times as grand. The hollow wall contains stone-built staircases that wind towards the roof level so that the occupants could command a view for many miles across the surrounding countryside.

The mere ruin of Gurness remains impressive. The impact it had in its pomp – standing at least 30 feet high and visible from miles around – can only be guessed at. Just inside the entrance is the setting for an iron-shod post that would have supported a massive wooden door. On either side are square recesses for a blocking timber that barred the door shut from the inside. Everything about Gurness Broch says, 'Keep Out'. There is little known about the people who lived there, except to say a succession of inhabitants used the place for hundreds of years.

Excavation has produced sherds of Roman amphorae of a kind that went out of use by AD 60. If fine Roman wine and olive oil were being enjoyed in Gurness during the first century AD, then perhaps the story of a King of Orkney in Colchester in AD 43 is right enough after all. In any case it seems safe to imagine Gurness was a seat of power for several lifetimes, and that it first came to prominence in the middle centuries of the Iron Age.

If iron is strangely absent from the picture in the Early Iron

Age, then evidence of where people were living is not. As well as brochs in the north of Scotland, tens of thousands of Iron Age settlements of different sorts have been identified by archaeologists, scattered all across the British Isles. It is these many and varied domestic sites as much as anything else that demonstrate the emergence of different regional identities.

Brochs are unknown outside Scotland. In other parts of Britain people found different ways to stake their territorial claims. Some favoured small, massively defended houses called duns; some in Scotland constructed crannogs, homes built upon platforms supported on stilts above the waters of lakes and lochs. In the south of England – as well as along the Welsh border and the east of Scotland – farming communities devoted some of their energies to the building of hill forts. Often these were on a colossal scale, housing hundreds of people.

In the world before metal – the Neolithic world – people had forged relationships by creating special meeting places. At first there were the so-called 'causewayed enclosures' and gradually these had evolved, defined by more and more elaborate boundaries; some had been further complicated inside by the building of circles of timber and stone. In any case they had mattered for millennia.

During the Iron Age all sorts of enclosed spaces began to matter again – but in different ways and for different reasons. Maiden Castle, the most complex Iron Age hill fort in Britain, was begun as a causewayed enclosure during the Neolithic period. Around 600 BC it was extended and remodelled to enclose an area of 16 acres. A century and a half later it was tripled in size by architects blessed with a real sense of grandeur. The Maiden Castle we see today, with its multiple sinuous banks and ditches coiled around a space the size of 50 football pitches, is the grandest of its kind not just in Britain, but also arguably in the whole of Europe.

Niall Sharples has argued that some of the later building phases reveal that relationships between communities were being established or reinforced during the Iron Age through the medium of labour. Limestone incorporated into the eastern entrance was quarried not within the confines of the hill fort itself but from a location some miles away on the far side of the South Dorset Ridgeway. There was no practical need for the limestone – especially from a source that only added to the logistical complexities of the construction project. Sharples has argued instead that it was built into the entrance as a highly visible display of the relationship between the inhabitants of the fort and people living on the other side of the Ridgeway. Rather than exchanging metal tools and weapons, people were demonstrating their mutual ties by co-operating on large-scale building schemes. By contributing raw materials – and perhaps the strength of their own backs as well – they were acknowledging and honouring their responsibilities to one another.

Hill forts started to appear in Britain from around 600 BC, often in lofty positions overlooking prime agricultural land. Also in Dorset are two more splendid examples, at Hod Hill and Hambledon Hill. On a wind-blasted peak on the Llyn Peninsula in Gwynedd, in north Wales, is one of the finest and most impressive to be found anywhere in Britain. Tre'r Ceiri – 'the Town of the Giants' – perches on an exposed ridge around 1,300 feet or so up Yr Eifl, 'the Hill of the Rivals'.

The climb up from the valley floor gives a person plenty of time to wonder what on earth possessed any people, in any age, to make life so exhausting for themselves. But finally you arrive on top of the ridge and at once the inspiration for living up a mountain is all around. There cannot be a better view in Wales.

Incredibly, parts of those revetments have survived at close to their original height of around 10 feet or more. Enclosed within the six-acre interior are over 100 dry stone houses, mostly survivors of the latter period of occupation by Rome. It is thought that at the height of the pre-Roman Iron Age, around 200 BC, there might have been 100 people in Tre'r Ceiri, living in perhaps 20 houses.

The term 'hill fort' can be misleading, as it implies defence in a time of war. Archaeologists believe the threat of conflict was not always the spur for their construction, however. More than places to defend, they were places in which to live. Their inhabitants' choice of elevated positions may have had more to do with their relationship to and stewardship over the surrounding fertile land.

Excavation of the houses in hill forts like Tre'r Ceiri reveals they were all more or less the same size. There is seldom anything that would have satisfied the ego of a 'big man' or a chief. Instead they evoke a sense of equality, of people pooling labour and resources, co-operating with one another to achieve ends that benefited all. Some archaeologists (notably those with left-wing leanings) even imagine our Iron Age ancestors living together in the sort of communist collective that would have appealed to any iron-worker who believed that property was theft.

Strange to say, it may also be the case that there was a direct relationship between the apparently isolated, inward-looking hill forts and the communal feasts of the midden sites. The livestock and other foodstuffs consumed at the great gatherings in the lowlands may have had their origin in the farms of those whose homes were on the hilltops. If their locations made them seem distant and cut off from their neighbours, then the connections established through the display and sharing of animals and grain would have served to close the gap.

These were farming communities and where there was plenty of grain or of livestock, it could be traded. Better yet, surplus grain from a good year might be set aside, in pits or other storage spaces within places like hill forts, for a rainy day. In this new, emerging world it was food and not objects of bronze that represented wealth. So it followed that larger tribes, larger communities could work more land, grow more crops and husband more animals – becoming more prosperous in the process.

By around 500 BC something else had changed as well: iron objects began to appear all across the country – and in useful quantities. Society had evolved in the absence of metal. Bronze had disappeared from the picture but life carried on, as it had to, and people had adapted. If its disappearance had torn a hole in the fabric of society, then within a couple of centuries it had been repaired. The pattern was different but it was every bit as strong as before, perhaps even stronger. By the time iron tools and weapons begin to appear in volume, Iron Age society was already fully formed. It was people and not iron that had made the difference.

Iron might have lacked the glamour of bronze, but it got the job done even better; and in the space of just a few hundred years its masters made some huge leaps forward in technology. The same site in Lincolnshire that produced tantalising evidence of human sacrifice in the form of 'Fissured Fred' also offered up evidence of a more workaday sort. But for all that the iron tools of the so-called Fiskerton hoard speak of the life of a working man, they are as evocative and as moving as any bronze sword.

The contents of a toolkit, they include an iron hammerhead, fragments of an iron saw together with its elegant horn handle and an iron file. I challenge anyone to hold those treasures in their hands and not feel a connection to them. Although corroded, the teeth on the saw blade are still plainly visible; the business ends of the hammerhead are battered and flattened by much use. Perhaps the file is most affecting of all, the individual cutting edges still sharp to the touch. If someone were to show you the Fiskerton tools and say they were from their grandfather's toolbox, you would believe them. They are utterly and unmistakably modern – and yet they were put aside for the last time 2,500 years ago.

By around 400 BC, the time of the Bronze Crisis (if there had ever really been a crisis) was a distant memory. The climate was reliable once more – enough rain to make the crops grow, enough sunshine to ripen them – and the fertility of the soil, plants and animals meant the human population could grow as well. It was agriculture and agricultural surplus that lay behind it all and the making and storing of surplus depended heavily upon the new metal – iron.

While the casting of bronze had been the preserve of secretive specialists, iron-working became a central part of village life. Men like Hector Cole – blacksmiths with the know-how that enabled them to make, maintain and repair the iron tools of day-to-day life – were right at the heart of it.

At Butser Ancient Farm, near Chalton in Hampshire, archae-ologists and other specialists are engaged in a longstanding project that seeks to recreate Iron Age agriculture – and the skills that made it possible. Dave Freeman has spent much of his life unpicking the weave of Iron Age life, learning to make and master the tools, understanding what was going on in the minds of the builders of roundhouses, the cultivators of fields.

He showed me the difference made to the lot of the Iron Age ploughman by the addition of an iron 'shoe' to the cutting edge of a simple scratch-plough, or ard. An ard is little more than a long wooden shaft supporting a wooden spike that points down towards the soil at an acute angle. Dragged behind a pair of oxen, the spike excavates a shallow furrow that may then be planted with seed. By adding an iron cover to the end of the spike – a cover with a cutting edge – its effectiveness is increased manifold, along with its lifespan. As well as cutting deeper, into heavier soils, the shoe can be mended or replaced whenever required. Suddenly the ard has been transformed into the kind of plough we might almost recognise today.

The Iron Age also saw the invention of some of the first 'machines' – tools with moving parts. The best of these were nothing less than some of the earliest labour-saving devices known to mankind. The saddle quern had been an absolute necessity for millennia. A large, flat, gritty stone provided the base plate upon which a smaller, rounded stone was rubbed back and forth. Grain trapped between the two was gradually ground into flour, but the 'daily grind' was a backbreaking chore. It was in the Iron Age that the rotary quern first came into play. Two circular stones, each with a hole through the centre, were loosely mounted, one on top of the other, on a wooden shaft. A wooden handle fitted on the side of the topmost stone meant it could be rotated on top of the lower, setting up an effective grinding action. Grain poured into the hole in the top was steadily forced – and so ground – between the two opposing surfaces. What eventually worked its way to the outer edges was coarse but usable flour.

Everything about the rotary quern shows a leap forward in thinking, in technology. It is a composite machine made from multiple parts and its use would have transformed the daily life of anyone keeping house in the Iron Age. More flour could be produced in less time, with less effort, and the production of the daily bread was made infinitely less arduous. They must surely have been treasured items in every home.

Another Iron Age innovation transformed surplus grain into a nest egg. Some or other genius discovered that freshly harvested grain sealed into a pit beneath an airtight cap of clay would be prevented from germinating. Held in a kind of suspended animation, such a cache could be kept for at least a year and potentially even longer. Grain pits – many of which are large enough to have been mistaken at times for subterranean shelters – have been found by the hundreds and thousands within the interiors of most excavated hill forts. By laying down stores in times of plenty a community could withstand the impact of a subsequent bad harvest. Better yet, an accumulation of such wealth might be traded with neighbours for other essentials or luxuries. A nearby community might one day come cap-in-hand, asking for help, and if they were bailed out with surplus grain they would be in debt. Such a marker might be kept in the back pocket, as it were, to be called in at some unspecified time in the future. In this way grain was transformed into something much more powerful than food. From now on it was a source of power and influence as well.

The Iron Age farmstead of Little Woodbury, just south of Salisbury, was found to have over 300 grain pits clustered around one large roundhouse. Excavated by the German archaeologist Gerhard Bersu just before the outbreak of the Second World War, Little Woodbury became for archaeologists the archetypal Iron

Age farming settlement – the model they subsequently applied everywhere else.

The Little Woodbury roundhouse revealed itself in the form of a circle of large postholes but Bersu, for all his undoubted talents, was unable to visualise what form the building they supported might have taken. He imagined all sorts, including a wigwam and a roof with multiple gables. Finally the English archaeologist Peter Reynolds, original director of Butser Ancient Farm, attempted a reconstruction. The solution he found – a simple conical roof supported on a low wall of posts – is so familiar now it is hard to understand why the form eluded archaeologists for as long as it did.

Bersu's work at Little Woodbury was cut short by the outbreak of war in 1939. He was interned on the Isle of Man as an enemy alien, along with many other German, Austrian and Italian nationals, and never returned to the site that had made his name.

From 400 BC there was something of a population explosion in Britain. Improved climate, better technology founded upon iron – the fields had never been so productive. Another chapter had been opened, one profoundly different in many ways from any that had gone before.

Bronze had created an elite. Iron was utterly and only practical but its edge, one that could be endlessly resharpened, carved Britain into a new shape. Iron technology put agriculture and the land at the heart of society. Wealth and power were no longer mysterious, or the unattainable preserve of a cosseted elite. Wealth could be grown and stored; power might be bought and sold.

We are the first creatures in the universe to pay attention to time and all that has happened. It was the unimaginable temperatures at the hearts of stars great and small, living and dying, that cooked the stuff of us. We have been 13 billion years in the making, from dust and scraps left over.

As of 2011, there were 118 elements in the periodic table. Iron is number 26. It was the Russian chemist Dmitri Ivanovich Mendeleev who first arranged the elements into that regular pattern,

like bricks in a wall. Such was his genius he left gaps for more –
elements yet to be discovered but which he knew must exist,
and whose properties he could predict. Of the 118 elements we
know today, 100 or so occur naturally. The rest, those heavier
than uranium, are the product of man-made nuclear reactions,
or carefully choreographed high-speed collisions in particle
accelerators.

Elements are made of atoms but atoms are not the least of it.
Within every atom is a nucleus and every nucleus is like an
infinitesimal planet, orbited not by moons but by electrons. Every
nucleus is made of neutrons and protons, and it is the precise
number of protons that gives each element its unique atomic
number. The nucleus of an iron atom contains 26 protons, and so
iron is number 26 in the periodic table.

All of this is fantastically complicated for a lesser mortal like
myself – hovering on the outer edge of my understanding – but
I persevere because it is important, and somehow revealing. In the
most fundamental, the most elemental way, iron is special. Nature
herself has decreed that its 26 protons combine with its neutrons
to make it incredibly stable. In fact iron is the most stable element
in the universe. Other elements – light ones like hydrogen and
helium, heavier ones like gold and uranium – have chaotic storms
raging in their tiny hearts; conflicting forces throwing them off
balance.

Iron is not like that. The heart of iron is a place of balance and
calm, where balance is restored. Every other element strives, wants
to be more like number 26, needs to be more stable and more
iron-like. Lighter elements like hydrogen would be more at peace
if only their atoms had more protons. Heavy ones like uranium
and polonium are so naturally unstable, with too many protons,
they fall apart in a bid to shed the excess – a physical breakdown
we call radioactivity.

Here, then, is the nature of the universe – ceaseless, restless
change as elements try to lose or gain protons, to become more
stable. Stable is what they and the universe want to be. It turns

out iron is the benchmark, the universal standard that makes the difference, all the way up and all the way down.

Change is the natural state of life on Earth as well. As a species we are driven by it. More than three millennia ago some of us, living in the eastern Mediterranean, discovered iron for ourselves. While bronze, its predecessor in our lives, had been all about magic and mystery, iron was practical and stable. After all those tens of thousands of years of flux, iron promised something reliable and enduring.

There was never any hope of a modern world built of a metal as fickle as bronze. A scaffold forged in iron, however – flexible and stable iron – might support any future we cared to design.

WARRIORS

'War was always here. Before man was, war waited for him.
The ultimate trade awaiting its ultimate practitioner.'
Cormac McCarthy, *Blood Meridian*

The Iron Age in Britain lasted from 800 BC until the arrival of the
Romans in AD 43.

Archaeologists make statements like that all the time, swiftly
bundling prehistory into tidy, manageable blocks – each with a
name or, more often than not, an age. The billions of empty years
after the Big Bang, the aeons required for the movement of tectonic
plates across the face of the Earth, the millions of years spent by
Mother Nature making the continents even vaguely liveable for
the likes of us – someone – cosmologists, geologists, archaeologists – had to try to put it all in order.

People, of one sort or another, began making stone tools around
two and a half million years ago, a few drops in the ocean of
geological time but an eternity for folk. After the Stone Age – an
expanse of time that found room for not one but several species
of humankind – came that of Bronze, beginning in Britain just
over 4,000 years ago. The iron tools that gave the Iron Age its
name were commonplace in these islands by about 500 BC. One
by one or in batches, the centuries could be filed neatly away.

Spend too much time thinking about 'Ages', however, and it is
easy to overlook the seconds, minutes, hours and days of which
human lives are actually made. Having contemplated billions,
millions and even thousands of years, a few hundred – like those

encompassed by the Iron Age – can seem like the stuff of moments. This is an unhelpful illusion, one that blinds us to the lives of individual men, women and children.

Silbury Hill, near Avebury in Wiltshire, standing 130 feet high and with a base that covers all of five acres, is one of the largest man-made prehistoric mounds in the world. It is often referred to, casually, as the work of 'Neolithic farmers', almost as though there were just a few of them and they all knew each other. Study of the construction process, however, has offered a variety of possibilities – most of which suggest the mound was generations in the making. Estimates vary from 100 to 500 years of work and it is at least certain the vast majority of the men, women and children who contributed to the building of Silbury Hill did not live to see it finished. If work was indeed under way there for 500 years, then it is as though the Millennium Dome, the O2 now squatting by the Thames in London, had been commissioned by King Henry VIII on the day of his coronation in 1509. It can be easy to make the mistake of compressing 500 ancient years, so that we trick ourselves into believing a mortal soul could see from one side to the other of such a vast landscape of time.

Some of the most recent thinking suggests the final shape of Silbury Hill – the finished article – was never the point anyway. Successive generations of architects and builders paid no heed to the objectives and motives of those that went before and instead set about putting their own identity, their own stamp on the thing. By the time work got under way on that most enigmatic of Neolithic creations, the surrounding landscape was peppered with tombs, circles, cursus monuments and long avenues of giant stones. Those farming peoples had a virtual mania for adding to, adapting and completely remodelling the man-made architecture that gave shape and meaning to their daily lives.

But then, as now, people were hardly likely to have seen them-selves merely as parts of a continuum, small cogs in a giant machine. Each generation does mostly what it wants. If the ancestors were invoked at any point, then surely it was only so their 'wishes' could be co-opted, exploited in line with whatever the dominant party had in mind anyway. The Neolithic farmers who were there at the start of Silbury Hill were dry bones and dust in the hands of those who took in the view from its summit.

From 800 BC until AD 43 is a span of almost eight and a half centuries – room for more than fifty generations of our species. If life expectancy in the Iron Age was 40 years – a generous estimate – then the era was more than 20 lifetimes long. Our own world is a consequence of the eighteenth-century Industrial Revolution. No more than fifteen generations have passed, just over three lifetimes of threescore and ten, since that tumultuous period – the Industrial Age – began and yet consider how much has changed and how distant seems the time of Richard Arkwright and his water frame, of James Watt and his steam engine.

The lives and times of people living in 800 BC were unimaginably lost and forgotten by the time the Roman Emperor Claudius arrived in Britannia with his elephants. The people living in the middle of the first century AD likely felt no more connection to the last of the bronzesmiths than we feel to those who gazed in wonder at Stephenson's Rocket.

The time of monument-building during the Stone Age, the duration of the Iron Age – these are spans of time we should struggle to comprehend. Does any living person anyway count themselves part of an age? The bigger picture is visible only from the distance provided by time. So when we look back at the centuries during which iron was or was not being used for tools we must allow that, at any given moment, people just like us were simply dealing with day-to-day life. The world turned and they coped with it as best they could, without bothering to notice whether or not theirs was an Iron Age.

The world has been home to people who are, first and foremost, individuals fighting to look after themselves and their close kin. Remembering this simple fact makes it possible to allow different interpretations for sites that are separated not just by geography but by time – even when they are remarkably similar in outward appearance.

When it comes to looking at sites separated by centuries, a word like 'hill fort', already loaded with connotations of warfare, becomes doubly misleading. Not only were hilltops occupied for reasons other than defence, they were also selected and used for different reasons at different times in our history. So the motivations of people choosing lofty locations in the Bronze Age, or in the early years of the Iron Age, might well have been quite different from those who settled similar places hundreds of years later.

People in Britain first thought about enclosing patches of land during the Neolithic, the New Stone Age. The causewayed enclosures and henges they created in those far-off days were probably inspired by the need to make contact with others. Scattered tribes and clans felt isolated in a mostly empty land and so took steps to establish places where they might congregate at special times of the year. The very act of coming together in the first place, to dig the encircling ditches and pile up the earthen banks, began the process of forging ties. Agreeing to meet there on pre-arranged days meant the connections could be maintained and deepened down through the years.

During the Bronze Age the population of Britain increased considerably. There may have been a contraction in the Late Bronze Age and during the early years of the Iron Age, due to a worsening climate, but the return of warmer, drier summers and the development of new farming technologies saw to it that numbers rose once more in the second half of the first millennium BC. After all the seemingly endless years of hunting and gathering and the time of the earliest farmers, when Britain was a land largely empty of people, some parts of the place actually began to fill up. For the first time there was genuine pressure on some of the available arable land. Instead of wanting ways to meet people and stay in touch, during the Middle and later Iron Age what folk needed was space, room to breathe.

Not every upland enclosure or henge was turned into a hill fort, that much is true. But as the years wore on, some people, in some of the busiest parts, must have looked up at the airy hilltops and ridges above them with fresh eyes.

Folk are always the same; it is their circumstances that vary. Now, instead of places at which all were welcome – for feasting, trading and negotiation – some of the high ground became valuable because it overlooked the fields, filled with crops and livestock. In some parts of Britain, notably in the south, land – and the animals and harvests that could be raised upon it – were the basis of wealth and power.

The earliest of the Iron Age hill forts were in use from around 600 BC. Crickley Hill in Gloucestershire – scene of that bloody battle during the Neolithic – was a fort again 3,000 years later. Inside were several roundhouses and one of them, close by the entrance, was conspicuously larger than all the others. Later the houses on Crickley Hill were all of a uniform size – suggesting that for a time social distinctions ceased to exist, as people battened down the hatches in the face of adversity and co-operated more closely.

Just as in the Neolithic, the fort on Crickley Hill was attacked and destroyed during the Iron Age, indicating that by the later years of the period defence was part of what at least some of the hill forts were about. Where they do appear defended, the houses and other domestic buildings were usually slight, almost ephemeral. When this is the case, the most noticeable and numerous structures inside are raised grain stores built of timber, and storage pits dug into the earth – suggesting that often the most important function of the interior of the later hill forts was the display of valuable surplus food supplies. It appears that as the Iron Age progressed, it became important to defend not just people, but food.

Archaeologists have struggled to understand how some of the vast earthwork and timber defences, elaborate though they were, could ever have worked in practice. Some of the hill forts – like Maiden Castle in Dorset and Danebury in Hampshire – are so huge it would have been impossible to man the miles of encircling ramparts effectively. Rather than working like castles – places within which to withstand a siege – hill forts make more sense as grand locations in which the arable wealth of a community was centralised ... where it could be seen and appreciated by all. A scattered population might have gathered behind the banks and ramparts during times of strife, finding strength in numbers, but the defences were likely always more about show than for any straightforward, practical military application.

If people's circumstances vary, then so do their responses to them. As the Iron Age progressed, the building and occupation of hill forts was more a feature of southern and western Britain. In eastern Britain, as far north as southern Scotland, settlement was often more open in character – villages and undefended homesteads surrounded by carefully organised fields.

There is a well-used maxim that goes, 'Absence of evidence is not evidence of absence'. Archaeologists have taken it almost for their own and it is certainly worth bearing in mind when looking at archaeological remains. The point is that hill forts in the most inaccessible locations would be those most likely to survive the passing of years. Modern farming and land use would tend to leave such sites alone, so they are still with us today. Defended sites built in the lowlands, within land that continued to attract farmers and the rest of the modern world, may well have long since been ploughed away or otherwise removed. This is an important caveat. Just because we do not find as many hill forts or other defended settlements in the generally lower land of eastern Britain, does not mean they were never there.

For all that, the absence of large-scale defended sites might be interpreted another way. It may be that people in the more open, arable landscapes of eastern Britain found other ways to get along with one another. The apparent tendency towards open settlements may well be a reflection of people coming together to make best use of the available land. The need for manned boundaries and distance – privacy even – may have been set aside, sacrificed in favour of the benefits to be had from tolerance.

Certainly the archaeological evidence in eastern England is of farmsteads and villages spread across wide areas. The differences are not hard and fast – there are some hill forts and some defended enclosures – but in the main it appears that in the east of England and into East Anglia, the trend in the Iron Age was for different communities to accept one another, to pool resources and put up with the consequences of greater population density without feeling the need to man the barricades against one another.

The presence of too many people has always provoked a variety of responses. The nineteenth-century scholar Thomas Malthus wrote, 'The power of population is infinitely greater than the power in the earth to produce subsistence for man.' That statement fell upon his world like a hammer blow – the first inkling for society that Mother Earth could not cope indefinitely in the face of unrestricted human breeding. Apparently there were limits, and one day they might be reached and breached. It seems pressures on land, as the Iron Age progressed from around 300 BC onwards, also encouraged ancient peoples across Britain to find ways to confront a new reality.

The archaeologist Richard Bradley has suggested that the surviving hill forts have skewed our view of how the majority of people were actually living in the second half of the first millennium BC.

By their very nature hill forts are impressive – suggestive of people in ancient times quite literally taking the high ground, the better to look down on those around and below them: the homes of an elite. It is impossible to walk around sites like Danebury, or Maiden Castle, or Hod Hill, and not feel as though the ancient occupants must have been nothing less than the lords of the land. But in *The Prehistory of Britain and Ireland*, Bradley questioned whether such places were ever really centres of civilisation for the majority. He wrote: 'They are strongly defended, they were built in dominant positions, and they enclose the sites of many round-houses, but it is difficult to see how they could have been inhabited continuously.' He added that it was 'tempting to suggest that these were aggregation sites, used on an occasional basis and possibly in the course of summer grazing'.

By virtue of their visibility in the archaeological record, hill forts may have attracted a level of attention from us that is disproportionate to their real significance. Large sections of the population in eastern and southern Britain were apparently living in open settlements in the lowlands, and such a lifestyle may have been just as representative as any centred around a hill fort. Wrote Bradley: 'For all the labour invested in their construction, the hill forts could have been a rather peripheral phenomenon'.

Suffice to say, hill forts have long preoccupied many archaeologists, but still there is little consensus concerning their function. Symbols of power; tribal capitals; places of refuge in a war-torn land; centralised grain stores; places of trade and manufacture – all of these labels and more besides have been invoked to explain why people expended so much effort enclosing hilltops. Perhaps all of the explanations have been correct . . . but at different times.

Why expect a single unifying explanation anyway? One hilltop may have been used several different ways, down through the years. Do we do justice to the life of a 70-year-old by understanding only how he lived out his last decade? What does seem to make sense is that the high ground of Britain has drawn people for millennia. The reasons for going there changed through the years and even today the locations of many of them continue to command our attention.

Sir Barry Cunliffe has been studying Danebury hill fort, in Hampshire, for the past 40 years. During that time more than half of the interior – a space covering around 12 acres – has been excavated, along with parts of the defences. It is one of the most comprehensively investigated hill forts in the whole of western Europe.

It has been established that Danebury was built early in the story of hill forts – around 600 BC – and then occupied continuously for the next 500 years. Around the same time that work got under way at Danebury, three other large hill forts were constructed in the surrounding countryside. On a clear day Bury Hill, Figsbury Ring and Quarley Hill are all visible from the summit of Danebury Hill. In a part of Hampshire where the land rarely rises more than 300 feet above sea level, all four sites occupy dominant positions. Danebury Hill is nearly 500 feet high, giving the hill fort commanding views over the surrounding farmland as well as towards the three neighbouring hill forts. They are equally spaced, all within similarly sized territories.

It is fascinating to imagine the world in which they were first built – to think that perhaps all four communities were at work at the same time, consolidating their territorial claims by digging deep ditches and raising great banks and ramparts of earth and timber. All the time they sweated and toiled, their neighbours might have been similarly employed; so that whenever a worker lifted his head from his labours he would have looked off into the distance to see the emerging chalk-white defences of one or all of the other three picked out against the green of the grass.

Sir Barry explained how the population living in that part of Hampshire in the middle years of the first millennium BC gradually filled the place to capacity. The farmland was good and rich and the agricultural practices of the time were producing more and more food. More food provided for yet more people and so the problems intensified.

Walking through the eastern entrance of Danebury today is still an unsettling experience. The drop from the top of the great sloping bank to the bottom of the accompanying ditch was once more than 50 feet. Two and a half thousand years of weathering have softened the profile somewhat, infilled some of the ditch and lowered the bank, but still they loom menacingly above the head of anyone seeking to pass through to the interior. The long curve of bank and ditch is no mere architectural affectation. If Danebury was designed to repel invaders, then would-be attackers had a lot of ground to cover before they even reached the stout wooden gates barred against them. All the time they passed in front of the bank they would have been at the mercy of defenders ranged above them, armed with slings and stones, longbows and arrows and spears.

Even an approach in a time of peace, to share bounty at a feast or to gather together with allies to reinforce ties, might have been intimidating. Being overlooked by the residents observing from above, friends or not, would have reminded the guests they were approaching an important place that was home to people of substance. All of it is cleverly designed to give the advantage – of status or of defence – to those in possession of the hill fort. If not purely defensive then at the very least there is something theatrical about a site like Danebury, so that at times people were 'on stage' there, performing roles that helped define relationships and pecking orders.

But according to Sir Barry, by 400 or so BC the time of the peaceful farming collective was over. In parts of Britain pressure on the land had pushed the emergent society to breaking point and a hill fort like Danebury was a visible response, a veritable clenched fist. Alongside all of the detailed evidence of life in the fort – grain pits and store rooms, roundhouses, shrines raised to honour gods or spirits – excavation has revealed copious evidence of awful dying there too.

Under a clear blue sky and a warm sun, Sir Barry unpacked cardboard boxes filled with Iron Age weaponry – along with piles of human remains that showed all too clearly the lethal use to which they had been put. It was a grisly haul, all of it collected from within Danebury itself. First there were beautifully crafted iron spearheads, long, slender shanks culminating in triangular points as big as beech leaves. One look at them confirms they were only ever intended for killing large animals, like men.

But if the weapons were chilling, they were as nothing compared to the butchered skulls. Sir Barry handed me the crown of one – the top halves of the eye sockets were clearly visible. It was punctured by a hole that exactly – exactly – matched the profile of the iron spearhead I had marvelled at moments before. If it was not the actual weapon that had done the deadly damage then it was one exactly the same, perhaps crafted by the same smith. It was a man's skull and it was easy to imagine him in action on some other bright day long ago in the moments before a well-aimed throwing spear arced down out of the blue. Then Sir Barry pointed out other, older damage on the same skull. At some point the warrior had received a fearsome blow to the top of his head from something like a hammer, or perhaps an axe. It had been enough to cave in a piece of bone the size of a man's thumb, but not enough to kill. Turning the crown upside down revealed how much hurt had been sustained on the inside. Heaven knows what kind of headache resulted, not to mention brain damage; but his skull had healed, the fragments knitting themselves together into a rough, pitted bump. It was gruesome, but graphic evidence of how much punishment a man can withstand.

The knowledge he had been so grievously wounded before painted an even more vivid picture of the man's life and death. On his last day on Earth he had gone into battle knowing full well what might happen, what he might have to endure in order to survive. He was not to be so lucky, however (if lucky is quite the right word), and instead he was felled for the last time, perhaps by a missile he never even saw coming. And there were plenty more bits and pieces to add further detail to a gory picture of at least one aspect of Iron Age life. Another skullcap bore evidence of multiple glancing sword wounds. On more than one occasion the individual in question had received the most radical of haircuts, right down to the bone. Whole flakes had been lifted from his crown before the moment came when the blade swung and a portion of skull as big as a child's hand was parted from his head, killing him instantly.

Sir Barry had chosen a spot near the elaborate eastern entrance for his demonstration – and just when I thought things could not get much worse for the Iron Age occupants of Danebury, he pointed to a part of the interior of the fort just yards away. 'Close to where we're standing was a very large pit into which they had thrown body parts – clearing up after a battle presumably. A large number of body parts and some of these skulls came from there.'

What he was describing was a charnel pit. When the death toll after a battle is too great to permit formal identification and separate handling of the fallen, there is sometimes no option but to heap the dismembered body parts and heads into a mass grave. Just such a horror had evidently unfolded at Danebury, on at least one occasion. So here had been a community well used to brutal hurt and death.

In our antiseptically clean, bubble-wrapped world we shy away from the wounded. News coverage of soldiers home from theatres of war like Iraq and Afghanistan can be hard to watch. Young men with faces destroyed, or missing limbs and condemned to lifetimes in wheelchairs – many of us find it easiest just to look away and forget.

But there have been times when some wounds were viewed differently. In the medieval world, for example, a man was hardly a man at all unless he had the scars to prove it – scars won in battle. Prince Henry, the future King Henry V, was lucky to survive the Battle of Shrewsbury, on 21 July 1403. Just sixteen years of age, young Hal was among a force of men-at-arms struggling to save the life of his father, Henry IV, when a rebel archer found his mark. Hal was felled by an arrow shot from a longbow, the missile penetrating his face 'overwharte' – meaning it came in from the side, Hal's left, plunging deeply into his cheekbone and burying the arrowhead in the bone behind his nose. It was five days before the royal surgeon, John Bradmor, was able to remove the thing, using a purpose-built tool he designed and made himself. The bespoke arrow-extractor was a fearsome-looking shaft of iron with a three-part head that Bradmor inserted into Hal's wound. By turning a screw on the other end, he was able to make the three wings open outwards, much like a rawlplug, so that they gripped inside the socket of the arrowhead. Once there was enough pur-chase, he pulled the offending article from the boy's face.

Needless to say, Hal was left with a scar that must have been disfiguring; but the war wound would have been worn with great pride for the rest of his life. Here was boy who had fought with men – and no ordinary boy, but a prince, and a king-in-waiting. His standing among his fellows – not to mention in the eyes of female admirers – would have been enhanced beyond words.

> 'Then will he strip his sleeve and show his scars.
> And say "These wounds I had on Crispin's day."'

Although we have no name or date for the Iron Age battle that filled a charnel pit with a heap of slain, it is reasonable to imagine the scarred survivors telling and retelling their stories with all the pride of any that stood with Henry at Agincourt 2,000 years later. Limbless or not, scarred or battered, they lived in a society that had learned to value the warrior, so that such men would have carried their wounds with a bearing won only in combat.

A charnel pit is indisputable proof that, for at least part of the Iron Age, might was right. Sir Barry described a time not of constant war, but of heightened tension. For some of the second half of the first millennium BC, Danebury, Bury Hill, Figsbury Ring and Quarley Hill were home to communities in competition with one another. The outer edges of their territories rubbed together, creating friction, and in that febrile atmosphere young men would have swaggered around, vying for respect and acknowledgement of status.

From time to time, said Sir Barry, raiding parties would have set out from one or other of the hill forts looking for trouble or just an opportunity to let off steam. When two such groups came together it would hardly take much before someone got hurt, perhaps badly. In the aftermath of such an incident – once word got back to the home fort of the wounded – outright, large-scale violence could well be the result. Around that time the great wooden gates of Danebury's eastern entrance were burnt to the ground on at least one occasion – yet more evidence of terrifying strife.

If the time of the peaceful farming collective really was over by 400 BC, then it is interesting to speculate about the kind of personality that might have prospered in the newly dangerous world. If the latest trade was war, then its natural practitioners would come to the fore, as they must.

We cannot know for certain, but it is tempting to imagine that, during times of peace, society was run by councils of elders, or by the headmen and women of prominent families. But cometh the hour, cometh the man and in times of violent trouble the leadership of communities would likely have fallen into the hands of those able to wield swords, defend and extend territories, bring troublemakers and upstarts to heel. If archaeologists like Sir Barry Cunliffe are correct, then during the Middle Iron Age Britain entered a period during which local power bases – like that at Danebury – fought it out for overall control, for power and for prestige. It was a time when individual status might best be established, improved and secured in battle.

The warrior was hardly invented in the Iron Age. At least as early as the Bronze Age, men were going to their graves accompanied by items that might suggest a martial life and death. The same is probably just as true for at least some of the Stone Age skeletons that have been found with flint knives, arrowheads and axes.

In 1834 a landowner excavated a burial mound on his estate near Scarborough, in north Yorkshire, and found the remains of a man buried within a tree trunk that had been hollowed out to form a coffin of sorts. Named Gristhorpe Man, after the farmland on which he was found, he has been described by modern archaeologists as a warrior chieftain.

In life he had reached a height of six feet. Given that he also had a full set of good teeth and had lived to an age of perhaps 40 years or more, it seems likely he had access to a privileged diet as well. Forensic examination of the remains concluded he had died of natural causes; but his bones bore the signs of many healed fractures, suggestive perhaps of the hard life of a warrior.

Just as evocative as the man's bones were the grave goods that accompanied them. The burial party had provided Gristhorpe Man with a vessel made of bark that had once been sealed and may have contained some sort of drink, along with a wicker basket that still bore the residue of food more than four millennia after it first went into the ground. There were also flint tools and a bronze knife that had been cast from Irish copper and Cornish tin. Analysis suggested that by the time it was made into a knife, the metal had been recycled many times over many years. It was probably imbued with untold power. A knife may also be interpreted as the tool of a hunter; but surely the ceremony and care that attended the death and burial of Gristhorpe Man speak of a figure revered for his fighting prowess and for his resilience in the face of many injuries suffered in battle, all of them survived.

In 2009 archaeologists excavating a Bronze Age site at Forteviot, in Perthshire in Scotland, found a unique warrior burial beneath a giant sandstone slab engraved with a spiral and an axe-head. Forteviot has mattered to people for millennia. It is where Kenneth Mac Alpin, a fabled Scottish 'king', is supposed to have died, in a palace, in the ninth century AD. For thousands of years before that the area inspired countless generations of prehistoric peoples to build monuments and bury their dead.

Sometime between 2300 and 2100 BC, a burial party was at great pains to create a last resting place fit for one of their finest men. First a grave was cut through to the subsoil and lined with slabs. Then the bottom was covered with a layer of white quartz pebbles and a lattice woven from strips of birch bark, before the dead man's body was laid down along with items including a copper knife in a leather scabbard, a carved wooden bowl and a second container made of leather and wood. The sandstone slab was six feet square, more than a foot thick and weighed four tons. The engravings were pecked into the underside, so as to face the dead man, and are instantly reminiscent of the burial within the Bronze Age cairn in Kilmartin Glen.

That such effort was spent, so much thought committed, makes clear the man beneath the stone was a leader of men. The knife in its sheath may well mean he was a fighter as well. Knives are always going to be slightly ambiguous grave goods. They may after all represent nothing more than the power to possess metal. Swords, on the other hand, are only for fighting and killing other people at close quarters. It is surely safe to assume that those facing eternity armed with such priceless items were either warriors, or those who wished they had been.

Three stunningly beautiful Late Bronze Age swords, together with a bronze pommel, a bronze chape from a scabbard and two bronze pins, were found at Tarves, in Aberdeenshire. Known as the Tarves hoard, the assemblage has been interpreted by archaeologists as an offering buried in memory of the warrior who owned and wielded them. They date from between 1000 and 850 BC – a time when formal burials were rare anyway. It seems believable that while the man's remains were disposed of elsewhere, possibly by excarnation, his retinue honoured his passing by sending his weaponry back to the Earth, or to the gods, or to the ancestors, in a grave of their own.

Sir Barry's investigation of the wider landscape of Hampshire suggests that while the other hill forts gradually went out of use after 400 BC, the community centred on Danebury prevailed. Survey and excavation has found Danebury was surrounded by scores of smaller farms and homesteads. It is likely the grain pits and storage buildings were the communal reservoir for the produce from all of those smallholdings.

Richard Bradley has suggested hill forts like Danebury might have been built almost as representations of giant roundhouses. 'Such places may have been conceived as the houses of an entire community who could have used them in much the same way as an early medieval assembly,' he wrote. 'Perhaps they were where the communal business was transacted and where important decisions were made.'

Gradually though, the smaller settlements were abandoned while Danebury itself rose in prominence. Sir Barry and others refer to places like Danebury at this time as 'developed hill forts' – although perhaps a term like 'mega hill fort' conveys more of a sense of their status. Maybe the charnel pit was filled – and the gateway torched by attackers – during a time when life in that part of Hampshire had reached a point where it was almost unbearable on account of population pressure and resultant violence. Maybe the occupants of the surrounding homesteads – those within the bailiwick of Danebury – were too exposed to constant raiding and so opted to move into the hill fort itself in search of protection.

Some observers have detected the presence of a chieftain in Danebury in the later Iron Age, presumably with some sort of elite around him. There are structures that have been interpreted as shrines, along with evidence of ritualised burials of animals, all suggesting there may have been something of a priestly class massaging the ego of the leader, his family and their followers.

It is a long, slow pull to the summit of Danebury Hill, up a fairly steep grass-covered slope. When Sir Barry first arrived at the site in 1969, it was an altogether different place, slumbering beneath a forest of trees that had sprung up in the ditches and across much of the interior during the millennia of abandonment. Many were diseased, making their clearance in advance of survey and excavation less of a quandary. Nowadays the fort and its surrounding slopes are the domain of dog walkers and sightseers. The ramparts – and the distance – give the advantage to observers at the top. Standing up there, watching people approach, you get plenty of time to check them out, assess their mood – alone or in couples or groups, walking fast or slow, heads up or heads down, arms swinging or hands in pockets. By the time they are close enough for eye contact you feel you have a real sense of their demeanour, and their intentions. As in so much of life, height confers advantage.

What can we say about Britain in the second half of the Iron Age, in the years before the hill forts fell from use and trees grew, like forests of thorns round enchanted castles? It was a country of disparate peoples living many different ways – ways dictated by their geographical circumstances and that made sense to them. By the time Danebury was a 'developed hill fort', some farmers in northern Scotland were brooding behind the barred doors of their broch towers. Elsewhere folk built more modest defended homesteads, thick-walled duns, and retreated inside them whenever strangers came calling. While communities in the east of Britain were growing their homesteads and farms into full-blown villages surrounded by open field systems, many communities in Scotland and Ireland felt it best to inhabit crannogs. Britain had become a land of strong regional identities, allegiance paid first and foremost to the tribe. The leaders were warriors now, chieftains controlling grain and people alike. It was also a populous place where as much as possible of the arable land was exploited to grow the crops and keep the animals upon which power and prestige were now based. There were strong ties, focused around trade as well as kinship, with Continental Europe.

If archaeologists and others have tended to lump centuries and millennia together and give them names, in an effort to impose some sense of order, then they have done something similar with the people as well. There has certainly been a mania for cataloguing the products of the past, making every broken thing fit into something like a periodic table. By ordering the artefacts – the pottery, the knives and swords, the brooches and pins – we have sought also to find neat labels for whole swathes of population.

One of the most problematic words in the archaeologist's lexicon is 'culture'. *The Oxford English Reference Dictionary* offers several definitions, including: 'the arts and other manifestations of human intellectual achievement regarded collectively ... the customs, civilisation, and achievements of a particular time or people ... the way of life of a particular society or group.'

In the endless quest to tidy the place up a bit, archaeologists have split past time into ages, determined by technological achievement. With greater audacity, however, they have had much fun defining past peoples by cultures. If enough similarities are found between two sets of artefacts, unearthed hundreds or even thousands of miles apart, then it is to be assumed those who made and used them must have been united across that distance by a shared set of values and beliefs. They were in a sense one people, unified by a culture.

It is not, of course, just the Iron Age that has been treated this way. The earliest copper and gold objects in Britain were recovered from graves alongside clay beakers. Similar graves found across Europe, containing metal artefacts and the same sort of drinking vessels, enabled archaeologists to define an entire 'Beaker Culture'. By now there is a culture to fit just about everyone. The nagging worry in all of this, however, is the fact that we cannot know how the people actually described themselves – who they considered themselves to be, what 'culture', if any, they felt they belonged to.

Archaeologists have pressed ahead regardless, posthumously unifying the departed into groups they have invented for their own convenience. Just as the Mormons have been in the habit of baptising the dead, giving them the benefit of the doubt and hope of redemption, so archaeologists examine the contents of graves and place their occupants into one culture or another.

In 1846 Johann Georg Ramsauer, a mining engineer by trade but an antiquarian on the side, found an ancient cemetery near the lakeside village of Hallstatt, in his native Austria. His excavations on the site eventually revealed more than a thousand graves, some of which contained items that had been imported from the Classical world of the Mediterranean. It was not long before archaeologists were spotting similarities between artefacts found elsewhere and those turning up in vast quantities in Ramsauer's astonishingly rich Austrian graves; and so the Hallstatt Culture was born. It is generally accepted that it was dominant in central Europe during the first half of the Iron Age – that people living in the swathe of territory now occupied by the modern countries of Austria, the Czech Republic, France, Germany, Slovenia and Slovakia in the years between about 800 and 450 BC – were all doing things the Hallstatt way.

During the second half of the Iron Age, however, the Hallstatt Culture seemingly evolved into something slightly different. Finds made in 1857 in the shallows of a lake in the Swiss canton of

Neuchâtel were identified as belonging to a younger culture –
called La Tène after the town nearest to the original finds – so that
now the entire Iron Age of much of central, northern and western
Europe could be seen in cultural terms. Hallstatt was an evolution
of earlier Bronze Age traditions and La Tène was its successor, each
seemingly shaping people's lives and thinking until the advent of
the Roman Empire. This is fair enough as long as we bear in mind
that the cultures in question are the creations of archaeologists, not
the people themselves. The Division Bell rings and the strengthless
dead of the Iron Age are ushered into one lobby or the other,
Hallstatt or La Tène.

All of which brings us to the problem of the Celts. If culture is
a concept to approach with caution, then the other 'c-word' is a
hazard of a whole different order of magnitude. Before considering
its many meanings, it may be better to start with some art.

Within the collections of the British Museum in London are
some Iron Age artworks that are considered to be without equal.
They were made in Britain by British craftsmen and the best of
them are nothing less than sublime. In among all else that was
going on – the building and rebuilding of hill forts, the storage
and display of grain as a basis of power, the outbreak of wars and
the rise of the warriors to fight them – domestic art too produced
its finest flowering.

Imagine my trepidation, then, on learning I was to have the
opportunity to handle a few of its priceless, irreplaceable creations.
Once the museum was closed to the public, I was ushered into
one of the quiet galleries. There, on a table covered with a black
cloth, lay an iron spearhead and a bronze shield. Just seeing them
outside their glass cases was a shock, but the knowledge that
I could actually touch them was enough to make my hands tremble
as I approached.

The spearhead had been recovered from the River Thames and
more than two millennia in wet mud have resulted in the loss of
most of one half to the slow smoulder of corrosion. There is more
than enough remaining of the whole, however, to take the breath

away. Apart from anything else, it is a testament to the care and skill of the conservator who has stablised the piece, putting the rust to sleep.

Longer than a man's hand, it is an elegant, slender leaf shape with a finely wrought spine running down its centre, giving it strength as well as symmetry. What makes it a marvel, though, are decorative strips of bronze, two on each face, that transform it from mere weapon into ceremonial talisman. Surely it was never meant for combat, commissioned instead by a warrior who had already triumphed and who could command the very best in honour of his prowess.

The craftsman has used a sharp-edged tool harder than the bronze, presumably one made of iron, to stamp the surfaces with a painstakingly fine pattern of curves, swirls and circles – designs typical of La Tène metalwork. The so-called River Thames Spearhead is thought to have been made between 200 and 50 BC and to hold it in your hands is to confront a reality more affecting by far than any abstract notion of a culture. Before the coming of the Romans there was an appreciation in Britain of fine things, the very finest, and whoever designed and fashioned that spearhead was already the master of anything the conquerors might seek to teach.

The shield exudes even more power. Pulled from the Thames, like the spearhead, it is called the Battersea Shield and is thought to have been made sometime between 350 and 50 BC. It is a boy's dream of a warrior's shield – shining like gold and lavishly decorated with all the extravagant flair a hero could wish for. If I am honest, my first thought was that it looked like a prop from a swords-and-sandals epic movie, like *Gladiator* or *300*.

Standing proud of the flat surface of the shield are three circular areas filled with ornate decorations. These are the roundels and each is an exuberant display of technical skill and artistic genius. Elegant curls and circles mirror each other on either side of the long axis. Some experts insist they can see, in the centrepiece, the stylised head and antlers of a stag. Much of the raised decoration has been created using a technique called repoussé, which meant hammering the bronze from the reverse side until the design stood out from the front surface. In a final flourish, 27 red enamel jewels were incorporated into the circles and swirls so that the shield appears studded with rubies.

Circles and swirls: something at the heart of human beings is possessed by the spin. The Megalithic art of the Neolithic is filled with them, etched and pecked into stones again and again. Then there were the stone and timber circles themselves, inspired perhaps by the movement of the night sky. Natural laws saw to it the circle was everywhere – from the shape of the sun and the Moon to the tiny depressions made by the stalks of wind-blown sea grass shivering in the sand.

Inside the passage grave of Newgrange – on a stone forming part of the chamber that is illuminated by the sun once every year – there is a triple spiral. This perfect form, three inter-connected spirals with no beginning and no end, occurred to artists again and again. The triple spiral – or triskele – is also a recurrent feature of Celtic art.

As far as artists were concerned, once the circle was set in motion it never stopped. W.B. Yeats was obsessed with it and referred to it over and over:

> 'Turning and turning in the widening gyre
> The falcon cannot hear the falconer;
> Things fall apart; the centre cannot hold;'

The vortex is also central to the universe. Physicists have their 'Law of the conservation of angular momentum', descriptive of the spin that set everything in place and keeps it there. It began billions of years ago and must not stop and since it is everywhere – from smallest to greatest, inside the nuclei of atoms and driving galaxies – it is hardly surprising someone noticed. Having spotted the spin very early on, it seems artists were especially taken with it.

Almost as impressive as the artistry is the inventiveness displayed by the metal-working itself. For one thing the shield has not been fashioned from a single sheet. Instead several individual pieces of beaten bronze have been fitted together with riveted joints that have in turn been concealed beneath the details of the roundels. The overall rigidity of the piece has been improved by an encircling strip of bronze around the outside rim that binds the whole.

What is not immediately obvious at first sight is that the Battersea Shield is in fact a shield cover. For all the evident skill of the smith, it is still just a hopelessly thin sheet of metal supporting three heavy roundels. What survives today would once have been fixed onto a wooden shield; but thousands of years in the Thames have ensured that only the metal has lasted. While certain to make the heart of any small boy beat faster, the Battersea Shield could never have been intended for action. Instead it is more likely it was carried by an already victorious warrior chief, perhaps at the head of a celebratory parade that made its way to the banks of the river for a service of thanksgiving. We can imagine some appropriate speech-making – thanking the gods for all their righteous energies – before the masterpiece was consigned to the waters for ever. Something similar happened to the spearhead as well.

It is not enough to gaze in wonder at great artworks like the Thames Spearhead and the Battersea Shield. We are also obliged to ask about their makers. Who were they and what inspired the glorious flowering of art and design in Britain that archaeologists have dated to the years after about 350 BC?

The simplest answer has long been that they were Celts, part of a culture said to have permeated and shaped the thinking of many of Europe's inhabitants for a thousand years or more before the eventual ascendancy of Rome. It was Roman historians and geographers who first used the label Celt – but they applied it only to tribes they encountered on Continental Europe. Those writers actually borrowed 'Celt' from the Greeks, who used their own word *Keltoi* to describe any foreigner, so that it meant anyone who was not Roman. It is even fair to say they used the word as an alternative way of referring to people they normally called

Gauls – meaning the inhabitants of the swathe of territory they named Gaul, occupied now by Belgium, France, northern Italy and Switzerland.

Inconveniently – and confusingly for us – they never used Celt or Celtic to describe the peoples of Britain after the conquest of them. It seems that whatever they knew, and then learned, of the inhabitants of the archipelago off to the north-west, all but lost in the seas that bounded the world that they called Oceanus – they always considered them significantly different from those barbarians they had encountered closer to home: different enough indeed to require their own name, and that name was 'Britanni'. So the Celts as the Romans understood them were land-locked, separate not just from the Britanni but also from another northern European population, known to the same writers as the 'Germani'.

During the Iron Age some of the Celtic leaders grew rich from trade along the great Continental rivers that gave them access to the wider world. Archaeologists see the influence of things Celtic spreading in time not just to the British Isles and Ireland, but also to parts of the Iberian Peninsula and as far east as Turkey. Whatever the truth of the Hallstatt and La Tène 'cultures', they were apparently influenced in turn both by the emerging Classical world to the south, and by that of the Scythians to the east.

The Scythians were horse-riding nomads who, during the first millennium BC, steadily spread westwards from their homeland on the steppes between the Black and the Caspian Seas. They were pastoralists to begin with, but climate change back home gradually turned their grasslands into dust. Driven to follow their herds into greener pastures, they encountered the peoples of eastern Europe – and found they were able to subjugate many of them. As they became more successful and dominant in their new demesne, they settled into the life of arable farmers and aggressive slavers.

This, then, was the rich mix flowing through the heartlands of the Celts. As well as enjoying imported luxury goods from east, west and south, they also developed a decorative style that was all their own. This was the birth of Celtic art.

Whoever the Celts were, whatever Celticness was, they and it were changed by Britain, made different. When artists in Britain began encountering Continental Celtic art around 350 BC, they used it as the seed crop from which to grow something unique. It has been said by art historians that the innovation and sophistication of British Celtic art was the single greatest contribution ever made by these islands to the world of design.

Evidence in support of that bold claim is to be found in the third piece of Iron Age artwork I was permitted to handle in the British Museum, alongside the spearhead and the shield – the so-called Kirkburn Sword. Found during the excavation of an Iron Age cemetery in east Yorkshire in 1987, it is regarded as perhaps the finest sword of the period to have been found anywhere in Europe. It was made between 300 and 200 BC and is as far removed from a cast bronze sword as is a Ferrari from a horse-drawn chariot.

It is a composite item, comprising a total of 70 separate pieces, all of which had to be designed and made before the finished object could be assembled. The hilt alone comprises 37 pieces of bronze, horn and iron. Once the more functional parts had been put together, the sword and its scabbard were decorated – with La Tène scrolls and curls cut into the metal, but also with pieces of specially made red glass that would once have suggested the grim lustre of freshly spilled blood. Even more fascinating, analysis of the metal has shown evidence of repairs, suggesting this was a working sword that was damaged in battle on at least one occasion.

The art of the European Celtic Iron Age is rightly celebrated. It was in the hands of artists and craftsmen in Britain, however, that it was elevated to a whole new level of mastery and sophistication. British Celtic art is unique, made different by the peoples of the islands in which it was made. It is also worth noting that British Celtic art finds its most exquisite expression not in jewellery but in the sorts of things desired and required by a new elite – the warriors. They had grown in stature so that by the later years of the Iron Age the most powerful among them could demand the very best, the most glamorous tools of their specialist trade.

The Kirkburn Sword was the property of a man known to archaeologists as the Kirkburn Warrior. In life he was the owner of that splendid sword and in death he was treated to an altogether special send-off. The burial party – surely his comrades-in-arms – laid him in his grave lying on his left side and accompanied by his sword. While the body was still exposed to the air, or only lightly covered with earth, three spears were thrust points-first into the grave. They may even have been thrust into the man's body.

Imagine the impact of that moment on those gathered to witness the funeral rite. (Archaeologists have established that the man was aged somewhere between 20 and 35 years old and there were no signs of injury on the body. Perhaps death by natural causes was deemed beneath the dignity of such a man, and those closest to him were moved to grant him the posthumous honour of a warrior's death.) Whatever the explanation, the shafts were left sticking out of the grave as it was backfilled. When they were finished, the mourners created a mound that bristled with spears – so it was clear to any who saw it that here was a great man, a man of war. The ends of the shafts appeared to have been scorched to black in the flames of a fire, the better to resist the effects of decay and so last longer.

The Kirkburn Warrior was not alone in his glory. Nearby in the same small cemetery a man of similar age had been buried with a disassembled chariot, another fighter no doubt. His body had been covered with a shirt of chainmail, laid upside down upon him so the hem of the garment was across the chest, the shoulders across the legs. He had been provided with food for the journey as well, a pig's skull neatly split in two.

At a time when most bodies were simply exposed to the attentions of scavengers, something quite different was happening in part of east Yorkshire. In the Wolds and in the East Riding are Iron Age cemeteries that seem out of place in Britain, even alien. Archaeologists have decided they represent nothing less than another culture – the Arras Culture – and its eccentricities have been the subject of fierce debate since the first graves came to light in the nineteenth century.

Arras is more familiar as the name of a city in north-eastern France and the battle fought in and around it during April and May 1917; and a French connection has long been cited as part of an explanation for what was going on in east Yorkshire during the later Iron Age. When archaeologists first came upon the cemeteries close by the east Yorkshire towns of Arras and Kirkburn, they assumed the different burial practices were evidence of invasion. Archaeologist Melanie Giles, however, has studied the cemeteries for several years and is among a growing number of experts who dispute the notion.

We spent some hours together weaving our way between the low, eroded barrows of an Iron Age cemetery at Scorborough, near the town of Beverley. The sky seemed low enough to touch and dank mist hung in the air or clung to our clothes and hair. It was the right sort of day for talking about the dead.

Giles explained that, while fairly common in parts of east and north Yorkshire, such barrows are unknown elsewhere in the British Isles and Ireland. Something similar, however – their nearest relatives, as it were – is to be found in the Marne-Moselle region of northern France. 'There are lots of different ideas about this, lots of different debates,' she said. 'Some people thought it was a massive invasion, a kind of war band coming across. But, in fact, most of these people look as if they are local. They were born and brought up here.'

'We might be looking at just a small group of important or powerful people coming across from the Continent,' said Giles. 'And some of the grave goods we find in the barrows reinforce that sense that there are contacts with the Continent.' Contact with the Continent – but no invasion. According to the work of archaeologists like Melanie Giles, the Celtic culture that came to represent an entire era of the history of ancient Britain may have had its genesis in the Continentally connected warrior elites of east Yorkshire. If they are right, then the handful of individuals that did cross from northern France to the east of England certainly left their mark. The locals may have been thoroughly impressed by the clothing and jewellery fashions of the incomers. If foreign meant exotic, and desirable, then local craftspeople might have sought to ape what they saw so as to appeal to their customers among the resident population.

When the incomers died it would have made sense for them to be buried in line with the customs they had brought with them from back home. A trend was set then for fashion in death as well as life and local funerary traditions may have been set aside in favour of new ones. The skeletons in the barrows face east, suggesting perhaps that in death it was thought best to face the direction from which the revered ancestors, and their ideas, had originally come. But, as usual, formal burial was for the few; and often in the British Celtic Iron Age the few were great warriors.

A few miles west of the market town of Driffield, still in the East Riding, is a Yorkshire Wolds village glorying in the unforgettable name of Wetwang. Despite what generations of comedians have said, it might mean nothing more than 'wet field' – in contrast to the 'dry field' of Driffield. The Iron Age is thick on the ground between Wetwang and nearby Garton, with settlements of roundhouses and a cemetery containing well over 400 burials.

During recent excavations archaeologists found three graves there of individuals who had been buried with those most enigmatic and evocative of two-wheeled vehicles, chariots. There is as much debate about 'chariots' as there is about the Arras Culture itself. Many specialists object to the word, saying it is too resonant of *Ben-Hur* and sure to make people think they were used only by warriors. Rather than mobile weapons platforms, driven into battle by spear-throwing, sword-wielding heroes, they may have been just carts for getting from A to B. It is also argued by some that when they are found in graves they ought to be seen first as the hearse and then as the coffin of the deceased. Suffice it to say, there is no agreement on whether 'chariot burials' are always 'warrior burials'.

The story of the Arras Culture, apparently limited to east York-shire, was further complicated by the discovery of a chariot burial just west of Edinburgh in 2001. A new traffic interchange was soon to be built close to the site of a Bronze Age cairn and, given the obvious sensitivity of the site, archaeologists were brought in to carry out survey and excavation in advance of the work. What they found on the outskirts of the Scottish capital was a chariot burial.

The Newbridge chariot had been buried intact – unlike the Yorkshire examples but in keeping with the tradition in Iron Age France. Although the human remains had long since decayed, leaving no trace, there was no doubting it was a high-status grave. Clearly at least one Continentally connected Yorkshireman had contacts in northern Britain as well.

One of the three chariot burials excavated at Wetwang was certainly a challenge to the idea they could only ever represent the rites accorded to fighting men. In grave number 2, lying on top of the wheels and cockpit of a chariot, was the skeleton of a woman. The story of so much ancient history is the story of men. Formal burial (where it occurs), and the grave goods that accompanied it, is usually redolent of masculinity. So often it is knives, spearheads, axes and arrowheads that go into the ground: boys' toys.

But the so-called 'Wetwang Woman' was altogether different, suggesting that by 300 BC or so, in east Yorkshire if nowhere else, the importance of the feminine was finally being recognised as well. Analysis of her skeleton revealed she lived well into her forties at least – an older, even an elderly woman by Iron Age standards. Her teeth were in good condition, indicating access to a privileged diet; so for all of her long life she enjoyed high status, free from the more mundane concerns of daily life 2,300 years ago.

The chariot had been taken apart before it went into the ground, the constituent parts laid out in a careful symmetry. The cockpit and central pole seem to have gone in first, before the two-spoked wheels were laid on top along with all the horse furniture of bits, traces and the like. The woman's body had apparently been laid down on the chariot parts towards the end of the whole process. Burial with a vehicle speaks of a journey as well as status. Perhaps it acknowledged how far she had come in life, as well as an immeasurable distance to be travelled into the unknown.

Wetwang Woman was also accompanied into the afterlife by several of her personal possessions. One was quickly dubbed the 'bean tin', and that is certainly what it looks like. On closer inspection it turns out to be a small canister made of thin sheet bronze, richly decorated with patterns of incised curves and lines and suspended from a fine bronze chain fixed at both ends. At the centre of top and bottom is a red enamel roundel. Fascinatingly, the bean tin is and was completely sealed. If it ever contained anything it must have been something small and organic, because it seems utterly empty now. There has been endless speculation as to its function. Perhaps it held a handful of beans or seeds so that it could be used as some sort of ceremonial rattle. Maybe it was fixed on her belt so that it rattled on her hip as she walked.

There was also a finely wrought iron object that has been called a mirror – understandably, since it has precisely the shape of the sort of thing you might find on a lady's dressing table. In this instance, however, there is no glass and the only reflection would have been that returned by the highly polished surface of the metal itself. It is badly corroded now, though, and so fragile I was not even permitted to touch it for fear it might crumble in my hands.

For me the word 'mirror' is unsatisfactory, suggesting as it does something frivolous and vain. More recently archaeologists like Giles have suggested that such items were intended not to reflect the likenesses and world of the living, but to provide a window on the world of the dead. Perhaps when she looked at that gleaming surface the woman glimpsed not her own reflection but something less than sharp and not quite perfectly remembered – not her own face but that of her mother, or her grandmother. A woman in possession of such an object, able to wield the power that comes from contact with other worlds, might have been feared and revered in equal measure.

Missing from the grave of Wetwang Woman – and most of the other chariot graves – are the horses. (The so-called 'King's Barrow' appeared to have contained a pair of animals, but that was unusual.) When we think of a time when mighty Celtic warriors roamed the land, surely we see them on horseback? We have the men and the weapons; and in Wetwang Woman perhaps we have the wisdom and guile of the seer who sent them forth and nursed their egos on their return. It was a find made not in Yorkshire, but back in that mega hill fort in Hampshire that at last completed the visual image of the Celtic heroes of legend.

Horses are rare throughout the prehistory of Britain, even on farms. Many horse bones, however – skulls in particular – were recovered during Sir Barry Cunliffe's excavations at Danebury. Often the heads had been deliberately buried as part of some or other ritual but analysis of a complete skeleton, by specialist Robin Bendrey, revealed indications that the animal had likely been rather more than a beast of burden. 'The lifetime activities of the horse will leave different markers in the skeleton,' he said. He added that a clearly visible band of white enamel on one of the animal's teeth showed it had been made to wear a bit; but more significant by far was a gaping fracture running across the centre of one of the vertebrae in its spine. 'This is evidence that this horse was ridden – and this is the first evidence we have for riding in prehistoric Britain.'

More than any polished stone axe or bronze sword, the ridden horse is a symbol of power. It is said that when some of the peoples of South America first encountered mounted Spaniards in the sixteenth century, they thought they were looking at creatures that were half-man and half-beast. The centaurs of Greek legend too are said to have been conjured up in the imaginations of the people of the Minoan Aegean after their first sight of nomadic horsemen making forays into their territory.

But as well as commanding that first shock and awe, men on

horseback would have enjoyed numerous practical advantages over those limited to two legs or being pulled on carts or chariots. 'The horse would have allowed people to travel further and faster,' said Bendrey. 'The horse would also have revolutionised warfare. It would have changed raiding. People could raid at greater distances – and faster. You could attack a neighbouring settlement, take control of their cattle. A man on a horse would have had major advantages over a man on foot.'

With this final piece of the jigsaw in place, our image of the Kirkburn Warrior might finally match that of the mythical heroes. He died in the prime of his life and was laid to rest beneath a green mound spiked with spears. But his comrades may have grown old and grey regaling their children, and their children's children, with stories of the great man they remembered from their youth. And perhaps when they closed their eyes and pictured him then, blood-soaked sword in hand, he was on horseback.

If the ridden horse was a relatively late development, then that other great companion of the hero, the hunting dog, was part of the British tradition for much longer. British dogs were famed on the Continent and their export would have been a huge earner for those tribes that had perfected the art of breeding the best of them. The Greek geographer Strabo wrote about hunting dogs being exported from Britain to Rome and described them as small, strong, rough-haired, fleet of foot and with a keen sense of smell. In the third century AD the Roman poet Nemesianus immortalised their quality in a work he called 'The Hunt': 'Besides the dogs bred in Sparta ... you should also raise the breed which comes from Britain, because they are fast and good for our hunting.' They may have been related to the Gaulish hunting dogs described by another Roman writer, Arrian. He wrote that they were called *vertragi* – a word he claimed meant 'speed' in the Gaulish tongue. Those beasts were muscular, lean, with broad chests and long necks and muzzles.

Hunting dogs from Ireland were also sought after, and on that island they were to become the stuff of legend. Warriors keen to show how courageous and loyal they were would even refer to themselves as hunting dogs. The real name of the great Irish hero Cú Chulainn was Setanta; but after he killed the best hound of the blacksmith Culann, in self-defence, he volunteered to serve as the beast's replacement. From that moment he was Cú Chulainn, 'Culann's hound'. He chose to retain the name for all his life, long after the debt to the smith had been repaid.

By around 200 BC, the so-called Celtic culture had spread right across Britain and Ireland. Power was increasingly in the hands of the sort of leaders able to draw fighting men to their sides in regional centres like Danebury hill fort; it was the time of the Celtic chieftain. But always there is that same burning question: just who were the Celts?

As a Scot I am used to hearing about my 'Celtic' roots. I have circumnavigated the coastlines of Britain and Ireland more than once and I can safely say there is a lively sense of Celticness in Cornwall, in Wales, all around both Irelands and drilled through much of my own homeland like veins of a precious mineral. The problem is I cannot be sure how old, and therefore how genuine, that feeling really is. There are those who believe the Celts were united by more than culture. Some are convinced they were – and remain to this day – a separate race of people. Proving or disproving that notion, however, is a challenge to say the least.

There is a sort of archaeology that involves digging not into the earth but inside the cells of our bodies. It is practised by scientists and they are looking for a substance called deoxyribonucleic acid (DNA). Curled inside the nucleus of every cell of every human body is an infinitesimal thread of DNA. Our bodies are built from simple proteins and it is that magical little thread, plaited like a corn dolly, that controls the process. Whether we are tall or short; dark-haired, ginger or blond; fair-skinned or dark brown and with blue, brown or hazel eyes – all of these and every other variation besides are the products of our DNA.

It sounds simple enough, but the principal difficulty for gene scientists lies in the fact that *Homo sapiens sapiens* is a very young species of animal indeed. Modern humans began in sub-Saharan Africa over 200,000 years ago and stayed snuggled in that warm cradle until as recently as 50,000 or 60,000 BC. It has taken no more than 60 millennia for us to spread across the entire planet, exploiting every nook and cranny.

From nature's point of view, therefore, we might as well have been born yesterday. Genetic differences evolve with glacial slowness and so in most of the ways that matter we are identical to one another – all 6.7 billion of us. From the point of view of our DNA, each of us shares 99.9 per cent of the stuff with everybody else – which means the differences between a ginger-haired Scot on the bus in Glasgow, a Japanese factory worker practising Tai Chi in a park in Tokyo and a Zulu farmer counting his goats in KwaZulu-Natal are lurking somewhere in just 0.1 per cent of that little plait. Every one of us has three billion blocks of DNA in our blueprint and 2.997 billion of yours are the same as mine. We might as well be clones.

To make matters even worse for the DNA counters, we are the products of a tiny original population. Archaeologists and palaeontologists have found reason to believe our species came terrifyingly close to extinction in the years before some of them chose to head north out of Africa. We may in fact be the descendants of just a few thousand survivors who clung on in the heartlands while all around them was disease, starvation and death. We are not quite inbred, but for a while there it was a close-run thing. Small wonder that, genetically speaking, we are still so tightly bound together.

Work carried out by geneticists over the last decade or so has already established something astonishing about the people alive in Britain today. With the obvious exception of the most recent arrivals – people whose families came here from their homes in Pakistan, the West Indies and suchlike in the last 60 years or so – the vast majority living in these islands are the direct descendants of those pioneers who reclaimed the land from the ice 12,000-odd

years ago. There have of course been a few invaders over the years –
a handful of Mediterranean Romans, some Angles and Saxons, a
few Vikings and some Normans. But the genetic fact is their DNA
has made about as much impact on the British bloodline as a few
teaspoonsful of water added to an overflowing bath.

Do not forget either that most of the 'Romans' who came to
Britain were not Italians, but men press-ganged into the legions
from territories just across the Channel. So the majority of them
were likely Gauls or Germans anyway – genetically indistinguishable from the Angles and Saxons who would arrive a few
centuries later. The Normans were Northmen, descendants of the
Vikings who had settled in France after their leader, Rollo, and
his men muscled their way into the territory in the ninth century
AD. It is called Normandy because it was settled by men from the
north.

And underlying it all is the certainty that the first hunters, who
walked onto the peninsula of Britain 12,000 years ago, were the
sons and daughters of tribes living in the same parts of northern
and western Europe that would later be home to Gauls and Danish
Vikings. In short, Britain has been invaded several times by the
same people. The British are a pack of mongrels, that much is
certain, and all pups are from the same two or three breeds. They
are still the same people they have always been.

With all of that in mind, consider how difficult it might be to
find a Celtic gene.

Undaunted by scientific reality, I sat in the arrivals lounge of
Heathrow Terminal 5 one afternoon in the summer of 2010,
swabbing the inside of my mouth with a lump of cotton wool on
the end of a little stick. I had flown down from my home in
Scotland specifically for the purpose. Somewhere within my saliva
would be cells, and within those cells my DNA. A young television
researcher waited patiently while I did so, before popping the
sample into a specially prepared sealable tube and heading back
off into London to find a suitable lab where it would be analysed.
For a little while it might be possible to isolate those relevant

fragments of my innermost chemistry and thereby begin to unpick a long, long story.

Our DNA is like a set of family heirlooms. Within some cells are mitochondria, little batteries that provide energy. It is thought mitochondria may have wormed their way into some cells long ago as independent bacteria looking for someplace warm to live. Having initially tried to evict or destroy them, the cells learned to take advantage of their invaders instead, enslaving their power to their own ends. Along with the energy to drive certain processes, mitochondria contain DNA (mtDNA) that is unique to the woman's bloodline and to her offspring. Women receive it from their mothers and pass it forwards to their sons and daughters. Only their daughters have the ability to pass it on to the next generation.

Fathers pass private information to their sons too, in the form of a package called the Y chromosome. As well as determining the maleness of men, the Y chromosome also contains DNA that is unique to the man's bloodline and his male offspring. While the mother passes what might be regarded as a genetic diamond ring to her daughters, the father hands down a gold pocket watch.

I have a daughter and two sons. My little girl has received my wife's mtDNA, just as my wife received it from her own mother. Our sons have the Y chromosome that was passed down to me from my father, and from his father before him, and so on back into the distant past. If a couple have only sons, the mother's mtDNA runs into a dead end – a little tragedy after surviving in an unbroken line for hundreds of thousands of years. Likewise if they have only daughters, the man's Y chromosome disappears from the world.

There was therefore something strangely intimate and uncomfortable about the experience of handing over so much personal chemical data – as though I was confiding family secrets I would rather have kept to myself. Some weeks later I met with Peter Forster, an expert in statistical genetic dating methods, to find out how much of my past he had been able to distill from those pieces of damp cotton wool.

The whole experience was bizarre, bordering on the surreal. We met in the beer garden of a pub in Shepherd's Bush in London, and there Forster attempted to explain where his analysis suggested my bloodline had its deepest roots. The subtleties and complexities were mind-boggling. In the simplest terms, he had been able to identify two strands of my DNA – one that let him follow my mother into deep prehistory, the other my father. By comparing my sample to those of tens of thousands taken from volunteers all over the world, Forster had been able to find the individuals alive today whose DNA most closely matched mine.

My mother's mtDNA – which is in my cells for all of my life, but going nowhere else – was most like that found in the blueprints of donors dotted across various parts of Scotland. In fact nothing remotely like a match was found anywhere outside that country. 'As you can see it is all over Scotland,' said Forster. 'It is not just one particular island, or location – so that argues for the presence of your mother's line in Scotland way back into prehistory thousands of years ago.'

In other words, the statistical likelihood was that my mother's descendants had arrived in Scotland in deep prehistory, perhaps (I like to think) alongside the first pioneers who recolonised the land after the last Ice Age 12,000 years ago.

The DNA in my Y chromosome had something quite different to say about my father, however. When the map appeared on the screen of Forster's laptop I looked instinctively at the British Isles, expecting more red dots like those conjured up by my mother's mtDNA. But there were no matches in Britain or Ireland at all, not a single one. Furthermore it appeared there was no connection to any of Forster's volunteers in the whole of northern Europe, even Scandinavia. Instead it turned out that the only people with DNA matching that of my father are alive and well and living in eastern Europe, even as far afield as Iran.

There is a lot of smoke and mirrors surrounding the science of

DNA analysis. It is virtually impossible for non-scientists to make
head or tail of it all. Forster's statistics are worked up from a base
of just tens of thousands of volunteers, meaning there are literally
billions of people missing from the picture. Those caveats aside,
it seemed statistically likely my Y chromosome had made it as far
as Britain only relatively recently – in genetic terms at least. While
my mother's ancestry showed all the signs of having been built
into these islands at the foundation level, the material from the
male half of my make-up had been out east for most of that time.
The individual or individuals who brought it into north-west
Europe had done so not very long ago at all.

On a personal level it all made a kind of sense to me – if only
in completely unscientific ways. My mum is and always has been
happiest close to home. She is most content in her own house,
surrounded by her family. I like to think now that she is fixed
there by a kind of genetic gravity. Scotland keeps tight hold of the
atoms of her skin and bones. My dad on the other hand is a born
wanderer, pulled towards distant places. He is a reader of maps
and a planner of journeys. Maybe the magnet that attracts his
particular DNA is someplace far away, up the hill and over the
lea, off towards the east. You couldn't prove a word of all that of
course, but I think it's true.

For all sorts of reasons people have been looking for proof of a
Celtic bloodline for generations. If I have a Celtic gene, it has yet
to be found. If it exists at all it is a minuscule splinter on the side
of Jacob's Ladder catching in the skin of some hands but not
others. All we can say with any certainty at the moment is that
ancestry – like mine, for example – is complicated. Each of us is
anyway more than the sum of our genetic parts. An Inuit raised
in Kensington would vote Tory; a Xhosa living in Soho would
work in the media.

Rather than a Celtic gene, it seems more likely there was once
a set of Celtic ideas and ideals. By the time of the Late Iron Age,
people were more mobile than they had ever been before. On foot
and on horseback they ranged easily across vast distances so that

customs, beliefs and artistic sensibilities were soon spread throughout Europe and beyond. So we can safely say there exists a Celtic
heritage. It can be demonstrated and proved archaeologically that
there was a shared appreciation of art and design as well as a
respect for status and hierarchy.

In the modern world the word 'Celtic' refers primarily to a
family of languages, all of them originally spoken only in the
British Isles and Ireland. All share a common ancestor-language
that likely travelled across Europe with the hunters in the years
following the end of the Ice Age. The mother tongue may well
have been a predecessor of the Sanskrit language of the Indian
subcontinent.

If the study of DNA is a kind of archaeology, excavating inside
ourselves in search of answers, then the study of language might
be yet another form of digging. Talk surrounds us every day,
flowing around us like a river. We learn it by rote and understand
it without wondering where the words came from – why they
mean what they mean. Some of the words are new, coined during
our own brief lifetimes. Others have been there so long they are
like the most elderly people among us: we take them for granted,
paying them no attention as they brush past us in the street. No
one else alive is old enough to remember when those ancients were
young, to care where they came from, to ask who they actually
are, or were.

Scots Gaelic, Irish Gaelic, Welsh, Cornish and the Manx tongue
of the Isle of Man are all ancient, and all related to one another.
The last of the Celtic languages, Breton, is spoken in Brittany in
northern France but was exported there in the Middle Ages, along
with emigrants from the British Isles. Language matters to students
of the history of ancient Britain because clues about our past lie
curled inside it, like fossils in rock.

Saint Michael's Mount, the rocky island off the south-west coast
of Cornwall, is called 'Carreg luz en kuz' in the old Cornish
language. It is a phrase that means 'the grey rock in the woods'
and might seem like a strange name for a little island in the sea.

From around 1500 BC, Phoenician ships tied up alongside the island to await consignments of precious tin, so it is clearly a very long time indeed since it was surrounded by anything other than waves.

Once in while, however, when the tide falls low enough, the remains of ancient tree stumps can still be glimpsed poking through the sand on nearby beaches. The Cornish language is therefore the custodian of a fascinating fact that might otherwise go unnoticed: that long ago, long before the tin traders came in their ships, the sea level around Britain was much lower and the dry land extended far beyond the rock that is now Saint Michael's Mount.

'Eenie, meenie, miney, mo ...' is familiar to everyone as the start of a rhyme learned in childhood, and likely dismissed by most adults as nonsense words coined for fun. In fact 'eeny, meeny, miny, moe' is one, two, three, four – parts of a counting system that is almost certainly Celtic in origin. To this day some old shepherds in East Anglia use 'ina, mina, tehra, methera' when counting their flocks. In Cornwall they say 'eena, mea, mona, mite' and in Cumbria – where some audacious scholars are even attempting to resurrect yet another 'lost' language – the sheep farmers can be heard muttering, 'yan, tan, tether, mether' as their beasts scamper past them.

The ancient past is fossilised too in the names of places and features in the landscape. We blithely accept a river name like 'Avon' without allowing for the fact that the word once meant something specific. Long before the Romans came, the people living in Britain had a word 'abona' in their own language – referred to by modern linguists as Brittonic – that meant 'river'. The same meaning survives in the Welsh 'afon'. Dover comes from 'dubris', meaning 'waters'; 'Kent' was once sounded as 'cantus', meaning 'border' or 'periphery'; and when the nomadic hunters first laid eyes on the River Thames, as they began the recolonisation of the land 12 millennia ago, they referred to that silent black barrier as 'Tamesis', the 'darkness'.

And so it goes on, words are all around us like ancient buildings left stranded here and there in modern cities, cut off from the time when their existence made sense in a bigger picture. Sometime in the fourth century BC, a Greek merchant and sailor called Pytheas travelled as far as the 'Tin Islands' before heading home to Marseille to write about what he had seen. Among much else he mentioned asking some Gauls about the people who lived on the other side of the water known to us as the English Channel. They apparently told him the island over there was 'Pretannike' and home to the 'Pretannikai'. Say 'Pretannike' out loud and you will hear a trace of something familiar in it.

In the British form of the language the inhabitants of the islands were known among themselves as 'Pretani' – a word meaning 'painted people' and a reference to their habit of tattooing their bodies. After the Roman warrior and Emperor-in-waiting Julius Caesar had spent some time fighting with the locals there, he wrote down the name of the troublesome new territory as 'Britannia' – so that even that most familiar of names, 'Britain', actually means something and is a connection to a story thousands of years in the telling.

'Welsh' is a corruption of an Old English word 'wealas', meaning 'foreigner' or more likely just 'not one of us'. The people there called themselves 'Cymry', by which they meant 'companions' or 'the community'. Their own word for the people living beyond the limits of Welsh territory was the 'Prydyn' – another reference to the fact the inhabitants had tattoos on their skin.

In time the Roman invaders would find a people in the far north of Britannia who continued to cover their bodies in designs long after all the other inhabitants of the island had abandoned the practice. The soldiers would label them 'Picts' – a disparaging nickname for a painted people. In fact the Picts and their ancestors were keeping up an ancient tradition, one that in their eyes had a very practical application. Pictish warriors fought naked – believing their gods would look down upon them, see the tattoos worn in their honour, and confer divine protection upon the wearers.

The tattoos were always blue, made from the juice of elderberries and sloes, and the chemicals contained in the fruit were natural aids to the coagulation of blood. A warrior's tattooed skin was therefore likely to heal more quickly in the event of injury.

These are the tattered fragments that remain when all else has been lost. Imagine what Iron Age Britain might have sounded like, with all those variations on the theme of a Celtic language. The words of ancient Britain are utterly unintelligible to us now, alien to all but a handful of scholars, and yet they were spoken in those islands for uncounted thousands of years before the advent of the Romans with their Latin, or the Angles and Saxons and the beginnings of what became spoken English.

Paul Russell, Reader in Celtic at Cambridge University, described how confused and disorientated a modern English-speaker would feel if somehow transported back to an Iron Age market-place where they could hear the language of the time. 'I think the most striking thing for them would be that they wouldn't understand a word of it,' he said. 'This is a language group that is unrelated, or only distantly related, to English.'

And just as a journey through Britain today from the south-west of England to the north-west of Scotland would take a traveller through scores of regional dialects of English, so the sounds of ancient Celtic would have varied across the land. 'That is probably the case, by virtue of the fact that this is a language that developed into different languages – Welsh as separate from Cornish, and so on and so forth.' 'So there probably was that kind of variation – so that mile on mile, neighbour to neighbour, they would understand each other perfectly well – but if you moved someone all the way from the south-west to the north-east they would probably struggle.'

More than anything else it was the advent of Latin Rome that sounded the death knell for the older languages. On mainland Europe, where the Roman grip was firmest, the Celtic tongues all but vanished. Only in the archipelago, on the islands of Britain and Ireland in relative isolation in Oceanus, did anything survive.

Beyond reach on the westernmost fringes – in Wales, in the deep south-west of England, in the north-west of Scotland and in Ireland – the last vestiges have clung on like rare plants in a lost valley.

The very word 'Celt' was buried away in the ashes of the fallen Roman Empire and not heard again until the 'Celtic Revival' of the early eighteenth century. The linguist Edward Lhuyd paid particular attention to the surviving Celtic languages as well as to relic traces in the Iberian Peninsula. His studies persuaded him that since the peoples along the Atlantic seaboard had spoken Celtic languages, they must themselves have been Celts. Soon public imagination was captivated by the thought of giving a name to Britain's original inhabitants – those who had raised the stone circles in the fields and made the tools and weapons occasionally fished from the rivers and lakes. The Victorian enthusiasm for the notion of a separate, older race – the rightful owners of the land – has never really gone away for some.

Celtic-speaking Britain – the Britain of Celtic art and Celtic sensibilities, of legendary swords and mounted warriors – was also a Britain of rival tribes. Two centuries after the life and death of the Kirkburn Warrior, the people might have been united by a common Celtic culture but they were still divided by all the tensions and stresses born of human nature.

In order to survive and to thrive, communities needed leaders who were warriors, skilled at defending and extending borders. If those leaders were themselves to survive and thrive, however, they required more than just a strong sword arm, and archaeological finds recovered from the waters of a Scottish loch make it clear that the dark arts of politics and public relations are as old as the hills.

The territory centred around Loch Tay, in Perthshire, has always drawn and held people. During the Neolithic it was the crags above the water that focused some of their attention. The slopes of the hill they call Creag na Caillich, formed of an easily splintered, fine-grained stone known as hornfels, or hornstone, are littered here and there with the rough-outs and flakes left behind by axe-makers. The axe factory is 2,000 feet above sea level, however, and nowadays there is a more accessible visitor attraction in the form of the Scottish Crannog Centre. The centrepiece is a completely convincing reconstruction of an Iron Age crannog, inspired by one of nearly 20 crannogs already discovered in the shallows of the Loch.

People all over Scotland and Ireland (and perhaps in Wales, though only one has been found there so far) began building and living in such dwellings at least 5,000 years ago, and found reason to go on doing so up until the 1600s. Where the builders had access to timber, the crannogs sit on platforms perched on huge piles driven into the bed of the Loch. If there were no trees around, then tons upon tons of rock were dumped into the shallows to create an artificial island on which a stone building could be erected.

The attractions of the crannog are fairly obvious. The inhabitants have the security of being surrounded by water, their home accessed only by an easily defended causeway. At times when arable land was at a premium, a home built over the water of the Loch was freeing up ground for crops and animals that would otherwise be occupied by buildings. Then there is the visual impact of such dwellings – a huge roundhouse seemingly floating above the water. A leader able to marshal the raw materials and the expertise for such a venture would advertise his status and power to all who laid eyes upon his home.

Nowadays crannogs survive only as mounds of material under several feet of water. Excavation of them is therefore undertaken only by divers. The reconstructed crannog on Loch Tay is the product of years of work by the Scottish Trust for Underwater Archaeology (STUA), and in the process they have amassed a huge amount of detailed evidence of life on the loch over 2,000 years ago.

Sealed beneath the waters for all that time, the organic materials used by the crannog dwellers have survived in unusually high quantities. Along with the materials used in the construction of the buildings and platforms, STUA archaeologists have also found personal belongings and even food remains. On one crannog site on Loch Tay they recovered traces of around 160 different edible plants – a unique insight into the diet of the Iron Age inhabitants.

What is immediately apparent is the absence of foods taken for granted in modern Britain. None of the familiar staples were available, so there are no potatoes, no onions. Instead it is clear that even after millennia of farming, foraging for wild foodstuffs was still key to a healthy and varied Iron Age diet. Edible wild greens like sorrel, chickweed and wild mushrooms were plentiful and popular, along with cultivated crops like barley. Meat was available as well, both from hunted animals and those kept in the fields.

As well as the food remains, the waters of the Loch have also preserved wooden plates – the sort of item that almost never survives on sites on dry land, where the processes of decomposition are so much more aggressive. All in all it is an assemblage of material that hints at the importance of food to Iron Age society – its production, collection and, most importantly of all, its distribution. Central to the control of power was the feast.

Human beings make eye contact with one another while they eat. This is unique in the animal kingdom. For every other creature, eating is a stressful business. Consider a pride of lions around a kill. Each knows his place – or if they do not, they will quickly learn it. It is all flashing teeth, furtive glances at those higher and lower in the hierarchy, bite, chew and swallow as fast as possible. For many beasts feeding is a solitary business. Get some food and then scurry away to somewhere safe and private where the eating can be done out of sight of prying eyes. Even our closest relatives, the chimpanzees and gorillas, avoid looking one another in the eye.

Homo sapiens sapiens evolved differently. Eating is sociable for us, friendly. Our companions are quite literally those with whom we share bread, from the Latin *panis*. Dinner parties are still the

Deep inside the Great Orme copper mine, at Llandudno in north Wales. Generations of Bronze Age miners burrowed for miles into the limestone in search of ore, leaving an awe-inspiring network of claustrophobia-inducing tunnels.

An aerial view of Gurness Broch – once a massively built stone tower that would have stood around 30 feet high, dominating the land for miles around.

Seemingly peaceful now, Lindow Man was killed by axe blows to the head. He was likely already dead when he was then throttled with a cord. In a final act of violence, his throat was cut before he was placed face-down into a shallow pond or bog.

As at home in our hands and time as in the Iron Age world in which they were made: the achingly familiar Fiskerton tools.

Made between 350 and 50 BC, the Battersea Shield is far too ornate and delicate for battle. Instead it was likely carried by a victorious warlord as a symbol of power – before being cast into the Thames as an offering to the gods.

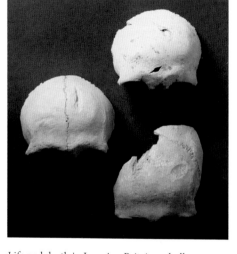

Life and death in Iron Age Britain – skulls recovered during archaeological excavations at Danebury hill fort bear fatal wounds inflicted by swords and spears. All were recovered from within a mass grave of battle dead.

In the Iron Age – as in every age before or since – at least some technological expertise was dedicated to the development of tools intended only for the taking of life. Spearheads recovered from Danebury hill fort matched wounds on the skulls of the dead.

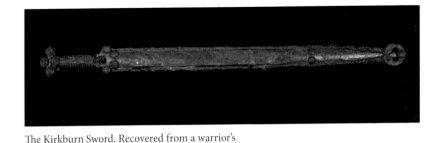

The Kirkburn Sword. Recovered from a warrior's grave in east Yorkshire, it is regarded as perhaps the finest Iron Age sword in Europe.

Around a century before the birth of Jesus Christ, the Llyn Cerrig Bach slave chain is a reminder of a time when these islands were a focus for the trade of human beings.

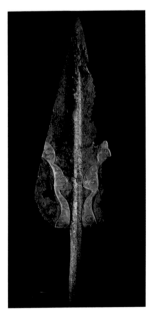

The Thames Spearhead was fashioned sometime between 200 and 50 BC. Before the arrival of the Romans, master craftsmen were producing items that may be regarded as the greatest contributions ever made by these islands to the world of art.

As mysterious now as when its final generation of builders turned their backs on it for the last time – Silbury Hill, near the village of Avebury in Wiltshire. Standing 130 feet tall and with a footprint of around five acres, it is one of the largest man-made prehistoric mounds in the world and comparable in scale to the pyramids built in Egypt in the same period.

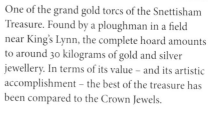

One of the grand gold torcs of the Snettisham Treasure. Found by a ploughman in a field near King's Lynn, the complete hoard amounts to around 30 kilograms of gold and silver jewellery. In terms of its value – and its artistic accomplishment – the best of the treasure has been compared to the Crown Jewels.

'Turning and turning in the widening gyre . . .' – one of the earliest examples of a perfect form known as a triple spiral – with no beginning and no end – pecked into one of the recesses in the passage grave of Newgrange.

The *lilia* defences on the northern side of the Antonine Wall at Rough Castle Fort, near Falkirk. Originally three feet deep, each pit would have contained sharpened stakes. Camouflaged with brushwood, they would have crippled charging men and horses.

With a large circular enclosure connected to a long narrow entrance, a class of Iron Age sites has been saddled with the name of banjo enclosures. While they may appear defensive, in truth it seems more likely they were simply homes for extended families.

A carved stone slab from Housesteads Fort on Hadrian's Wall showing an item of clothing dubbed the original duffel coat. Known to the Romans as the *birrus Britannicus*, it was apparently worn by the natives to ward off the enervating cold of the northern winters.

Irish examples of the enigmatic and mysterious class of artefacts known as divination spoons – rare finds attributed by some to the ritual practices of druids.

Not bad for a first attempt – the hoard of gold jewellery found near Stirling in 2009 by a man trying his hand at metal-detecting for the very first time. What was unearthed was nothing less than the most valuable hoard of Iron Age gold ever found in Scotland.

A tiny silver minim found at Silchester. One side bears the name of Verica, a warlord or king who ruled a territory in southern Britain around the time of the Claudian invasion. In a bid to secure his position, he had styled himself 'Commius Filius', CF, on the reverse of the coin – meaning son of Commius, and therefore a reference to an earlier British ruler supported by Caesar.

The Falkirk Tartan – a fragment of woven woollen fabric found in 1934 alongside a pot full of Roman silver coins. It is thought the cloth was originally used as a cover or seal. The simplicity of the fabric, coupled with its similarity to familiar modern tartans, has made the find a potent symbol of the people who wove it and wore it around 1,800 years ago.

Hell no fury hath ... a curse tablet recovered from the sacred waters of Bath, begging vengeance for love lost: 'May he who has stolen Vilbia from me become as liquid as water.'

Two silver handles from the vast hoard found on Traprain Law, in East Lothian, home of the Votadini tribe. A leopard and a panther, perhaps designed and made as a pair and buried between AD 410 and 425.

height of sophistication. Going out for dinner with friends is a high point of the day, or the week, and while we sit around the table eating and drinking, we chat and look each other in the eye.

It was in the later Iron Age in Britain that people first began thinking about individual place settings, about accompanying food with alcoholic drinks. We know that people then were in the habit of eating communally. What is fascinating is the way Iron Age communities used food and feasting as key tools for brokering power. Social standing was no longer demonstrated only by the wearing of ostentatious jewellery or fine swords. It was also about the ability of a leader (or would-be leader) to draw supporters to his side and keep them there. A chieftain in control of surplus food would therefore be able to use a feast as an opportunity to show his generosity and, more specifically, to make it clear who was in favour with him and who was not. The feast was almost a ritual in its own right, with a clearly defined etiquette. Every guest at the table, as well as everyone looking on, would have read and understood every nuanced move. Who was seated closest to the chieftain? Who was served first and who was served last? Who was offered the finest cuts of meat and who was fobbed off with the cold shoulder? A skilled operator, a chieftain with the resources and the confidence to carry it off with style, would leave no one in any doubt about the status quo.

At the centre of the feast was the firedog – an elaborate piece of ironwork upon which the meat, be it pork, lamb or a side of beef, might be suspended over the flames of the hearth for cooking. Sometimes they were displayed in pairs, either side of a fire and helping to keep the burning timbers in place. The mere sight of such things would have been impressive – unmistakable status symbols and a clear sign that here was the home of rich and powerful man.

One of the most impressive ever found is the so-called Capel Garmon firedog, found in a field at Carreg Goedog Farm in Capel Garmon, in Conwy, north Wales, in 1852. It had been laid on its side in a deep hole, deliberately buried as a gift to the gods.

Comparison with firedogs from elsewhere suggested the Capel Garmon example had been made and used sometime between 50 BC and AD 75. Such was the complexity of the work – with elaborate animal heads depicting a bull and a horse – it may have taken as much as three years to make.

Capel Garmon was not the only site of a buried firedog. In 1967, workmen using a bulldozer to clear the way for a new road in the town of Baldock, in north Hertfordshire, turned up what they initially thought was just a lump of scrap metal. Archaeologists were later called in to investigate and found not one but two iron firedogs. They were in a circular grave containing cremated human bone together with a Roman amphora, a bronze cauldron, two wooden buckets, two bronze basins, half a pig and bones from a bear's paw. It appeared the departed had been dispatched into the next world after a feast in his or her honour. The bear bones suggested either the corpse had been wrapped in a bearskin when it was cremated, or that a bear had been the main course. Burials like this, alongside all the apparatus of a feast, are described by archaeologists as Welwyn-type and are an occasional feature of the later Iron Age. Whether the feasts were shared by the mourners – or intended for the dead person and the ancestors – will never be known.

Britain had been reshaped – if not by iron then by the more modern world of which it was a part. A warrior elite had arisen, men whose status was displayed by the weapons they wielded. By the final years of the Iron Age, power was centralised in the hands of regional chieftains, those who controlled the land and the food it produced. Warriors themselves, they drew towards them other men of war and, by force of personality, had them do their bidding. They dominated the hill forts in the south, the brochs and crannogs in the north. It is thought that by around 100 BC, some of these chieftains had risen to an even more exalted level. They were likely few in number but each controlled so much land and so much trade they became the first of the super-rich.

During the first century BC, modern-day Norfolk was the

territory of the Iceni tribe. It seems that, by perhaps 70 BC, their leader exerted a gravitational pull so powerful he had drawn towards himself treasures that were beyond the dreams of avarice.

In 1948 a ploughman working in fields outside the village of Snettisham, a few miles north of King's Lynn, turned up a large, shiny piece of metal. Responsible man that he was, he showed it to the farm manager, who took one look at the thing and said it must be part of a brass bedstead. The ploughman kept on plough-ing – and kept finding more and more pieces of metal. Soon a whole pile lay scattered around the original find, on the grass by edge of the field. Heaven knows how long they might have lain there if it had not been for the arrival of a visitor, who spotted the pile and realised at once the metal was old, and possibly valuable. When the hoard was carted into Norwich Museum in search of an expert opinion, the curator must have fallen off his stool. The ploughman had found a huge hoard of Iron Age gold jewellery.

Buried gold is like that. Because it never corrodes it comes out of the ground in the same condition as when it went in. After hundreds or even thousands of years in the soil it looks brand new; a quick brush with a cloth and it is ready to wear. Usually when people find ancient gold – while digging a ditch perhaps, or waving a metal detector around – they persuade themselves it must be fake, or at least not very old. Gold looks too much like gold actually to be gold.

Between 1948 and 1973, the gold just kept coming out of the ground at Snettisham. For a while there were no more finds and it was assumed the field had given up all its secrets. Then, in 1989, a local metal detectorist was given access and soon began finding more of the same; modern technology was penetrating well beyond the reach of any plough. Experts from the British Museum were called in and soon the Snettisham Treasure had doubled in size.

It turned out the field had kept the best for last. Just when the archaeologists thought they had swept the site clean, they found a shallow pit containing a number of bronze and silver torcs. Then, like something out of a movie, the 'bottom' of the pit collapsed into a void beneath. Shining in the loose soil below were two bronze bracelets, two torcs made of silver and 10 made of pure gold.

The Snettisham Treasure is astonishing, almost beyond belief. It amounts to nearly five stones of gold and silver and fills whole display cases in the British Museum. Much of it is in the form of broken pieces, scrap waiting to be made into something new, but the rest is a stunning collection of torcs and solid ingots bent into bracelet shapes. There are also more than 230 gold and silver coins.

Shining brightest of all are the torcs – thick necklaces of twisted gold or silver. A grand total of 175 were found, 75 more or less complete and the rest in pieces. Some of the Snettisham Treasure has been placed on a par with the Crown Jewels. I have had the privilege of handling one or two of the grandest torcs and I would say they are of such dazzling brilliance it is hard to accept they are real. No matter how many times you tell yourself they are made of pure gold, your eyes continue to insist they must be fakes. They simply look too good, too weighty, to be true.

The intricacy of the design, the skill of the goldsmiths – the whole effect is overwhelming; and that is the impression they make on someone born in the twentieth century. Their impact on a population of farmers 2,000 years ago can only be guessed at.

No traces of a settlement contemporary with the treasure were ever found. To all intents and purposes the hoard had simply been buried in a field. It has been suggested the gold and silver were indeed 'crown jewels' – the stored wealth of the ruler of the Iceni in the decades before the coming of Rome. What is undeniable is that even one of the torcs would have represented extreme wealth. A man seen wearing such a treasure – while he led his warriors into battle, or while he addressed his followers at some grand occasion – would surely have seemed more than a mere chieftain. In his own eyes, and perhaps more importantly in those of his followers, he was their king.

It was not just about the leader's personal adornment either. While a gold torc worn around the neck would underline an individual's authority in the eyes of those who saw him wearing it, something more pervasive was going on at the same time. During the first century BC, coins of gold, silver and bronze – portable symbols of authority – were passing through the hands of at least some of the people.

Coins are viewed as evidence of increasing levels of contact between Britain and Gaul between around 125 BC and 50 BC. They are often discovered as hoards, whole collections buried in the ground either for safekeeping or as offerings to the gods. The earliest of them were Gallo-Belgic 'staters' – coins minted in northern France or Belgium – and crossed the English Channel either as payment for trade goods or as gifts exchanged between chieftains. It has even been suggested by some numismatists that the Gallo-Belgic staters of mid-first-century date arrived in Britain as payment for mercenaries and other supplies sent to Gaul to support the struggle against Rome.

In any event, by the time such coins reached Britain, they were already part of a long story. Study of their designs has revealed the Gallo-Belgic tradition had its origins in coins made hundreds of years earlier by Macedonian Greeks. What started out in the fourth century BC as a coin with the head of King Phillip II of Macedon on one side, and a horse-drawn chariot on the other, had gone through a stylistic evolution in the hands of the Celtic tribes during the intervening centuries. The gold staters that crop up in the south-east of England in the first century BC feature heads that are so stylised as to be almost unrecognisable as representations of anything human. Similarly the chariot is played around with until it features usually as an abstract horse surrounded by bits and pieces that may or may not be parts of a vehicle.

When the British chieftains started commissioning their own coins they continued the practice of retaining the original elements of Continental coins, while reflecting their own artistic sensibilities at the same time. It must have been a tricky business. On the one hand individual leaders wanted unique coins; but on the other they had to pass muster in the wider world. (The practice of copying coins from elsewhere – particularly those regarded as trusted currency – was one that would continue for centuries. A gold coin made during the reign of the eighth-century Anglo-Saxon King Offa has 'OFFA REX' on one side and the inscription 'THERE IS NO GOD BUT ALLAH ALONE' on the other. For a while it was claimed by some as evidence Offa had converted to Islam – until it was identified as a copy of an Arabic coin. Islamic gold coins of the Abbasid dynasty were the most trusted in the Mediterranean world at the time and Offa's coin-makers were simply giving their own output the best chance of being accepted as credible tender.)

British coins had to be suitable for circulation in Roman markets as well and so increasingly began to feature Classical designs and motifs. British chieftains had developed tastes for Mediterranean luxury goods including wine, olive oil and pottery and so in addition to declaring their status at home, their coins gave them access to yet more prestige items available from the Classical world to the south.

Underlying all of it was the power of the emergent state. By the time coins were in general use, for buying and selling among individuals in Britain, they were a constant reminder of the power of the leader. A coin might secure a purchase; but since it bore the likeness or name of the chieftain it also made clear the transaction had been validated in some way by his authority.

So much of what archaeologists find tells the story of men – hunters, warriors, chieftains. The picture is also unhelpfully skewed in favour of the elites, the rich. Those accorded burials of the sort that survive to be found thousands of years later were clearly special people singled out for unusual treatment and sent into eternity accompanied by treasures of their time. It is therefore not just women who often seem invisible, but also the rank and file. And if the mass of men and women have disappeared without a trace, the lot of the poorest of the poor is even worse.

For every king or queen, every chieftain or warlord enjoying Roman luxuries, there had to be hundreds or even thousands of men and women whose lives were so hard as to be all but unbearable. Hardest of all were the lives of the lowest of the low – the slaves.

For most people in modern Europe, slavery is an evil associated with Africa. But it happened in Britain and Ireland too. In relatively modern times – at least from the seventeenth century onwards – Barbary pirates preyed on those coastlines. The examples are as numerous as they are heartbreaking. In 1631 the entire population of the village of Baltimore, in County Cork in the south-west of Ireland – 109 men, women and children – were taken by African pirates, loaded onto ships and sold in the slave markets of North Africa. Not one of those souls ever saw the old country again and between 1630 and 1730 it is estimated Barbary pirates took a million Europeans from their homes and sold them into slavery.

Some of us seek to distance our own nations from the business of African slavery – or at least shift responsibility for it – by pointing out that the African chiefs were active slave-sellers. The argument goes that since they were selling their own people, or at the very least their neighbours' people, then their descendants cannot simply blame the 'middlemen' of Europe who bought them and shipped them to the New World. But the unavoidable fact is that during the Iron Age our own ancestors were themselves valuable trade items. In the European markets one commodity above all else was in great demand – tall, strong, British manpower.

Back in the National Museum of Wales in Cardiff, close by the display featuring those first iron treasures of the Llyn Fawr hoard, is proof of part of the price that had to be paid for all those Continental luxury goods imported into Britain during the first and second centuries BC.

During the building of the airfield at Valley, on the island of Anglesey, during the Second World War, workmen found scores of ancient iron and bronze objects sealed in peat. The peat had formed in antiquity, as an ancient lake had dried up, and the artefacts – eventually numbering more than 150 – had been votive offerings thrown into the water to honour and appease the gods.

This was the Llyn Cerrig Bach hoard – a rival to that found at La Tène. Alongside numerous swords and fragments of at least one shield, horse gear and the metal parts of chariot wheels, blacksmithing tools, spearheads, iron ingots and parts of cauldrons, were two lengths of heavy iron chain. The links were still strong – so strong in fact the chains were put to work pulling trailers behind tractors – and at first no one guessed their darker purpose.

The Llyn Cerrig Bach chains were made for the restraint of human beings. Made around 90 BC, they are as chilling as they are impressive. Just a foot and a half of chain would have separated each person in the line. The links are still a great weight in the hands and the dull clanking sound they make now is an echo of the same that would have accompanied the shuffling steps of whichever souls were imprisoned by them 2,000 and more years ago. The parts shaped to go around the neck are quite small and would have all but throttled anyone larger than a child.

Just a few hundred years earlier, many people in Britain had lived in egalitarian farming communities. By the time of the slave chains of Llyn Cerrig Bach, all of that had changed. As the last century before the birth of Christ progressed, Britain was a land of hard social divides. For every petty king with a golden torc around his neck, there were uncounted thousands of men, women and children more accustomed to the chafing of tight-fitting iron.

By now the days of the hill forts were numbered too; even giants like Danebury were in decline. A privileged few had grown accustomed to great power and great wealth. They had acquired a taste for Mediterranean cuisine and the stylish bowls from which it was to be eaten and drunk.

By the middle of the first century BC, many of the tribes of southern Britain had grown comfortable with the thought of all the luxuries they could obtain from across the water. Archaeological sites around the south-east of England yield amphorae of the sorts that were in use from perhaps 100 BC onwards. It was these that contained the wine and oil so desired by the first of the British nouveaux riches. Some of it was from the vineyards and groves of Rome itself.

Those commodities were a feature of Britain at the height of the Celtic Iron Age, with all its warring and kingly display and sophisticated art. But by the middle of the century, Rome was on the move. Gaul, just across the English Channel, she had already taken for her own. Not content just to trade with her neighbours, Rome wanted domination and ownership as well.

Around AD 98, Tacitus would finish '*De vita et moribus Iulii Agricolae*', better known to us as 'the *Agricola*', a biography and tribute to his father-in-law Gnaeus Julius Agricola, conqueror of much of Britannia. During Tacitus's account of the defeat of the Caledonians at the Battle of Mons Graupius in AD 84, Calcagus (almost certainly a fiction created by the author for dramatic effect): exclaims: 'Romans . . . Brigands of the world . . . the wealth of an enemy excites their greed, his poverty their lust for power . . . Robbery, butchery, rapine . . . they create a devastation and call it peace.' Tacitus understood not just how powerful the Empire was, but also how it was seen by others.

Whether or not the British tribes and their chieftains knew it, they might soon have to finish their drinks and pick up their swords for one last, climactic battle – this time against the Brigands of the world.

There was a storm coming.

INVASION

'So the Britain the Romans found in AD 43 was a country split up among warring tribes, some of whom could find men and money with which to build extensive defences and engaged in foreign trade, even though they lived in flimsy huts in rather sordid conditions. In some areas conquered groups nursed vengeance in their hearts and bided their time, ready to turn on their oppressors, while others lived in fear of imminent attack. Further north among the hills and moors of the highland zone, more tribes led a still harder life, snatching a scanty living from the poorer soil or leading a pastoral existence with their flocks and herds. No foreign imports found their way to them, even iron tools were a luxury, and some still used the stone axes or flint blades of their forefathers.'

Joan Liversidge, *Britain in the Roman Empire*

Britain and the British struck terror into the hearts of Romans in 55 BC – not into the heart of Julius Caesar perhaps, but those of the rank and file faced with the prospect of invading the place. We can imagine their fear, unfocused and amorphous, and all the darker as a result. The fear born of suspicion, of the sort that citizens of modern, civilised states often harbour about places where things are done differently, by people with beliefs they regard as unholy or at least unclean.

The Roman world was bounded by Oceanus and any lands within or beyond that ocean-sea were at best mysterious and at worst forsaken by the gods themselves. The archipelago to the north and west of Gaul was therefore a kind of Ultima Thule – a furthest land – and surely there were good reasons why those islands were cut off from the civilised world?

In many ways the inhabitants of Britain liked it that way. The society that had evolved there by the mid to later Iron Age was insular in the extreme and obsessed with boundaries, with drawing lines that defined who was within and who was without. It was good to import wine, olive oil and other luxuries from the Continent, but there were limits to how much actual contact was needed or wanted. (It is one thing to enjoy the fruits of a delivery from a supermarket's online service, quite another to contemplate having a megastore built at the end of the road.) Each tribe had what you might call a very clear sense of its own personal space. They were xenophobic, almost paranoid.

It seems to me that the people of Celtic Gaul understood and let them be. Many archaeologists working in the first half of the twentieth century imagined successive invasions of southern Britain by Gallo-Belgic Celts, but now it is thought cultural behaviour crossed the Channel without the people themselves.

From 800 BC three states had begun to emerge in the Mediterranean – the Greeks, the Phoenicians and the Etruscans. The Etruscans had their centre on the Italian peninsula, but in 509 BC the warriors of Rome, their southern neighbour and one-time subordinate, finally overthrew them. During the following two hundred years or so, the Romans took control of more and more territory, like a cuckoo in the Mediterranean nest. By the middle of the second century BC, they were all-powerful, having eclipsed and overwhelmed both the Greeks and the once-mighty Phoenician city-state of Carthage.

For hundreds of years the Mediterranean world of the south had developed alongside that of the Celtic world in the north. Each had fed something into the other – through trade and also by a certain amount of cultural osmosis. But the time finally came when the Romans were no longer content just to be trading partners and interested observers.

Around 100 BC the English Channel was more of a gateway than a barrier, and therefore a comfort to those living on either side. For the people of Britain it acted like a kind of customs point, through which trade goods and travellers could pass in both directions but with a reassuring element of control.

The presence of the European mainland, visible from the south coast of England on a clear day, therefore presented the chieftains of Late Iron Age Britain with something of a quandary. For while on the one hand they were obsessively protective of the borders of their territories, on the other they needed prestige goods with which to impress their neighbours. Finds made as far north as Scotland reveal it was not just the rich men and women of southern and eastern Britain who had developed educated tastes in the finer things in life.

Just eight years after the discovery in 2001 of the Arras Culture-style chariot burial at Newbridge, in Edinburgh, a metal detectorist made the discovery of several lifetimes beside a farmer's field outside Stirling.

David Booth, a game warden at the Blair Drummond Safari Park a few miles outside the city, had decided to spend a day off practising with his latest purchase. He had just taken delivery of his first-ever metal detector and had previously tried it out only in his kitchen and garden. Having decided to really see what it could do, he first located a likely looking field and then sought permission from the landowner before driving over in his car and parking at its edge.

Picture the scene if you will: it is a pleasant day in the late September of 2009 and Booth has just climbed out of his car. He is parked on an area of clear, flat ground and he decides to check the gadget is working properly. 'I thought, "I'll just scan this first before I head out into the field",' he said. So he switches on the metal detector, takes half a dozen or so steps away from the car and hears his first 'bleep'. Pleased and encouraged, he sets down the machine and starts digging.

It was one of those metal detectors that, while not top of the range, could at least distinguish between precious metals and scrap. The machine indicated it had located gold, but such signals – from the more basic models – usually turn out to be no more exciting than the brass caps on the ends of spent shotgun cartridges.

What Booth found, however, six inches down, is the most valuable hoard of Iron Age gold ever recovered in Scotland. Glinting in the soil, as lovely as the day they went into the ground 2,000 or so years previously, are four solid gold torcs. Booth described his 'disbelief' in an interview with a reporter from *The Times* some weeks later. 'I saw a glimpse of one of them, then uncovered the rest of the hoard. They were in a wee group. Half of me was saying, "that does look important", but I was thinking I couldn't be that lucky on my first go. 'I took them home, gave them a wee clean up and went online. I looked at some torcs and kind of guessed this was Iron Age history.'

Most archaeologists look down their academic noses at metal detectorists – and the illegal activities of so-called 'nighthawks', those who raid archaeological sites without permission and under cover of darkness are indeed beneath contempt – but Booth's behaviour was quite different and he played completely by the rules. For a start, he immediately reported his find to the authorities. Having emailed a photograph of one of the torcs to the National Museum of Scotland (NMS) in Edinburgh, he was joined on site by the experts within hours.

Now in the care of the museum, the Stirling hoard has given archaeologists an unexpected insight into the tastes of at least one individual, or perhaps a handful of individuals, living in Scotland in the later years of the Iron Age. Two of the torcs, single ribbons of elegantly twisted gold, are typical of the sort of jewellery known to have been made and worn in Scotland 2,300 years ago. The other two are different. One find is in two pieces and amounts to approximately half of a broken torc. It is of an ornate style previously unknown in Britain and appears to have been imported from the Toulouse region of southern France, where similar items have been found.

The prize among prizes, however, is the fourth torc, a wonder created by twisting together eight separate delicate strands of gold and fixing them into two elaborate terminals decorated with tiny swirls and coils of gold wire (it even features a gold safety chain, making it clear the item was valued then just as it is valued now). Iron Age specialists at the NMS believe it represents a fusion of traditions – some elements home-grown in Scotland and others inspired by fashions among metalsmiths trained in the Classical world of the Mediterranean.

Whether it was made by a local goldsmith who had trained in workshops far away in the Roman world or was something commissioned and imported from there by a local worthy, it speaks of international connections at a time when the tribes of northern Britain were traditionally believed to have been especially inward-looking. The find in the past decade of both a hoard of exquisite gold and a chariot burial make clear the reach of Rome was great, and welcome, long before anyone thought about invasion.

Subsequent investigation suggested the torcs had been buried beneath some sort of circular building. Stirling sits at the centre of Scotland, both geographically and historically. The castle there was home to kings and queens long before Edinburgh rose to prominence, and all around are sites of all periods that make clear the area has long been a hub for lives and events. Stirling has been described as the brooch that fastens together the Lowlands and the Highlands of the country and so it seems appropriate that such a rich find should have come to light there.

Archaeologists have estimated that by about 100 BC Britain was home to between one and two million people, ruled over by perhaps a score of men best described either as great chieftains or little kings. At that time those leaders had much in common with their peers in Gaul, including the opinion that Rome presented not a military threat but an economic opportunity.

It was during those halcyon days that Hengistbury Head, in

Dorset, rose to become, for a while at least, the busiest port in Britain. A great promontory of sandstone, it juts out eastwards into the English Channel. A narrow spit of land turns abruptly northwards from the end of the headland to create the narrow entrance into the sheltered waters of Christchurch harbour. Viewed from high above it looks like a finger curled in the act of beckoning the Isle of Wight towards it. It is easy to see why the place was attractive to mariners plying their trade along the south coast. Tall cliffs provide protection from storms and from 100 BC onwards, the settlement that grew on the level plain on the leeward side of the headland turned into something of a boomtown.

The human history of Hengistbury Head neither starts nor finishes in the Iron Age. A mining company extracted ironstone from the headland in the nineteenth century and modern excavations have found evidence of large-scale flint tool-making there as early as the Upper Palaeolithic. (These were people of the same sort – the same vintage – as those who carved the little likeness of a horse's head onto a rib bone in that cave in Creswell Crags, near Sheffield.)

Hengistbury Head is just a tourist attraction now, mainly drawing walkers and beachcombers, but in the long story of Britain's history that headland has had important lines in key scenes since the very beginning.

The lifeblood of the Iron Age boomtown was international trade. Only a small part of the interior has been excavated, but there is enough to suggest a whole complex of homes, shops and workshops. In the centuries before the Roman invasions, the place would have been a hub, busy with the sounds and smells of cooking, of metal, glass and leather-working, of jewellery-making. Merchants and traders from all over the known world would have spent time there, browsing the wares and haggling over prices. For native Britons Hengistbury Head must have been a real thrill: exotic and tantalising smells from all that unfamiliar food; the sounds of talk and banter in foreign tongues; the sight of men and women with different-coloured skins and differently shaped features, wearing all manner of outlandish clothes.

According to the Greek writer Strabo, the native peoples of Britain were in the business of exporting cattle, corn, gold, animal hides, hunting dogs, iron, silver and slaves. In return they were importing all manner of European luxuries. It may well be that the first wine tasted in Britain was enjoyed at Hengistbury Head. Archaeological finds also feature copious evidence of glass-making, including blocks of coloured glass that would themselves have been extremely valuable. The site was clearly one of the doorways through which the future entered Britain.

However much Britain benefited from all the to-ing and fro-ing at Hengistbury Head, from the import and export business that made many of them rich, it could not last for ever. Between 50 and 60 BC, the flow of wine, along with much else, slowed to a trickle and then stopped completely. This was the period when Caesar broadened his offensive against the Celts of Gaul to take in the native tribes of Britain as well. For the time being, the good times were apparently over.

It has been said by some that in the early days it was Celtic sophistication and civilisation that impressed the Romans, rather than the other way around, and that in time they became what they had once beheld. Whether or not that is true, as the first century BC wore on Roman attitudes towards their northern neighbours began to harden.

Julius Caesar was the prime mover against the Celtic tribes. The Republic already controlled a part of northern Italy they called Cisalpine Gaul and before ending his term as a Roman consul (a senior government leader) he made himself Governor of the place. Students of Roman history say Caesar then made war on the rest of the Gallic tribes as a cynical ploy to raise both cash (to help pay off the many debts he had spent buying friends in high places) and his political standing. Gallic tribes had threatened Rome in the past, however, and his homeland's best interests may have played at least some part in his thinking.

In any event he was at war with one tribe after another from

58 BC onwards – and was soon infuriated by the support being supplied to his enemies by the inhabitants of the British Isles. Mercenaries and other resources were being sent across the water in return for Gallic coins and it could only be a matter of time before a belligerent like Caesar sought revenge for the meddling.

By the late summer of 55 BC, with much of Gaul under control, he had 20,000 soldiers aboard a fleet of nearly 100 ships, ready to conquer a new territory – Britannia. But while the move made perfect sense to a political and tactical genius like Gaius Julius Caesar, for his men it meant a voyage into the heart of darkness.

Apart from anything else, the islands across the water were known to be under the thrall of a mysterious priestly caste called druids. The Romans had encountered them before, among the Gauls. They were keepers of knowledge of all kinds, including medicine, as well as judges and arbiters, advisors to kings. Apparently they had means of divining the future but, worst of all, they presided over human sacrifices. As well as seeing to it that enemy captives were put to death, they meted out the same fate to their own people whenever the gods required it.

Everyone today thinks they know what druids look like – odd characters in robes, usually to be spotted mooning about ancient sites like Stonehenge during mid-summer. The truth of their existence in antiquity, however, is harder to find.

Archaeologist Miranda Green, of Cardiff University, is an expert on druids, among other things. She said the historical references that do survive make clear they were in some ways more important than tribal leaders, or even kings. 'They were right at the top of society,' she said. 'We know that the kings listened to their advice. They were like Old Testament prophets. 'One of the things that made them important was that they overarched society – so that you might have kings of tribes but the druids would connect with each other through huge areas of Europe, so they acted like a sort of Celtic glue.'

According to Green the druids were so respected and feared they had the power to start and to finish wars. 'They even intervened in times of warfare. They could walk out into the middle of a battlefield – and stop the fighting. To go against a druid would be almost as bad as being dead, because you would be exiled. Nobody would speak to you and you were then beyond society – because of the word of a druid.'

The druids apparently wrote nothing down. Caesar himself recorded that their secret knowledge – their lore – was learned by rote and held only in the memory. All of the contemporary references to druids are therefore the work of a few Greek and Roman writers, so that our image of them is a distortion seen through the lens of biased observers. They seemingly conducted their religious services in the open air and their sacred places were often close to water and oak trees, especially those bearing mistletoe. Animals and humans were sacrificed during their ceremonies and Caesar wrote about the use of the Wicker Man, a giant wooden effigy within which people were burnt alive.

Much is made of their ability to see or rather to divine the future and there is even a class of archaeological artefact, mostly found in Britain and Ireland, that has been cited as evidence for the practice. Since the nineteenth century a total of 15 enigmatic little bronze spoons have been recovered from a variety of contexts. Usually they occur in pairs and the majority came to light in the days before anyone bothered much about recording the precise circumstances of their discovery. Two sets have more recently been excavated from within graves and one from a bog close by a natural spring of water. Most of the others are believed to have come from small hoards deliberately buried or placed in boggy or watery places. Only one pair have been found on Continental Europe, in the grave of a woman excavated on a site in the Marne region of France; and even those are thought to have been British or Irish in origin.

They are the queerest little objects. Called 'spoons' because they feature a shallow bowl, they are actually of a form that is quite unique and distinctive. To me they suggest the shape taken on by a leaf cupped in the hand to hold water. One end is gently pointed, the other straight-edged so that it forms a simple handle. In all but the French examples, one bowl of the pair has an incised cross that divides it into four equal quadrants, while the other is plain but for a tiny hole off to one side (in the case of the French spoons, one bowl is completely plain while the other has both a cross, and a hole drilled or punched where the lines intersect). Sometimes the 'handles' are decorated with typically Celtic artwork, but in truth they are too few and far between to allow many generalisations to be made.

Most archaeologists are agreed the spoons look as though they were used for ritual purposes. Best guesses suggest they were held together, either with bowls facing one another like castanets or with one inside the other, bowl within bowl. Liquid or powder could then be dripped or blown through the hole and, depending on its dispersal among the quadrants on the lower bowl, assumptions made about the future, or the will of the gods.

Green described the likely scene, with the druid being consulted by the chief or petty king about what was likely to happen next. The whole affair was obviously open to exploitation by the man in the long robe. 'Having heard the question, the druid would have the choice of what to say in response,' she said. 'So I think what you've got here is a way of manipulating the future and manipulating power.'

In a manner wholly befitting characters for whom mystery and intrigue were stock in trade, the druids have all but managed to disappear. Little else but 15 spoons scattered between Britain, Ireland and France sounds like a pretty clean getaway. The only other evidence is in the form of the graves that provided the contexts for three of the little caches of cutlery.

The French grave was that of a woman; and if she was a member of that priestly class of advisors and seers, then her existence at least suggests not all druids were men. The graves of two men, one in Burnmouth in the Borders and another at Mill Hill, in Deal, Kent, contained the other pairs. That they too were accompanied into the next world by such unusual objects suggests they were unusual people, members of an unusual sect.

A second burial from Mill Hill contained the skeleton of a man whose grave goods might have suggested that in life he was a warrior. He was in his early to mid thirties when he died, sometime around 200 BC, and had been laid on his back, partly covered by a large shield. The wood of the shield had long since decayed and its existence was revealed only by telltale surviving bronze fittings. Alongside him was an iron sword inside a scabbard decorated with more fittings of cast bronze. There was a brooch as well, also made of bronze and decorated with coral.

On his skull was a piece of headgear that, given the sword and shield, might have been taken for a helmet. Closer examination of the find, however, revealed it was a dainty thing, a loop of bronze to fit around the skull and a band curving over the crown from ear to ear. Great skill had been required to make the pieces, rivet them together – and then to apply a fine tracery of Celtic curls and lines to the outer face. A few of the dead man's hairs were found snagged in the band, making it clear there had been no leather or other padding between the metal and the head. In short, it was no helmet, rather some sort of headdress.

Then there was the skeleton itself. It was small for an adult male – the bones of the pelvis and skull left no room for doubt about the sex – but at least one of the excavators remarked upon the 'feminine' nature of the slender bones. The burial has gone into some of the archaeological literature as that of the 'Deal Warrior' but it seems unlikely he would ever have swung that sword of his in anger. So who was he?

Iron Age specialist Ian Stead looked at the headdress and found it most closely resembled ceremonial gear worn by religious leaders in Roman Britain fully 200 years later. His burial had been within a cemetery but set some distance away from all of the other graves. Was he set apart from the mass of men in death, just as he had been separate from them in life?

There seems enough about the circumstances of his burial to

suggest that, rather than any kind of warrior, he was a man whose status was born of something other than physical strength or martial prowess. Perhaps he fought his battles on behalf of the spiritual well-being of his people, and when he died they laid their druid in the ground armed and garbed to keep fighting on their behalf.

Archaeologists found another enigmatic grave in a cemetery at Stanway, outside Colchester. Excavated during the 1990s, the collection of burials appeared to be of people regarded as special by those who laid them in the ground. They died in the few years either side of the Roman invasion of AD 43 and yet nothing about their graves or the personal items buried with them suggested they actually were Roman. Rather they were native Britons who had knowledge of Rome and who valued some of the luxury items available from there. Among the grave goods were a pottery inkwell – implying knowledge of writing at least, if not the ability actually to write; an amber-coloured glass bowl and an elegant blue-glass jar that may once have held make-up of some sort. Both vessels likely came all the way from Rome.

One man's grave in particular captured the imaginations of the archaeologists. Alongside his mortal remains were a dinner set, with vessels of both red and black pottery, and two wooden boxes. None of the organic material survived, but the hinges and other fittings revealed their shadows. One box contained bronze drinking vessels, the other a mysterious gaming board with glass beads for gaming pieces. Placed on top of the board were rods of bronze and iron, some interpreted as divining rods – tools for looking into the future – and others more identifiable as those of a surgeon – forceps, scalpel and the like. Some have looked at the finds and called him a doctor; others prefer to think of him as a druid.

Whoever they were and whatever became of most of their bodies when they died, the British druids were real and a cause of much anxiety for those tasked with invading their land. The Romans had practised sacrifice in their time – of people as well as animals –

but had consigned it to the past long before they contemplated the conquest of Britannia. They were determined from the outset to destroy the druids, whom they regarded as powerful and hard-line Celtic insurgents and who would not prove easy prey.

Even as the first century AD drew to a close, the Romans were still in the messy, frightening business of bringing them to bay. Tacitus, who gifted that legendary speech to Calgacus, the first named Scot, also recorded a climactic encounter between Roman soldiers and druids on the island of Anglesey in Wales:

'On the beach stood the adverse array, a serried mass of arms and men, with women flitting between the ranks. In the style of the Furies, in robes of deathly black and with dishevelled hair, they brandished their torches; while a circle of druids, lifting their hands to heaven and showering imprecations, struck the troops with such an awe at the extraordinary spectacle that, as though their limbs were paralysed, they exposed their bodies to wounds without any attempt at movement. Then, reassured by their general, and inciting each other never to flinch before a band of females and fanatics, they charged behind the standards, cut down all who met them, and enveloped the enemy in his own flames. The next step was to install a garrison among the conquered population, and to demolish the groves consecrated to their savage cults; for they considered it a pious duty to slake the altars with captive blood and to consult their deities by means of human entrails.'

All of that lay far off in the future – during the lifetimes of the great-, great-, great-grandchildren of those Roman soldiers who contemplated Britannia in the middle of the first century BC. Sensed from the coastline of Gaul, it seemed a strange place. It was a strangeness thousands of years in the making, much of it the product of separation from the European mainland by just 21 miles of cold, grey water.

Julius Caesar's invasions of Britain in 55 and 54 BC are so familiar they feel like touchstones. Told and retold down the centuries, the words and dates have become their own memorials. For all that, some portion of it bears retelling here.

The oft-repeated account has it that early on the morning of 23 August 55 BC the first of 98 transport ships, carrying two legions of professional foot soldiers and a cavalry force, appeared on the horizon off the coast of Kent. Caesar led the campaign himself and initially made for Dover. Word of what the general had in mind had gone before him, however, spread by merchants with contacts on both sides of the Channel, and the Romans were expected. Apparently the sight of thousands of British warriors lining the tops of the White Cliffs made any attempt at landing there unappealing to say the least, and the fleet headed a few miles round the coast instead, looking for an open beach suitable for disembarking the men.

Wherever they went, the defenders followed, armed with shields and long swords. There was to be no unopposed landing and it seems likely that Roman and British blood finally mingled for the first time that late summer in the shallows off Walmer Beach. By any standards it was a scrappy first encounter. Eventually the Romans got enough men ashore to establish a beachhead; but since their cavalry could not get off their ships to drive home any advantage, a stalemate developed. Caesar would later crow about how the Britons had been cowed by his arrival on their shores – that they quickly capitulated and offered him hostages as proof of their good will – but he was undoubtedly being economical with the truth. Many of his ships were damaged by waves pounding onto the beach, as late summer turned to autumn, and soon there was a real threat of finding his troops stranded without means of returning to Gaul. More indecisive fighting followed – the British attacking, the Romans defending their position – until finally Caesar withdrew, back onto the remains of his ships.

Before the year's end they were back on the other side of the Channel again. What might have been regarded as failure was successfully spun the other way by the general and Emperor-to-be.

As it turned out, the mere fact that he had actually gone to Britain – and landed an army on the beach there – was enough to persuade the Senate back in Rome his efforts were deserving of a ceremony of thanksgiving.

Having licked his wounds, Caesar spent the winter of 55 BC and the spring of the following year preparing to return and finish what he had started. By 7 July 54 BC, by his own account at least, he was back in Kentish waters with a fleet of 800 ships and a fighting force comprising five legions of soldiers and 2,000 mounted men – an army perhaps 50,000 strong.

This time the landing was unopposed. Those resistant to Caesar awaited him elsewhere, inland. But for the British there was a problem: some of them hated each other far more than they hated Rome. The classic account becomes then a tale of hubris – of a land and its peoples undone and undermined by petty rivalries. At a time when the independent tribes of Britain needed to set aside their squabbles in favour of tackling the greater foe, they allowed themselves to be blinded to the bigger picture by selfishness and by hopes of personal gain.

It was the tribes in the south and east of England who faced the onslaught first. These were the Cantiaci, who in time gave their name to Kent; the Iceni in Norfolk; the Trinovantes in Essex and, most powerful of all, the Catuvellauni, who controlled an extensive territory north of the River Thames. The biggest obstacle in the way of a united front was a bitter, long-running feud between the Trinovantes and the Catuvellauni, neighbours and deadly rivals.

A coalition of some of the tribes had gathered around the leadership of Cassivellaunus, fearsome and bellicose chieftain of the most fearsome and bellicose Catuvellauni. Rather than fight them on the beaches, Cassivellaunus had taken his army inland in hope of sustaining a guerrilla war of ambush and lightning strikes.

Whatever chance of success such a force might have had in the face of 50,000 highly trained infantry and cavalry, it was hopelessly compromised by human frailty. The Trinovantes from south of the Thames believed their own chieftain had been murdered by men of the Catuvellauni and put revenge ahead of inter-tribal unity. While Cassivellaunus hoped his superior knowledge of the geography of his home turf would give him an advantage, the Trinovantes sided with the invaders and offered to show them the way into the Catuvellauni heartlands.

Cassivellaunus had drawn up his troops on the north bank of the Thames at the point occupied today by the west London suburb of Brentford. In 54 BC it was, as the modern name suggests, a shallow ford at the confluence of the Thames and Brent rivers. It was the only point where men and horses could hope to cross and Cassivellaunus might have prayed the Romans would never find it – that the deep, black barrier of the water itself would hold back the foe. With the help of their new-found friends, however, Caesar and his legions were there in no time.

A battle duly ensued but, for all the undoubted bravery of the defenders, there was never any real chance of withstanding the onslaught. The front rank of any Roman army fought for no more than 15 minutes before being pulled back to the rear to recover their strength. Fresh men stepped forward to replace them and in this way any enemy found itself fighting a foe that never tired, never weakened. It was an enervating battle of attrition and in time the British warriors were overwhelmed and forced to break and run. Everyone could see which way the wind was blowing and one by one the tribal leaders made terms with Caesar. Cassivellaunus retained the loyalty of his own closest followers and they withdrew to fight another day. But it was over.

Here was the lesson that later Britons would learn from. By failing to stand together, the British tribes had defeated themselves. It would become part of the lore of the British people – that in the fight to defend British people from the tyranny of dictators, unity and loyalty were everything.

The names of those peoples sound as foreign to us now as those of any Native American Indians – indeed only the Romans' latinised versions survive – and yet they were part of the story for hundreds if not thousands of years. Among the missing are the

Atrebates in Hampshire; the Brigantes, their name meaning 'hill-dwellers', in the Pennines – likely a confederation made up of smaller tribes like the Corionototae, the Lopocares, the Tectoverdi and the Setanti; the Parisii in east Yorkshire; the Carvetii in Cumbria; the Dubunni in the Cotswolds; the Deceangli, the Demetae, the Ordovices and the Silures in Wales. On and on goes the roll-call of peoples lost to us, and yet still in our DNA somewhere. In Scotland were the Novantae in the south-west; the Damnonii in Strathclyde; the Votadini in the south-east; the Venicones in Tayside and the Epidii in Kintyre and on the islands of Arran, Islay and Jura. Imagine, too, the language that went with those names, that could string them together like beads on a necklace.

For now, though, in 54 BC the inescapable fact was that Britain's doors lay open to the invader. It might have been easy to imagine that, in the aftermath of such a decisive defeat, all Britain would quickly have fallen under Roman rule. But of course it was not quite like that. Caesar stayed for just three months. Having contented himself with pledges of allegiance from the tribes of southern Britain, he loaded his army back aboard their ships and returned to Gaul.

That, in abbreviated form, is the familiar version of the events of 55 and 54 BC taught to countless generations of schoolchildren. It is a version of the truth (myths and legends form like pearls around grains of sand, or like raindrops around specks of dust), but it is certainly less than the whole story. For one thing it has the Romans leaving in 54 BC without so much as a backward glance. The schoolchildren are expected to believe that after all that effort – with a view to adding Britannia to the Roman demesne – Caesar just cut the place adrift once more. The next significant date in the story is AD 43 – the best part of a century later – and we are traditionally told that Britain was left to its own devices for all that time. But if that is what most of us think, the scholars know different.

Key to their deeper understanding is the coinage. When some

numismatists look at the coins circulating in Britain in the middle of the first century BC, they spot a clean break. After the Roman invasion of 54 BC, the old Celtic coins disappear and are replaced with new ones – suggesting one hierarchy had been replaced by another.

In his wonderfully readable *Britannia: The Creation of a Roman Province*, John Creighton identifies three ways in which the new coins differ from the old. Firstly there is an abrupt change in the familiar depictions of a human head on one side and a horse on the other. After Caesar's time in Britain, the imagery suddenly mimics that of coins minted in Gaul. The second change is in the amount of gold in gold coins: where once the gold content was highly variable, suddenly it became carefully regulated and consistent. Thirdly, says Creighton, hoards featuring both old and new coinages are rare – making it likely that the old coins were withdrawn and replaced wholesale by the new version. 'The combination of these three changes in the gold coinage, all happening at the same time, suggests a radical restructuring of the political arrangement of south-east Britain at this date, even though otherwise in the archaeology we see little alteration,' he wrote. 'A recoinage across all of south-east Britain required the mobilisation of a significant degree of power or authority.'

Creighton infers the 'radical restructuring of the political arrangement' went further than just issuing new coins. He believes the Romans also installed two Gallic aristocrats as kings of two new territories, one south of the Thames and one in the east.

Caesar himself refers to a figure named Commius, a Roman-approved king of the Atrebates tribe back in northern Gaul. Caesar trusted Commius and sent him to Britain as part of the build-up to his invasion in 55 BC, with instructions to win over as many as possible of the British tribes. While his diplomatic mission was a failure – he was captured on arrival – he retained the general's support. Returned to Caesar as a bargaining chip, he was subsequently rewarded with fresh territory in Gaul. 'My reading of the evidence, therefore, would be to view Commius as being appointed king over several of the political groups that surrendered to Caesar on his expeditions to Britain,' wrote Creighton.

Commius is the name on some of the first of the new coins issued in southern Britain, along with that of a figure named Tasciovanus. Creighton suggests the former was made king in the south, while the latter was put in place in the east. The use of placemen was the Roman way, after all – demonstrating so much more finesse than the blunt edge of invasion. That the Republic was so polished, so experienced in the business of takeovers, somehow makes it seem even more sinister, even more irresistible.

Details like these make the story infinitely richer and more satisfying than before – reminding us that powerful states use wit and guile just as readily as brute force in pursuit of their objectives. Better yet, they expose as nonsense the idea the Romans left the best part of 100 years between phase one and phase two of their plans to conquer the islands. In the years after 54 BC, a new chapter was opened in the history of Britain. In many practical respects it was truly momentous – in fact, the end of our prehistory. From then on, to a greater or lesser extent, the land was under the gaze of those in the habit of writing things down.

It is true to say Roman forces had touched only a small part of Britain. But while the tribes in the north and west likely felt Caesar's adventures and intrigues among the Trinovantes and the Catuvellauni were distant concerns, those in the south and east came face to face with a new reality. And just as the tale told by the coins would be easy to overlook, the effects of those first decades of Roman suzerainty on the fabric of life in southern Britain are less than obvious at first glance.

Silchester, in Hampshire, became one of the most important Roman cities in Britain. They knew it as Calleva Atrebatum – a latinised form of a Celtic name meaning 'the wooded place' – but it was a fully functioning town for generations before Emperor Claudius arrived in Britain to celebrate the official conquest of the new colony in AD 43. Today it is the site of one of the largest archaeological excavations currently under way in Britain and evidence already recovered has proven beyond doubt that Calleva was something previously unknown: a town founded, built and run by Britons.

What is surprising about the place is that as early as 25 BC it featured streets laid out like a modern city, on a regular grid pattern – something archaeologists previously believed arrived only when the Romans came to stay, in AD 43. (Something similar is suggested at Fishbourne, in West Sussex, where some of the excavated pottery dates to around 20 BC; there is an early mosaic showing the Iron Age town laid out in a grid pattern.)

Fascinatingly, at Calleva the town planning – and that is what we are talking about – is a fusion of British Iron Age and Roman sensibilities. For while the main axis of Roman towns ran from north to south, at Calleva the alignment was east to west. Iron Age traditions gave priority to the path of the sun, with house entrances facing east; so that although the planners had clearly acquired some of the new ideas, they clung stubbornly to important elements of the old. Iron Age Silchester is nonetheless the earliest known example of town planning anywhere in Britain.

Who then was responsible for such quasi-Roman behaviour, on an island apparently abandoned by the Romans 30 years before? The answer is to be found back on the beach at Walmer, with Caesar in 55 BC. By his own account he demanded and was given 'hostages' from the tribes as gestures of their good will and their intention to behave themselves. Those individuals, likely to have been the sons or close relations of the chieftains, were then spirited away, all the way back to Rome. But the use of the word 'hostages' – so loaded with notions of imprisonment and threat to life – is unhelpful. It just happens to be a convenient translation of the Roman word *obses* and has tended to remain stuck in the literature ever since.

In fact the lot of the *obsides* was far from unhappy and it is more accurate to think of them as exchange students. *Obsides* were educated in the Roman way, mixed freely with Roman citizens and were generally encouraged to become Roman in their dress, outlook and behaviour. Once their makeover was complete –

perhaps many years later – they were sent home. It was hoped that they would take Rome with them, and that consciously or unconsciously they would educate the people back home, persuade them the Roman traditions and practices were best.

In the case of the founding of a city like Calleva, the chronology fits. Perhaps we should picture the return to Hampshire of men who had last seen Britain when they were mere boys. By dint of an adolescence and young manhood spent in the Classical world, they must have returned as strangers to a strange land. They were still the sons of chieftains and aristocrats, but now their strongest allegiances may have been to Roman foster families a thousand miles away – certainly to Roman ways.

Homesick for another world, they might understandably have used their influence to try to create, among the fields and round-houses, some shadow of all they had left behind. They did not just bring back a taste for ordered streets either. The new city was soon filled with new sights and smells as well. Evidence from the Silchester excavations shows the inhabitants acquired a taste for Mediterranean exotics like coriander, dill and anchovies.

Jonathan Swift is one of several people credited with the line, 'He was a brave man that first ate an oyster.' At various times in prehistory they had been an important and plentiful food, but during the Iron Age of southern Britain they were off the menu. In Calleva, however, they were being consumed by the barrow load and so the locals had to have acquired that habit from somewhere. The somewhere was Rome, where oysters were as popular as ever.

The archaeologists have found coins in the Silchester excava-tions as well. A tiny silver minim, about the size of the nail on an adult's little finger, has on one side the head of a man and the name Verica. He is styled like a Roman emperor, but on his head he bears an unmistakably Celtic torc. The other side reveals more about his identity: another torc encircling the letters CF, standing for 'Commius Filius'. This then is a coin minted under the authority of King Verica, a descendant of

Commius – surely the same Commius set in place by Caesar himself.

Coins like that minim, tiny though it is, would have had a huge impact on the people of Calleva and on the wider world of southern Britain. It is hard for us to imagine the power coins once had. We see tokens for buying a newspaper, or to drop into a busker's hat. Increasingly now we do not even bother to bend down and pick the lowest denominations if we drop them. They are close to being meaningless and valueless.

But 2,000 years ago they bore messages as effectively as do texts on mobile phones today. Celtic coins used images, pictures to tell people who was in charge. When there was a change at the top, there would have to be a new image. The coinage recovered from Silchester is even more important because it features the written word as well. In the last decades of the first century BC, the mass of people living in Britain had never seen writing before. For such marks to start appearing on coins would have been truly radical.

If the cosmopolitan port of Hengistbury Head had been a shock to the locals during the first half of the first century BC, then the impact on the senses felt by native Britons on first encountering Calleva would have been of a whole different order of magnitude. These would have been people who, for the most part, were familiar only with roundhouses and field boundaries. Occasionally they might have visited a hill fort, but by the end of the first century BC those were in sharp decline. So to leave their farmsteads and villages and arrive at a city – a full-blown, planned city of interconnecting streets lined with houses, shops and workshops, and home to hundreds of people – would have left them wide-eyed and speechless with sensory overload.

Wonders though they surely were, pockets of early British uptake of Roman mores would have been few and far between in the decades after 54 BC, limited to the south-east. Two foreign dynasties had been established and their impact had been made visible on the coins and with the creation of at least one Romanised city. Elsewhere, Celtic life continued as it always had.

Perhaps in the territories to the north and west Rome was a talking point, fuel for gossip and speculation. Caesar's efforts had secured a foothold on Britannia – had opened a door through which Roman ways began to seep like rising water. In some ways it was a decades-long phoney war that followed. An aggressive and acquisitive Empire, brooding just across the water, had made its presence felt and its intentions clear. In most of the British Isles, though, life continued as normal. Farmers sowed their crops and then harvested them. The sun rose and set, illuminating round-house doorways in the morning and setting them into shadow in the evening.

Rome had, anyway, rather bigger business to attend to else-where. Around the time the foundations of Calleva were being laid in Hampshire, Rome installed Juba II as client king of the territory of Numidia, in north Africa. By then the 500 years of the Roman Republic were over and Rome had her first emperor. Caesar had been assassinated in 44 BC and his will named his grand-nephew Octavius as his adopted son and heir. Octavius was first supported and then challenged by Caesar's friend and ally Mark Antony – who had also taken the dead man's lover, Cleopatra, for his own. Matters were settled by the climactic sea battle of Actium in 31 BC. Defeated on water and then on land at Alexandria, the doomed lovers took their own lives.

From the moment in 27 BC when Octavius was named Augustus, meaning great or revered, by the Senate he was Emperor in all but name. Augustus it was who placed Juba II on the throne – the throne of his father, Juba I – and then made him the gift of a wife as well. Cleopatra had had three children by Mark Antony: sons Alexander Helios and Ptolemy Philadelphus, and a daughter, Cleopatra Selene.

All three were descendants one way or another of Ptolemy I, best friend and one-time bodyguard of Alexander the Great. Augustus had adopted them following their parents' death and raised them in his own household. Egypt had been Alexander's gift to Ptolemy and the Ptolemaic Pharaohs his legacy. Cleopatra

Selene, child of immortal legends, was given in marriage to Juba II and then disappeared from history for ever.

The Roman territory of Judaea, roughly equivalent to modern Israel and Palestine, was ruled as part of the neighbouring province of Syria until 40 BC when it was made a kingdom again. Herod the Great was the Roman placeman on the throne, eventually controlling a territory that also included Galilee, until his death in 4 BC. When he died, the Romans honoured his wishes that his kingdom be split between three of his sons. Archelaus was granted Judaea, Philip was gifted a portion of the northern territory and Herod Antipas, who in time would have a role to play in the executions of John the Baptist and Jesus Christ, ruled Galilee.

Antony and Cleopatra, the birth of the Roman Empire itself were unwitting steps towards the creation of a religion that would change the world. With such events, and more besides, unfolding elsewhere in the Empire, the fact that Britannia was not always at the top of the agenda is perhaps less of a surprise.

Eventually, though, the eyes of the Empire turned towards Britain once more. The softly, softly policy of leaving territories under the control of sympathetic client kings, which had been a feature of Roman business practices in the later years of the Republic, was less attractive to the emperors. In AD 9 three whole legions – 15,000 men – were wiped out in a battle east of the Rhine in Germania. It was a jarring blow for imperial morale. Until that moment the advance of the Empire had seemed natural and limitless, almost preordained. After the German disaster Roman minds began thinking about security, about tightening the nuts and bolts holding their demesne together. In Britain the situation was exacerbated by civil strife and unrest among the tribes.

Augustus thought about invading on three separate occasions but never actually put any plans into action. Emperor Gaius Julius Caesar Augustus Germanicus (better known to history as Caligula, a soldiers' nickname for him, meaning little shoe) came close in AD 40 and went so far as to assemble an army on the coast of Gaul.

Accounts of what happened next are dominated by later Roman writers who sought to portray Caligula as a madman; and he is variously reported as ordering his men to attack the waves, or to collect seashells. It seems more likely his preparations were rather more measured and sensible and modern historians and archaeologists have credited his efforts with laying much of the groundwork for the successful invasion by Claudius three years later. Archaeological investigation of the foundations of a lighthouse Caligula ordered to be built at Boulogne, for instance, in advance of the departure of his landing craft, has revealed it was used as the blueprint for one later erected at Dover.

After Caligula, Claudius was a new Emperor in need of a success to thrill and impress the citizens of Rome. He also needed to underline the difference between himself and his immediate predecessor. By AD 43, in short, Britain's card was marked.

Given that the eventual invasion of AD 43 is such a landmark in British history, it is a surprise to learn no one seems to know for certain where the four Roman legions, under the command of the distinguished senator and general Aulus Plautius, actually came ashore. Richborough, in Kent, is a popular choice but wherever it was, the force that splashed onto the British beaches nearly 90 years after Caesar's men departed had come to stay.

Despite all the years of client kingdoms, there was still a spirited resistance from at least some of the Kentish tribes. Elsewhere too, beyond the territories of those friendly towards the Romans, there was much blood to be spilled. The whole of the south-east was subdued within a matter of weeks, but the rest of the invasion was to be the stuff of years, lifetimes, and the Romans likely knew it from the start. It was now, with the invaders bent upon nothing less than total conquest, that the already ancient and venerable hill forts of the south were pressed into service one last time.

As warriors the forts had probably grown old and drowsy. By AD 43 southern Britain had enjoyed a century or more of relative peace and the forts were mostly given over to trade, to ceremony and to worship. But at the sound of the carnyx, the great howling war trumpet of the Celts, they roused themselves as best they could. Legend would later have King Arthur asleep beneath a green hill, ready to rise and ride out whenever he was needed. As the legions advanced, 500 years before his time, it was the hills themselves that briefly reared up in defiance.

Archaeological evidence recovered from some of the hill forts of Dorset reveals the reality of the last stands. Hod hill fort was the spiritual home of the Durotriges tribe. Excavation close by the north-east entrance found the remains of a young woman buried in a pit. This was interpreted as a 'foundation' burial – something like an offering to the gods in hope of good fortune for the settlement. Similar burials, though of young men, were found in pits inside the hill forts of Maiden Castle and also South Cadbury, in Somerset. Many other people had been buried within Hod hill fort over the years. Excavation found another within part of the ramparts and a dozen more, including infants, within pits dotted across the sites. Squares of postholes suggested either raised grain stores or perhaps platforms used for the excarnation of the dead. Hill forts were places that mattered to their tribes in profound ways, made as they were, to some extent, of their own flesh and blood.

Inside Hod was evidence of as many as 200 roundhouses, as well as a tracery of 'streets'. Excavation suggested work was under way to strengthen the defences even as the Romans advanced towards them. Two buildings surrounded by a small enclosure may have been the compound of the chieftain. There the archaeologists found the iron tips of numerous Roman ballista bolts fired from mechanised crossbows. By concentrating their fire on the home of the leader, the attackers likely hoped to weaken morale. The tactic worked. The defenders, by pitiful contrast to the artillery ranged against them, had amassed pits filled with rounded stones to launch from their slings. The fact that they had lain unused – together with few signs of fighting – suggested the people of Hod showed little resistance. Soon the Romans had underlined their dominance by building their own fort inside the tamed ramparts.

The peoples of the west and north faced a dreadful choice. If they were to roll over in the face of the aggressors, accept a future as part of the Empire, then they risked losing an identity that had been thousands of years in the making. But if they chose continued independence and defied Rome, if they stood behind sharpened stakes planted on the rounded slopes of their hill forts, they risked losing their lives.

Hod had come under attack from the Second Legion, commanded by Vespasian – a general in AD 43 but later Emperor. He had earlier taken Maiden Castle, again in the face of muted resistance, as well as several other hill forts to the south. The brutal efficiency of Vespasian and his ilk survives in the bones of some of those Britons cut down to make way for the future. Sometimes there are the iron heads of ballista bolts still imbedded in spines. Bones from hands reveal defensive wounds, likely caused by desperate attempts to grab the sword blades of Roman attackers. It was not just Celtic men who felt the sharp edge of Roman aggression either. Savage wounds to the backs of the skulls and leg bones of women reveal they were cut down while trying to run away.

When the famous English archaeologist Sir Mortimer Wheeler excavated Maiden Castle between 1934 and 1937, he was convinced he had found evidence of a bloody clash between Romans and defenders. There were traces of burning at the hill fort's complex eastern entrance, huge collections of sling stones and, most sensationally of all, victims of the horror: 'Men, women, young and old, were savagely cut down, before the legionaries were called to heel and the work of systematic destruction began ... the survivors crept forth and, in darkness, buried their dead ... in that place where the ashes of their burnt huts lay warm and thick on the ground.'

It was all fabulously dramatic stuff and since Sir Mortimer was a born storyteller, gifted with the ability to enthral the general public with a subject that might otherwise have passed them by, his version of events became a staple of archaeology for years to come.

More recently, Niall Sharples of Cardiff University, has disputed some of Sir Mortimer's interpretation. While he agreed the fort's defences had probably been damaged by the Romans after they had gained access to the place, he was less convinced by other parts of Sir Mortimer's account.

Examination of the burials suggested that, rather than being hurriedly laid to rest under cover of darkness, the bodies had been buried in an existing cemetery and in line with the usual funerary practices of the inhabitants. According to Sharples, the evidence of burning was more likely to have been caused by peacetime metal-working than by any wholesale destruction of the interior. Furthermore he believed the 'arrows' that were cited as evidence of Roman attack were of a type that predated the Roman conquest of Britain.

This sort of re-evaluation of evidence is what the science of archaeology is all about – how the subject continues to advance our understanding of the ancient past. In this instance, however, the older, and undoubtedly more exciting, version of events at Maiden Castle in AD 43 seems to have won out.

Work on the skeletons by specialists Rebecca Redfern from the Museum of London and Andrew Chamberlain of Sheffield University appears to indicate they went into the ground in the aftermath of something 'catastrophic'. They said the fact that the dead had been given formal burial, and in an existing cemetery, was no reason to dismiss brutal conflict as the cause of death. 'Examination of the human remains found overwhelming evidence for targeted blows to the head and body, assault injuries and overkill,' they wrote. 'Skeletal evidence for trauma was identified in adolescent and adult individuals, suggesting that both sexes and older sub-adults were exposed to and/or engaged in martial activity during the Late Iron Age. The organised burial of these members of the Durotriges tribe suggests that we should not assume that formal burials in the Late Iron Age excluded victims of the conquest ... we consider that large-scale conflict was a major contributor ... that the majority of the individuals buried at Maiden

Castle were most likely killed during the Roman invasion of Britain in AD 43.'

For all the shock and awe of the military, the Roman advance was really much more about patience, planning and a genius for the science of logistics. From the moment they marched up the beaches from their landing craft, the Romans knew that the transformation of the land of the Britons into the province of Britannia would be the work of decades. It is tempting to imagine the Roman army sweeping across the islands like a great wave, washing all resistance before it, but the reality was different.

Britain had felt the power of a tsunami before – in 8000 BC, when the forces of nature had made the place an island once and for all. But if the Roman advance resembled anything it was an older force still, that of the glaciers. Rome would remodel Britain gradually, grinding forwards relentlessly. The generation that arrived in AD 43 would retire and die, to be planted in British fields, but there would always be others following behind. Rome was not built in a day and neither was Roman Britain. Its architects had time on their hands and the stamina and patience to match.

So the legions marched out of the south-east, heading north and west, to fight their battles and erect their forts. Behind them came the engineers who would eventually construct more than 2,000 miles of roads for easy marching and easy tax collection; they built towns and cities for the all-important bureaucrats who would fill in the forms and count the money. Wherever they went the Romans had to plan and build more and more, until in time they would create an entire infrastructure.

At least as impressive as anything else they conceived are their roads – famously straight, uncompromising routes connecting the new cities. It had long been assumed that, until the arrival of the Romans, Britain was a land of tracks and pathways – ancient and familiar but ephemeral, maintained only by the imperceptible wear of footsteps and the wheel rims of chariots.

The ghost of a barbarian Britain is a hard one to lay to rest. Never mind that amphorae full of Roman wine were enlivening the long winter nights in Gurness Broch on Orkney, or that a king of those islands was named on a triumphal arch raised in Rome, as one who bothered to bow to Claudius at Colchester. Forget too that gold jewellery in the tradition of the Classical world of the Mediterranean was sought by the well-to-do in the land that would become Scotland, perhaps a couple of centuries before Claudius's birth. The discovery of a taste for fancy bangles, made of southern European coloured glass, at Hengistbury Head in the century before Caesar apparently matters not. Despite all the evidence to the contrary, it is still easiest to imagine Britain spurning all the changes and advances happening elsewhere, the mass of her peoples resisting civilisation just as they would resist the Romans themselves.

Modern Britons' reluctance to let go of their inner barbarian is tightly bound to the British sense of independence. Britons need to know they are different – and that, furthermore, they have always been different. But an archaeological discovery in Shropshire in 2009 is yet another nail in the coffin of that unquiet spirit.

A long, straight earthwork running for miles through the Shropshire countryside had long been regarded as part of the Roman road network. English archaeologist and Roman specialist Ivan Margary was the expert on the subject in the 1940s and 1950s and classified the Shropshire stretch as something akin to a Roman B-class road. If Margary said it was a Roman road, then that was that. An excavation in 1995 had looked at a small section of the thing and drawn the same conclusion.

But 14 years later, when the Tarmac Company proposed to quarry away a 400-yard-long stretch of it, archaeologists were called in to take a second look. To begin with, the team was persuaded they were indeed dealing with a Roman road. It had the familiar profile of a few feet of clay and hardcore topped with a cambered surface. There was a drainage ditch on each side into which passing travellers had flung the usual assortment of Roman-period rubbish. But, more interestingly, there were signs the road had been rebuilt on more than once occasion, and samples were collected in hopes of obtaining dates for the various phases of construction. Rather than dating to a time after the invasion, however, the road had been built sometime in the second century BC – and then repaired and rebuilt for the last time long before the Romans were even in Kent.

That the Romans found perfectly usable British roads in some parts of the land seems fairly certain now: we have already seen the long, straight metalled road at Silchester in 25 BC. Perhaps the soldiers, and some of their more worldly superiors as well, were surprised by how much they did recognise. Britannia may have been off the radar for most of them – and for all of their lives until they splashed ashore on the south coast – and yet there they were marching for some of the time at least along metalled roads through a landscape of ordered fields and trackways. Sometimes the roads passed through towns – *oppida* in their own Latin tongue – where they might find bathhouses in which to wash and soothe aching muscles, as well as innumerable craftsmen, artists and specialists in mysteries like medicine. If they had expected such towns to be chaotic and disorganised – if they expected them to exist at all – then they were wrong again. Those towns they encountered had clearly defined zones, with places of industry kept separate from places where people lived. There was ritual and religion as well – unfamiliar and foreign to Roman soldiers' eyes no doubt, but no less sophisticated and complex than their own.

Those legionaries might have known next to nothing about the British, so how disconcerting for them to find the British seemingly knew a great deal about them.

There were coins in circulation as well – much like the sort used in Gaul – and the invaders would have noticed how the local kings were styling themselves in the Roman manner. They might have seen the petty kings from time to time and they would certainly have noticed how many of the native men and women were wearing clothes and jewellery modelled on those worn in Rome, if not actually imported from there.

That the little kings of Britannia were dressing like Romans can only have worked in the Empire's favour in the long run. The first time a Briton saw one of his own dressed that way – or the first time they clapped eyes on a Gallic import like a Commius or a Tasciovanus – the garb might have seemed strange. Soon, though, they would have grown used to it, and by the time the first king was succeeded by a second and then a third, they might have paid more attention to the clothes and the crown rather than to the man or the woman.

This is the genius of uniform; and the raiment worn by kings and queens is just that, a uniform. Once the subjects understand the office denoted by the crown, they might become less interested in the face beneath it. The king is the king because his outfit says so, and that is all a person needs to know. This is a process that can make puppets interchangeable. (There is a story, perhaps apocryphal perhaps not, that the American film studios conceived of the Lone Ranger as a masked man for one very good reason: the audience never got to see the actor. If the actor got ideas above his station and started asking for more money, he could swiftly be replaced and his adoring fans would be none the wiser. The same was surely true for puppet kings and queens. If the crown no longer fitted the wearer in imperial eyes, then it could be moved onto the head of the next man.)

If the time came when the Republic, or later the Empire, sought to replace a native king with a home-grown governor – to change an 'independent' kingdom into a province – then that might be accomplished without any of the subject population even noticing the sleight of hand.

Whether or not they recognised aspects of the landscape around them, the Romans set about the business of remodelling the place in their own image. With a military infrastructure of forts in place, the planners and engineers got to work building towns and cities. In the comparatively safe south-east they established Colchester, London and St Albans, and on the frontier beyond they founded Exeter, Gloucester and Lincoln. If these were under way relatively quickly, it would take decades to expand that frontier. Wales was first and then the north. York was founded in AD 71 and then Carlisle, deep in bandit country, by AD 79.

After around 35 years of marching, fighting and building, much of the template of the Britain we recognise today had been carved from the ancient landscape. Superimposed upon the old bones of the place was a new skin carefully sculpted so as to be recognisable as an adopted daughter of the Empire.

One of the very first of the new towns was Camulodunum, founded in AD 49 and known to us as the city of Colchester. It was near here, in the 1990s, that archaeologists found the grave of the man called doctor, or druid. The Romans must have asked the locals what they called the native settlement that already thrived on the site on their arrival. When they were told it was dunum – the fortress – of Camulos – the god of war – the soldiers merely latinised the name. Here had been the royal stronghold of the Trinovantes – the same that had felt so threatened by their neighbours, the Catuvellauni, that they opened Britain's doors to Caesar in 54 BC.

In AD 65, more than a century after that betrayal, a huge triumphal arch was built through the walls of the Roman town that supplanted the Iron Age settlement, dedicated to the glory of Emperor Claudius. A single archway still stands today, made of red Roman bricks. This is the Balkerne Gate, the oldest surviving and most complete Roman gateway in the whole of Britain. It is a strange relic today, like a hanging valley left high and dry above the modern traffic thundering past on the A134 dual carriageway below. There is a pub beside it and people bustle obliviously through the ancient gateway, mostly heading to and from the walkway that carries pedestrians over the road.

But for all that it is lost in the modern world, it still carries some of its old power. Any Celtic Briton used to a village of roundhouses would have been stunned into obedience by such a structure. Having passed through something like the Balkerne Gate you would hardly have to feel the sharp edge of a Roman sword to understand that the people who could build such things were the people in control.

For every Briton cowed by Camulodunum, there would have been a Roman soldier returning from the front, or a bureaucrat employed to count taxes, who took great comfort from entering a town little different to any in the Empire. These were the *civitates* built in the image of Rome and for Romans and they were symbols of permanence. The first of them were established as colonies for retiring soldiers and if the veterans of the conquest were staying put, so was everyone else.

Anyone seeking a memorial to those anonymous souls crushed beneath the Roman machine need only look around a place like Colchester. Built into its 2,000-year-old foundations are their skulls and bones. In an annexe of Colchester Museum I was given permission to examine all that remained of two men who lived and died in the town around AD 50 – just when Camulodunum was being built.

Neither of them died naturally. Only their skulls survive and those were found during the excavation of a ditch in the 1970s. They make for grim viewing: one features a thumb-sized depressed fracture of the crown, caused by a crushing blow from a blunt instrument like a cosh or a hammer. It had been a mortal wound. The other man's skull was even worse, with two or three deep cuts made by something heavy and sharp, an axe or a sword. These showed the man had been the victim of a clumsy decapitation.

These are the remains of two British men who met their deaths in Camulodunum before the paint was dry. It is highly likely they represent some of the hundreds, thousands of locals pressed into duty as labourers and builders of the new town. In some long-forgotten manner they fell foul of their overlords and were messily butchered. Their severed heads may well have ended up on the ends of sharpened poles, a warning to all of the fate awaiting any who, by accident or design, got in the way of the march of Rome.

Dead men like those were details anyway, as far as the Roman Empire was concerned. The whole point of the exercise, the reason for expending all that effort to make a province of Britannia, was to take advantage of all the land had to offer. The islands had been known, since the time of the first Greek map-makers at least, as the Tin Isles. It was well known too that there was copper aplenty in the wild lands of Wales, as well as on the neighbouring island of Hibernia – Ireland. Where such mineral wealth existed there might well be all the rest as well: gold and silver.

Celtic Britain had been a source of slaves. Rather than kill the men and women of your defeated foe, it made much more economic sense to sell them on instead. The Celts had made a profit from such human misery and the Romans were more than happy to keep the business going.

In the Mendip Hills of Somerset the Roman prospectors quickly found rich reserves of galena, the naturally occurring mineral form of lead. Within six years of their arrival in Britain, a large-scale lead mine was in business in an area known today as Charterhouse. The scars on the landscape, long since overgrown and reclaimed by nature, are on such a scale they appear like the work of nature. Great trenches called 'rakes' up to 30 feet deep and as much as 100 yards long were hacked out of the bedrock to expose the galena. The mine was soon the biggest lead-mining operation in the whole of the Empire and the output was on such a colossal scale it brought protests and demands for cuts in reduction from rival mines in Roman Spain. What was achieved by the Romans during their tenure would not be equalled in the Mendips for 1,000 years after their departure in the fifth century.

While the native Britons had used lead as a constituent of bronze and pewter, the Romans had many more applications for the stuff. The Latin word for lead is *plumbum*, and the Romans certainly employed the metal in their plumbing – in pipes for their homes and bathhouses as well as for their grand viaducts. Lead is toxic – a fact that may or may not have been known in ancient times – but nonetheless it was used by the Romans to line their cooking pots and even as an ingredient in some of their cooking.

Ingots of lead, some weighing as much as 15 or 16 stones – as much as a grown man – were produced in the Mendips and transported all the way back to Rome. Some were stamped as the property of the Emperor himself – and not because he coveted the lead itself necessarily, but another metal contained within. Lead contains silver, crucial for Roman coins, and with this in mind the metal was processed within heavily defended forts. Like gold, lead is so heavy it provides its own security – you would be hard pushed to make off with 16-stone ingot of the stuff – but it was the prospect of silver that explains the scarred landscape of the Mendips.

The promise of gold drew the Roman miners and engineers towards known reserves in Devon, Scotland and Wales. But the biggest prize lay further west. Around 30 years after they arrived in Britain they had brought the Welsh to heel. Right away they set about extracting gold on a huge scale at Dolaucothi, in Carmarthenshire in south Wales.

Gold was being collected from the rivers and streams by the locals there as early as the Bronze Age, but the Romans brought truly industrial techniques into play. Having surveyed the terrain, they understood the gold ran in veins through quartzite rock. The problem was how to get at the quartzite without expending thousands of man-hours stripping the trees, turf and soil that cloaked the hillsides.

Their solution was to divert the natural streams and rivers along specially built aqueducts and leats, some of them as much as seven miles long, and into huge clay-lined earthen tanks dug into the hillsides. By opening sluice gates, millions of gallons of collected water could be directed downhill in thundering torrents, completing the task of exposing the bedrock in seconds. Known today as hydraulic mining – or hushing – the technique was in use in Britain from time to time until the nineteenth century, and in parts of Africa until the twentieth.

The exposed veins were then exploited by hand, by miners. No doubt much of the manpower was slave labour – local populations pressed into servitude underground. The area was exploited again by the Victorians and remained open until 1938. It was while digging their own tunnels and galleries that modern miners broke through into spaces excavated nearly 2,000 years before. The walls and roofs were pitted throughout with the scars left by ancient iron picks. As well as forcing the locals underground, the Romans routinely sentenced their convicts to lifetimes in the mines, so that the fortunes in British gold that went into the Roman exchequer were soaked in sweat, blood and tears.

As the Roman machine spread out across Britain, more and more of the native population was faced with choices – and dilemmas. There was an obvious and understandable temptation to get into gear with the machine, to seek to profit from it. Back in Dorset in the former lands of the Durotriges – some of whom would await the Roman advance from within their capital at Hod hill fort – archaeologists have found evidence that not everyone there lived in fear of Rome.

At a place called North Down, deep in the Dorset countryside, a team from Bournemouth University has been excavating one of a class of settlements known as banjo enclosures. Viewed from the air such sites bear a superficial resemblance to a banjo, with a circular ditch enclosing the shape of the body, connected to a long narrow neck that provides the entrance. Banjo enclosures might look defensive but in fact they are anything but – in truth just undefended farming settlements providing homes for extended families.

As well as mineral wealth and slaves, the Romans wanted to take advantage of southern Britain's rich farmland. In later centuries Dorset would be known as the 'breadbasket' of England and the Romans viewed the place in much the same way. Dorset grain would be exported by the Romans as far as Hadrian's Wall and the Rhine Valley. But at North Down the picture being built up by the archaeologists is of Iron Age Britons living peaceably through the transition from independence to domination by Rome.

Scattered across the site are as many as 30 large, deep pits, dug straight down into the chalk. Their primary function was the storage of grain like oats and barley, but it seems the farmers also used them as a means of entering into some kind of transaction with the gods, or with nature herself. Having emptied a pit of grain, the farmers then made offerings of pieces of pottery and other valuables, including pieces of Roman amphorae. Sometimes they placed cuts of meat or even their own dead into the spaces left by the food. It seems they felt an obligation to give something back into the earth in return for that which had been gained.

As well as native grains and animals, the pits occasionally offer up exotic imports like chicken. Such birds are commonplace on our own tables but in Iron Age Britain they were a luxury that could only be obtained through people with connections to Europe and the Mediterranean.

Since so much of the old way of life, the Celtic way of life, continued unmolested and unabated, it is tempting to imagine some people there living prosperously, making themselves rich by selling their grain to feed the hungry armies of Rome. All the while they mixed with the foreigners they picked and chose from those aspects of the new life that attracted them – new styles of clothes and jewellery perhaps, new foodstuffs – but they continued to inhabit the same sorts of settlements they always had, and to practise their own rituals and religions. At North Down at least, the indications are that the Romans left them to it.

Rather than an unbroken wave of conquest, then, the coming of Rome was a process. The armies meted out violence – that much is certain; but it was hardly a time of endless battles. By AD 60, having spent nearly two decades in Britannia, the Romans were even lulled and lured into dropping their guard from time to time. Given the scale of the new province, they could hardly defend every town, every city – and surely they deemed that unnecessary anyway. In the south-east, after all, the Roman presence was so well established it had engendered among its Roman, or Romanised, inhabitants a fair degree of complacency.

Camulodunum had been established first of all as a colony for retired soldiers. Despite the military background of its original inhabitants, it was undefended for the first 11 years of its existence. It was also quite unique in Britain in that it was independent, self-governing and semi-autonomous. Completion of military service was rewarded with Roman citizenship and in the first century it was a prosperous, cosmopolitan place with a population made up of people drawn from all over the Empire. Nearing completion in AD 60 was an enormous temple, the biggest in Britain, dedicated to Claudius. Camulodunum was, by any measure, a town on the up.

But if all was well in the busy streets, shops and comfortable homes of the oldest Roman town in Britannia, something was rotten in the way at least one of the nearby tribes was being treated. The Iceni, occupying a territory roughly the same as modern Norfolk, had long been friends of Rome. Their king, Prasutagus, had grown wealthy by association. He may have been one of those who bowed down before Claudius alongside the King of Orkney, but his loyalty had served him well in any case.

Wily politician that he was, he drew up a will stating that in the event of his death his estate was to be split – half for his two daughters and half for Emperor Nero himself. He was not the first native king to attempt the ploy: such tactics had become relatively commonplace as local leaders walked the tightrope between their people and their masters. The Romans, as it turned out, were having none of it. Despite all of Prasutagus's efforts to ensure a future of peace and prosperity for his family and for his people, when he died the local officials helped themselves to everything he left behind.

Prasutagus's widow was named Boudicca. History paints her as the British pride incarnate, but she was a woman who had played the game and married well. She was as much a part of the establishment as an opponent of it. Whatever the truth of her motivations, she apparently complained bitterly about the treatment meted out to her family, the disrespect being shown to her dead husband.

According to the ubiquitous Tacitus, Boudicca was publicly

thrashed, 'disgraced with cruel stripes'. Worse still, her daughters were raped by Roman soldiers while she was made to watch. More worrying for the mass of the Iceni, however, was a demand that they surrender their swords and other weapons. This was part of the so-called Pax Romana – Roman Peace – whereby the inhabitants of Roman provinces all across the Empire were forbidden to bear arms. While an apparently reasonable suggestion in principle, for Celtic warriors raised over countless generations to see their weapons as visible manifestations of their independence, the surrender of their swords was unthinkable, an intrusion bordering on a personal slight.

If the Roman authorities thought they had dealt with matters by doling out rough justice, they were mistaken. In the words of Tacitus: 'Exasperated by their acts of violence, and dreading worse calamities, the Iceni had recourse to arms. The Trinovantes joined in the revolt. The neighbouring states, not as yet taught to crouch in bondage, pledged themselves, in secret councils, to stand forth in the cause of liberty.'

Tacitus levelled much of the blame for the uprising that followed on the conduct of the veteran soldiers settled in Camulodunum. 'These men treated the Britons with cruelty and oppression; they drove the natives from their habitations, and, calling them by the names of slaves and captives, added insult to their tyranny,' he wrote. 'In these acts of oppression, the veterans were supported by the common soldiers; a set of men, by their habits of life, trained to licentiousness, and, in their turn, expecting to reap the same advantages.'

Gaius Cornelius Tacitus is every bit as fascinating as the times and characters he wrote about. A senator and historian, he was almost a manifestation of Rome's conscience as well. Born more than a decade after the Claudian invasion of Britain, he lived until AD 117. It was not until AD 98 that his written works began to circulate, but from then until the end of his life he kept the revealing light of his intelligence trained on the triumphs and disasters of the Empire.

Tacitus – a name that, ironically, means silent – was especially exercised about the often-corrupting nature of power. He saw the citizens of Rome getting rich on the proceeds of tyranny and apathetic about the moral cost of so much easy wealth. More than anything else it seemed he feared an unchecked, unaccountable Empire would become a monster.

Time and again he watched Romans sowing a bitter crop in the soil of those they have chosen to abuse. 'While the Britons were preparing to throw off the yoke, the statue of Victory, erected at Camulodunum, fell from its base, without any apparent cause, and lay extended on the ground with its face averted, as if the goddess yielded to the enemies of Rome,' he wrote.

Having raised an army tens of thousands strong, Boudicca quickly turned her attention towards the nearest symbol of Roman oppression. With its giant temple to Claudius, Camulodunum fitted the bill perfectly. The timing was ideal as well: the Roman Governor of Britain, Gaius Suetonius Paulinus, was on campaign in Wales with most of the army, fighting druids on the island of Anglesey.

Within Camulodunum there was an atmosphere of rising panic. There were a handful of serving soldiers in the town but nothing capable of mounting any kind of realistic stand against thousands of Britons. Such was the complacency of the inhabitants of the town, they had built the place without any practical defences: 'No fosse was made; no palisade thrown up; nor were the women, and such as were disabled by age or infirmity, sent out of the garrison,' wrote Tacitus.

Boudicca and her rebels laid waste. Those sheltering at home, in mostly timber buildings, were quickly dispatched. The temple was the only structure erected of stone and it was a massive edifice – taller in its day than the Norman castle that occupies the site now. It was windowless, the only way in or out being through massive bronze doors that could be barricaded from the inside. It was behind those walls that perhaps thousands of men, women and children took refuge, holding out for two days.

Finally the rebels managed to break in. None was spared and later the whole town was set ablaze. Only the stone walls of the temple survived the inferno. Fragments of burnt human bone, along with piles of charred Roman Samian Ware pottery, are still being excavated from the foundations of Colchester – testament to an atrocity committed nearly 2,000 years ago. Evidence of the burning of Camulodunum can still be seen. All across modern Colchester, when holes are dug down through the Roman deposits, a black layer of ash a foot and a half thick is clearly visible.

The razing of Camulodunum was not enough to satisfy Boudicca. Word of the horror had been sent to Paulinus, but before the Roman army could double-time it back from Wales the bellicose queen led her warriors on a campaign of murder and destruction. Londinium – as the Romans called their new town – was wiped out, along with Verulamium, the town known today as St Albans.

It is estimated that something like 70,000 people died at the hands of Boudicca's warriors in Camulodunum alone. Noble-women were apparently singled out for special treatment. In line with Celtic tradition, inspired by the druids, female captives were taken to sacred groves of trees and put to death. Their breasts were then cut from their bodies and sewn over their mouths before their corpses were impaled on long spikes driven into the ground. Whether this actually happened – or if it was an invention on the part of Roman writers seeking justification for wiping out the druids – is anyone's guess.

Boudicca's self-righteous rage was not enough to protect her indefinitely. Suetonius Paulinus returned from Wales and, though outnumbered by his enemies, brought them to bay. The location of that final battle is unknown, but many suggest it may well have taken place somewhere between London and St Albans. The Britons were blood-soaked and charged with adrenaline, and so confident of victory they had brought their families to watch the predicted slaughter of the Romans.

According to Tacitus, Boudicca appeared before her warriors with her two daughters, riding a chariot. Just as he would do for Calgacus the Scot in the moments before the Battle of Mons Graupius, he imagined what the wronged and vengeful queen might have said – what he presumably thought she should have said:

'This is not the first time that the Britons have been led to battle by a woman. But now she did not come to boast the pride of a long line of ancestry, nor even to recover her kingdom and the plundered wealth of her family. She took the field, like the meanest among them, to assert the cause of public liberty, and to seek revenge for her body seamed with ignominious stripes, and her two daughters infamously ravished. "From the pride and arrogance of the Romans nothing is sacred; all are subject to violation; the old endure the scourge, and the virgins are deflowered. But the vindictive gods are now at hand ... Look round, and view your numbers. Behold the proud display of warlike spirits, and consider the motives for which we draw the avenging sword. On this spot we must either conquer, or die with glory. There is no alternative. Though a woman, my resolution is fixed: the men, if they please, may survive with infamy, and life in bondage."'

Those are the sentiments every leader wishes he or she might convey. Shakespeare would do the same favour for Henry V before Agincourt; Elizabeth I found her own words for her men when she addressed them as 'but a weak and feeble woman' at Tilbury as the Spanish Armada loomed in 1588. There are echoes of it all in Churchill's speeches to the British people during the Second World War as well.

There would be no triumph for Boudicca though. Suetonius, seasoned warrior that he was, drew up his men with their backs to a forest, so they could not be attacked from behind. The Celtic warriors sought individual glory on the battlefield and so had no concept of working together towards a common goal. A disciplined wedge of legionaries advanced into the high-spirited mêlée and slowly, but surely, cut their enemies to pieces. Roman writers would claim a death toll of 80,000 among the Britons, so that their army was virtually wiped out. Boudicca fled the field and died, depending on what account is followed, either of self-administered poison or illness.

The events of AD 60–61 are often referred to as the last British rebellion against Roman rule. That may have been true for the south, but there were other parts of the archipelago – Ireland, for example, and in the north of Britain – where in some senses the rebellion never stopped. If the tribes of much of southern Britain were firmly under Roman control by the end of the first century, there were peoples elsewhere living in territories beyond the effective reach of the Empire.

Mainland Britain is today split into unequal parts by the borders between England, Scotland and Wales. Imagining the Romans' northward advance through their province of Britannia is therefore complicated by our deep-rooted awareness of those three separate nations. It is important right from the start to bear in mind that, to begin with at least, the Romans saw no such divisions. As far as they knew and understood it in the early years, Britannia was one land populated by many disparate tribes. All would have to be confronted and dealt with sooner or later – those in the far north as well as those in the south.

By AD 71 there was apparently a Roman concept of Caledonia – encapsulating the *terra incognita* of the far north. It was in that year, under the governorship of Quintus Petillius Cerialis, that efforts were originally made to push forwards into that unknown land.

First contact was probably with the Votadini tribe, occupying a vast tract of land on the eastern side of the country stretching from Northumberland in the south to the southern shore of the Firth of Forth in the north. For their own reasons the Votadini decided co-operation was their best option and ushered Cerialis's forces through their territory. They would be allies of Rome from then on, growing ever richer and more powerful on wages paid in Roman silver. On the northern side of the Forth were the lands the Romans understood to be occupied by the Caledonii. Attempts to make sense of the place and the people, far less bring them under Roman control, would continue without success and without conclusion for the next three and a half centuries.

Gnaeus Julius Agricola, father-in-law of Tacitus, took up the post of Governor of Britannia in the summer of AD 78. He was more obsessive about the Caledonii than his predecessor and within two years he had built himself a base-camp for continued operations – a fort called Trimontium, 'three mountains', in the shadow of the triple-peaked Eildon Hills near the modern town of Melrose in the Scottish Borders.

He finally got his wish, drawing the massed army of the Caledonians into a pitched battle in the shadow of another mountain, Mons Graupius, the Grampian Mountain, in the late summer of AD 84. Their leader, Calgacus, stepped out of the mists and into history that day. According to Tacitus, 'the swordsman' had 30,000 men at his command and the significance of the moment was not lost on him: 'Battles against Rome have been lost and won before, but never without hope; we were always there in reserve,' said Calgacus. 'We, the choicest flower of Britain's manhood, were treasured in her most secret places ...'

For all the fine, brave words, the battle that followed was a rout. Tacitus would later claim 10,000 Caledonian dead, but he did at least concede that many more were able to disappear back into the trackless mountains from which they had come.

In many ways the victory at Mons Graupius was a high point the Romans would never reach again in Caledonia. They garrisoned tens of thousands of men in the northern territories, built forts and roads and imported all the grain and wine and other foodstuffs required by an army of occupation. But the truth of the matter was the tribes of the north were unwilling to trade their independence for Roman coins; and the occupation was costing the Romans more than they could hope to recoup in taxes or anything else. To some extent Mons Graupius had been a Pyrrhic victory and they had simply bitten off more than they could chew (or even wanted to).

If the Romans started out calling the people of the northern tribes Caledonii, sometime during their attempted occupation they started referring to the locals as 'Picts', in reference to their tattooed skins. Whoever they were – descendants of the Caledonii, or a confederacy of many hitherto unknown tribes brought together by a shared commitment to rid themselves of the Romans – we do not even know what they called themselves. The Picts seemingly emerged from nowhere, a fully formed people who would feature in the history of Scotland until the tenth century, when they were subsumed by the Gaels, to whom they were related.

Unable (or simply disinclined) to reach any sort of accommodation with the Picts, the Romans decided instead to shut them out – literally. Between AD 118 and 122, the Roman Governor of Britannia was Quintus Pompeius Falco and just as his term of office was coming to a close he hosted a visit from Emperor Hadrian. The Governor had lately fought off yet another uprising by some of the northern tribes and the decision was taken to build a wall from one side of the country to the other. In honour of the visiting Emperor it would be Hadrian's Wall. The stubbornness of the Picts was therefore the inspiration for one of the most famous constructions of the ancient world – as well as the most northerly, the most elaborate and the most heavily fortified and defended frontier in the whole of the Roman Empire.

Built between AD 122 and 136, Hadrian's Wall stretches 74 miles (or 80 Roman miles, based on *mille passuum*, 'a thousand paces') from Wallsend on the River Tyne in the east to Bowness-on-Solway on the Solway Firth in the west. Constructed largely from limestone, it varies between 10 and 20 feet wide and between 11 and 20 feet high. The original execution saw a stone wall between the Tyne and the River Irthing, 40-odd miles towards the west, and then a turf wall from the river to Bo'ness. At some point, however, the decision was made to rebuild the turf section in stone. As well as the wall there were 80 'mile castle' fortlets and perhaps as many as 17 full-sized forts, each containing between 500 and 1,000 soldiers.

Most of the construction work was completed within six years, all of it by the men of the three occupying legions. By any measure it is a wonder, striding for mile after mile up hill, down dale, across rivers and over cliff tops. On the southern side of the wall a deep ditch called a *vallum* defines a broad stretch of no-man's land preventing anyone even approaching the border without permission. Once the entire length of the wall was rendered in white limewash so that it would have been a shining barrier, dazzling and humbling to any who laid eyes on it.

Hadrian's Wall served many functions. For one thing it precisely defined the limits of what the Romans regarded as the civilised world. Beyond was perdition, the land of the barbarians – here be dragons, as it were. Because there were gateways through the wall, it could function as a kind of customs control as well. Trade was permitted, actively encouraged in fact – and in both directions – so the wall gave the Romans the opportunity to tax anyone heading north or south.

From time to time the Picts attacked the wall, sometimes breaking through, sometimes not; but usually it was a place where Romans and tame Britons co-existed peacefully. The threat from the north may have necessitated the presence of tens of thousands of soldiers, but for the tribes south of the wall the forts and their captive populations of soldiers were a goldmine. The men needed food, drink and entertainment and around forts like Housesteads and Vindolanda whole settlements sprang up, populated by those able and willing to keep them supplied with whatever they needed and wanted.

But if Hadrian and Pompeius Falco thought Rome had pushed as far north as was practical, they were followed within a few years by an Emperor and a Governor with different ideas. Emperor

Antoninus Pius ordered his Governor, Quintus Lollius Urbicus, to advance once more into the territory of the Picts and from 138 onwards much of southern Scotland was reoccupied. Lollius Urbicus rebuilt old forts and added new ones besides, and by AD 141 he was crowing about his success.

Part of the campaign involved embarking upon the construction of another wall – this one comprising a deep ditch and a steep-sided earthen bank stretching for 37 miles between Bo'ness on the Firth of Forth in the east and Old Kilpatrick on the Firth of Clyde in the west. The Antonine Wall took took a dozen years to build. As well as the barrier itself, there was the matter of building a total of 17 forts – one every two miles – to keep it manned and operational.

So much talk of dimensions and years, the numbers blurring into one another, can somehow diminish the work involved. As an archaeology student at Glasgow, I visited one of the forts on the Antonine Wall – known today as Rough Castle Fort – and was stunned by the inventiveness of the builders. Located just outside Falkirk, it is the best-preserved of all the forts on the wall. The main defences were built of turf, the same as the wall itself, but inside were once-substantial stone buildings including the commander's house, the headquarters, a granary, a barracks for the men and a bathhouse. A bathhouse! Think of that. Deep in the heart of Pictish territory, a hundred miles further north even than Hadrian's Wall (which was, anyway, already the back of beyond in the eyes of those posted there), every serving soldier had access to steam rooms and warm baths.

The attention to detail did not stop there either. Archaeologists excavating the gateway leading through the wall itself, out into the badlands beyond, discovered a regular series of row upon row of pits. These were a defensive feature known as *lilia* – literally 'lily pads' – and would once have been filled with sharpened stakes, and camouflaged so as to be invisible to approaching attackers. Just like the punji pits deployed by the Viet Cong during the

Vietnam War, the *lilia* were a cruel deterrent laid down to help defend the most vulnerable point in the fort.

It was long assumed the Romans must have made a major impact on Scotland – almost by dint of the sheer force of imperial personality. That may or may not be the case. More recently, scholars have taken the view that Scotland was largely unaffected by its contact with Rome, and that society there continued to evolve along lines laid down in her own distant past. Those lines and grooves were deep, as deep or deeper than any valley cut by ancient ice, and the people would not be jolted out of them by Rome or anyone else. For one thing, the Romans built no towns there, and would never even have dared to try. The main story in the land that would become Scotland appears to be one of continuity, in which the Romans appear only as a minor disruption. In terms of agents of social change, they may have had less impact than the perennial midges.

I do wonder, though, what they made of Scotland, those soldiers, and what it all meant to them, if anything. Some of them were legionaries, full Roman citizens, while others were recruited from among the peoples of the provinces. Many of those who spent time in Britannia would have been born and raised in provinces in northern Europe – France, Belgium, Germany and the like.

Once constructed, the walls were manned by auxiliaries, pulled in from the same territories again and with fewer rights still. I try to imagine the Caledonia, the Scotland, they marched through. The books are full of doom and gloom about the weather, about how the soldiers must have suffered and grumbled, and just bided their time until they might be moved to somewhere else, somewhere warmer, or at least drier. But I have seen France and Belgium and Germany and, while I appreciate the scenery in those places, I cannot help but think Scotland must have struck some of them as an astonishing place.

Much was made by their superiors of the great impenetrable forest of Caledon; modern scholars, however, have wondered whether it was a myth created as an excuse for failure. But maybe there really were trees there that had been free to grow for thousands of years, making shade for bears and wolves.

I wonder what they thought of the slow, black rivers, and of the mountains that were ancient even then. Some of the soldiers must have rowed and sailed their ships past the islands off the west coast, islands to the west of time where the sun set, or into fjords cut by glaciers and flooded long ago by rising seas. For every soldier that moaned, and remembered only smothering rain and achingly cold winds, there must have been others who were changed for ever and stayed for good.

But regardless of how much Scotland changed them – or they changed Scotland – I am also impressed by how much of their world they were able to carry with them; so that their sojourn in inhospitable territory was much less uncomfortable than it might otherwise have been. One famous tablet from Vindolanda proves the soldiers were careful to wear *subligaria*, underpants. What the Romans could not bring from home, to alleviate the misery of service in that wind-blasted, rain-sodden land of the Picts, they either invented or acquired from the locals.

In the lands between the walls the natives shared such enthusiasm for one item of clothing, historians have suggested it may even have formed the basis of a cult. Judging by its depiction on engraved stones and the like, the *birrus Britannicus* was a forerunner of the duffel coat. Figures cloaked and hooded in some sort of one-piece garment crop up again and again, often suggestive of a deity. It seems the Roman soldiers stationed in Caledonia found the garment was the only solution to the enervating cold. They certainly wore them and may even have exported the idea back home. (Elsewhere it has been shown Romans in Britain wore socks with their sandals. What with that and duffel coats it seems the Italians must have earned their reputation for sartorial style much more recently.)

Like Hadrian's Wall, the Antonine Wall provided a means of taxing people moving north and south, as well as stopping tribes in the north uniting with their southern counterparts in hope of making mischief. Despite all the hard work, however, despite the ambition of the Emperor and the determination of his Governor to do his bidding, the Antonine Wall proved a step too far. The Romans in Scotland might have drawn a parallel between their own efforts and those of the mythological Greek king Sisyphus, doomed by the gods to push a huge boulder uphill. By AD 160 a permanent presence so far north had proved uneconomic and unsustainable. In due course the Romans pulled everyone back to the great wall raised in Hadrian's name.

Two centuries had passed since those first landings in Kent. But by the time the Roman auxiliaries were accepting Hadrian's Wall was their line in the sand, Caesar was a distant memory. To be Roman was no longer to be just an invader. It was to be immersed in something much more complicated – an exchange of ideas flowing in both directions. Southern Britain had emerged from the turbulence of the past as home to something quite new – a Romano-British culture that was a unique synthesis of both.

In the north, however, beyond the wall, it was and would remain a different story. To the mystification of the Romans, their version of civilisation simply was not wanted there. And yet the incomers had changed that part of the world too. Celtic Britain had been the natural development of all that had gone before. Just like those in the south, the tribes of the north had evolved their own territories, separate from one another but also sharing one unifying Celtic culture. Now the Romans had changed that as well.

When their engineers and surveyors made their plans for the wall, the line they drew across the country was largely arbitrary. Look on the map and you will see they were connecting east to west at the narrowest convenient point they could find, between the Tyne and the Solway. Contrary to popular opinion, Hadrian's Wall is not the same as the modern border between Scotland and England – although pretty close in places, the wall is entirely in England. That line drawn across the country by some foreign surveyors looking for the easiest place to build a wall would help shape events in Britain long after the Roman hold on the place was over.

By AD 160, mainland Britain had been cleaved in two, between Britannia in the south and Caledonia in the north. Nothing would ever be the same again.

8

ROMANS

'What we've got here ... is failure to communicate. Some
men you just can't reach.'

The Captain, *Cool Hand Luke*

For Fernand Braudel, human lives were ephemeral flecks of foam
riding upon the waves of a deep ocean. We are therefore powerless
and inconsequential in the unfolding of that *longue durée* – the
'long term' – subject always to the impossibly languid motion of
time.

This is an image worth bearing in mind when we think about
the world we have built, and upon which we depend. The story
of the Britain we live in is deeper than any ocean. Every square
foot of the land has been touched and modified by us or by our
forebears during perhaps a million years of human habitation.
Britain's principal cities – London, Glasgow, Birmingham,
Manchester, Leeds, Liverpool, Cardiff, Edinburgh, Newcastle,
Nottingham, Sheffield – all of them have been busy urban centres
for at least a thousand years. Much the same is true for the towns
and villages as well. Most have been home to people, one way or
another, for thousands of years at least.

The depth of history in Britain is remarkable – and not necessarily repeated everywhere. In *Notes From A Small Island*, Bill
Bryson observed there were more seventeenth-century buildings
in Malhamdale, his adoptive village in the Yorkshire Dales, than
in the whole of North America. All this means Britons are walking
every day upon the very stuff of their own history as a people.

It is all around us, whether or not we pay it any heed. In Edinburgh there are people who talk quite seriously about an underground city, a metropolis of streets and houses lost somewhere in the darkness beneath the modern hustle and bustle of tourists and traffic. There is a truth to what they say, in that the residents of Edinburgh have always found ingenious ways to make the most of all the land available to them for building.

The High Street – the long, straight thoroughfare that runs downhill from the Castle to the Palace of Holyroodhouse, known to tourists as the Royal Mile – sits on top of a natural ridge of sandstone. It is a part of the same geological processes that created the Salisbury Crags that so captivated the eighteenth-century genius James Hutton and led him to see, for the very first time, the great age of the world.

Edinburgh Castle sits upon a crag of extremely hard volcanic basalt. Behind the crag, a softer tail of sandstone was therefore protected from the advance of glaciers during subsequent Ice Ages and survived behind its shield to form the ridge upon which a sloping street might later be built. At least two thousand years ago, the people of the Votadini tribe may have found the sandstone was soft enough for tunnelling. They certainly built on its surface, all the way along the ridge and on Castle Rock itself, where they raised the first of many fortresses.

The crag and tail were continuously occupied from then on, later builders blithely burying the homes and bones of those who had gone before them. In the aftermath of Scotland's defeat by the English at the Battle of Flodden in 1513 – the same that saw King James IV himself slain alongside a slew of nobles and churchmen – there was panic in Edinburgh. Fears of an invasion inspired the building, in double quick time, of a wall to protect the city. By the time the townsfolk had raised their Flodden Wall it enclosed a space just one mile long and a quarter of a mile wide. For the next 250 years, not a building was erected beyond that barrier. They built gates through the wall of course, and beside the site of one of them – the Netherbow across High Street itself – there sits an old pub called the World's End. It was a joke and not a joke, for the feeling was that beyond that gate was nothing.

Edinburgh's inhabitants were sealed inside a tiny world within which the only options were to build up or down. As well as creating the first skyscrapers – the tallest in Europe at up to 130 feet high – they had to burrow downwards as well, underground.

Many centuries later, during the eighteenth-century Scottish Enlightenment, the city fathers saw fit to commission a whole new town. The old one had grown rank and pestilent – an overcrowded shambles known to residents and visitors alike as 'Auld Reekie' – and the time had come to create somewhere grand enough to fit the aspirations of the sons and daughters of genius. This so-called New Town would be a marvel of the world, built from scratch on open land between the Old Town and the Firth of Forth. In time it would earn the nickname 'the Athens of the North', not least because so many of its architects favoured the Classical Greek style.

Like Rome, Edinburgh is a city built on seven hills, although you would be forgiven for failing to notice that now. During the late eighteenth and early nineteenth centuries, civil engineers constructed five gigantic bridges that spanned the gaps between five of the hills – Bunker's Hill, Heriot Hill, Moultree's Hill, St John's Hill and St Leonard's Hill. While Edinburgh is still dominated by two summits – Calton Hill (home to both the Royal Observatory and an unfinished replica of the Parthenon, dubbed 'Edinburgh's Shame') and Castle Hill – the rest were cleverly made to disappear. The others are still there, of course, but now they form parts of the foundations for the great arches and spans of George IV Bridge, King's Bridge, North Bridge, Regent's Bridge and South Bridge.

Those five massive structures helped create an entirely artificial level plain of masonry upon which the New Town steadily grew. In the voids beneath, in the valleys below the bridges, yet more buildings sprang up so that eventually there was a second city underneath the first. More building in the early decades of the nineteenth century steadily filled in the rest of the gaps beneath the spans until in time it was hard to remember that, beneath it all, there were spaces, huge spaces.

Eventually the phases of building blurred into one another until there was indeed an underground city – some of it made inadvertently by eighteenth-century town planners, some burrowed and scratched out by British tribesmen and women 2,000 years before, and much of the rest built higgledy-piggledy during the centuries in between. Along the way many of the vast vaults, serpentine tunnels and dank passages and alleyways – as well as whole streets that were once home to thousands of people – were gradually lost to the world above. Even when the darkness beneath was absolute, still there were those who found need of the shelter provided by the shadows. Far below the rattle and hum of the bright world above they lit their fires, lamps and candles and made good use of those otherwise forgotten places.

During the first decade of the twentieth century, G.K. Chesterton would be moved and affected by what he called the 'abruptness' of the city of Edinburgh, without quite managing to put his finger on an explanation for it all: 'It seems like a city built on precipices: a perilous city. Although the actual valleys and ridges are not (of course) really very high or very deep, they stand up like strong cliffs; they fall like open chasms. There are turns of the street that take the breath away like a literal abyss. There are thoroughfares, full, busy and lined with shops, which yet give the emotions of an alpine stair. It is, in the only adequate word for it, a sudden city.'

That the sequence of events, the process by which old Edinburgh was buried beneath new, was invisible to an observer within 50 years of the completion of the building job goes some way towards illustrating how quickly we forget and move on.

Much of the rest of our man-made landscape has a similar story to tell, and nowhere more emphatically than London. When Julius Caesar first encountered the area in the middle of the first century BC, he noted it was already home to a large population and that the ground there was 'thickly studded with homesteads'. It was already old in Caesar's day then, and in truth it is almost impossible to know quite how old, quite how long people of one sort or another have found cause to spend time there.

If Scotland's capital grew up around seven hills, then the first version of Great Britain's principal city came to occupy the land around three. Cornhill, Ludgate Hill (where St Paul's Cathedral now sits) and Tower Hill form a long, sharp triangle lying on its hypotenuse along the north bank of the River Thames. Between Cornhill and Ludgate Hill runs another river, a tributary of the Thames called the Walbrook, long since forced underground and out of sight along with so much else.

Here then was the nucleus of the place that would be known in time as London, but it is impossible to pinpoint precisely when people first found meaning or importance there. A great river like the Thames would have been one of the first major natural barriers encountered by the hunters who walked into the southern part of the British peninsula 10,000 or 12,000 years ago, once the ice had retreated. Then, as now, it would have made sense to follow its route ever deeper inland, so that the territory later occupied by London was long defined by a well-trodden path, carrying people into and out of Britain.

The land around those three hills, watered by three rivers (the Thames, the Walbrook and also the Fleet) would have been fertile. When people turned towards farming as a way of life, they would have found yet more reasons to settle there, perhaps reassured too by the presence of the high ground provided by the nearby slopes.

Much later, by the zenith of the Celtic Iron Age, the Trinovantes tribe had their territory on land that included much of what is known now as Greater London, north of the Thames. The twelfth-century cleric and writer Geoffrey of Monmouth would claim in his *Historia Regum Britanniae* that the original name of London was Trinovantum, from Troi-novantum, meaning 'New Troy'. He was therefore able to tie London to the ancient myth of Britain's foundation by (and even named after) Brutus, a refugee from the

Trojan War. Such stories sound fanciful to us, but it is likely they have lasted so long because they contain some or other fragment of a truth.

Plentiful streams and rivers, along with marshlands and other forbidding nooks and crannies, would have provided the druids of the Trinovantes with sacred places for secret rites. There were springs and wells too – Sadler's Wells and Clerkenwell to name but two – known for their medicinal and curative powers right up into the modern era, and doubtless home to gods and goddesses in their time as well.

So our cities are testament to the *longue durée*. Down in their depths is where the bronze and iron swords of warriors glint and glimmer like fish. Too deep for memory, London – the name sounding like heartbeats, Lon-don … Lon-don … Lon-don – may have been marking the time as long as any. The modern streets and buildings are only the youngest carapace to have hardened on the city's back and all the old flesh lies beneath, sealed and pre-served beyond the reach of decay. Nothing was ever cleared away, it seems, just knocked flat and covered over to provide a level surface for the building of something new.

In the foundations of a derelict building, on the corner of King's Arms Yard and Token House Yard in Moorgate, deep in the heart of Old London Town, I had the opportunity to catch a rare and surreal glimpse of an ancient version of London.

The façade of the building itself, tucked out of sight now on a back street, was grand enough, and will be preserved as the outer skin of the new. The rest of it, however, will be razed to the ground, and once inside it was easy to understand why. If the interior was ever possessed of any grandeur, it was long gone. There were occasional patches of something promising – some Edwardian or Victorian wood panelling on a wall, a well-turned banister on a staircase – but successive occupants had interfered with the layout to such an extent it was mostly just a depressing maze of soulless, low-ceilinged rooms, subdivided by walls covered in layer upon layer of woodchip paper, thick as calluses on overworked hands. Vandals had been into the place as well, and their obligatory tags were spray-painted everywhere I looked.

It was only in the foundation levels that anything of worth survived. I could hear the archaeologists long before I could see them, the sounds of their voices and their tools echoing up from deep within the wrecked interior. For want of anywhere else to put it, they had piled the spoil from their excavations into rooms in the basement, and it was as I passed the last of those heaps that I began to notice the long shadows cast by high-powered arc lights. Finally I arrived at a series of hatches that gave access to a deep rectangular pit cut down through the lowest foundation levels of the building and into the ancient earth beneath.

This was the surreal part. What they had created looked like every other archaeological dig – people in hard hats and overalls, wheelbarrows and shovels, surveying equipment on tripods, trowels and brushes carefully deployed – and yet it was all happening indoors and deep underground, among shattered walls of brick and concrete and under the artificial glare of electric light. Above their heads were criss-crossing steel joists supporting the ground floor of the building, the whole mass of it pressing down and creating a feeling of claustrophobia. It was hot and airless down there too, all those blazing lights coupled with the sweat of hard physical labour, so that the place almost seemed to steam.

What archaeologist Alison Telfer and her team were uncovering in that bizarre bearpit of a site, however, was nothing less than a fragment of Roman London itself. If that grand name suggests buildings of dressed stone, elegant statuary and the like, then picture something much more humble. Beneath modern Moorgate were the remains of a modest row of timber-built shops and workshops laid out along a straight street – a shopfront if you will – and separated one from another by wooden fences. The whole lot of it sloped gently downwards, behind the row, towards the course of an ancient stream, and it was the dampness from that old waterway that had worked a miracle of preservation.

As well as the carefully worked timbers that formed the foundations of the buildings, the archaeologists had found considerable amounts of leather. Rough-outs of soles, with holes punched for stitching, along with piles of off-cuts, made plain that this part of Roman London was once home to craftsmen making and selling shoes. More amazing even than the sight of the pieces, was the smell of them. After the best part of 2,000 years, the comforting, familiar scent of leather was unmistakable.

What has been revealed there is planned, urban development: the town that grew up in the years following the Claudian conquest of AD 43. Whatever settlement Caesar had found nearly a century before, he presumably left more or less alone. During the second half of the first century AD, however, the impact of foreign ideas began to make more of a mark on the place. As early as AD 50, the soldiers built a timber bridge across the Thames, at a site just a hundred yards or so to the east of the present London Bridge. This engineering achievement alone may have been awe-inspiring for the locals. No doubt the Celtic Britons believed a river as mighty as the Thames must be home to a mighty god; and to see the Thames tamed in such a way must have made them wonder just what else those incomers were capable of.

Whatever reaction that first London bridge provoked, it would have become a hub of activity, and quickly. Since the river could now be crossed, Roman London would have grown along both banks. No doubt there was an existing British settlement somewhere close by, soon absorbed within what would have grown into a busy town of ordered streets laid out in a simple grid pattern. The Romans could hardly have failed to notice either that the Thames led to an estuary served by a double tide, making it particularly useful for sea-going trade.

The conquest of Britannia was about trade, after all – taking control of British resources and extracting them for export all over the Empire. British minerals, metals, crops and manpower were to be sent not just into Europe but as far as Africa and the Middle East as well. At the same time, foreign exotics would arrive in a settlement like Londinium ready for onward dispersal into the rest of the ever-expanding province.

It seems that this place between three hills, watered by three rivers, was destined from the start to be the capital of a greater Britannia. If it started small and modest, it did not and could not stay that way for long. As well as cargoes of Samian Ware, wine and olive oil and the rest, the boats arriving at the first harbour, possibly near Billingsgate, brought administrators as well. These were the bean-counters who would organise and oversee; making sure every last ounce of value was squeezed from Rome's latest acquisition.

There were setbacks along the way: sometime around AD 60 the residents of Londinium were slaughtered by Boudicca's warriors, their homes and other buildings set aflame. More flames would follow, of course. London's foundations form a cake of many layers and several of those are black as coal. These are the ashes of the great fires – some few of Boudicca's no doubt and some from the most famous of all the infernos, which consumed the old city in 1666. Archaeologists find that haunting proof of the Great Fire every single time they open a deep trench within the City of London. Ironically it is the viewing platform at the top of Sir Christopher Wren's monument to that particular fire – a column of Portland stone standing a few minutes' walk from the northern end of London Bridge – that gives the best sense of the scale of the Roman city.

During the second century AD Londinium rose to become Britain's first metropolis, home to perhaps 40,000 people. It stretched from where St Paul's sits on Ludgate Hill, all the way across to where the Tower of London still stands defiant among younger usurpers in a crowded skyline. Together with the soldiers – tasked variously with the defence of territory already held and the ceaseless advance into the north and west – there were all the sorts of people that make up any town or city. As well as merchants and businessmen, administrators and clerks – those who create an ordered place in which to live – there would have been all the characters who make places worth living in, like artists, artisans, writers and technologists.

It was not just Londinium that was on the up during the first century of the Roman occupation of Britannia. Other towns were growing too, thriving in those years when people realised it was possible (and beneficial to the purse) to be Roman and British at the same time.

The advent of urban living was not limited to the south-east. From Bath in the west to York in the north, Roman ways were, by around AD 200, deeply rooted in many parts of Britain. In the far north, the domain of the Picts, the Empire had still to be on a war footing from time to time. But elsewhere the violence of conquest was a distant memory. Where once there had only been garrisons of occupying soldiers surrounded by camp-followers, now there were towns co-ordinating and administering the settled government of perhaps three million people.

For many of those it had been a long time since they had felt themselves victims of an invasion. Instead they were willing accomplices of the most impressive, the most technologically advanced empire the world had yet seen. The Roman infrastructure was firmly embedded in the landscape by then. The roads were no longer solely for the movement of advancing armies; now they were just as important for the passage of merchants and their trade goods, moving between the towns and cities.

There was already an aspirant middle class with an appetite for all things new and modern. Along with much else, the Romans introduced the benefits of mass-production to Britain, and as well as tableware made of pottery, that meant glass too.

Consider glass for a moment, something as commonplace as a window pane. For the Celtic Britons, light was allowed inside a building through openings that let in wind and rain as well. Perhaps thinly stretched skins or other organic membranes might have been used for weatherproofing the holes from time to time, but in the main, light was admitted at the expense of warmth. Then imagine what it might have felt like to stand inside a building in front of a glass window – to be proofed against the elements and yet bathed in sunlight at the same time. (It is thought the invention of glass was a happy accident to begin with, an almost natural event spotted and adapted by some observant soul. Keep a cooking fire burning on a sandy beach for a few hours – a sandy beach that happens to include a fair amount of ground-down, lime-rich seashells – and clumps of a glass-like material might form among the embers. The development of the kind of glass we take for granted, however, was the stuff of millennia of experiment and refinement.)

The Phoenicians had invented blown glass by around the middle of the first century BC, only for the Romans to acquire it for themselves. By using simple clay moulds, into which glass could be blown to a regular shape and size, and with a ready-made decoration impressed into the sides, it was possible to mass-produce bottles and other items likely to capture the imaginations of the buying public. Glass bottles and jugs would have been as wondrous as glass windows. Where before liquids had been held within pottery vessels, visible only from above, now it was possible to see wine and oil through a solid material.

For a while it must have seemed as though the wonders would never cease. The list is endless and only scattered examples may be chosen to illustrate the range. Iron padlocks and the keys to open and close them are to our eyes so commonplace as to be almost invisible, but once just the proof of their existence would have taken the breath away. Consider such a notion – ushering in the possibility of the locked door. From now on there might be truly private property, or a money box.

Everywhere Britons turned, in that world made new, there were dazzling demonstrations of power and technical superiority; science fiction all of it. There were soon statues as well, gazing down from their plinths outside public buildings, life-size and lifelike representations of fellow human beings. From time to time you might actually have recognised the subject of the effigy. No one in Britain (unless they had ventured abroad into longer-held

Roman territory) could have conceived of such things.

Here, then, was yet another truly startling innovation; and as if it were not unsettling enough to be confronted by such images, not all of them stopped at just life-size. From time to time archaeologists come across bits and pieces of metal giants that must have adorned temples and other buildings in the first decades after AD 43. Imagine what it was like for Britons to walk through the walls of a Roman town or city and be confronted by gilded bronze statues 20 or even 30 feet high.

Not everyone in Britain was exposed to the wonders of Rome quite so directly. Beyond the heavily Romanised south of England, and also Wales, the impact of the new goods – and the new culture of which they were part – would have been much less. But for those living in and around the new urban centres, the Classical civilised Roman world might have touched every part of their lives. Rather than seeming foreign, alien or in any way threatening, it must surely have been utterly intoxicating and seductive.

If the new towns, filled with shops offering exotic goods, populated by people from every part of the Empire and all sheltered beneath the shield of Roman authority – if all that were not enough to beguile and to persuade – then there was something else. The Romans brought mass public entertainment to the people as well, often on a truly massive scale.

A chariot-racing track – known to the Romans as a *circus* – was discovered south of Colchester town centre in 2004. Aside from a possible, but unconfirmed, circus in the evocatively named Knightrider Street, just south of St Paul's in London, it is the only find of its kind in Britain and only the sixth known in the north-west provinces of the Empire (the others being at Arles, Lyon, Saintes and Vienne in modern France, and at Trier in Germany).

It is the sheer scale of the circuses that makes them impressive. Classically they comprise an elongated oval track with two long, straight sides. One end is left open for the chariots to get in and out, while the other describes a tight curve. Tiered seating several storeys high flanked the straights and the curve and, running down the centre of the track, was a low barrier called a *spina* that prevented the chariots running headlong into one another. At the open end there were traps, or starting bays. The walls were of banked earth and rubble, faced front and back with stone walls or timber revetments. It is thought the Colchester circus was around 500 yards long – a little less than a third of a mile. It was well over 80 yards wide, with terraces several storeys high and capable of seating as many as 15,000 people at any one time. It is the single largest Roman building ever found in Britain.

Nothing of the Colchester circus survives above ground. The only evidence for the structure has been produced by excavation and in fact I was present on site while a tiny slot was opened in a likely spot in a temporary car park. Once the Tarmac was removed and a few feet of modern rubble shovelled away, the telltale traces of Roman brick and masonry began to appear. Those were almost certainly parts of the foundation of the circus and it was salutary to think that a building which would have dwarfed anything in the modern city had been made to disappear so completely.

Of all the games and sports in the Roman world, chariot racing was the oldest and the most popular. The Greeks seemingly started it all but the Romans acquired it from the Etruscans, their own predecessors as rulers of the Mediterranean world, and then took the entertainment to its greatest heights. Anyone could go to the circus and the crowds might contain everyone from slaves to governors. Mostly they were run by private management, for financial gain, but their main purpose was to keep the people happy – and distracted from anything else that might otherwise have stopped them thinking and behaving like good Romans.

Anyone who has seen the film *Ben-Hur* can imagine the thrill of watching the sport for real. Charioteers were protected only by helmets, shinguards and light chest plates for the duration of seven exhausting laps of the track, and faced the constant threat of horrific injury and death. All of the dangers were offset, however, by the prospect of acquiring fame and truly eye-watering fortunes.

Most of the competitors were drawn from the lowest echelons

of society, often poor illiterates for whom the racetrack offered a chance of escape from lives of grinding poverty; and the wealth amassed by the greatest of the champions makes the incomes of the greatest of today's F1 drivers look almost modest by comparison. The greatest of the great – probably the best-paid athlete of all time – was a man named Gaius Appuleius Diocles, born in the second century AD in Lusitania, a province that comprised parts of modern Spain and Portugal. When he retired, at the age of 42, his fans and fellow charioteers were moved to erect a monument in his honour, detailing his triumphs – and his earnings.

In 2009 the US golfer Tiger Woods was estimated to have earned over a billion dollars. During the course of a 24-year career Diocles, who made his name primarily in the Circus Maximus in Rome, pulled in 35,863,120 sesterces – the equivalent of 15 billion US dollars or nearly 10 billion pounds. To put it another way, he could have paid the salaries of every single Roman soldier, at the height of the army's imperial powers, for over two months – and that was purely prize money, without any of the modern sponsorship deals and endorsements that make up the bulk of the pay packets of modern sporting heroes.

The Colchester circus was likely built during the second century AD, perhaps around the time when Diocles was rising to greatness, and is on such a scale its principal excavator, archaeologist Philip Crummy, has suggested it might have been beyond the resources of anyone but the Emperor himself. Crummy has pointed out that since the visit to Britannia by Emperor Hadrian in AD 122 coincided with a great deal of new building in the province – including the wall raised in his name – Colchester's circus may have been built around the same time. So massive was it, so substantially built, Crummy also thinks it may have survived, albeit in a ruinous condition, until the time of the Norman occupation of Britain in the eleventh century.

If the thrill of the circus was not enough to keep the people of Colchester entertained, it seems there were other distractions on offer as well. As it had been founded as a colony for retired Roman soldiers, many of its population would have had an interest in combat in all its forms, and a vase found there in 1848 revealed evidence of fans of gladiators.

Called the Colchester Vase, it was excavated from a grave at West Lodge in the city. It was made sometime around AD 175, probably in Colchester itself, and is regarded as one of the very finest pieces of Roman pottery yet found in Britain. My hands shook as I handled the thing and part of what makes it so obviously valuable and unique – and therefore irreplaceable – is the way it suggests the mind either of its maker, or its original owners, or both. As well as a hunting scene, it vividly depicts two gladiators in action. On the left of the fight is a *secutor*, protected by shin guards, helmet and shield and armed with a short sword called a *gladius* (from which the name gladiator is derived). He is faced by a *retiarius*, much more lightly protected and traditionally armed with a trident and a net, as well as a dagger.

On the Colchester Vase, the contest is reaching its conclusion. The 'net-man' has been disarmed – his trident is on the ground – and the secutor is bearing down, sword raised above his head ready to deliver the coup-de-grâce. The defeated gladiator has a hand raised towards his foe, as though asking for mercy.

The Colchester Vase is made all the more affecting by the addition of names. Scratched into the fired clay, at some time after the vase was completed, are the names Secundus, Mario, Memnon and Valentinus – surely real-life heroes or champions known to the owner.

A Roman amphitheatre big enough to seat as many as 30,000 spectators was discovered in London, near where the Guildhall stands now, in 1988. Others have been found in Chichester, Cirencester, Dorchester and Silchester. All would have witnessed the spectacle of gladiatorial combat.

Circuses filled with the sounds of thundering horses and chariots, and of cheering crowds of onlookers . . . amphitheatres where men were pitted against each other and against wild animals in the name of entertainment. Britain during the centuries of Roman rule was a land in the process of being quite rapidly transformed. Ancient, pre-Roman Britain had evolved on its own over thousands of years, but within just a couple of centuries a substantial part of the country had been reshaped in the image of a far-away land.

While time, effort and money were spent providing the populations with distractions, the aims of the Empire remained the same as they had always been. British resources – like those of every province – were required to feed a giant animal that was growing bigger and hungrier all the time. The Roman Empire exerted a massive gravitational pull, drawing crops, precious metals and human beings in ever-increasing numbers – all of them united in a single, intricately connected economy. All the roads led to Rome, primarily so that all the money could get there as quickly as possible. While the circuses and amphitheatres kept the masses looking the other way, it was the administrators and the civil servants – not the soldiers – who were responsible for the lifeblood of the Empire.

London – Roman Londinium – became Britannia's commercial gateway and also its political nerve centre. While the army kept the peace, the men tasked with counting pieces of silver and gold built for themselves another giant structure, indeed eventually one of the largest and most impressive in the whole of the Empire. This was the basilica – part town hall, part tax office, part courthouse and part records office and therefore a genuinely frightening building for any citizen, law-abiding or otherwise.

The administrative heart of any Roman town was the forum, a square or rectangular marketplace surrounded by buildings on all four sides. As well as a temple, banks, offices and shops, part of the forum was always given over to the basilica. By around AD 70 there was a forum in London, just east of the River Walbrook and centred around what is now Gracechurch Street in the heart of the modern City of London. Grand though it undoubtedly was, and encapsulating an area 100 yards long by 50 yards wide, it was soon regarded as too small, altogether too modest to suit the status of somewhere like Londinium, and more particularly the egos of the men who ran the place. Work on the second forum began just 20 years or so after the first, and was to take 30 years to complete. In its finished form the basilica was a massive, three-storey structure more than 180 yards long on each of its four sides – proportions generally in keeping with that part of the city today. It was one of the largest Roman buildings north of the Alps and impressive enough to grace any Roman city anywhere.

Grand or not, nearly 2,000 years of subsequent building works have obliterated the forum above ground. Astonishingly, however, a visit to a hairdresser's salon at 90 Gracechurch Street provides an opportunity to glimpse a tiny stub of the thing – behind a smoked-glass door in the basement.

The heat from the hairdryers and a lack of ventilation lends a vaguely tropical atmosphere to the room in which the foundation layer of the forum now sits. It is altogether disorientating to be many feet below the modern road level and yet simultaneously at the heart of Roman London. It is all just testament to the sheer depth of building that has gone on in the city down through the centuries and millennia. Having spent some minutes beside that fragment of the ancient world – a few feet of mortared masonry, standing approximately waist-high – I stepped back into the salon, locked the door and returned the key to one of the stylists. Climbing back up the stairs and out onto the pavement meant the Roman stonework felt like something left behind in a dream.

The Romans built a fort in Londinium around AD 120, where the Barbican sits today, and something like 80 years later they encircled the whole town with a great wall – the London Wall. A construction of that kind, something to shelter behind, seems to speak of troubled times but in truth there is no written explanation for its creation. Whatever the motivation, the engineers plotted and the labourers sweated until they had looped a three-mile-long boundary around all they cared to call Londinium. It was 20 feet high, the best part of 10 feet wide and enclosed 330 acres of land.

Behind the wall were all the things you might expect inside a city: shops, bathhouses, temples and so on – but also large areas of open ground and pasture.

Through the wall they first built five gates, known now as Aldgate, Bishopsgate, Cripplegate, Ludgate and Newgate. After 150 years or so came Aldersgate. A seventh and final opening – Moorgate – was added sometime later, in the medieval period. Dots and dashes of the London Wall remain still, fragments of Morse Code punctuating phrases of more modern architecture.

In Londinium, Rome had created a provincial capital – as far as they were concerned, the capital of a single, unified territory. This was the concept of Britannia and therefore an idea that endures to this day. Like so many of the landmarks on the road out of ancient Britain and towards the present, it was about something quite new. Whatever else Celtic Britain had been, however much it might have been united by a shared set of cultural ideals and values, it was still a fractured land. Individual chieftains or petty kings ruled their own jealously guarded independent territories. But the Romans had a bigger idea, a modern idea – that of a single entity, an Empire of which Britannia was just a part – an important part, but a part just the same.

As far north as York – called Eboracum by the Romans, 'the place of the yew trees' – visitors would have known what to expect within the walls and would not have been disappointed on arrival. Just a hundred miles south of Hadrian's Wall, effectively at the end of the world, York had all of the infrastructure required of a fully functioning Roman town. Rather than feeling they were out on the edge of civilisation, its inhabitants were right to believe they were very much within an exotic, internationally connected world.

Such a grand idea was as hard to control as it was to conceive of and some of what happened within its frontiers may have been unexpected even by its architects. For one thing the towns and cities became melting-pots, attracting anyone and everyone from all parts of the Empire.

In York Museum are the remains of a woman known to archae-ologists as Ivory Bangle Woman. When she died, around AD 250, she was still in her early twenties, or even younger. Her bones reveal no signs of stress caused by poor diet or chronic illness, and no injuries of the sort that might have left their marks on a skeleton. The cause of her death, while so young and apparently healthy, remains unknown.

We are to believe she was a wealthy young woman because alongside her in her grave were items of considerable value. An exquisite blue glass jug, the work of a highly skilled specialist craftsman; a necklace of finely shaped and faceted blue-glass beads; a bracelet made of Whitby Jet, that most captivating of materials. Anyone who saw her in her finery would have realised at once she was a woman of substance, from a rich and powerful family.

But if the Jet is local, from the coast of Yorkshire itself, one of her belongings came from much farther afield. The find in question is a delicately turned and carved bangle made from ivory and sourced originally, in all likelihood, from somewhere in Africa. Her time on Earth was short and yet the evidence she left behind suggests a fascinating life for all that. She may even hold the explanation for the mystery, quite literally, in her own head – for the shape of her skull has its own fascinating story to tell, or at least hints to make. For one thing her forehead is quite flat and therefore reminiscent of the skulls of black Africans. Her nose, however, seems more typical of a white European. Chemical analysis of her teeth has in fact suggested Ivory Bangle Woman may have grown up some-where in north Africa – perhaps in Libya or Tunisia.

Was she the wife or daughter of a centurion or other high-ranking soldier posted to Britannia with his family? The thought of her, with her youth and perhaps beauty too, head held high and hips rolling as she strolled around York in all her expensive jewellery, makes her seem exotic even today. The possibility alone of such a woman in such a place so long ago is tantalising to us, and yet even if she was a woman of mixed blood, part black African and part white European, and a rich one at that – in the multicultural melting-pot that was Roman York in AD 250, she would not have been unusual.

Around 50 skeletons recovered during excavations in York in the late 1960s formed the basis for a recent scientific study of the likely origins of those people and the authors of the subsequent report, published in 2009, believed their findings suggested 'a heterogeneous population'. 'The combined results lead archae-ologists to believe that the population of Roman York comprised individuals from a broad spectrum of ancestral heritage and geo-graphic origin,' they wrote. 'Given the history of Roman Britain, this is precisely what we should expect. In the north of England, urban centres such as York were populated by both military and civilian personnel from all over the Empire and were often founded specifically to accommodate these individuals. The ... data iden-tified individuals with both European and African ancestry, in addition to a number of individuals with a mix of characteristics suggesting a degree of admixture.'

Some of the skeletons reveal the likelihood they were the second- or even third-generation offspring of African migrants, and as well as skeletal evidence of Africans in York there are occasional finds there of African-style cooking stoves.

As Ivory Bangle Woman so elegantly demonstrates, being Roman was not about where you had been born. Instead it was about how you lived, how you dressed, the values you held. There was a sense in which the Roman Empire would allow a person to make his or her own way in the world. There was no need to feel shackled to some or other ancestral heritage. If a person made the decision to leap wholeheartedly out of the world of their birth and into the world defined by the frontiers of that empire, then all well and good. Ivory Bangle Woman also makes it plain that status was not related to colour. It was about whether you were a Roman citizen, or a free non-citizen, or a slave. Hers was not the only burial that implied high status; others alongside had also enjoyed privileged lives.

Whatever barriers Rome might have put in front of a person,

skin colour was not one of them. After all, Septimius Severus, Roman Emperor from AD 193 to 211, was born in the city of Leptis Magna, in modern-day Libya.

Along with everything else we do not know about Ivory Bangle Woman, we have no way of saying for certain what language she learned at her mother's knee. A place like York, with its fort on one side of the River Ouse and its civilian town on the other, would have echoed to the sounds of many different tongues. But we do know that all of the inhabitants would have been united under one common language, the language of Rome and the Empire – Latin.

What made Latin special was that as well as being spoken, it was written down. Its arrival on these shores meant that for perhaps the very first time the people faced the prospect of having their words and actions – their very existence – recorded for posterity. The advent of writing, this alone, is what truly defines the break between prehistory, the domain of archaeologists who must reassemble the ancient past from objects and burials – things left behind – and history, the domain of historians who have recourse to documents, diaries, letters and all the other products of the written word – thoughts left behind.

The problem is the paucity of written words from this earliest period. For the most part there are just abbreviated inscriptions above doorways and beside gateways, on tombstones and so on. What you want to see is evidence of the everyday, of random, idle jottings that give a sense of what people were actually thinking about at any given moment of their lives.

Precisely those sorts of insights are contained within a unique collection of 'postcards' found during excavations at the Roman fort of Vindolanda, on Hadrian's Wall, in 1973. Called the 'Vindolanda Tablets', they are in fact thin slivers of locally grown birch, oak and alder, about the size of the postcards we know today. More than 500 were excavated during the 1970s and 1980s, within a waterlogged dump close by the site of the commanding officer's house, and yet more have been unearthed since.

When they first started coming to light they were almost dismissed as no more than wood shavings – until one of the excavators found two stuck together and bothered to pull them apart. Preserved on the inside surfaces was handwriting in faint ink. The processes of decay had meant the writing on most of the others was all but invisible and certainly indecipherable to the naked eye. Only modern imaging techniques using infra-red light have made it possible to read once more what was on the minds of some of the officers, soldiers and wives who spent time on Hadrian's Wall in the first and second centuries AD. It seems the practice was to score each card down the middle, write on the two halves with quill-like pens and a carbon-based ink, and then fold the thing in two so that an address might be written on the outside.

Most were composed by officers and seem to relate to the running of the fort. Some seem almost like 'hand-over' documents left behind by outgoing men for the benefit of those taking their places: 'The Britons are unprotected by armour. There are very many cavalry. The cavalry do not use swords, nor do the wretched Britons mount in order to throw javelins.' The Latin word in use there was actually 'Brittunculi', a soldier's typically derogatory nickname for an awkward foe – in this case one that will not stand and fight but who strikes and runs in the manner of the guerrilla.

Elsewhere there are examples of the usual gripes: 'My fellow soldiers have no beer. Please order some to be sent.' Perhaps most famous of all of the Vindolanda Tablets is one written by a woman. Claudia Severa was the wife of the commander of a fort elsewhere on the wall and sometime around AD 100 she wrote to Sulpicia Lepidina, the wife of the commander at Vindolanda, to invite her to her birthday party.

Alan Bowan of Manchester University was one of the scholars who succeeded in translating the tablets and he explained how, together, the collection offers a unique insight into the life of the fort and its occupants. 'We've got one tablet that shows the price paid for pepper. We have another example in which a writer refers to someone he's trying to help ... a man who's "a lover of literary culture" – a remarkable phrase to be using on the northern frontier of Britain at this time.' Alan also explained the important role of the Latin language itself in bringing together the disparate peoples of Roman Britain. 'In Britain itself there was a large number, in the pre-Roman period, of different tribal units, different small kingdoms and fiefdoms. The Roman presence brings them all under one system, and that system was run in Latin.'

It was all a remarkable change from the way things had operated in Celtic Britain. For Celts, it appears tribal identity – the blood-line and family to which a person belonged – underpinned every-thing else. Under Rome, however, a person might have much more control over 'what' or 'who' they were. To some extent, and for the people with the freedom to do so, there was an element of choice. There were still those whose birth was interwoven with their destiny – slaves and the children of slaves for example. But for others it was a question of whether or not they wanted to act as Romans did, to live urban lives or not.

Roman ways even reached out into some parts of rural Britain as well. As a Roman citizen a person could legally own land and property; and such holdings could also be bought, sold and inherited, all within the letter of Roman law. In the south and east of Britain, for the very rich at least, all of this gave rise to something that, while it sounds and seems so commonplace now, was truly astonishing then.

The Roman villa operated exactly like a Victorian country house. It was a luxurious home at the centre of a working estate that generated a rich income for its owners. As well as providing accommodation for the family itself, there would also have been space set aside for domestic servants and for those who worked the land. If all of that sounds familiar then it is necessary to remember once more the impact of such a concept on native Britons.

Even after decades, even after a couple of hundred years of Roman rule, the majority of Britons were still used to round-houses – simple, single-roomed homes where all the business of life was performed in one open space centred around a hearth. The Roman villa by contrast was everything we visualise when we think about somewhere to live: rectangular buildings with straight walls and corners; separate rooms with doors providing privacy; corridors linking one space to another; more than one way in or out; glazed windows; tiled floors and tiled roofs; running water.

It was a world away from all that had gone before and yet another example of how everything before the Romans seems ancient and of the past, while everything after their arrival feels familiar and somehow part of the present.

Bignor Roman Villa in Sussex was occupied between around AD 250 and 350. Precisely how long the buildings were upstanding will never be known, but in time they disappeared from sight completely. It was only in 1811, when farmer George Tupper felt the blade of his plough collide with a buried stone, that daylight fell once more upon a small wonder of Roman Britain. What Tupper had hit, and then uncovered with his bare hands, was in fact one side of a hexagonal water fountain set into the floor of a lavish dining room.

The whole site was gradually excavated by John Hawkins, a local landowner, and an antiquary by the name of Samuel Lysons. Eventually revealed were parts of what was once a huge villa sited within a large estate quite close to a Roman road connecting London and Chichester. Evidence excavated over the years suggests part of the wealth created at Bignor was based on supplying the Roman military with grain as they passed up and down on the road nearby.

Originally arranged around a large, square enclosure, the buildings provided accommodation that was luxurious even by modern standards. The original Georgian excavators went to the trouble of erecting buildings to protect the floor surfaces they had uncovered; and it is those floors that reveal how wealthy the inhabitants must have been.

What survives at Bignor are some of the very best mosaic floors anywhere in Britain. Around the fountain unearthed by Tupper are brilliantly executed depictions of topless dancing girls; at the other end of the room Jupiter, in the guise of an eagle, has Ganymede grasped in his talons ready to be carried back to Olympus for service as cupbearer to the gods. In other rooms winter appears as a doleful woman, cupids fight as gladiators and, best of all, there is the face of Venus, regarded as one of the finest mosaics anywhere.

The Venus and gladiator images appear in a room set aside from the rest of the villa. It is entered by its own door, directly from outside, and seems likely to have served as the place where the man of the house would have conducted serious business. Part of the mosaic floor has collapsed in antiquity and, while that might be regarded as a tragedy by fans of mosaics, it provides a wonderful view of the underfloor central heating system, known as a hypocaust – literally 'heat from underneath'.

The floor sits on brick piles that create a network of subterranean channels. All of these were once connected to a furnace built outside the building itself and powered by charcoal. Flues in the walls, connected to the passages under the floor, then drew the hot air from the furnace so that it heated floor and walls alike. Apparently the system was so effective that the floor would become warm to walk on with bare feet.

All of that in the English countryside in AD 250: underfloor central heating in every room, indoor plumbing, glass windows. When the inhabitants of Britain forgot about central heating, after the time of Roman rule was over, they would not embrace the idea again for around 1,600 years.

As well as the finest home comforts, the owners of villas would have enjoyed the best Roman-inspired cuisine as well. The man of the house at Bignor would likely have gathered his guests around that octagonal fountain in his summer dining room, where they would have relaxed on couches drinking wine and toasting Bacchus. The topless dancers on the mosaic floor would have drawn their eyes, while the soft tinkling of the fountain's waters helped them relax and unwind.

It was in such an atmosphere that the food would have been served and according to Roman cookery expert Sally Grainger, the treats would have been like nothing ever tasted in Britain before. 'What they [the Britons] were doing was roasting a lot of meat, drinking a lot of ale and eating a lot of bread,' she said.

The Romans, by contrast, introduced spices like coriander and cumin – the dominant flavours in Indian curry today. They used a lot of lovage, a plant whose leaves could be used for salads and soups, whose roots could be cooked as vegetables or grated, and whose seeds provided yet another spice. The chefs would have to be careful with it, though, since too much would render any dish bitter and unpalatable. Like Thai cooks today, the Romans were extremely fond of a powerful fish sauce they called *garum* and used it as a base for sweet as well as for savoury dishes. They introduced lentils to Britain, as well as chicken.

The French like to claim the invention of fine dining and attribute the emergence of the first of their professional chefs to the greatest chopping implement there ever was – the blade of the guillotine. The story goes that since the nobles kept staffs of highly trained chefs and cooks, the Revolution denied most of those artists their employers, and therefore their incomes. Suddenly needing paid work, they made their way to the nearest auberge and offered their services. Soon every drinking den in France was providing food prepared by the finest chefs – and a legendary reputation for cuisine was born.

As it turns out, however, the Romans were way ahead. They too had their chefs – slave chefs right enough, but every bit as talented and well trained as any Frenchman, and even given to writing cookery books such as 'Apicius', a collection of Roman recipes from the late fourth or early fifth century AD.

In Britain the Roman chefs and cooks soon had access to carefully cultivated orchards of apples, cherries, plums and pears. They planted other novelties like green vegetables including cabbages, leeks and peas. There were herb gardens too, within a few years so that the very best of Roman fine dining was being enjoyed in villas all over the south and east.

It was a culinary revolution more than a millennium and a half before any serious chopping got under way in France. All that remains uncertain is how many Britons actually got to taste it. For the rich it probably became commonplace. For the mass of the population no doubt it was, 'Let them eat roasts . . . and bread . . . and drink ale,' just as before. So far just around 800 villas have been identified in Britain, accounting for only one per cent of all rural settlements in southern England.

I have to say the sample menu prepared for me by Chef Sally Grainger was fantastic. There was belly of pork slathered in a paste of pepper and spices and roasted in a portable two-piece clay oven that sat over the flames of the hob, and a pudding that consisted primarily of eggs and what I initially considered to be a worrying quantity of that ubiquitous fish sauce. My fears were proved groundless, however. The pork was perfect and the pudding tasted of many good things, none of them fish.

Regardless of how delicious the Roman cuisine may or may not have been, the truth of it all was that, out of a population of perhaps three or four million in the third century AD, only a fraction lived in towns, even fewer in villas like Bignor. For at least 90 per cent of the people, therefore, life during the Roman period – food included – was much the same as it had always been.

Chysauster is a wonderfully preserved ancient village in the West Penwith area of Cornwall, not far from Penzance. Only a relatively small section remains, a few houses and workshops, but it is hugely evocative and atmospheric. Walk around the place, without reference to the information boards, and I promise you would swear you were looking at a settlement built during the Bronze Age – even the Stone Age. It has much of the feel of Skara Brae on Orkney.

The homes are cellular, built of dry stone and laid out around courtyards that were likely where most of the day-to-day work was carried out. Around the courtyard are various buildings, some for living in, some for keeping animals, some for general storage.

But excavation and analysis of finds at Chysauster reveal it was established in the early part of the second century AD, probably by members of the local Dumnonii tribe. While Britons in Colchester were enjoying chariot racing at the circus, hearing tales of the legend that was Diocles, and while the inhabitants of London watched a great wall being built around their town, the folk of Chysauster 250 miles or so to the west were quietly growing crops and tending their animals, just as they always had.

They had access to tin, in nugget form in the streams and rivers, and since it was still a valuable commodity they could have used ingots of it to barter for whatever they could not make or grow. Their village was inhabited for just 100 years or so – four or five generations, and right in the middle of the Roman occupation of Britain – and yet it would appear they were mostly untouched by most of what was new.

There would have been Romans nearby, possibly garrisoned in a fort. Their taxmen would have come around at regular intervals demanding coins. And as long as the residents of Chysauster and other places like it had bothered to exchange enough animals and crops for the requisite currency, then those taxmen would have taken it and been on their way.

Another part of the secret of Roman success, then, was to leave people to live the way they wanted, provided they paid their dues and made no trouble. Far away from the urban centres, people had much more choice about just how Roman they actually wanted to be; and so a place like Chysauster could survive and even thrive, as a sort of relic of the old Britain. You might almost describe the unremarkable, unremembered lives lived in such places as a biddable, passive resistance to the centralised authority of Rome.

From time to time there are burials too that suggest unspoken defiance, continuing commitment to older rites. Roman dead were laid to rest flat on their backs, ideally in designated cemeteries set apart from where people were living. When archaeologists find skeletons placed in the ground within settlements during those centuries, curled on their sides like babies, perhaps with traditional Celtic grave goods, they suspect something old, something retained from times past, that flourished only at the end.

Back at North Down in Dorset, inside that banjo enclosure where a farming family had grown wealthy trading with the Roman invaders, but on their own Celtic terms, was found the skeleton of a young man. He was buried sometime in the second half of the first century AD a few decades after the Romans arrived in Britain. For all that his family were happy to sell their surplus grain to the incomers, to acquire tastes for Roman fashions, jewellery and food, they stayed faithful to many of their old ways. There was no obvious cause of death for the young man – no wounds or signs of disease. In any event, when he came to die he was buried in the foetal position, knees pulled up towards his chest and arms tucked in front of him. He was not set apart then either, in the Roman way, but kept close by and still at the heart of his family.

There is always something touching about such graves, cut and filled at that time. They make a person wonder whether perhaps a flicker of defiance of Rome was enacted in life or saved quietly for death. In any event they speak of deeply held beliefs and truths, of true colours worn. In their hearts – in the hearts of those found dead, and in the hearts of those that put them in the ground out of sight at last – they were never Romans, only Britons.

More of the same was demonstrated by the excavation of a Roman villa at Thruxton, in Hampshire, near the hill fort of Danebury. The site was already famous for its stunning mosaic floor, which was removed in 1899 for display in the British Museum. The mosaic, which features the god Bacchus, also reveals that the occupants seem to have considered themselves both Roman and British at the same time. The inscription, Quintus Natalius Natalinus et Bodeni, suggests Thruxton was home to a man named Natalinus who was descended from a native British family called Bodeni. It might be reasonable to assume the Bodeni family were farming land there or thereabouts long before either of the Roman invasions.

Work on the villa began towards the end of the second century. For a while it was a fairly modest affair, essentially just a rectangular hall with a pitched roof supported by upright posts and horizontal trusses. During the fourth century however, there was a change. One end of the building was set apart from the rest and subdivided into three rooms. It was in the last of these – a room now entirely separate from the hall and accessible only from the outside via its own door – that the mosaic floor was laid down.

Thruxton was excavated by Sir Barry Cunliffe and he was of the opinion that the room functioned as a shrine. Outside the shrine, but quite close to it, was a grave containing the remains of a man who had been buried with Late Iron Age Celtic jewellery. Nearby was a pit full of animal bones that also returned a Late Iron Age date. Most intriguing of all, the builders of the villa had gone to the trouble of erecting a wooden fence that surrounded the grave and the pit and then connected it with the outside wall of the building – so that all were joined together as one.

Surely the intention of all that effort is quite clear. The Bodeni family might have adopted Roman ways, but they remembered who they were. They were the descendants of an ancient British family and when they created their Roman shrine they were careful to incorporate within that sacred space the grave of an ancestor buried nearby and still revered.

Sir Barry suggested that for the Bodeni family, the Roman invasion of AD 43 had mattered little. 'There would, of course, have been new taxes to pay, a new range of consumer durables available in the distant market towns, and soon a new network of highways making travel much easier for those with time and inclination. But for the most part life was little changed,' he wrote. 'Farms continued to be owned and worked by families whose ancestors may have broken the land many centuries earlier – perhaps even before iron had come into general use.'

The story of the Romans in Britain is complicated to say

the least. Characters make their appearance and we think we understand their backgrounds and therefore their motives. Then, suddenly, there is a twist and all at once we have to consider a different angle, allow for behaviour we had never suspected. Sometimes we realise the picture we had in our heads is quite wrong, and late in the day we have to allow for the possibility that everything was subtly different all along.

The enduring and popular impression of the Roman arrival in Britain is one of invasion. Rapacious and acquisitive, they set their sights on Britain – and persevered until it was theirs. The ways of Rome were made the ways of the new province as well.

But we have only to look at our own modern world to be reminded that regime change is almost always a process of Byzantine complexity. By the time one country is invaded by another – or by a union of others – a great deal of politicking has probably already gone on behind the scenes and out of sight of the public. To put it another way: if you find yourself watching a shotgun wedding, it is pretty obvious the couple already know each other well enough, whether or not the families seem genuinely thrilled.

So as it turns out, when Emperor Claudius decided to send his legions across the Channel in the summer of AD 43, he had some reasons for believing his advances were expected – even desired. Back in Caesar's day the name of Commius, King of the Atrebates, had been crucial. He it was who had acted as go-between, shuttling back and forth between Caesar and the British tribes in hopes of striking a deal acceptable to all parties.

By the time of Claudius, it was a descendant of Commius who played the key role. Verica – whose name and likeness appeared on that tiny silver minim excavated from Silchester, and who styled himself 'CF' for 'Commius Filius', son of Commius – was a king with a problem in AD 43. Just as in Caesar's time, it was the Catuvellauni tribesmen in Essex that were making waves. Back then it had been the antipathy of their bellicose King Cassivellaunus towards his neighbours, the Trinovantes, that sparked war. More recently the Catuvellauni had been led by Cunobelin; and now they were at daggers drawn with the Atrebates, whose territory was spread across modern Berkshire, Hampshire and Surrey.

By AD 43 Cunobelin was dead and it was his sons Togodumnus and Caratacus who were carrying the torch of war. It was either fear or desperation or both that drove King Verica of the Atrebates to cross the Channel then and seek help from the Roman Emperor. Deliberately or not, willingly or not, Verica had given Claudius the excuse he needed.

Now take a moment to view Britain from where Claudius was standing. Better yet, replace him in your mind's eye with any recent President of the United States of America (and, just for the sake of it, have him backed by any twenty-first-century British Prime Minister and the leaders of some other members of the United Nations) and then ruminate on the way the West views the wider world.

Do not for one moment derive anything negative about that comparison. By as early as 27 BC the Romans had established their Pax Romana – Roman Peace. It would give rise to more than two centuries of relative calm for the ancient world. Life might well have been nasty, brutish and short for most people back then, but at least under Roman rule there was a nod to hot baths and an outside chance of some decent food.

From where Claudius was standing, the island of Britain looked like a place in danger of descending into the kind of turmoil that was bad for business. He was new in the job as well, still warming the seat of the imperial throne, and he needed a good war to secure some votes at home. Rome needed British grain and metals and all the rest, and petty feuding between bad neighbours was something best snuffed out sooner rather than later. Left alone it might lead to a civil war and that could have all sorts of consequences – not least the kind of conflagration that could pull in any number of different tribes and lead to unrest elsewhere as well. Viewed from that perspective, the so-called Roman invasion begins to look much more like an intervention to ensure a return to stable government.

Most archaeologists have long accepted Richborough in Kent as the place the Romans first made landfall in AD 43. Apart from anything else it would have made for a short crossing. More recently, however, there has been a groundswell of support for another site, near Chichester in Sussex.

Around a mile and a half from Chichester itself is the famed Fishbourne Roman Palace, a villa par excellence. Established as the site of a fort soon after the invasion, it had been developed into a luxurious 'palace' before the end of the first century. The site was discovered by accident in 1960, but more recent excavations, in 1995 and 2002, have unearthed artefacts that may suggest the place was home to Verica himself.

Since the Romans were en route to support Verica and his Atrebates in Sussex during their time of need, it would have made perfect sense for them to land and establish their beachhead in the backyard of the man himself. Since the days of Commius at least, the safe anchorages around Chichester had been familiar to Roman traders. When the dust of invasion settled, however, it was seemingly not Verica who was anointed by the Romans. He was an old man by then and it was a younger noble of the Atrebates – one Tiberius Claudius Cogidubnus – who emerged as the Empire's placeman. Perhaps Verica's reward, soothing ointment for his otherwise bruised ego, was the gift of a grand pile built and paid for by his Roman guests. Fishbourne is certainly unusual. Unlike other villas it does not appear to have been at the centre of agriculture, so the source of its income is unclear. Some have suggested it was the home not of Verica, but of Cogidubnus. Whoever first occupied the first palace, it certainly outlived them. Fishbourne was being inhabited and modified until around AD 270, when it was gutted by a fire. The damage was seemingly too great for repair and thereafter the place seems to have been taken apart.

The Romans were at least as good at politics as they were at war. No wonder, then, they understood that the iron gauntlet of violence was a clumsy tool. If a hammer is all you have got, you tend to treat everything like a nail. So if the Celts were strongly attached to some customs, then let them keep them. As long as the grain kept ripening in the fields and the mines kept producing gold, silver, lead, copper and tin, such tolerance was good for business.

No matter how reasonably a leader behaves, or appears to behave, however, there will always be those who consistently and stubbornly refuse to get the message. Nothing will work with them, in fact – neither reason nor flattery, nor violence. Some people are so set in their ways and so unshakeably confident of their own position, they will not be moved, not even by the threat of death. Sometimes their commitment comes from deeply rooted tribal identity and blood ties. Sometimes it is just a characteristic woven through an individual's DNA like a bright thread through cloth.

In the film *Cool Hand Luke* the eponymous hero refuses to submit to the regime in a Florida prison camp. He is a prisoner himself and apparently powerless in the face of the guards and, more particularly, the camp governor, known as the Captain. On the face of it, Luke has nothing with which to fight and nothing much to gain by fighting; yet he will not submit to the rules, even when by doing so would seemingly be to his benefit. Playing cards with his fellow inmates one night, he bluffs his way to winning the pot even though he has nothing of value in his hand. But as he explains to his fellow inmate, Dragline, 'Sometimes . . . nothing can be a real cool hand.'

Even after hundreds of years of Roman control of the south of Britain, much of the northern third of the island refused to accept the regime. The Romans called their province Britannia and no doubt they liked to pretend it was a single, unified entity. But it was an illusion and they knew it. Britannia was a fractured land. Despite the efforts of soldiers and administrators alike, despite thousands of miles of roads, hundreds of forts, shining towns and cities, despite the presence of a Romano-British elite living in villas, drinking wine and eating spiced meats – despite all of that and more besides the project remained unfinished, the picture imperfect.

Ever since AD 136 there had been a livid scar across the face of Britannia. It was a lime-washed white blemish called Hadrian's Wall that advertised, upon a billboard 74 miles long and 20 feet high, Rome's failure to subdue the peoples of the north. During the second century AD Rome had to station 40,000 auxiliary soldiers on that wall just to keep the barbarians at bay. Hadrian's Wall marked the end of civilisation but, worse than that, it under-lined the truth that Rome's reach exceeded her grasp.

It was in AD 297 that the name Pict – or rather Picti – was first recorded in writing. The credit goes to a Roman writer named Eumenius, more famous for his speeches than for references to obscure peoples beyond the reach of Empire, but who nonetheless made a reference to all the strife those people were causing. Having first encountered the Caledonii, it was the Picts who became a more abiding and troublesome obsession for the invaders as time wore on. And given that they left behind no written words of their own, we have to be grateful to the Romans for at least making a note of the existence of the people of the designs.

Despite the fact that they kept no records, the Picts are remembered too in place names. In his *Historia ecclesiastica gentis Anglorum – The Ecclesiastical History of the English People* – the Venerable Bede noted that the Picts spoke a language of their own. Bede was writing in the early eighth century AD, but he was able to tell us there were five languages spoken in Britain at that time. While he was happy to report that 'all are united in their study of God's truth by the fifth – Latin – which has become a common medium through the study of the Scriptures', he did at least make room for the other four, namely Anglo-Saxon English, Brittonic Welsh, Gaelic and Pictish.

The words of Bede are backed up by those of another cleric, Adomnán, Abbot of Iona. In his hagiography of his predecessor

Columba, he described his master's visit to the northern kingdom of Brude, a Pictish king based near the River Ness. Columba spoke Gaelic – the language of much of Scotland and Ireland – but Adomnán points out that he needed a translator in order to be able to speak to the king, so the Pictish language must have been quite different from his own.

Norse, the language of the Vikings, would be written into the landscape in later centuries. Gaelic has left its mark too, with words like 'cill', meaning chapel or church, as in Kilmarnock; 'dun', meaning fortress, as in Dundee or Dunkeld, the fortress of the Caledonians; 'inver', meaning the meeting of the waters, as in Inverness, the meeting of the waters of the River Ness, and 'tigh', meaning house, as in Tighnabruaich, the house on the hill.

But while Scots Gaelic is still spoken by a few tens of thousands of people, Pictish survives only in words on maps, or engraved on stones. 'Pett', or 'pit', is a Pictish word meaning a portion or a share, as in Pittenweem or Pitlochry; 'carden' means a thicket, as in Kincardine, and 'aber' means the mouth of the river, as in Aberdeen.

There are even suggestions in the Roman writings of a grudging respect for their painted foes. In AD 211 there were negotiations between the Romans and a Scottish tribe called the Maeatae, who occupied lands around the modern towns of Stirling and Falkirk and also towards the south and west. At some point in the talks a meeting took place between a woman referred to only as the wife of the Maeatae chieftain Argentocoxus, and Roman Empress Julia Domna, wife of the Emperor Septimius Severus.

Heaven alone knows what the women must have made of each other – one a tattooed tribal queen, the other a haughty Roman of the highest rank. According to the Roman writer and historian Cassius Dio, it seems Julia had learned that the tribeswomen were in the habit of brazenly sleeping with men other than their husbands, and threw this in her rival's face. 'We fulfil the demands of nature in a much better way than do you Roman women,' replied the chieftain's wife. 'For we consort openly with the best men, whereas you let yourselves be debauched in secret by the vilest.'

I am writing this chapter in the attic bedroom of my wife's parents' house in Dumyat Drive, Falkirk, and from the windows I can see the long ridge of the Ochil Hills (from 'uchel', meaning high). The highest point in the view is a flattened summit shaped like a thick pancake. This is Dumyat Hill and the story goes that the name is a corruption of Dun Maeatae, the fortress of the Maeatae, so that even the writing of this book has a shadow of the ancient past across it, perhaps a Pictish shadow at that.

It was in Falkirk in 1934 that workmen digging a seven-foot-deep ditch unearthed a find that immediately resonated through Scottish hearts and minds. It is now in the care of the National Museum of Scotland in Edinburgh, and it is called the Falkirk Tartan. It has to be said, it is not much to look at. What the workmen actually found was a reddish clay pot containing a hoard of almost 2,000 silver Roman coins – the largest hoard of its kind ever found in Scotland.

The coins themselves cover a range of dates, from 83 BC through to AD 230. Many of them are worn thin and look as though they were in active circulation for a long time before finally being collected together and put into the ground inside their pot. The workmen had been digging in a spot just 400 yards or so north of the Antonine Wall and best guesses by archaeologists suggest the cache belonged not to any Roman, but to a native tribe or family. The coins may have been paid as a series of bribes, over several generations, to secure co-operation – always cheaper than war. Why the hoard was buried will remain a mystery.

Alongside the coins – and presumably originally covering the mouth of the pot – was a small piece of the simplest woven fabric imaginable. Specialists in tartan have described the pattern – or sett, to use the more precise term – as the 'shepherd's check'. It comprises just two colours of undyed wool, brown and off-white or cream, and that it survived at all is miracle enough. Somehow the fact that it is such a meagre scrap of a thing only adds to its potency.

Tartan is a powerful word in modern Scotland, and modern is the key word here. The traditional dress of the Highlander, until it was banned after the defeat of the Jacobite rebellion of 1745/46, was the 'breacan an feileadh', the belted plaid – 12 yards of plaited and folded woven wool fabric that was kilted, literally 'tucked up' around the body and fixed in place with a buckled leather belt around the waist.

But while the makers of the plaid in those pre-Culloden days came up with patterns composed of many colours, achieved with dyes made from local plants and minerals, there never were any 'clan tartans'. They never functioned like football strips – team colours that let a MacDonald differentiate himself from a Campbell, or a Stewart from a MacNeill. In times of inter-tribal warfare, members of a clan might identify themselves to one another by all wearing a sprig of the same plant or flower in their bonnets, but that was as far as it went.

The whole 'cult of tartanry', as it has been described, was largely the invention of John Sobieski Stolberg Stuart and Charles Edward Stuart, two Polish brothers who turned up in Edinburgh during the feverish run-up to the visit to Scotland's capital city by King George IV in 1822 – the first by a monarch since that of Charles II in 1650. Brandishing what they claimed was an ancient text called 'Vestiarium Scoticum', 'Scottish Costumes', they claimed not only that they were the grandsons of Bonnie Prince Charlie himself, but that they and they alone knew the significance of tartan.

Conmen, salesmen – call them what you will; but the brothers succeeded in making a fortune by persuading well-heeled Scottish gentlefolk to buy tartans described in the Vestiarium (a book they showed briefly once and that never saw the light of day thereafter). Each of the hundreds of different patterns matched a different proud Scottish surname. And so an entire industry, and a legend, was born.

All of this tomfoolery is why the modest nature of the Falkirk Tartan matters so much. While they bear no resemblance to the bright, regimented colours of the modern plaids so beloved by tourists, patriots and nationalists, the soft hues of the Falkirk Tartan have something quiet to say that is actually worth listening to.

That scrap of woven wool speaks of the people who made it and wore it nearly 1,800 years ago. Within yards of that abandoned Roman wall were people who lived according to their own ways and beliefs and damned the consequences. For generations the Romans had had to hand over coins to them and others, the better to keep the peace. But while the silver bought co-operation, it was never enough to buy the culture, far less the independence, of the Picts.

So by AD 250, the painted people were still a thorn in Roman flesh. There had been the abortive experiment of the Antonine Wall, begun in AD 142 and abandoned 20 years later; but pretty much everything north of the Roman town of Carlisle was then, and would remain ever after, hostile territory.

It had not been for want of trying either. As well as building their more northerly turf barrier, the Romans had sallied forth again and again, north of that line, in hope of securing final victory. But anyone who has visited the north of Scotland – particularly the wild and mountainous north-west – will easily understand the logistical and tactical difficulties to be faced there by any would-be invader.

Whatever else they were, the Picts were certainly the descendants of those hunters who had walked ever northwards while the ice retreated, many thousands of years ago. The rocks and the waters of the place were therefore in their bones. They understood the landscape like no recent incomer ever could and probably saw themselves as belonging to it more than it belonged to them. Every mountain, spring, river and bog had its god or spirit to guide them and reward them as well. They covered their skins in patterns only they and their gods could read, and when it came to fighting they willingly stripped naked, the better to be seen and so protected by their guardians. How does anyone hope to conquer that?

They were guerrilla warriors, emerging from folds and shadows in the landscape to torment the foreigners before melting away again into the mists and mountain fastnesses that were their home and their inspiration.

In time the Romans realised what the Picts had always known: that the land was poor. There was barely enough nourishment in the thin soil to grow handfuls of oats and barley, or to satisfy a few head of scruffy cattle. There might have been some gold, but only a sprinkling in the gravel of a few streams and rivers. The land mattered to the Picts and the rest of the tribes for reasons unfathomable to the Romans. They would never recoup enough in taxes or plunder to justify the cost of keeping whole armies in the field there and so in the end they withdrew for ever. In short, the Picts had nothing – at least nothing the Romans wanted or needed. But sometimes nothing can be a real cool hand.

In the wilds of the north something old had survived, the Celtic Iron Age. It was something out of reach and long forgotten in the south and east of Britannia but it would not die.

If the silver coin hoard in Falkirk had been a collection of bribes – paid to the Maeatae perhaps, or to another of the recalcitrant tribes – then they certainly were not the only ones in receipt of pieces of Roman silver. Also within the collections of the National Museum in Edinburgh is a hoard that makes the Falkirk coins look like the contents of a charity bottle on a pub bar.

The Traprain Law Treasure amounts to 53 pounds of silver. There is enough of it to fill several museum display cabinets and it is the most blatant evidence so far discovered of the lengths to which the Romans would go to keep at least some of the northern tribes sweet.

Traprain Law is a 700-foot-high whale-backed volcanic hill that breaches the surface of an otherwise calm sea of arable farmland beside the old A1 road connecting Edinburgh to Dunbar (a name meaning 'the fort on the summit'). Covering a footprint of around 30 acres, the hill is visible from miles around and would have attracted people from the very beginning. There are Neolithic cup marks pecked into the bedrock on its summit. Sometime in the Bronze Age, perhaps 1,500 BC, people with bronze tools found their way there too, possibly in the summertime when the weather was more amenable. More recently a great unsightly bite has been taken out of one end by quarrying for road metal.

It was during the Iron Age that the Votadini tribe chose Traprain Law as the location for one of their huge hill forts, encircling much of the summit with a third of a mile of earth and timber ramparts. Like the Brigantes who held much of northern England, and who caused a great deal of trouble for the Romans until at least the middle of the second century AD, the Votadini were probably a confederacy of many smaller tribes whose individual names were not deemed worthy of recording.

They held lands stretching from Northumberland to the southern shore of the Firth of Forth and the hill fort at Traprain may even have served as their capital for a while. These were the same that laid claim to another volcanic rock, a few miles to the west. Visible from Traprain, it was once called Din Eidyn, although it is Edinburgh Castle Rock now. Centuries later, the descendants of the Votadini, called by then the Gododdin, would sally forth out of Din Eidyn and into legend. Their subsequent defeat by Angles at the Battle of Catraeth, was a fall commemorated in a poem by their bard Aneirin, called Y Gododdin.

'Three hundred gold-torced men attacked,
Guarding their land, bloody was the slaughter,
Although they were slain, they slew;
And until the end of the world they will be honoured.
And all of us kinsmen who went together,
Sad, but for one man, none escaped.'

Perhaps their bloody destruction in 600 was come-uppance for their forebears' dalliance with Rome. In 638 even Din Eidyn fell to the Angles, so their downfall was complete.

In any event the Votadini mattered once and in the years before the coming of the Romans they had hundreds of roundhouses on top of Traprain Law, together with workshops where they crafted things of metal and also enamel. Archaeological excavation has established there was a sudden rush to augment the defences sometime around AD 80 – perhaps in preparation for the coming of the foreigners. When it came to it, however, there was no fighting and instead the Votadini chose to welcome the Romans with open arms, giving them safe passage through their territory all the way to the Forth.

Archaeologists of the Royal Commission on the Ancient and Historical Monuments of Scotland rate Traprain Law as nothing less than 'by far the most important place in the late prehistory and early proto-history of Scotland, and of a wider area including NE England'. The Votadini citadel on Traprain Law was on such a scale as to merit the title *oppidum*, the Latin word the Romans used to describe the principal native centres they encountered as they explored their new provinces. Such places were few and far between in the north of Britain and the only others to rival that at Traprain were Yeavering Bell in Northumberland and Eildon Hills, which glower over the modern town of Melrose in the Scottish Borders. Even Eildon was abandoned either just before the Romans arrived or very soon thereafter.

That Traprain Law survived and indeed thrived throughout the Roman period is testament to how careful the Votadini were to stay onside with the incomers. Their capital remained a free British town and its occupants apparently grew rich on Roman bribes along the way.

This, then, is the context for the Traprain Law Treasure. Archaeologists know it as a hacksilver hoard because the precious metal was acquired as scrap that could be melted down and cast into new objects. Once-stunning objects – jugs with handles shaped like dolphins and panthers, huge plates and other items bearing Classical motifs – had been crudely cut into pieces using shears or some sort. Fine tableware, drinking goblets, wine jugs, military buckles – all of it was put deliberately beyond use.

Hacksilver hoards have little if anything in common with other collections of metal found buried in the ground or deposited in water. Most other hoards contain precious swords and cooking pots that were ritually broken – made useless to the world of men before being offered to the gods. In the case of the Traprain silver the archaeologists are certain the objects were cut up by the Romans themselves before the whole lot was handed over to the Votadini as bullion, its value based only upon its weight.

Fraser Hunter, of the National Museum of Scotland, said the Traprain Law Treasure was a diplomatic gift made to a client king as part of a long-running effort to maintain the Votadini as a buffer between Hadrian's Wall and the troublesome Pictish tribes further north. Two silver coins were found among the hoard – one dating to between AD 364 and 378 and the other to between AD 395 and 423. Clearly the tribe was in a position to continue to extract payments right up until the Romans lost control of Britannia altogether. 'The late dating of the hoard suggests that this relationship was sustained by both parties until the very end of the Roman period in Britain,' said Hunter.

The Brigantes had slugged it out with the Romans until the bitter end, but their northern neighbours preferred to reach an accommodation that left their swords in their sheaths and their independence sold for Roman silver. It had been classic manoeuvring by the invaders, using a military tactic that is as old as the hills: namely the undermining of inter-tribal loyalties – divide and conquer.

Fighting Rome was like fighting the Hydra, the many-headed serpent of Greek legend. If a tribe managed to beat off the soldiers, then a ruthlessly organised division of administrators and money men would emerge to bamboozle and bribe. If that failed then the allure of Roman civilisation itself – with all its fine clothes, fine foods and luxury – might prove beguiling. The success of the Roman machine was therefore down to how many levels it operated on. Finally, if they could neither coerce nor seduce, then they simply excluded – building walls that clearly defined who was in and who was out. If the Roman advance was not physically overpowering, then it was at least confusing. All the while one tribe held out, their neighbours might succumb. For proud and independent people it must have been infuriating as much as anything else.

The Romans would change the layout and organisation of your land. They wanted to change your way of life. By the time they were in Britain they were past masters too in the art of handling the tribulations of culture clash, of massaging perceived differences until they were made to disappear. And as well as dealing with the day-to-day, they had also learned how to overcome a potential obstacle that was deeply personal to every individual they encountered: that of religious belief.

In Britannia they knew the people were part of the Celtic tradition they had already encountered in the provinces of Gaul. Each British tribe would have had its sacred places in the landscape, watched over by gods that demanded to be appeased by the giving of gifts, and of sacrifices.

When the Romans arrived, they brought their own pantheon of gods: Apollo, god of the sun and Diana, goddess of the Moon; Mars, god of war, Venus, goddess of love and Saturn, god of time. There were deities for all needs and ruling over them were Jupiter and Juno, King and Queen of the gods.

The Romans worshipped their gods as faithfully and fearfully as the Celts worshipped theirs and so it might be assumed the invaders sought to impose their own beliefs on those they encountered. It was either that or accept that the local gods held sway, which would surely have been unthinkable. In fact the Romans, pragmatic as always, found a solution that avoided either extreme.

The modern city of Bath, in Somerset, is built around a natural wonder, the only one of its kind in the whole of the British Isles. Rainwater falling on the Mendip Hills sinks into the soil and then begins slowly, so slowly, to percolate down through the limestone.

By the time it has descended to around 14,000 feet, the water comes in contact with natural geothermal energy emanating from the Earth's core that raises its temperature to nearly 100 degrees centigrade. Now under pressure, the near-boiling water begins its journey back to the surface through fissures and faults in the rock. By the time it emerges as the hot, mineral-rich spring that is the whole reason for Bath's existence, the temperature has lowered to an extremely pleasant 46 degrees centigrade. Every day the best part of a quarter of a million gallons of this naturally produced bath water gushes forth. It has been going on for millions of years and will likely continue for millions more.

The people of ancient Britain had no way of understanding how it was happening, and were simply drawn by the wonder and the pleasure of it all. By the time the Romans arrived, the locals had long since decided it was the work of a goddess they called Sulis and were in the habit of appeasing her with prayers and with gifts thrown into the spring.

The Romans were just as impressed as everyone else and between AD 60 and 70 they set about building their own baths around the spring. They would continue to develop and augment the site for the next three centuries, eventually creating a lavish structure housing a *caldarium*, hot bath, a *tepidarium*, warm bath and a *frigidarium*, cold bath.

The Roman baths were lost for centuries, submerged beneath more recent streets and buildings. Then in the middle of the eighteenth century a lady house owner began complaining about the water that was always flooding her basement. The local authority of the day investigated the problem and, in so doing, redis-covered the fourth-century foundations, in 1755. Since 1987, the City of Bath has been recognised by UNESCO as a World Heritage Site.

The local goddess, Sulis, was apparently concerned with healing, wisdom and insight and when the Romans heard this they were immediately reminded of their own deity, Minerva, who looked after medicine, wisdom and magic. Rather than cause offence by evicting a local girl and replacing her with a foreigner, the Romans cleverly combined the two – creating a goddess called Sulis-Minerva. Everyone was happy and able to continue with the business of seeking help and comfort from the mistress of the hot spring.

At Bath, just as at other similar sites scattered all across the Classical world, people appealed to Sulis-Minerva by scratching messages onto little squares of lead. These were then folded in half and usually thrown into the water for the attention of the goddess. Classicist Roger Tomlin has been studying those recovered from Bath for the past 25 years and he explained the very specific nature of the language used.

For a start he said the messages were best described as 'curse tablets', since people were usually appealing to the goddess in hope of revenge. The whole concept is fascinating because so many of the 'wrongs' seem trivial – and therefore wholly understandable. Tomlin said it was important to remember that the Roman world was 'badly policed' and that people had to find their own ways of recovering stolen property or seeking redress for insults and slights.

He has deciphered all manner of curses, and usually they were invoked for the theft of towels and clothing, or occasionally of a ring or other piece of jewellery. The strategy seemed to be to make over ownership of the stolen property to the goddess herself so that it would then be in her interest to reclaim it. If you could not have the item back yourself, at least there would be the comfort of knowing the thief would lose it too, and hopefully be savagely punished at the same time. The most potent were written back-wards, or otherwise encrypted, so that only the goddess would understand them.

'May he who has stolen Vilbia from me become as liquid as water,' or,
'To Minerva the goddess of Sulis I have given the thief who has stolen my hooded cloak, whether slave or free, whether man or

woman. He is not to buy back this gift unless with his own blood.'

Or how about,

'I curse him who has stolen, who has robbed Deomiorix from his house. Whoever stole his property, the god is to find him. Let him buy it back with his blood or with his own life.'

The venom goes on and on. Around 130 curse tablets have been deciphered from the Bath collection and since they have been delivered to a goddess of healing it comes as no surprise to learn the requested punishments include everything from blinding, to failure of vital organs, to an inability to eat, drink, sleep, sit, lie down, urinate or defacate. For all the curative and relaxing properties of the baths, these people were often furious indeed.

Elsewhere in Britannia disgruntled citizens sought similar help from other deities. On the foreshore of the Hamble Estuary in Hampshire, a metal detectorist found a curse tablet dedicated to another pairing of gods, this time Niskus, thought to be a local water god, and Neptune, the Roman god of the sea.

'Lord Neptune, I give you the man who has stolen the *solidus* and six *argentioli* [gold and silver coins] of Muconius. So I give the names who took them away, whether male or female, whether boy or girl. So I give you, Niskus, and to Neptune the life, health, blood of him who has been privy to that taking away. The mind which stole this and which has been privy to it, may you take it away. The thief who stole this, may you consume his blood and take it away, Lord Neptune.'

Twinning of gods and goddesses was a tactic the Romans employed all across their Empire. It was a cosy set-up and it served them well. But a quite different challenge was presented by a cult that began spreading out of the Middle East during the first century AD. It emerged from the province of Judaea and at first most Romans were unconvinced to say the least. For one thing it demanded obedience to a single god. The very idea seemed absurd. But there was a problem: followers of the cult were being assured of something no one had ever even dreamed of before – eternal life. Anyone and everyone – from emperors to slaves – was being promised they could survive death itself. No Roman god had ever made such an offer before. It was a powerful message and as the followers grew more and more numerous, their cult was outlawed by Rome. Now its followers had to practise in secret.

Like everything else that touched the Roman world, Christianity eventually reached Britain. Since the religion was banned, any merchant or traveller bringing the new teaching across the Channel was taking a terrible risk. Nonetheless the religion found its way into the province of Britannia and the proof of its presence is revealed by objects bearing the first two letters of the Greek spelling of Christ – 'chi', which usually appears as an 'X', and 'rho', represented with a 'P'. The chi-rho symbol was used rather like a secret sign by which Christians might recognise one another.

In February 1975 a ploughman working in a field in the village of Water Newton in Cambridgeshire unearthed a metal hoard, damaging several of the items in the process. All but one of the objects are made of silver; the other, a small disc, is made of gold. There are nine silver vessels – cups, jugs, dishes and the like – but the rest of the artefacts are thin triangular plaques. Now in the collections of the British Museum, the so-called Water Newton Silver is thought to date from the fourth century AD.

The little plaques would, at first sight, suggest pagan worship and similar items have often been found dedicated to gods like Jupiter and Mars. Several of the Water Newton pieces, however, bear the chi-rho symbol and the hoard is therefore regarded as the earliest collection of Christian liturgical silver found in Britain so far. The village of Water Newton is close to the site of the Roman town of Durobrivae and it is thought that a congregation of

Christian Romans living and worshipping there found cause to hide their precious silver – and then never had the opportunity to recover it.

Many similar items have been recovered over the years, either bearing the chi-rho mark or sometimes the Greek letters alpha and omega, first and last and therefore also symbolic of the Christian message.

Unlikely though it may seem for a religion based around events that unfolded in the Middle East at the start of the first century, a key turning point for early Christianity happened in Britain. In AD 305 Emperor Constantius I arrived in Britain and headed north. His objective was a military campaign against the Picts and within a year he was proclaiming victory – as well as awarding himself the grand title 'Britannicus Maximus'. Still puffed up with his triumph, he withdrew south of Hadrian's Wall and was wintering in York when he was suddenly taken ill. Sensing he would not recover, he urged the army to accept his son, Constantine, as the new Emperor. This they were apparently happy to do and Constantine I – later styled Constantine the Great – was duly proclaimed by the legions at York.

Not everyone in the Empire was happy with the turn of events, however, and soon a power struggle ensued. Constantine's principal challenger was Maxentius and their rival forces finally had their climactic showdown at the Battle of Milvian Bridge, just outside the gates of Rome, in AD 312. Legend has it that before the battle Constantine looked up at the sky and saw a fiery cross. That night Christ visited him in a dream saying, 'By this sign conquer'. Realising what he must do, Constantine ordered his men to adorn their shields with the chi-rho symbol and to march into battle behind a Christian banner. They were victorious and from that moment the future of Christianity within the Roman Empire was transformed. By 313 the worship of Christ was officially approved and his followers were freed from the fear of persecution.

Even then the struggle for supremacy was not over for Constantine. Only after another bloody civil war did he finally emerge,

in AD 324, as the undisputed (and first Christian) Emperor of the
Roman Empire. He it was who established a new Christian Rome,
named Constantinople, on the Bosphorus, and by championing –
or at the very least, accepting – Christianity, he allowed it to
change the world.

Some of the sources suggest Constantine had been introduced
to Christianity by his mother, Helena. According to some, she was
the daughter of an innkeeper and had married Constantius when
he was a junior officer stationed at Naissus, on the Danube. It was
there that Constantine was born, on 27 February AD 272. Some
scholars have suggested his decision to accept Christianity was just
another shrewd political move. By bringing the new religion into
the fold, along with its already uncountable numbers of followers,
it could be organised and therefore controlled by the state. In any
case Christianity began to flourish and by AD 391 it was the old,
pagan religions that were banned. The time of goddesses like
Sulis-Minerva had come and gone and her spring at Bath was
abandoned, left to silt up and overflow, her temples to fall into
decay.

Soon Christianity was making a more overt mark on Britannia.
At Lullingstone Villa in Kent the mosaic floor is augmented with
Christian motifs and there are also paintings of people in prayer.
The chi-rho symbol is there again in the mosaics from the villa at
Hinton St Mary, in Dorset, alongside a face that may represent
Christ himself. At Frampton Villa nearby there are three mosaics
featuring a fusion of pagan and Christian symbolism. Whatever
else the villa owners were enjoying in fourth-century Britannia,
many of them were being careful to make the worship of Christianity a part of it all.

Yet another ploughman, this time at Mildenhall in Suffolk in
1942, found one of the most famous silver hoards in the country.
It comprises fabulously extravagant serving platters, bowls, ladles
and spoons, mostly decorated with Classical motifs. Of the eight
silver spoons, three bear Christian symbols including the chi-rho
and also alpha and omega. Two of the spoons have the word

vivas, meaning 'may you live', another sign popular among early followers of the Christian faith.

All the while Christianity's star ascended, the light of Rome began first to flicker, and then to dim. In AD 367 a co-ordinated attack by Picts from Caledonia, Scoti warriors from Ireland and other barbarians including Saxons from Germania inflicted a terrifying blow. It is said that disgruntled Roman soldiers on Hadrian's Wall colluded with the northern tribes and opened the gates. A whole swathe of northern Britannia was overrun and countless civilians slaughtered. It was not until the end of the following year that the Romans were able to regroup and defeat the uprising. By the winter of AD 368, the barbarians had been driven back into the sea or beyond Hadrian's Wall once more.

For all the Roman celebrations of victory, Roman supremacy in Britannia had been rattled to its foundations. By the time Emperor Theodosius died in AD 395, the sun had already begun to set on the rest of the Empire as well. During his time in office he had succeeded in fighting off yet more barbarian attacks around his demesne, but the mere fact that so many felt confident enough to rear up at all meant Rome no longer wielded absolute authority. The Empire began to depend more and more on mercenaries to defend her boundaries. Even the role of Emperor was eclipsed. After Theodosius they were heads of state more than real leaders and effective power was wielded by senior military figures.

The Empire had been split in two by Diocletian in AD 285 – eastern and western. The eastern half became known as the Byzantine Empire and would survive in some form until 1453, when it fell to the Ottoman Turks of Sultan Mehmett II. The soldier in charge of the western empire was Flavius Stilicho, a Vandal by birth and married to Theodosius's niece. In Britannia there was increasing trouble from Caledonian Picts, Irish Scots and Saxons from the Continent. The Romans fought back against them as the fourth century drew to a close, but in truth they were doing little more than manning the barricades. By AD 398 Stilicho had bigger problems than those being posed by the Picts in Britannia.

Increasing levels of barbarian attacks on the mainland of Europe left him no option but to begin pulling men back out of Britannia so they might be more usefully deployed elsewhere.

For a while during the fourth century, Britannia had seemed like a safe haven, far from the troubles afflicting the Empire on the mainland. Many Roman citizens, senior military and political figures among them, had even retired there, taking their valuables with them for safekeeping. That time had passed, however. An already volatile situation finally came to boiling point in AD 409 when yet more barbarian attacks – and the likelihood of more to come – led to nothing less than a full-scale rebellion by the Roman soldiers tasked with keeping a lid on it all. Even the civilians rose in protest, railing against the Empire.

By the time Alaric, King of the Visigoths, finally achieved what had previously been unthinkable and broken through the gates of Rome itself in AD 410, the isles of Britain were Britannia no more. Britain would survive and prevail – she always had – but nearly four centuries of direct Roman rule had come to an end. That much was over.

Amongst everything else the Romans did for us, they herded us across the bridge that separates prehistory from history. Whatever might happen on these islands from now on, there was at least an outside chance of it being written down somewhere. In the end we had lost nothing. Like so many people before them, the Romans had arrived in Britain expecting to change it – and were themselves changed too. Roman Britain had been a unique place, a uniquely modified version of the Roman idea. This is what Britain has always done – Britain the island, the mountains, valleys, lochs, lakes, fields, forests and coastline of the place; she accepts all comers but quietly transforms them, shapes them in her own image. Britain has had a history of making things British.

Roman rule in Britain lasted, give or take, for four centuries. Counting back four centuries from 2011 leads all the way to 1611 – the year William Shakespeare's *The Tempest* was performed for the very first time. It was also when the Authorised King James Version of The Bible was published after seven years of dedicated work by a team of 47 scholars. The King James in question was James I of England and VI of Scotland, son of Mary Queen of Scots.

A span of time like four centuries seems an eternity when looked at that way; and yet it may have taken our Neolithic forebears five centuries to build the great mound of Silbury Hill. Fewer years separate us from Cleopatra than separate Cleopatra from the building of the Great Pyramid. Time is all about perspective.

It is more than 2,000 years since Caesar's legionaries first splashed ashore on a beach in Kent; 4,500 since the arrival of people with metal tools; 12,000 since the first hunters after the ice and 33,000 since the time when the oldest modern human being we know about lived and died here. It is half a million years since Boxgrove Man closed his eyes for the last time on a Britain roamed by elephants, lions and hyenas.

At the time of writing it is the 50th anniversary of Yuri Gagarin's first orbit of the Earth. We wonder at the experiences of those who spend time now in the International Space Station, watching 16 sunrises and sunsets every 24 hours. Few of us indeed will ever have the benefit of that view downwards from so very high above the blue marble upon which we all depend.

But we are flecks of foam on the surface of the blue. Beneath us is an ocean of deep time and we can gaze down into it whenever we want, from wherever we are. It is a more revealing view by far than any to be had from space, which only reminds us where we live, how small our home is and how vulnerable. The space station orbits the marble every 90 minutes – so anyone looking out for the British Isles from up there will see them come around 16 times every day. Everything that matters is therefore too small, too far away and moving too fast.

As flecks of foam we have all the time in the world. By contemplating the ocean of time beneath us we are reminded that people, gradually evolving to be more and more like us, have found ways to survive for millions of years. Our existence in the here and now is no fluke. It has been the work of the ancestors, all the nameless individuals who somehow lasted long enough to make the people who made us. How they achieved that is no secret. It is all right there. We have only to remember to look down.

Bibliography

Chapter 1

AMS radiocarbon dating of Ancient Bone using ultrafiltration
http://oxford.academia.edu/TomHigham/Papers/424234/
AMS_radiocarbon_dating_of_ancient_bone_using_
ultrafiltration

Baker, D. 'Results from Radiocarbon Measurements' (letter),
Research Laboratory for Archaeology and the History of Art,
Oxford, 2010

Bell, M. *Goldcliff Mesolithic Footprints* (Research Design, 2010)

Conneller, C. 'Becoming Deer: Corporeal Transformations at Star
Carr' in *Archaeological Dialogues*, 11: 37–56 (Cambridge University
Press, 2004)

Conneller, C. 'Inhabiting New Landscapes: Settlement and Mobility in Britain after the Last Glacial Maximum' in *Oxford Journal
of Archaeology*, 26 (3): 215–237 (2007)

Conneller, C., Warren, G. *Mesolithic Britain and Ireland: New
Approaches* (The History Press, 2006)

The evolution of modern humans
http://www.nhm.ac.uk/nature-online/life/human-
origins/modern-human-evolution/index.html

Genetics and the origins of the British population
http://www.onlinelibrary.wiley.com/doi/10.1002/
9780470015902.a0020804/pdf

Gordon, J. E. 'Aucheneck' in *Geological Conservation Review*, 6 (13):
Western Highland Boundary Site: AUCHENECK (GCR ID:
832) http://www.thegcr.org.uk/

Mithen, S. *To the Islands* (Two Raven Press, 2010)

Mithen, S.J., Wicks, K. and Hill, J. 'Fiskary Bay: A Mesolithic Fishing Camp on Coll' in *Scottish Archaeology News*, 55: 14–15 (2007)

Chapter 2

Beginnings of farming in north-western Europe
http://www.novelguide.com/a/discover/aneu_01/aneu_01_00064.html

The big dig: Hambledon Hill
http://www.britarch.ac.uk/ba/ba107/feat3.shtml

Bogaard, A. and Jones, G. 'Neolithic Farming in Britain and Central Europe: Contrast or Continuity?' in *Proceedings of the British Academy*, 144: 357–375 (2007)

Bogucki, P. and Crabtree, P. *Ancient Europe 8000 B.C.–A.D. 1000. Encyclopedia of the Barbarian World* (Charles Scribner's Sons, 2003)

Callaghan, R., Scarre, C. 'Simulating the Western Seaways' in *Oxford Journal of Archaeology*, 28 (4): 357–372 (Blackwell, 2009)

Caulfield, S. et al. 'C14 Dating of a Neolithic Field System at Céide Fields, County Mayo, Ireland' in *Proceedings of the 16th International C Conference*, 40 (2): 629–640 (University of Arizona, 1998)

Collard, M. et al. 'Radiocarbon Evidence Indicates that Migrants Introduced Farming to Britain' in *Journal of Archaeological Science*, DOI: 10.1016/j.jas.2009.11.016 (2009)

Leary, J. 'Perceptions of and responses to the Holocene flooding of the North Sea Lowlands' in *Oxford Journal of Archaeology*, 28 (3): 227–237 (Blackwell, 2009)

Lost in space: The origin of the Orkney vole
http://orkneyjar.com/archaeology/dhl/papers/kd/index.html

O'Connell, M., Molloy, K. 'Farming and Woodland Dynamics in Ireland during the Neolithic' in *Biology and Environment: Proceedings of the Royal Irish Academy*, 101B (1–2): 99–128 (Royal Irish Academy, 2001)

The origins of agriculture
  http://www.comp-archaeology.org/AgricultureOrigins.htm

Schulting, R., Tresset, A. and Dupont, C. 'From Harvesting the Sea to Stock Rearing Along the Atlantic Façade of North-West Europe' in *Environmental Archaeology*, 9 (2): 131–142 (Maney Publishing, 2004)

Sheridan, A. 'The Neolithization of Britain and Ireland: The "Big Picture"' in *Landscapes in Transition* (Oxbow Books, 2010)

Sheridan, A., Field, D., Pailler, Y., Petrequin, P., Errera, M. and Cassen, S. 'Breamore Jadeitite Axehead and Other Neolithic Axeheads of Alpine Rock from Central Southern England' in *Wiltshire Archaeological and Natural History*, 103: 16–34 (2010)

Smith, D. 'Tsunami: A Research Perspective' in *Geology Today*, 21: 64–68. DOI: 10.1111/j.1365-2451.2005.00501.x (Blackwell, 2005)

Smith, M. 'Bloody Stone Age: War in the Neolithic' in *Current Archaeology*, issue CA 230 (Current Publishing, 2009)

Tresset, A. 'French Connections II: of Cows and Men' in *Neolithic Settlement in Ireland and Western Britain* (Oxbow Books, 2003)

Weninger, B. et al. 'The Catastrophic Final Flooding of Doggerland by the Storegga Slide Tsunami' in *Documenta Praehistorica*, XXXV. *Neolithic Studies*, 15: 1–24 (2008)

Whittle, A. 'The Neolithic Period, c. 4000–2400 cal BC: A Changing World' in Hunter, J., Ralston, I. (eds) *The Archaeology of Britain* (Routledge, 2009)

Whittle, A., Bayliss, A., Wysocki, M. 'Once in a Lifetime: the Date of the Wayland's Smithy Long Barrow' in *Cambridge Archaeological Journal*, 17: 103–121 (2007)

Whittle, A., Pollard, J., Grigson, C. *The Harmony of Symbols: the Windmill Hill Causewayed Enclosure* (Oxbow Books, 1999)

Chapter 3

Burl, A. *The Stone Circles of the British Isles* (Yale University Press, 1976)

The 'cathedral' at the heart of Neolithic Orkney
  http://www.orkneyjar.com/archaeology/nesscathedral.htm

Clarke, D. 'Once Upon a Time Skara Brae was Unique' in Armit, I., Murphy, E., Nelis, E. and Simpson, D. (eds) *Neolithic Settlement in Ireland and Western Britain* (Oxbow Books, 2003)

Edmonds, M. *The Langdales: Landscape and prehistory in a Lakeland valley* (Oxbow Books, 2004)

Eogan, G. *Knowth and the Passage Tombs of Ireland*
http://www.knowth.com/

Neolithic temples of the Northern Isles
http://www.archaeology.co.uk

Parker Pearson, M., Pollard, J., Richards, C., Thomas, J., Tilley, C. F. and Welham, K. 'The Stonehenge Riverside Project: Exploring the Neolithic Landscape of Stonehenge' in *Documenta Praehistorica*, XXXV: 153–166 (In Press, 2008)

Ruggles, C., Burton, B., Hughes, D., Lawson, A. and McNally, D. *Stonehenge and Ancient Astronomy* (Royal Astronomical Society, 2009)

Scarre, C. *The Megalithic Monuments of Britain and Ireland* (Thames and Hudson, 2007)

Sharpe, K. 'Rock-art and Rough-outs: Exploring the Sacred and Social Dimensions of Prehistoric Carvings at Copt Howe' in Mazel, A., Nash, G. and Waddington, C. (eds) *Art as Metaphor: The Prehistoric Rock-Art of Britain* (Archaeopress, 2007)

Sheridan, A. 'Green Treasures from the Magic Mountains' in *British Archaeology*, 96: 23–27 (Council of British Archaeology, 2007)

Skara Brae: the discovery of the village
http://www.orkneyjar.com/history/skarabrae/index.html

Stonehenge Riverside Project 2008
http://www.bbc.co.uk/history/programmes/stonehenge/

Stout, G. 'Monumentality and Inclusion in the Boyne Valley, County Meath, Ireland' in Darvill, T., Field, D. and Leary, J. (eds) *Round Mounds and Monumentality in the British Neolithic and Beyond* (Oxbow Books, 2010)

Thomas, J. et al. 'The Date of the Greater Stonehenge Cursus' in *Antiquity*, 83 (319): 40–53 (Antiquity Publications, 2009)

Watson, A. 'The Architecture of Sound in Neolithic Orkney' in Ritchie, A. (ed) *Neolithic Orkney in its European Context* (McDonald Institute Monographs, 2000)

Chapter 4

The Amesbury Archer and his world
http://www.templeresearch.eclipse.co.uk/bronze/ab.htm
Britain in the age of warrior heroes
http://www.britarch.ac.uk/ba/ba46/ba46feat.html
British Archaeology issue 101
http://www.britarch.ac.uk/ba/ba101/feat1.shtml
Casting methods in Bronze Age Britain
http://www.templeresearch.eclipse.co.uk/bronze/casting.htm
The first weapons devised only for war
http://www.britarch.ac.uk/ba/ba22/ba22feat.html
Fitzpatrick, A. P. 'In his Hands and in his Head: The Amesbury Archer as a Metalworker' in Clark, P. (ed) *Bronze Age Connections: Cultural Contact in Prehistoric Europe* (Oxbow Books, 2009)
Fitzpatrick, A. P. 'The Amesbury Archer' in *Current Archaeology*, 184: 146–152 (Current Publishing, 2003)
Hughes, S., Quinnell, H. and Richards, J. *A Bronze Age Roundhouse at Bellever Tor, Dartmoor Forest, Devon* (AC Archaeology, 2009)
Johnston, R. 'Copper Mining and the Transformation of Environmental Knowledge in Bronze Age Britain' in *Journal of Social Archaeology*, vol. 8, 2: pp. 190–213 (Sage, 2008)
Johnston, R. *Life in Bronze Age Britain and Ireland* (The History Press, 2011)
Molloy, B. *For Gods or men? A Re-appraisal of the Function of European Bronze Age Shields* (UCD, 2009)
Molloy, B. *The Cutting Edge: Studies in Ancient and Medieval Combat* (Tempus, 2007)
Neolithic Axe 'Factories' and Flint Mines: Towards an Ethnography of Prehistoric Extraction www.saa.org/Portals/0/SAA/Meetings/Programs/Program2006.pdf
Roberts, B. 'Creating Traditions and Shaping the Technologies:

Understanding the Earliest Metal Objects and Metal Production in Western Europe' in *World Archaeology*, 43: 354–372 (Routledge Online, 2008)

Roberts, B. et al. 'Development of metallurgy in Eurasia' in *Antiquity*, 83: 1012–1022 (2009)

Sharples, N. *Social Relations in Prehistory* (Oxford University Press, 2010)

Sheridan, A. 'Towards a fuller, more nuanced narrative of Chalcolithic and Early Bronze Age Britain' in *Bronze Age Review*, 1: 57–70 (British Museum Online Journal, 2008)

Topping, P. 'The Evidence for the Seasonal Use of the English Flint Mines', presentation to the 2nd International Conference of the UISPP: Madrid, 14 October 2009

Tower, J. et al. 'An Investigation of the Origins of Cattle and Aurochs Deposited in the Early Bronze Age Barrows at Gayhurst and Irthlingborough' in *Journal of Archaeological Science* (Elsevier, 2009)

Van de Noort, R. 'An Ancient Seascape: The Social Context of Seafaring in the Early Bronze Age' in *World Archaeology*, 35: 404–415 (Routledge, 2003)

Vander Linden, M. 'What Linked the Bell Beakers in Third Millennium BC Europe?' in *Antiquity*, 81: 343–352 (2007)

Chapter 5

Amesbury, M. J. et al. 'Bronze Age Upland Settlement Decline in Southwest England: Testing the Climate Change Hypothesis' in *Journal of Archaeological Science*, 35: 87–89 (Elsevier, 2008)

Armit, I. and Ginn, V. 'Beyond the Grave: Human Remains from Domestic Contexts in Iron Age Atlantic Scotland' in *Proceedings of the Prehistoric Society*, 73: 113–134 (2007)

Barber, K. *Peatland Records of Holocene Climate Change* (Elsevier, University of Southampton, 2007)

Brown, T. 'The Bronze Age Climate and Environment of Britain' in *The Bronze Age Review*, 1: 7–22 (British Museum Press, 2008)

Carr, G. 'Excarnation to Cremation: Continuity or Change?' in

436 A HISTORY OF ANCIENT BRITAIN

Haselgrove, C. and Moore, T. (eds) *The Later Iron Age in Britian and Beyond* (Oxbow Monograph, 2007)

Celtic art in Iron Age Wales
http://www.museumwales.ac.uk/en/rhagor/article/1938/

Collis, J. Interview

Coombes, P. and Barber, K. *Environmental Determinism in Holocene Research: Causality or Coincidence?* (Royal Geographical Society, 2005)

Cunliffe, B. *Iron Age Communities in Britain* (Routledge, 2009)

Cunliffe, B. *Iron Age Britain* (Batsford, 2004)

Great Orme http://www.greatormemines.info/ca2002.htm

Haselgrove, C. *The Iron Age in the Archaeology of Britain* (Abingdon, 2009)

Huth, C. *Metal Makes the World Go Round: The Supply and Circulation of Metals in Bronze Age Europe* (Oxbow Books, 2000)

The Iron Age settlement: discussion
http://www.sair.org.uk/sair24/sair24-11-iron-discussion.pdf

James, S. and Rigby, V. *Britain and the Celtic Iron Age* (British Museum Press, 1997)

Johnston, R. 'Copper Mining and the Transformation of Environmental Knowledge in Bronze Age Britain' in *Journal of Social Archaeology*, 8 (2): 190–213 (Sage, 2008)

Mulhall, I. 'Presenting a Past Society to a Present Day Audience: Bog Bodies in Iron Age Ireland' in *Museum Ireland*, 17: 71–81 (2007)

Needham, S. 'The Great Divide' in Haselgrove, C. and Pope, R. (eds) *The Earlier Iron Age in Britain and the Near Continent* (Oxbow Books, 2007)

O'Conner, B. *Llyn Fawr Metalwork in Britain: A Review* (Oxbow Books, 2007)

Pope, R. Conversation, 2010

Pope, R. E. 'Ritual and the Roundhouse: A Critique of Recent Ideas on Domestic Space in Later British Prehistory' in Haselgrove, C.C. and Pope, R. E. (eds) *The Earlier Iron Age in Britain and the Near Continent* (Oxbow Books, 2007)

Prehistoric mining at the Great Orme
   http://www.greatormemines.info/MPhil.htm
The religious symbolism of Llyn Cerrig Bach and other early sacred
   water sites http://people.bath.ac.uk/liskmj/living-spring/
   sourcearchive/ns1/ns1mg1.htm
Sharples, N. 'Iron Age Midden Sites: An Attempt at Social Reconstruction Following the Bronze Economic Fallout', notes from
   2010

Chapter 6
Ancient British language
   http://en.wikipedia.org/wiki/British_language
Andover Museum: Danebury hill fort
   http://www3.hants.gov.uk/museum-of-the-ironage
Armit, I. 'Hillforts at War: from Maiden Castle to Taniwaha pa' in
   Proceedings of the Prehistoric Society, 73: 25–40 (2007)
Bendrey, R. 'Horse' in Sykes, N. and O'Conner, T. (eds.) *Extinctions
   and Invasions: A Social History of British Fauna* (Windgather Press,
   2010)
Bendrey, R., Hayes, T.E. and Palmer, M.R. 'Patterns of Iron Age
   Horse Supply: An Analysis of Strontium Isotope Ratios in Teeth'
   in *Archaeometry*, 51 (1): 140–150 (2009)
Bendrey, R., Taylor, G.M., Bouwman, A.S., Cassidy, J.P. 'Suspected
   Bacterial Disease in Two Archaeological Horse Skeletons from
   Southern England: Palaeopathological and Biomolecular Studies'
   in *Journal of Archaeological Science*, 35: 1581–1590 (Elsevier,
   2008)
Fitzpatrick, A. 'The Fire, the Feast and the Funeral: Late Iron Age
   Mortuary Practices in South-Eastern England' in *Revue du Nord.
   Hors série. Collection Art et Archéologie*, 11: 123–142 (2007)
Giles, M. *Iron Age Chariot Burials of Britain* (Sheffield University,
   2009)
Gwilt, A. Conversation re: Iron Age artefacts in NMW
Hamilton, S. 'Cultural Choices in the "British Eastern Channel
   Area" in the Late Pre-Roman Iron Age' in Haselgrove, C. and

Moore, T. (eds) *The Later Iron Age in Britain and Beyond* (Oxbow Books, 2007)

Harding, A. 'The Development of Warrior Identities in the European Bronze Age', paper 2
http://www.scribd.com/doc/46514337/Harding-The-development-of-warrior-identities-in-the-European-Bronze-Age

Hill forts in Wales http://www.museumwales.ac.uk/

Iron Age chariot burials
http://www.yorkshirehistory.com/chariot_burials/index – a.htm

Moorhead, S. *What can we discern about Iron Age Britain from a study of the coinages?* (Portable Antiquities Scheme, 1996)

Ralston, I. *Celtic Fortifications* (NPI Media Group, Exeter, 2006)

Redfern, R.C. accepted. 'A Re-appraisal of the Evidence for Violence in the Late Iron Age Human Remains from Maiden Castle Hillfort, Dorset, England' in *Proceedings of the Prehistoric Society*

Chapter 7

Atrebates http://www.gallica.co.uk/celts/tribes.htm

Birrus Britannicus http://www.unc.edu/~css/Exhibition_paper.html#Hoods,%20eggs

City of the dead: Calleva Atrebatum
http://www.bbc.co.uk/history/archaeology/excavations_techniques/city_dead_01.shtml

Creighton, J. *Britannia: The Creation of a Roman Province* (Routledge, 2006)

Crew, P. 'Bryn y Castell Hillfort: A Late Prehistoric Iron Working Settlement in North West Wales' in Cleere, H. and Scott, B. G. (eds) *The Crafts of the Blacksmith* (Belfast, 1987)

Email between Ellie James and Paul King, 5 August 2010

Fitzpatrick, A. 'Druids: Towards an Archaeology' in *Communities and Connections* (Oxford University Press, 2007)

Fulford, M. Phone conversation, 13 July 2010

Haselgrove, C. *The Later Iron Age in Britain and Beyond* (Oxbow Books, 2007)

Iron Age coins www.predecimal.com

James, S. and Rigby, V. *Britain and the Celtic Iron Age* (British Museum Press, 2007)

Redfern, R. and DeWitte, S. 'A New Approach to the Study of Romanization in Britain: A Regional Perspective of Cultural Change in Late Iron Age and Roman Dorset Using the Siler and Gompertz-Makeham Models of Mortality' in *American Journal of Physical Anthropology*, DOI: 10.1002/ajpa.21400 (2010)

Roberts, C. A. and Cox, M. *Health and Disease in Britain: From Prehistory to the Present Day* (Sutton Publishing, 2003)

Works of Tacitus, Book XIV. Queen Boudicca revolts against Rome, AD 60–61
http://www.mytimemachine.co.uk/boudicca.htm

Chapter 8

Archaeology http://www.hadrians-wall.org/page.aspx//About-the-World-Heritage-Site/Archaeology-

Chenery, C., Muldner, G., Evans, J., Eckardt, H. and Lewis, M. 'Strontium and Stable Isotope Evidence for Diet and Mobility in Roman Gloucester, UK' in *Journal of Archaeological Science*, 37 (1): 150–163 (Elsevier, 2009)

A Corpus of writing-tablets from Roman Britain
http://www.csad.ox.ac.uk/rib/ribiv/jp4.htm

Curse tablets – c/o Centre for the Study of Ancient Documents
http://curses.csad.ox.ac.uk/

Eckardt, H., Chenery, C., Booth, P., Evans, J., Lamb, A. and Muldner, G. 'Oxygen and strontium isotope evidence for mobility in Roman Winchester' in *Journal of Archaeological Science*, 36 (12): 2816–2825 (Elsevier, 2009)

Jackson, R. *Cosmetic Sets of Late Iron Age and Roman Britain* (British Museum Research Publication, 2010)

A Lady of York: Migration, Ethnicity and Identity in Roman Britain
http://antiquity.ac.uk/ant/084/ant0840131.htm

Leach, S., Lewis, M., Chenery, C., Muldner, G. and Eckardt, H. 'Migration and Diversity in Roman Britain: A Multidisciplinary

Approach to the Identification of Immigrants in Roman York, England' in *American Journal of Physical Anthropology*, 140 (3): 546–561 (Wiley InterScience, 2009)

Roman empires and frontiers
http://www.hadrians-wall.org/page.aspx//About-the-World-Heritage-Site/Roman-Empires-and-Frontiers

Romano-British settlement Chysauster, Cornwall
http://www.roman-britain.org/places/chysauster.htm

Wheatley, G. *Chysauster Ancient Village: Information for Teachers* (Palladian Press, English Heritage, 2008)

White, D. What the Romans Found: The Picts
http://www.suite101.com/article.cfm/ancient_british_history/46697

Wilson, P. *The Archaeology of Roman Towns* (Oxbow Books, 2003)

Index